Applications of Artificial Intelligence in Libraries

Iman Khamis
Northwestern University, Qatar

A volume in the Advances in Library and Information Science (ALIS) Book Series

Published in the United States of America by
IGI Global
Information Science Reference (an imprint of IGI Global)
701 E. Chocolate Avenue
Hershey PA, USA 17033
Tel: 717-533-8845
Fax: 717-533-8661
E-mail: cust@igi-global.com
Web site: http://www.igi-global.com

Library of Congress Cataloging-in-Publication Data

Library of Congress Cataloging-in-Publication Data

Names: Khamis, Iman, 1982- editor.
Title: Applications of artificial intelligence in libraries / edited by Iman Khamis.
Description: Hershey, PA : Information Science Reference, 2024. | Includes bibliographical references and index. | Summary: "The book provides a comprehensive exploration of the different ways in which AI technologies are being integrated into library operations and services"-- Provided by publisher.
Identifiers: LCCN 2024010154 (print) | LCCN 2024010155 (ebook) | ISBN 9798369315736 (hardcover) | ISBN 9798369344941 (paperback) | ISBN 9798369315743 (ebook)
Subjects: LCSH: Artificial intelligence--Library applications.
Classification: LCC Z678.93.A77 A67 2024 (print) | LCC Z678.93.A77 (ebook) | DDC 020.285/63--dc23/eng/20240401
LC record available at https://lccn.loc.gov/2024010154
LC ebook record available at https://lccn.loc.gov/2024010155

This book is published in the IGI Global book series Advances in Library and Information Science (ALIS) (ISSN: 2326-4136; eISSN: 2326-4144)

British Cataloguing in Publication Data
A Cataloguing in Publication record for this book is available from the British Library.

Advances in Library and Information Science (ALIS) Book Series

ISSN:2326-4136
EISSN:2326-4144

Editor-in-Chief: Alfonso Ippolito, Sapienza University-Rome, Italy, Carlo Inglese, Sapienza University-Rome, Italy

MISSION

The **Advances in Library and Information Science (ALIS) Book Series** is comprised of high quality, research-oriented publications on the continuing developments and trends affecting the public, school, and academic fields, as well as specialized libraries and librarians globally. These discussions on professional and organizational considerations in library and information resource development and management assist in showcasing the latest methodologies and tools in the field.

The **ALIS Book Series** aims to expand the body of library science literature by covering a wide range of topics affecting the profession and field at large. The series also seeks to provide readers with an essential resource for uncovering the latest research in library and information science management, development, and technologies.

COVERAGE

- Social Networking Technologies
- Digital Rights Management (DRM)
- Alternatives to Dewey Decimal System
- Information Literacy
- Open Access
- Gaming in Libraries
- Outreach, Promotion, and Advocacy
- Virtual Reference Services
- Intellectual Freedom
- Resource Sharing in Libraries

IGI Global is currently accepting manuscripts for publication within this series. To submit a proposal for a volume in this series, please contact our Acquisition Editors at Acquisitions@igi-global.com or visit: http://www.igi-global.com/publish/.

The Advances in Library and Information Science (ALIS) Book Series (ISSN 2326-4136) is published by IGI Global, 701 E. Chocolate Avenue, Hershey, PA 17033-1240, USA, www.igi-global.com. This series is composed of titles available for purchase individually; each title is edited to be contextually exclusive from any other title within the series. For pricing and ordering information please visit http://www.igi-global.com/book-series/advances-library-information-science/73002. Postmaster: Send all address changes to above address.

Titles in this Series

For a list of additional titles in this series, please visit:
http://www.igi-global.com/book-series/advances-library-information-science/73002

Examining Information Literacy in Academic Libraries
Sabelo Chizwina (North-West University, South Africa) and Mathew Moyo (North-West University, South Africa)
Information Science Reference • © 2024 • 313pp • H/C (ISBN: 9798369311431) • US $230.00

AI-Assisted Library Reconstruction
K.R. Senthilkumar (Sri Krishna Arts and Science College, India)
Information Science Reference • © 2024 • 363pp • H/C (ISBN: 9798369327821) • US $235.00

Challenges of Globalization and Inclusivity in Academic Research
Swati Chakraborty (GLA University, India & Concordia University, Canada)
Information Science Reference • © 2024 • 301pp • H/C (ISBN: 9798369313718) • US $225.00

Multidisciplinary Approach to Information Technology in Library and Information Science
Barbara Holland (Brooklyn Public Library, USA (Retired)) and Keshav Sinha (University of Petroleum and Energy Studies, India)
Information Science Reference • © 2024 • 345pp • H/C (ISBN: 9798369328415) • US $245.00

Handbook of Research on Innovative Approaches to Information Technology in Library and Information Science
Barbara Holland (Brooklyn Public Library, USA (Retired)) and Keshav Sinha (University of Petroleum and Energy Studies, India)
Information Science Reference • © 2024 • 427pp • H/C (ISBN: 9798369308073) • US $285.00

For an entire list of titles in this series, please visit:
http://www.igi-global.com/book-series/advances-library-information-science/73002

IGI Global
PUBLISHER of TIMELY KNOWLEDGE

701 East Chocolate Avenue, Hershey, PA 17033, USA
Tel: 717-533-8845 x100 • Fax: 717-533-8661
E-Mail: cust@igi-global.com • www.igi-global.com

Table of Contents

Detailed Table of Contents

Due to AI, libraries have changed operations and user service swiftly. AI is becoming more important in education and research. Organizational improvements have enhanced product quality, consumer behavior prediction, inventory management, and AI data analysis. Mobile phones and search engines employ AI. Libraries may become big data hubs, analyze data, and provide remote access. Ability-enhancing AI is employed. Libraries read books and other materials to visually challenged persons using AI-driven text-to-speech technology. Library staff can focus on research because AI can perform regular chores. This chapter describes AI-assisted library administration. Most science fiction and movies include intelligent machines. AI is now commonplace. Several sectors need automation prep. Library AI development is slower than other institutions. Schools increasingly include it in their programs. Library AI development is studied. Librarians' automation-era potential and problems must be considered. This chapter covers librarianship's many obligations and opportunities.

This chapter discusses the implementation of artificial intelligence (AI) in academic libraries and the impact of AI related technologies on various library services. AI impacts research and educational activities in academic institutions so they can

Modern libraries involving AI present improved productivity, user experiences, and resource management. Responsible AI approaches are crucial because of ethical factors including algorithmic biases and patron data privacy. Organizational barriers provide serious difficulties that necessitate strategic ways for successful implementation. The integration scenario includes budget limits and expenditures related to AI technologies. Adoption of AI is made more complicated by regulatory factors, such as adherence to data protection laws and potential legal ramifications. Through the synthesis of extant research, this article offers a thorough comprehension of these intricate challenges. Technical, ethical, organizational, financial, and regulatory aspects provides insightful information for researchers, politicians, and librarians. In order to promote responsible AI integration in libraries and optimize the advantages of emerging technologies, the evaluation seeks to provide guidance for future strategies, policies, and decision-making procedures.

This chapter aims to present to the readers the point of view of the managers of the world top universities' libraries as compiled by topuniversityranking.com. After an introduction presenting the special relevance of the academic libraries and the importance of the respondents, an analysis of data is conducted to verify the application of Rogers theory in the special context of AI. The survey used the standard scales from the theory and applies them to the introduction to AI, after qualifying respondents in terms of knowledge. The theory explains the adoption by using five factors affecting innovation: relative advantage, compatibility, compatibility, complexity, trialability, and observability. Since AI is a relatively new technology in many libraries, a better understanding of the leaders will be beneficial.

Artificial intelligence has played an important role in reference services for academic libraries. This chapter reviews 40 journal articles published between 2000 and 2023. It reports that artificial intelligence technologies of machine learning, robots, and natural language processing have all played an important role in providing personalised services in information literacy, sentiment analysis, information retrieval and recommendations on library materials. In addition, the review reported an increased usage of ChatGPT among academics and reference librarians in academic libraries. The review generally showed a limited adoption of artificial intelligence for reference purposes in the developing world due to several limitations such as lack of knowledge and skills, lack of finance and limited infrastructure among these institutions.

The use of artificial intelligence (AI) has transformed several industries, including research and education. Due to relevance and global competitiveness, in the present scenario incorporation of artificial intelligence in library workflow is inevitable. Libraries are changing in the age of information explosions to keep up with technological improvements and provide access to the greatest information while avoiding obstacles. This chapter provides a thorough description of the use of artificial intelligence (AI) tools and techniques in distinct sections of Library management and services. Creating devices that can imagine and work like humanoid brains is the aim of artificial intelligence. Artificial intelligence integration has the potential to improve library space intelligence and eliminate physical obstacles. The chapter offers a complete grasp of how AI could alter library infrastructure and services in the future, leading to better outcomes for readers, educators, researchers, and students.

Libraries face the difficulty of maintaining huge volumes of information while offering users effective resource discovery in the fast-expanding digital world. The incorporation of artificial intelligence (AI) has emerged as a significant change in library administration. This chapter explores the use of AI, with an emphasis on recommendation systems and knowledge discovery. AI-powered recommendation systems provide personalized ideas, increasing user engagement and making content research easier. AI-powered resource discovery technologies extract important insights from enormous collections, assisting in trend analysis and resource summaries. The collaboration of these AI-powered technologies transforms the library experience, making it more user-centric, efficient, and enriching. This chapter demonstrates how AI-powered recommendation systems and resource discovery may convert libraries into dynamic, responsive organizations at the forefront of information distribution.

This abstract investigates how libraries are changing in the age of artificial intelligence (AI). It explores how new technologies are changing how libraries operate and provide services. Recommendation systems driven by artificial intelligence (AI), natural language processing (NLP) for improved user engagement, text analysis and data mining for knowledge discovery, AI-driven metadata management, and AI-driven preservation initiatives are some of the major themes in this field. Furthermore, RPA, or robotic process automation, simplifies library operations. The chapter focuses on how these technologies are transforming user experience, library administration procedures, and information access, so influencing how libraries will function in the digital era.

Preface

In the ever-growing landscape of library and information studies, the integration of artificial intelligence (AI) seems to be an inevitable shaping force, that will be reshaping the manners that we are currently operating in our daily lives as librarians and library professionals. This book, *Artificial Intelligence in Libraries*, aims to bring together insights from various experts across the world, offering an examination of how AI technologies are being implemented in library settings.

When I was editing this book, I had two goals. First, I hoped to provide library professionals with an understanding of the current AI technologies changing information management and user services. Second, I aimed to build a guide for implementing the new emerging technologies in libraries of all types and sizes, ensuring they remain relevant in our daily work.

The chapters in this book cover a range of topics, from basic introductions to AI in libraries to in-depth analyses of specific applications such as automated cataloging, user interaction enhancements, and data-driven decision-making processes. The chapters are authored by various authors from different backgrounds and perspectives, showcasing successful case studies and practical advice.

Chapter 1: This chapter provides a comprehensive overview of how AI has revolutionized library operations, from enhancing user services to optimizing organizational efficiency. Through AI-driven technologies, libraries have evolved into dynamic hubs for data analysis, predictive modeling, and accessibility improvements. The chapter also highlights the potential of AI in addressing challenges such as resource management and accessibility for visually impaired individuals, while emphasizing the need for librarians to adapt to the automation era.

Chapter 2: Exploring the intersection of AI and academic libraries, this chapter examines the profound impact of AI-related technologies on research, education, and library services. As academic institutions strive to meet the demands of personalized education and collaborative research, AI emerges as a critical tool for enhancing library operations and supporting diverse curricula. Librarians are not only users but also co-creators of AI-driven services, necessitating a deeper understanding of AI literacy and its implications for communication in the digital age.

Chapter 3: Delving into the ethical dimensions of AI adoption in libraries, this chapter addresses the potential risks, including bias, discrimination, and privacy violations. By exploring the ethical implications of AI-driven library services and human-machine interactions, it underscores the importance of ethical frameworks and safeguards to mitigate potential harm.

Chapter 4: In the digital era, cybersecurity awareness is paramount for libraries as they serve as crucial hubs for accessing digital resources. This chapter emphasizes the multifaceted nature of cybersecurity, including data security, privacy, and threat mitigation. By examining real-world consequences and strategies for enhancing cybersecurity awareness, it highlights the urgent need for libraries to safeguard valuable digital assets.

Chapter 5: Addressing the challenges of responsible AI integration, this chapter explores the technical, ethical, organizational, financial, and regulatory aspects of AI implementation in libraries. By synthesizing existing research, it offers valuable insights for researchers, policymakers, and librarians seeking to navigate the complexities of AI adoption while promoting ethical and responsible practices.

Chapter 6: Drawing on insights from top university library managers, this chapter examines the application of Rogers' theory to the adoption of AI in academic libraries. By analyzing factors such as relative advantage, compatibility, complexity, trialability, and observability, it offers valuable perspectives on the challenges and opportunities associated with AI adoption in library management.

Chapter 7: This chapter reviews the role of AI technologies in providing personalized reference services in academic libraries. By examining the adoption of machine learning, robots, and natural language processing, it highlights the potential of AI to enhance information literacy, sentiment analysis, and information retrieval. However, limited adoption in the developing world underscores the need for addressing barriers such as knowledge gaps and infrastructure limitations.

Chapter 8: Exploring the transformative potential of AI in library management, this chapter examines how AI tools and techniques can enhance library services and infrastructure. By envisioning devices that emulate human brains and eliminate physical obstacles, it offers insights into the future of libraries in the age of AI.

Chapter 9: Focusing on AI-powered recommendation systems and knowledge discovery, this chapter explores how AI technologies are revolutionizing resource discovery in libraries. By providing personalized recommendations and extracting insights from vast collections, AI enhances user engagement and transforms the library experience into a dynamic, responsive ecosystem.

Chapter 10: This chapter investigates the evolving role of libraries in the digital era of AI. By exploring technologies such as recommendation systems, natural language processing, text analysis, and robotic process automation, it highlights the transformative impact of AI on library operations, user experience, and information access.

As the editor, I have guided this project from conception to its final stages. My journey has been facilitated by the contributing authors and brought a joyful experience of collaboration among the contributors, peer reviews, and a shared commitment to advancing the role of libraries through emerging technologies.

This book is intended for librarians, information science professionals, and researchers interested in the intersection of library science and artificial intelligence. Whether you are looking to advance your understanding of AI applications in libraries or seeking inspiration to start on your own AI projects, this book will serve as a valuable resource.

We hope that *Artificial Intelligence in Libraries* will not only inform but also inspire our readers to explore the potential of AI to transform library services and enhance the user experience.

Thank you for joining us on this exciting journey into the future of libraries.

Editor

Iman Khamis
Northwestern University Qatar, Qatar

Chapter 1
A Futuristic Perspective:
The Utilization of AI in the Field of Library Management

Geetha Manoharan
https://orcid.org/0000-0002-8644-8871
SR University, India

C. V. Guru Rao
https://orcid.org/0000-0002-9210-6122
SR University, India

M. Nivedha
Robert Gordon University, UK

ABSTRACT

Due to AI, libraries have changed operations and user service swiftly. AI is becoming more important in education and research. Organizational improvements have enhanced product quality, consumer behavior prediction, inventory management, and AI data analysis. Mobile phones and search engines employ AI. Libraries may become big data hubs, analyze data, and provide remote access. Ability-enhancing AI is employed. Libraries read books and other materials to visually challenged persons using AI-driven text-to-speech technology. Library staff can focus on research because AI can perform regular chores. This chapter describes AI-assisted library administration. Most science fiction and movies include intelligent machines. AI is now commonplace. Several sectors need automation prep. Library AI development is slower than other institutions. Schools increasingly include it in their programs. Library AI development is studied. Librarians' automation-era potential and problems must be considered. This chapter covers librarianship's many obligations and opportunities.

DOI: 10.4018/979-8-3693-1573-6.ch001

INTRODUCTION

The domain of artificial intelligence (AI) has attracted considerable interest from both the general populace and the academic library community owing to its notable technological progress. Given the early stage of research and public adoption of this technology, there is an opportunity to examine a representative sample of librarians in order to explore their perspectives on artificial intelligence using the Diffusion of Innovations model. As of now, there exists a dearth of scientific publications within the subject of library and information science (LIS) that have undertaken a study of comparable scale and scope. The performance of such an analysis has the potential to provide useful information pertaining to the diffusion of innovations theory and the attitudes exhibited by academic library workers towards artificial intelligence (AI) within a wider framework. The findings of this study may prove advantageous for academic library directors and technologically inclined personnel aiming to enhance the adoption and utilization of artificial intelligence (AI) technology inside their respective libraries.

Libraries presently function within a dynamic milieu that is characterized by ongoing fluctuations. Users face a multitude of complex obstacles, including the exponential expansion of information, the transformative impact of information technology, the continuous development of networks, constrained financial resources, escalating document costs, heightened user expectations, and the diverse array of information resources accessible in different media formats. The field of Information Technology (IT) offers a wide range of opportunities that hold promise for addressing substantial challenges. The rapid advancement of modern technology has greatly improved the capabilities of storing, processing, retrieving, repackaging, communicating, sharing, and managing the huge growth of information in libraries, leading to improved effectiveness and cost-efficiency. The incorporation of Information and Communication Technology (ICT) within libraries has become a crucial necessity in the present era, which is marked by an abundance of information and the advent of numerous new technologies. The integration of various systems and technologies is necessary in order to adequately address the dynamic and complex information needs of library patrons. Libraries have used information technology (IT) in a comprehensive manner, particularly focusing on computer technology, to enhance efficiency in many administrative and technical processes. The aforementioned advancements encompass the evolution of databases, online public access catalogues (OPACs), and networks, all of which collectively contribute to the augmentation of services provided to library consumers. The adoption and integration of information and communication technology (ICT) in diverse library environments have witnessed significant expansion in recent years, resulting in improved techniques for managing information. The widespread adoption and integration of information and communication technology (ICT) within libraries has had a profound impact on all aspects of the modern library environment. The incorporation of Information and Communication Technology (ICT) within libraries undeniably presents a substantial advantage to our society. However, in order to attain success, the effective implementation of this system requires the steadfast dedication of librarians, as the human resource element plays a crucial role. The development of a favourable mindset among library personnel toward the integration of Information and Communication Technology (ICT) is of utmost importance. The domain of technology, which encompasses both computer hardware and software, is distinguished by its rapid rate of development, resulting in the swift obsolescence of contemporary knowledge. It is imperative for librarians to be abreast of evolving technological breakthroughs. To keep pace with and adapt to technology changes, humans must continually engage in educational endeavours to learn new skills. Librarians frequently experience a range of obstacles that are commonly referred to as technical stress or techno tress, as described in numerous instances.

Librarians have identified multiple concerns related to technology, Librarians have identified multiple concerns related to technology, (Abdulwahid et al., 2023) encompassing apprehensions regarding the technological infrastructure, the financial implications of errors, the ability to acquire essential skills, job security, reduced opportunities for social engagement, the rise of a surveillance society, and potential health effects such as visual impairment, discomfort in the hands, pain in the neck and shoulders, backaches, migraines, and overall fatigue. While it is indeed accurate that a substantial proportion of library workers may possess a favourable disposition towards the utilization of information and communication technology (ICT), it is imperative to recognize that there are cases where certain individuals demonstrate a pessimistic attitude towards it. There exists a prevailing notion that the nature of professions within the library sector is susceptible to ongoing modification as a result of automation, which has the potential to influence levels of job satisfaction. Another concern that emerges relates to the training of existing people in computerization. There exists a discernible degree of opposition among individuals, namely those who had their vocational education several years ago and have limited exposure to information and communication technology (ICT). Therefore, it is apparent that the emergence of technological revolution might lead to personnel issues and substantial disruptions in work processes.

Requirements of AI Technology in Library

The integration of artificial intelligence (AI) technology into a library setting has the potential to enhance operational efficiency and elevate the overall user experience.

The following are certain considerations that should be taken into account while using artificial intelligence (AI) technology within a library setting:

The field of data management encompasses the processes, policies, and technologies involved in the collection, storage, organization, and retrieval of data.

The utilization of AI technology necessitates substantial quantities of data in order to effectively train models and generate precise predictions. In order to facilitate the implementation of artificial intelligence (AI) applications, it is imperative for a library to possess a meticulously structured and readily available database including its collections and user information.

The development of a resilient and reliable artificial intelligence (AI) infrastructure is of paramount importance.

The design of an AI infrastructure should be tailored to adequately address the requirements of the library, encompassing hardware, software, and connectivity aspects.

Proficiency in Artificial Intelligence Development

Libraries will be required to engage the services of proficient AI developers through employment or contractual agreements in order to construct and sustain the AI systems. Proficiency in AI programming languages, data analytics, machine learning techniques, and associated tools is deemed essential.

The dataset used for training purposes.

In order to effectively train AI models, it is important for libraries to possess data sets of high quality. The data utilized should possess contemporaneity, pertinence, and accurately reflect the library's holdings and user demographic.

The topic of concern is data privacy and security.

Given the handling of sensitive user data by libraries, it is imperative to establish robust processes for data privacy and security in order to safeguard user data and adhere to data protection rules.

The utilization of artificial intelligence (AI) has become increasingly prevalent in various domains, showcasing its potential in numerous applications.

Libraries should undertake the task of identifying distinct use scenarios for artificial intelligence (AI) within the library environment. The potential applications encompassed under this domain encompass the automation of library operations, the provision of individualized user experiences, the utilization of recommendation engines, and the delivery of additional services powered by artificial intelligence.

The incorporation of new systems into pre-existing infrastructure.

In order to ensure a smooth integration of AI technology within the library, it is imperative that the technology seamlessly aligns with the library's current systems. This is essential to prevent any disturbances in the library's operations and to facilitate the adoption of the new technology by both staff and users. In order to effectively integrate AI technology into a library setting, it is imperative to engage in meticulous strategic planning, allocate substantial financial resources, and maintain continuous assistance from domain specialists.

Utilization of Artificial Intelligence (AI) in the Provision of Library Services

Artificial intelligence (AI) has the potential to be utilized in several domains of library services, encompassing cataloging, categorization, recommendation systems, reference services, information discovery, and preservation efforts. For instance, artificial intelligence (AI) has the potential to assist librarians in automating the task of metadata production and extraction. Additionally, AI can contribute to improving the overall quality and consistency of bibliographic entries by identifying and rectifying errors and inconsistencies. Artificial intelligence (AI) has the potential to assist librarians in offering customized and pertinent recommendations to library users, taking into account their individual preferences, behavioral patterns, and situational context. Artificial intelligence (AI) has the potential to support librarians in addressing intricate and varied inquiries by employing techniques such as natural language processing and semantic analysis. In addition, artificial intelligence (AI) has the potential to assist librarians in identifying novel and developing subjects, trends, and patterns within the realm of information through the utilization of data mining and machine learning techniques. Furthermore, artificial intelligence (AI) has the potential to assist librarians in the preservation and digitization of their collections through the utilization of image recognition and optical character recognition (OCR) technologies.

Implementation of Artificial Intelligence in libraries Has Several Challenges

- At present, the extent to which artificial intelligence systems are applied in libraries is constrained. The implementation of artificial intelligence systems in libraries is subject to many constraints, which can be outlined as follows:
- The user's text exhibits an academic tone and structure. The library staff lacks the necessary technical expertise to effectively utilize and operate artificial intelligence systems. There is a lack of adequate financial allocation for the expansion or acquisition of artificial intelligence systems inside library environments. Libraries frequently encounter limitations in their ability to select and acquire systems due to the constrained availability of hardware and software resources.

- The user's text is already written in an academic style and does not require any more revising. The costs related to the establishment and maintenance of artificial intelligence systems in libraries are significant.
- The provided material is incomplete and lacks sufficient information to be analyzed or rewritten in an academic manner. Please provide a complete sentence or paragraph for me to assist you further. Could you please reword the following sentence in an academic manner: "I think the research findings are really interesting." The problem of unreliable electricity provision in libraries, particularly in developing countries, presents a significant obstacle to the efficient functioning of artificial intelligence systems.
- The user's text is lacking in completeness. I apologize for the confusion. Could you please send the content that you would like me to rewrite in an academic style? The development of expert/artificial intelligence systems is marked by intrinsic challenges. The user's content does not supply any information to rewrite in an academic style the limitations of natural language processing.
- The user's text is already written in an academic style and does not require any more revising. The functional capabilities of intelligent systems are constrained by the lack of a shared foundation of human knowledge.
- The user's text lacks sufficient information to be revised in an academic manner. The level of effort and technical expertise required for the creation of artificial intelligence systems within library environments. There exists a clear relationship between the level and nature of effort necessary for the creation of an intelligent library system and the system's effectiveness and complexity. This suggests that there exists a positive correlation between the level of intelligence exhibited by a system and the financial resources necessary for its growth and upkeep. Presently, there exists a deficiency in the availability of adequately skilled personnel possessing the necessary expensive development tools or procedures essential for the construction of sophisticated intelligent systems inside library settings. Consequently, libraries are encountering a deficiency in these systems.

THE LITERATURE REVIEW

The aim of this forthcoming study, to be done in 2023, is to investigate the impact of artificial intelligence (AI) on the facilitation of future library services. The primary objective of this study is to evaluate the extent of readiness exhibited by librarians working in university libraries across Africa in effectively deploying artificial intelligence (AI) technologies. The current investigation employed an interpretive methodology known as content/document analysis to scrutinize literature sourced from many databases, such as Scopus and Web of Science. The utilization of artificial intelligence (AI) has promise for various facets of information management, including circulation, serials management, reference services, and selective dissemination of information, among other functionalities. The use of this notion covers the facilitation of novel services aimed at recognizing various library activities, such as addressing research queries, arranging and classifying library materials, and overseeing the library system software that encompasses several databases within the library systems. The study's findings suggest that artificial intelligence (AI) is likely to continue being a universally applicable solution for future library services, irrespective of their geographical location. The identification of AI's utility in supporting future library services stems from its origins in the sector of engineering, which is known for its constant information expansion. The field of library science has experienced the integration of intelligent computer systems that demonstrate human-like behaviour, albeit not being genuine human entities, due to the positive reception and use of these systems in library service provision. This has enabled continuous interactions between librarians and these technologies. The incorporation of robots and artificial intelligence (AI) into jobs that need human involvement has resulted in significant progress in the management of intricate processes, communication, knowledge representation, decision-making, and task optimization across several work domains. The study's findings indicate that forthcoming library services should take into account the crucial significance of human interaction in the operation of AI systems. This comprehension is taken from the disciplines of computer science, information science, and information systems. The societal implications of breakthroughs in artificial intelligence (AI) pertain to the capacity to augment user engagement and interest among individuals from various backgrounds. The aforementioned functionalities can be accomplished by means of the conversion of intricate tasks, including but not limited to processing, communication, knowledge representation, decision-making, and idea generation. The authors were driven to investigate the role of artificial intelligence (AI) in enhancing library services in light of the empirical evidence derived from recent studies that examined diverse job operations. Librarians have been required to adapt their methods of providing services in order to meet the increasing demands of library patrons. The emergence of these advancing technology has also led to modifications in teaching approaches. Consequently, the present surge in service innovations propelled by digital technology has ushered in a novel paradigm for education and research. Given these alterations, librarians are actively seeking distinctive and groundbreaking technology in order to enhance user experiences within their libraries. These entities serve as catalysts in the assimilation of contemporary and sophisticated technology, consistently adapting to present-day technologies that enhance their services.

The research undertaken by Ivashkevych (2023) aimed to achieve a certain objective. The purpose of this study is to provide a comprehensive analysis of the accomplishments, potential for transformation, and challenges associated with implementing systems, elements of artificial intelligence (AI), and the corresponding algorithms in national library and information institutions. The study utilizes a research approach that integrates the principles of systematicity, generality, objectivity, and the established methodologies of scientific research. These methodologies include analysis, synthesis, comparison, and analytical monitoring of artificial intelligence (AI) components within libraries nationwide. The main objective of this work is to provide a comprehensive understanding of the difficulties involved in incorporating artificial intelligence (AI) intellectual resources into library operations in modern contexts. The focus is directed towards fundamental attributes that impede this integration. In conclusion, it may be deduced that... This article presents a comprehensive examination of the progress, key uses, and justifications for limiting the widespread integration of artificial intelligence (AI) systems and components into library operations. This study investigates the attributes and pragmatic ramifications of integrating artificial intelligence (AI) elements within the framework of national libraries, specifically emphasizing the potential of ultra-high-frequency technology. The practice outlined above maintains major importance in libraries, especially during periods of martial law and large societal transformations. The execution of this program will augment the accessibility of knowledge to the general populace and foster self-directed learning. Additionally, this will provide libraries the opportunity to access state-of-the-art technical improvements, facilitating their integration of digitalization and adjustment of their operations accordingly. Moreover, it will cultivate a holistic comprehension of the industry's influence on society and promote inventive strategies for library-user interactions, taking into account the complexities presented by civilization. The analysis of developing trends in the incorporation of intelligent systems and artificial intelligence components will support the implementation of technological initiatives in library and information institutions. This study investigates the feasibility of integrating intellectual components into the operations of the library business, taking into account the specific circumstances of the country. Additionally, it puts out a comprehensive plan of action for the long term. The incorporation of artificial intelligence (AI) in library environments has emerged as a subject of considerable interest and importance. This scholarly discussion centres on the integration of different artificial intelligence (AI) systems and components into libraries, along with the revolutionary technologies that are enabling the transformation of intellectual resources. Furthermore, this discourse explores the challenges that emerge during the implementation of artificial intelligence in library operations.

AI apps commonly utilize ML/DL (Machine Learning/Deep Learning) models to effectively perform certain AI tasks. The researchers indicated above, namely Liu et al., (2023) have undertaken investigations in this particular field. According to the study, it is a prevalent practice among application developers, who generally lack specialized knowledge in artificial intelligence (AI), to opt for the use of pre-existing machine learning (ML) and deep learning (DL) models as libraries for their AI-related assignments. The field of Artificial Intelligence (AI) is characterized by its dynamic nature and attracts considerable scientific interest, leading to a major annual output of scholarly papers. A multitude of research articles have presented machine learning and deep learning models that have been specifically designed to tackle particular challenges, along with comprehensive explanations of their implementations. However, developers may face difficulties when attempting to find machine learning and deep learning packages that are suitable for their particular needs. This chapter addresses two key concerns: the rapid progress of AI application areas and methodology, and the limited availability of full information on libraries, including environmental dependencies and supporting resources. This study offers an empirical inquiry conducted on the online platform Stack Overflow, with a specific focus on inquiries pertaining to libraries associated with machine learning and deep learning. The primary aim of this study is to gain a comprehensive understanding of the distinct requirements and anticipated outcomes of developers in regards to machine learning and deep learning libraries. The outcomes of the study propose the implementation of an MLTaskKG method, which is a task-oriented recommendation system for ML/DL libraries. The system produces a comprehensive knowledge graph that incorporates several aspects of artificial intelligence, including tasks, machine learning and deep learning models, implementations of these models, repositories, and the relationships between them. This is accomplished through the retrieval of information from many sources, such as specialized websites focusing on machine learning and deep learning resources, scholarly articles, frameworks for machine learning and deep learning, and repositories. The MLTaskKG system leverages the knowledge graph to offer developers suggestions on machine learning and deep learning libraries. The accomplishment of this objective is attained through the alignment of the developers' requirements about tasks, model properties, and implementation details. The evaluation completed indicates that a significant proportion of the sampled tuples obtained from the resultant knowledge graph, specifically 92.8%, demonstrate a high level of accuracy. This finding suggests that the knowledge graph has noteworthy quality. Another experiment was conducted to illustrate the potential of MLTaskKG in aiding developers to efficiently find suitable machine learning and deep learning libraries. The investigation revealed a substantial reduction in time by 47.6% compared to traditional methods. Furthermore, the utilization of MLTaskKG resulted in a higher satisfaction rate of 68.4%.

The scientific work produced by Maranchak (2023) aims to investigate the global adoption of artificial intelligence (AI) in the context of digital marketing in libraries. The study seeks to analyze the extent to which AI is being utilized in this domain on a worldwide scale. The main objective of this study is to ascertain the principal domains, possible prospects, and obstacles related to the implementation of these technologies in Ukraine. Moreover, the primary objective of this study is to offer suggestions for the successful incorporation of artificial intelligence (AI) into the digital marketing tactics implemented by libraries in Ukraine. The subject of inquiry relates to the field of research technique. In order to achieve our stated goal, we utilized various scientific approaches such as analysis, substantiation, systematization, comparison, and generalization. To acquire empirical data, a comprehensive examination was conducted on relevant literature and case studies concerning worldwide libraries that have integrated artificial intelligence (AI) into their digital marketing strategies. The collected data underwent statistical analysis, and the results were utilized to formulate recommendations for Ukrainian libraries regarding the efficient integration of artificial intelligence into their digital marketing plan. The notion of scientific novelty pertains to the degree of originality or innovativeness exhibited by a scientific investigation or breakthrough. The essay presents a fresh perspective on the incorporation of artificial intelligence in libraries to facilitate the implementation of digital marketing strategies. This study presents a proposition that involves analysing worldwide experiences to identify strategies and technology that can be utilized to effectively enhance the promotion of library services in the digital realm. Furthermore, the essay highlights the potential of artificial intelligence technologies in addressing the challenges faced by the library industry in Ukraine, while also offering practical recommendations for their successful integration. In conclusion, it may be deduced that... The present study has successfully identified and delineated five fundamental sectors in which artificial intelligence is employed within the specific context of digital marketing for international libraries. The fields encompassed in this context consist of chatbots, recommendation systems, smart libraries, digital archives, and user behaviour analysis. The integration of artificial intelligence (AI) presents a multitude of possible benefits. These capabilities encompass the capacity to customize user experiences through the provision of content recommendations that are in line with individual preferences and search histories. Moreover, artificial intelligence has the potential to improve search functionality by delivering more accurate and relevant outcomes. The utilization of chatbots for real-time interaction has the potential to enhance user engagement. In addition, artificial intelligence (AI) allows for the examination of user behaviour, so easing the creation of focused marketing campaigns. Additionally, it streamlines the analysis of large datasets, facilitating the detection of patterns and trends. Finally, artificial intelligence has the capability to automate operations that are repetitive in nature, in addition to other advantages. One of the main challenges faced while employing AI technology is the lack of necessary resources, technical and technological direction, as well as the relevant expertise and skills. Libraries has the capacity to forge partnerships with experts in the field of artificial intelligence (AI) or other libraries that have already included AI elements into their operations. This collaboration has the potential to facilitate the identification of areas that require improvement and investment. Furthermore, libraries have the capacity to find workers who possess the necessary abilities and expertise to proficiently oversee and provide assistance for intelligent technology. Furthermore, it is imperative for libraries to explore the potential of information and communication technology (ICT) devices in order to enhance the effectiveness and efficiency of their information service delivery. Moreover, it is imperative to strive towards improving the effectiveness of information and communication technology. Libraries should continually endeavour to increase their competencies and engage in ongoing assessment and adjustment of their services and technologies in a proactive manner. In conclusion, it is crucial for libraries to establish a clearly defined marketing strategy and an implementation plan for artificial intelligence (AI) that are in accordance with the library's aims and objectives.

The future obsolescence of libraries in the twenty-first century hinges on their capacity to proficiently employ emerging technology and augment the provision of information and services (Oyetola et al., 2023). The study aims to explore the potential applications and implications of artificial intelligence within the framework of contemporary library services in Nigeria. Methods: This study utilizes an expository research approach to evaluate the adoption and effects of artificial intelligence in contemporary library services, specifically focusing on the Nigerian setting. The present study investigates the possible application of artificial intelligence (AI) in academic libraries with the aim of improving and streamlining library services. This research employs a systematic review of pertinent literature to explore this topic. The results of this study underscore the limited uptake and utilization of artificial intelligence (AI) inside university libraries in Nigeria, despite its considerable potential for augmenting library services. The scarcity of scholarly investigations about the relationship between artificial intelligence (AI) and librarianship can be ascribed to a dearth of knowledge and restricted integration of AI's importance within library environments. It is imperative to acknowledge that the conclusions articulated in this column are the writers' own unique ideas and do not rely on any copyrighted materials. The editorial proposes the adoption of artificial intelligence technology, including chatbots, barcodes, RFIDs, and robots, as a means to improve the quality of services provided by academic libraries in Nigeria. Moreover, it is imperative for libraries to capitalize on the potential advantages presented by artificial intelligence in order to reestablish connections with their geographically distant users and consequently restore their prominence within the user community.

The library management landscape has experienced notable transformations in recent years due to the increasing use of Artificial Intelligence. The utilization of artificial intelligence (AI) technology holds great potential in enhancing the efficiency, accuracy, and user contentment in the domains of library cataloguing, management, and operations. The aim of this study is to investigate the influence of artificial intelligence (AI) on library management and its practical implementation. The increasing integration of artificial intelligence (AI) within libraries can be ascribed to developments in technology and a heightened acknowledgment of the potential benefits it presents. The advantages encompass enhanced precision and efficacy in the administration of library data, heightened user satisfaction, and decreased expenses. This presentation will additionally provide a provisional timeline of the increasing integration of artificial intelligence (AI) in library management and operations in the past few years. The present study will finish by analysing the limitations and challenges that arise during the deployment of artificial intelligence (AI) in library settings. Moreover, this chapter will elucidate key considerations that libraries must consider when integrating artificial intelligence (AI) into their operations. According to Bisht et al. (2023), this study is expected to provide valuable insights into the influence of artificial intelligence (AI) on the advancement and utilization of library management systems. As a result, these findings will empower libraries to make educated decisions regarding their investments in technology and operational approaches.

A study by Lin et al. (2023) found that the advent of advanced intelligence has significant implications for the evolution of library services. It highlights the challenges and opportunities that library services must address through mandatory restructuring. The outsourcing of the library's digital reading promotion service will be delegated to a third-party entity. The businesses responsible for providing services to enhance the dissemination of digital reading materials are frequently referred to as "data aggregators" within the industry. The present phenomena of digital reading has become increasingly prevalent in the evolution of libraries. There is a notable trend of individuals participating in online book reading, hence eliminating the need to purchase physical copies. As a result, there has been a consistent increase in the number of individuals who participate in daily reading activities. In order to accommodate to the requirements of these readers, libraries should give them high-quality services, a goal that can be fulfilled through the employment of artificial intelligence technology. AI technology has the ability to enhance the services supplied by libraries by successfully distinguishing the interests and reading patterns of library clients. This enables libraries to offer more specialized suggestions based on customers' interests and past reading behaviour, even in circumstances when the duration of each book or reading session is unknown.

Artificial intelligence (AI) is a notable technological achievement in contemporary times (Hussain, 2023). The technology in question has been tied to numerous industries such as commerce, defence, health, and education. However, its impact on library services is intended to enhance informed decision-making. Artificial intelligence (AI) is a widespread technology applied in library services, capable of changing the provision of high-quality services within the context of the information technology era. The purpose of this research is to highlight the application of artificial intelligence (AI) in the arena of library operations. Numerous studies have been undertaken relative to this topic; yet, they generally focus on a limited number of applications. This research intends to explore the advantages and downsides of artificial intelligence (AI) in the context of library services. The relationship between AI and libraries is significant; nonetheless, there are still questions concerning the utilization and comprehension of AI in library services, which will be investigated in this study. This study intends to provide significant insights for policy makers, librarians, and scholars in the field, enabling them to proactively handle the highlighted difficulties prior to the application of AI in library services. The present study adopts a qualitative approach and incorporates content analysis techniques as its methodology. The existing corpus of literature relevant to the subject matter was thoroughly studied and given to analysis in the context of this study. This study intends to explore the advantages and disadvantages of artificial intelligence (AI) in the context of library services, as well as provide alternative cures for the observed issues. The results of this study demonstrate that artificial intelligence (AI) is a dynamic technology with potential applications in library services. Nevertheless, various hurdles, such as insufficient financing, librarians' attitudes, and technical competence, impede the efficient integration of AI in library operations. The results additionally suggest that the incorporation of artificial intelligence (AI) into library operations will speed the evolution of libraries in a favourable trajectory. Moreover, this study elucidates a multiplicity of applications that can be done without paying any resources. This study intends to explore the comprehension of artificial intelligence (AI) within the context of library services, with the intention of supporting librarians and information professionals in efficiently deploying AI technology in diverse library contexts. Moreover, the introduction of artificial intelligence (AI) in library services is predicted to provide advantageous consequences. The societal repercussions of this study are predicted to serve as a catalyst for library professionals to embrace the utilization of artificial intelligence (AI) in their services, thereby supporting the advancement of library operations in a good trajectory.

The future of Libraries With Artificial Intelligence

Artificial intelligence (AI) has exerted a considerable influence on university libraries, resulting to a paradigm shift in their operational procedures and a fundamental transformation of the services they provide. There exist various key manners in which artificial intelligence (AI) is having influence on university libraries.

Enhanced Information Retrieval

The usage of AI-powered algorithms results in better efficiency and accuracy in the retrieval of information. Through the evaluation of substantial data and user behaviour, artificial intelligence (AI) systems have the power to deliver search outcomes that are more pertinent. This ability enables students and researchers in promptly and successfully locating the relevant information. This method significantly conserves time and increases the overall user experience.

Personalized Recommendations

Artificial intelligence algorithms have the power to assess user preferences, browsing history, and academic interests in order to deliver specialized suggestions for books, articles, and research papers. The deployment of a personalized strategy increases the ability of students and researchers to unearth innovative resources and explore into areas that they may not have previously contemplated. This technique promotes an environment that stimulates continuing education and the growth of intellectual capacities.

Intelligent Resource Management

Artificial intelligence (AI) technology, such as natural language processing and machine vision, have the power to automate cataloguing processes, digitize items, and efficiently arrange information within libraries. The adoption of this strategy promotes the efficiency of administrative activities and facilitates the ease of access to resources, thereby widening their availability to a more extensive range of individuals. Artificial intelligence (AI) has the ability to contribute to the optimization of collection development through the analysis of consumption patterns and the forecast of future demand for certain resources.

Virtual Assistants and Chatbots

AI-driven virtual assistants and chatbots give quick support to patrons of libraries. The librarians possess the ability to handle regularly requested issues, give help for research-related concerns, and offer guidance in accessing library services and relevant materials. These virtual assistants provide 24/7 guidance, increasing the entire user experience and providing quick assistance for students and researchers.

Dashboards for Libraries

The **core purpose** of any dashboard library is to communicate actionable information at a glance, you need to figure out the far-reaching goals of analysis and define metrics or KPIs to measure in a specific department. Employees often spend hours trying to compose meaningful reports with inconvenient tools, creating a big drain on efficiency in the team. To prevent this from happening, one can provide them with **ready-to-use data dashboard libraries** equipped with **interactive features** and **intelligible visualizations**. The advantage of this is one can control all the aspects of a dashboard (both visual and functional) and customize it whenever required. The data dashboard can consist of many elements of varying complexity: *charts, tables, maps, graphs, networks, diagrams, word clouds, timelines, widgets*, etc. Key characteristics of a full-featured dashboard library are the *ease of customization* and displaying trends in data.

Data Analysis for Decision-Making

Artificial intelligence (AI) improves the application of data analytics within libraries, thereby boosting their ability to make educated and improved judgments. Through the evaluation of consumption patterns, artificial intelligence (AI) algorithms have the power to deliver valuable insights regarding resource utilization. This, in turn, allows libraries to optimize their collections, distribute funding in a more efficient manner, and tailor their services to better respond to the wants of their consumers.

Collaboration and Knowledge Sharing

Artificial intelligence (AI) plays a significant role in boosting collaboration and fostering knowledge exchange among library users. One indication of the potential benefits of AI-powered platforms is their capacity to create connections among users who share common academic interests. This skill has the potential to build interdisciplinary alliances and promote a feeling of community within the academic setting.

In general, artificial intelligence (AI) is having a dramatic impact on university libraries. It includes refining the process of retrieving information, delivering individualized recommendations, optimizing the management of resources, improving the user experience, supporting data-driven decision-making, and promoting cooperation and the sharing of knowledge. The aforementioned enhancements contribute to sustain the vital function of libraries in promoting academic research, instruction, and knowledge acquisition within the setting of the digital era. Although making predictions on the future of any profession is highly difficult, this study will seek to do so by a combination of reviewing the available literature, and unique research. While there has been significant discussion and academic research regarding the potential future consequences of automation, and attempts to evaluate public attitudes to this, there has not yet been a study focused explicitly on library staff and users' opinions of robotics and AI. The unique study carried out for this dissertation has thus attempted to do this, utilizing the hybrid approach of an online survey and a focus group, and building on some of the related research that has already been carried out. It is hoped that this original research, combined with an analysis of the literature and previous studies, will be able to draw out some interesting issues related to libraries and automation, reflecting on the past, evaluating the present situation, and looking ahead to what the future may hold for libraries, and library workers in particular.

CONCLUSION

The application of Artificial Intelligence (AI) in libraries has the capacity to radically revolutionize library operations and improve user experiences. The following article presents a comprehensive assessment of the numerous applications of artificial intelligence (AI) technology inside libraries. These applications encompass AI chatbots, intelligent libraries, robotics, and a spectrum of AI-based services applied in library environments. The results of this review reveal that artificial intelligence (AI) has the ability to enhance information retrieval, streamline repetitive tasks, adapt user interactions, and offer unique services. Artificial intelligence (AI)-driven chatbots have proved their ability to properly manage customer queries and give rapid service, therefore boosting overall user happiness. Integrating AI technology into libraries can optimize the operations of cataloguing, classification, and recommendation, thereby simplifying effective information retrieval for library users. The integration of artificial intelligence (AI) in libraries involves a collection of difficulties and considerations. Ethical considerations, concerns over privacy, and the obligation to assure equitable information access are essential factors that necessitate thorough attention. Libraries are faced with the issue of creating a delicate equilibrium between the advantages afforded by AI technologies and the maintenance of human-centric values. It is imperative to ensure that AI serves as a supplementary tool that amplifies and improves the efforts of librarians, rather than rendering their roles obsolete. In order to increase academic understanding, it is necessary to do additional investigation that looks into the enduring implications of artificial intelligence (AI) on library operations, user habits, and information services. Furthermore, it is imperative to emphasize the significance of collaboration among libraries, academics, and technology developers in order to propel the progress of artificial intelligence (AI) solutions that are specifically customized to cater to the unique requirements of libraries and their varied range of users. It is vital to prioritize programs targeted at boosting knowledge dissemination and facilitating the exchange of exemplary techniques in order to speed the incorporation of artificial intelligence (AI) technology within library environments. Artificial intelligence (AI) possesses the capability to revolutionize libraries by converting them into interactive environments that prioritize the needs of users, ensuring convenient access to information and personalized services. Through the utilization of artificial intelligence (AI), libraries have the potential to optimize their operational effectiveness, broaden their scope of influence, and provide novel and inventive encounters for their clientele. As artificial intelligence (AI) progresses, it is imperative for libraries to adopt and integrate new technologies into their operations, while also adhering to their fundamental principles of ensuring fair and comprehensive availability of knowledge to all individuals. The existing body of literature pertaining to the utilization of artificial intelligence (AI) methodologies inside library settings remains quite constrained, exhibiting a dearth of academic investigations in this particular domain. The authors highlight the significance of artificial intelligence (AI) in enhancing the accessibility of digital collections and facilitating novel avenues for research. The conclusion underscores the interdependent association between artificial intelligence (AI) and libraries, positing that libraries have the potential to make valuable contributions to the ongoing advancement of AI.

REFERENCES

Abdulwahid, A. H., Pattnaik, M., Palav, M. R., Tilak Babu, S. B. G., Manoharan, G., & Pandi Selvi, G. (2023). Library Management System Using Artificial Intelligence. *2023 Eighth International Conference on Science Technology Engineering and Mathematics (ICONSTEM)*, Chennai, India. 10.1109/ICONSTEM56934.2023.10142904

Bisht, S. R., Nautiyal, A. P., Sharma, S., Sati, M. D., Bathla, N., & Singh, P. (2023). The role of Artificial Intelligence in shaping Library Management and its Utilization. *2023 International Conference on Disruptive Technologies (ICDT),* (pp. 467-472). IEEE. 10.1109/ICDT57929.2023.10150520

Hussain, A. (2023). Use of artificial intelligence in the library services: Prospects and challenges. *Library Hi Tech News*, *40*(2), 15–17. doi:10.1108/LHTN-11-2022-0125

Ivashkevych, O. (2023). *Artificial Intelligence in Acoustics of Library Functioning in Ukraine. Scientific journal "Library Science*. Record Studies. Informology.

Lin, X., Sun, Y., & Zhang, Y., & R, K.M. (2023). Application of AI in Library Digital Reading Promotion Service. *2023 IEEE International Conference on Integrated Circuits and Communication Systems (ICICACS),* (pp. 1-6). IEEE.

Liu, M., Zhao, C., Peng, X., Yu, S., Wang, H., & Sha, C. (2023). Task-Oriented ML/DL Library Recommendation Based on a Knowledge Graph. *IEEE Transactions on Software Engineering*, *49*, 4081–4096. doi:10.1109/TSE.2023.3285280

Maranchak, N. (2023). The Use of Artificial Intelligence in Digital Marketing of the Library Industry in Ukraine: Foreign Experience and Prospects. *Digital Platform: Information Technologies in Sociocultural Sphere*. IEEE.

Olusegun Oyetola, S., Oladokun, B. D., Ezinne Maxwell, C., & Obotu Akor, S. (2023). *Artificial intelligence in the library: Gauging the potential application and implications for contemporary library services in Nigeria*. Data & Metadata.

Chapter 2
AI in Academic Libraries:
Success, Pitfalls, Perceptions, and Why We Need AI Literacy

Stefka Tzanova
York College, CUNY, USA

ABSTRACT

This chapter discusses the implementation of artificial intelligence (AI) in academic libraries and the impact of AI related technologies on various library services. AI impacts research and educational activities in academic institutions so they can provide adequate operations and collaborative technologies in order to support diverse curricula and research. The complexity of research workflows and their variability couples with increasing demand for effective personalized education, so it acts as a driving force for application of AI related technologies. AI assisted library services demand reimaging traditional libraries' roles, so that librarians would become not only users of AI technologies but also co-creators and experts capable of conceptualizing AI driven services to library patrons. That requires librarians to promote AI literacy as a framework encompassing research literacy and data literacy, and understood as a necessary skill set for effectively communicating in an AI driven medium.

INTRODUCTION

Artificial intelligence (AI) is defined as intelligent performance expressed by artificial body. Typically, the AI is associated with some brainy behavior demonstrated by a "system", where the latter is normally a computer program. From libraries'

DOI: 10.4018/979-8-3693-1573-6.ch002

perspective AI is a technological implementation of the synergy between computing and psychology which can be used to increase librarians' productivity by providing techniques to conduct tasks quicker and in better way; to improve quality of library services; to enhance the quality of information yields and to advance the communication with patrons. Successful adoption of AI is still debatable due to the fact that there are many requirements to be met (Harisanty et al., 2023). AI in libraries is focused on improvements of reference services, cataloging, classification of data, indexing, document delivery and communication with users, but is used in a way that preserves "human centric" entity of the library – namely intuitiveness, cultural sensitivity and emotions. For the libraries the human centric context together with need to improve effectiveness on various levels define the subset of AI technologies applicable to library operations. All implementations fall under the umbrella of human-centered AI (HCAI), but use various technologies most suitable for libraries' services. That include rule based and fuzzy logic-based systems, natural language processing systems (NLP), machine learning (ML), pattern recognition and robotics. It is important to mention that other AI associated with perceptual tasks or theorem proving etc., are of little use for academic libraries. The above mentioned AI technologies are current in a systems associated with library automation such as library robots and with systems allied with core library services such as reference, collection development, scholarly communication, cataloging and indexing, and information retrieval. The latter services are the focus of this text.

DEFINITIONS AND TYPES OF AI

The term "artificial intelligence" (AI) is both an opaque and yet powerful expression which startles many librarians. The definition given by John McCarthy in 1956, at the first ever AI conference, describes AI as "the science and engineering of making intelligent machines". That characterization, however, diverges significantly from modern understanding of the entity of AI. The confusion comes from the fact that the term has at the same time scientific, technical, and social designations. Consequently, there are formal and informal AI definitions which exist in parallel. The informal definitions are associated with humanistic perspective of AI and thus typically counterpoint machine-based AI to native human intelligence. This designation seeks to answer the fundamental question "Can machines think?", formulated in the late 1950s by Alan Turing. He invented a test named after him (Turing test) to determine machine's "intelligent behavior" by looking at whether or not "the system acts like a human". Per this test the intelligence assessment of the machine is based on the computer's ability to produce responses indistinguishable from the ones generated by a human in a course of human-computer interaction. The humanistic approach focuses on generated knowledge concerning the interaction between machine and human intelligence including technologies. This view caused some researchers to introduce other definitions of AI inspired by different characteristics of human and machine rooted intelligence. Thus, De Cremer and Kasparov (2021) juxtapose machine associated AI to Authentic (human) Intelligence and define a third type of AI –Augmented AI (AuI). The latter is a machine-complemented Authentic Intelligence in which the machine deals with voluminous data tasks and calculations, but the human takes a leading role in switching from short term to long term strategies using his/her ability to anticipate, feel, and judge. It is important to mention that De Cremer and Kasparov drive the distinguished line between machine intelligence and human intelligence based on types of tasks suitable for one or the other. Thus, machine AI is understood only as useful for closed management systems with well-defined scenarios while the openness was attributed only to human rooted intelligence.

Technical definitions sway away from philosophical descriptions and define AI in terms of its scope, output and/or mode of use. From that perspective AI is considered to cover two large classes: weak AI, sometimes called Artificial Narrow Intelligence (ANI), and strong AI. ANI is dedicated to performing specific tasks such as Amazon's Alexa or Apple's Siri assistants. Strong AI is the theoretical arrangement of AI and includes Artificial Super Intelligence (ASI) and Artificial General Intelligence (AGI), and it targets to provide systems with self-aware perception and accordingly with the ability to solve complex problems independently, to learn multipart concepts, and to plan for the future. It is important to mention that more than 90% of current AI implementations are of the ANI type.

From the perspective of AI output the technical descriptions articulate generative AI (GAI) and predictive AI (PAI). The former is a set of ML models that can generate new data, i.e., the output are objects that look like the ones on which model is trained, while the latter deals with predictions over the existing data set. The common characteristic of all GAI implementations is that they convert input into a series of tokens, each of which represents a chunk of data. Then the program manipulates these tokens and generates new data that looks similar to training instances. ChatGPT is the most popular perception of GAI and operates in the same way as well-known Markov Chains, but with essential differences of vast complexity and huge number of parameters. Thus, ChatGPT cuts text in statistically meaningful chunks using probabilities for words and sentences learned in training phase. The pattern of obtained blocks is then used to propose whatever comes next. It is important to mention that ChatGPT is not universal AI and has its limitations. First, ChatGPT is only Large Language model (LLM) and thus it does not have cognitive and self-aware abilities. Therefore, it cannot provide or understand logical or common-sense reasoning in generated text if the former is not covered in training. In practice, the longer the ChatGPT response is, the more likely it will lack coherence and guiding logic according to Houston and Corrado (2023). Second, ChatGPT is designed and is finely tuned to generate text and thus is inferior to other LLM models such as Google's BERT, RoBERT and Microsoft XLNet when the task is analyzing and understanding some text. In principle, it is important to mention that GAI solutions are not always the best algorithm for all types of data; e.g., many non-generative traditional ML methods perform much better on highly structured data (i.e., tables). In addition, GAI tend to propagate and even enhance the bias that occurs in training data sets.

"Generative Adversarial Network" (GAN) is another variety of generative AI associated with image manipulations. The underlying "Diffusion Models" (DM) are ML models that can generate new data samples that resemble the ones in a training set. DM have been used to create realistic-looking images and for text-to-image generation in StableDiffusion system (Meng, C., et al., 2023).

AI IN LIBRARY SERVICES

AI in library services is associated with the adoption of AI enabled applications to support library services and the eventual changes to libraries and librarianship. There are two distinct classes of AI implementation in library services. The first one is AI-enabled "back-end" systems such as library robots. These machines are preprogrammed autonomy systems which can execute such tasks (i.e. select and deliver books) and can learn the optimal ways to do it (Cox, 2022). The second one is AI-enabled implementations dealing with "front end" library services. These implementations took decades to mature, despite the fact that some areas (cataloging and indexing, acquisition and collection development, reference services, information literacy) were ready since the 1990s (Lancaster & Smith, 1990). The main reason was that AI technologies reached current maturity after decades of development. Consequently, under expanding AI abilities, the topic of applicability and scope of intelligent technologies to library services remained an active field of research in the last couple of decades. Early researchers tried to predict the collective impact of AI on library services and consequently to identify possible areas of application of AI in libraries (Balleste, 2002). Some scholars conducted case studies focused on the use of AI technologies in specialized libraries, e.g., law libraries (Balleste, 2006). In addition, some researchers study the benefits of AI only in terms of particular (current at that time) technology. For instance, Alberico (2011) analyzed the use of expert systems in libraries in a context of five areas: knowledge institutions, knowledge media, modes of disclosure, knowledge industry, and implications. Recently the landscape of AI technologies used in library services was studied by Asemi (2018). It was reported that the natural language processing technology is still faintly represented in AI assisted library services, and that more traditional AI techniques (ML, ES etc.) are predominant. In particular the authors found that recommender systems are the most commonly used AI assisted tools in library services. To handle data uncertainties, these tools utilize various fuzzy models and apply fuzzy, but not Boolean logic in inference. The output is typically a list of resources tailored to particular user(s) and/or project. For example, the reported SIE2IN system (Porcel, C., et all., 2009) uses Fuzzy Language Models (FLM). The system demonstrates 63% precision in resource identification compared to librarians' recommendations to a group of users. In a context of referral services Butkovich (2019) reported development of fuzzy ES coupled with natural language processing module. The system was used in reference services at Texas A&M University. The system accepts the natural language requests from students and outputs "list of titles, call numbers, locations, types of sources, and broad subject headings". Some of the AI assisted library services grew and developed together with AI technologies themselves. The system CiteSeerX (Wu, Kim, Giles, 2016), was the first application using AI in a digital library search engine. The system was commissioned in 1998, but for over twenty years it underwent re-design and expansion of the AI algorithms. The team added algorithms for citation parsing, table extraction, author name disambiguation, document classification, and data cleansing. (Wu, Liang, Yang, et al., 2019).

The adoption of AI in library services sparked concerns about its impact on libraries and librarianship. The key question was whether AI may cause a loss of the humanitarian nature in libraries. Some researchers perceive AI as an avenue to corrupt the library mission (Massis, 2018); others argue that AI assisted services will lead to decline of the roles of librarians since patrons will not seek their expertise anymore (Johnson, 2018); some others advise toward needed regulations of AI (Oyelude, 2017). The latter are seen as necessary dealings to preserve the human-centered landscape of the library. In that context Miao (Miao, 2019) investigated the impact of AI in the context of human rights ethics. The question of preserving human control over AI enabled tools in the library's workflow boils up to the implementation of AI tools designed under HCAI principles. Margetis et al. (2021) define these as use of explainable AI (XAI), semantic, cognitive and perceptual computing, visual predictive analysis, interactive machine learning and federated learning. Several university centers already develop pioneer AI enabled applications for libraries utilizing above mentioned HCAI principles. Among them are the Computer Science and Artificial Intelligence Lab at MIT, Digital Skills Lab at the University of Oklahoma, Artificial Intelligence Lab at the University of Rhode Island and Stanford's HAI Institute to name few of them (Schmager, Pappas, Vassilakopoulou, 2023).

Another noteworthy issue related to AI in library services are the ethical implications of AI, namely privacy, transparency and balance between efficiency and human involvement (Hodonu-Wusu, 2024). Unfortunately, the use of ethics principles has not been systematically used in AI development, because the businesses apply AI-ethics checks on per-product basis, despite of chance to waste money and time. (Blackman, 2020). For instance, the Smart City, a Google's project for Toronto, was abandoned because the algorithm cannot guarantee absence of discrimination against women (Filion et al., 2023). Often the developers are not educated to answer ethical questions systematically, exhaustively, and efficiently. Consequently, as instructors and mentors, the librarians should focus on training the students to spot ethical problems caused by technology. Such approach can incorporate ethics in the AI development process indirectly and on personal level. Another aspect of AI ethics is the embedded bias. Programmers may introduce subconscious and conscious bias(es) in algorithms in addition to ethical problems caused by incomplete, incorrect or biased training sets. Librarians' ability to correct one or other bias "on the fly" depends on type of underlying AI. For instance, unsupervised ML is inaccessible, while supervised ML allows human intervention leading to more ethics-driven outcome. Librarians analyze the system output – namely how often and in which context the output is correct – and they compare it to their own practical experience. This way even without being direct participants in AI development process, the librarians can evaluate the "trustworthiness" of particular technology and further prepare guidelines and policies. The use of AI-enabled technologies in library and information services obliges librarians to inform and educate users about the capabilities, interfaces and limitations of AI. However, the lack of explicit formulation of AI ethics in academic and research libraries guiding documents (e.g. Framework for Information Literacy for Higher Education) negatively impacts the incorporation of ethics in Information Literacy classes (Nayyer & Rodriguez, 2022). De-facto the Information literacy for Higher Education Framework (Board, ACRL, 2016), deals with ethics only implicitly via its formulated principles. More recent (2019) "Ethics Guidelines for Trustworthy AI" published by European Commission addresses ethics responsibilities of developers and researchers, institutions and research librarians in a context of AI (Nikolinakos, 2023).

The scope of AI caused ethical dilemmas are also technology dependent. That requires specific skills and knowledge from librarians in addition to familiarity with ethics. For all AI-ethical issues such as plagiarism, copyright, equity and inquisition, transparency, etc. the librarians must have a grasp of core AI-driven services and teach patrons about possible negative implications of given AI application. For example a ChatGPT application may raise ethical concerns about transparency and privacy. Then the librarians can rise patrons' awareness about possible privacy leakage due to the underlying reinforcement learning algorithm and lack of transparency by design (Wu et al., 2023).

AI in Cataloging and Indexing

Cataloging is one of the core library activities requiring manual work from staff. The practice is tedious, time consuming and error prone, but it is guided by explicit rules. This "rule centric" nature of the cataloging process and accumulated knowledge and experience in development of ES in various areas inspired first attempts to create cataloging ES. It was assumed that MARC format, AACR2 rules, and OCLC guidelines interpretations are well-structured and understood data that can be easily represented as knowledge instances in a cataloging ES database.

The first cataloging ES (1984) was reported as unsuccessful with the reason cited as inadequate hardware which could not hold all of AACR2 (Hjerppe & Olander, 1989). However, the following attempts to apply ES in cataloging also proved themselves mostly unsuccessful and lacked accuracy despite the availability of comprehensive and complex rules (Šauperl & Saye, 2011). The problem was twofold: first, AACR2 rules and MARC records were identified to have structure and organization which imposes ambiguities for inference machine of rule-based ES; second, the process of expert knowledge transfer to ES produced bad results since human experts typically cannot translate their empirical expertise in formal terms, and thus to convey accurate knowledge to ES. The pursued solutions include redefining of cataloging rules and their division in smaller classes; using predicate languages such as Prolog to permit dynamic generation of ES rules (simple yes/no dialog) (Davies & James,1984); use of cataloging maps to better match limitations of rule based ES (Ercegovac & Borko, 1992). Unfortunately, none of the proposed cataloging ES (Olmstadt, 2000) was effective. The setback was rooted in the use of incompatible AI technology incapable to handle multifaceted knowledge which requires different representations (in particular the used ES built decision trees by applying production rules to token stream data base). In the case of representation of complex knowledge this organization leads to building of multiple deep decision trees which are very difficult to traverse. In addition, the system lacked flexibility due to token stream model – if the first character of the stream differs the whole match gets discarded.

AI based cataloging was revived with the appearance of ChatGPT in 2022. One may expect ChatGPT to perform better on cataloging, in comparison to ES, because the former uses forward neural network (NN) and thus is free from manipulating heavy decision trees. Recently Brzustowicz (2023) claimed that ChatGPT successfully resolved several cataloging tests and spawned correct MARC records. However, the reported results and highly touted "silver bullet" cataloging capabilities of ChatGPT were reviewed and strongly criticized by Amram, T., and colleagues (all cataloging librarians). The team analyzed Brzustowicz's results and concluded that the reported outcomes are "intrinsically" flawed and incorrect (Amram, Malmud &

Hollingsworth, 2023). The team pointed out that ChatGPT is simply a large language model which generates text by predicting the next word based on the list of calculated probabilities of each word in a given text vs. training texts. ChatGPT does not have the capabilities of self-understanding or self-consciousness. Consequently, when generating new objects, ChatGPT tends to propagate and even amplify the bias/error from the training set. The mathematical explanation of ChatGPT is beyond the scope of this text, but a good rationalization can be found in Steven Wolfram's work (Wolfram, 2023).

ChatGPT is based on forward NNs which are implementations of the mathematical models defined by McCulloch and Pitts (1943). As language model, ChatGPT is similar to the Markov model (1906), but achieves remarkable results because of its own complexity, huge number of parameters and extensive training on the whole web.

In the area of indexing AI was summoned to automate the tedious and error prone process of concept identifications and their translation into verbal descriptions using controlled vocabulary terms. The simplest approach in designing AI-assisted indexing system is to couple automatic content analysis with a thesaurus in order to spawn sets of keywords in addition to those proposed by humans. In reality, AI-enabled indexing systems combine AI methodologies with statistical methods processing the statistical associations and correlations, syntactical techniques targeting design of noun phrases and semantic procedures dealing with identification of context-bearing words and knowledge-based systems. The extensive classification of indexing systems can be found in *Encyclopedia of Library and Information Science* (McDonald & Levine-Clark, 2017). From the perspective of AI, the current designs utilize NLP, classification, reasoning, automatic content analysis, inference mechanisms and set of ML algorithms for data manipulations and data mining. The particular set of applied AI technologies vary across systems and is determined by the system's desired scope, functionality, original design and level of development. For instance, one of the most advanced indexing systems was developed by the National Library of Medicine and is called Medical Text Indexer (MTI) (Mork, et al., 2013), (Aronson et al., 2004). The system is alleged to replace humans in indexing and to provide fully automated service. It uses various AI technologies to capture human skills and experience; i.e., it uses NLP to seize human capabilities for the task of curation of biomedical literature. For the jobs of large texts categorizations and for chores of comparison between categorizations the MTI incorporates a ML module capable of meta-learning. In addition, in the core of MTI are Medical Subject Headings (MeSH) thesaurus and Meta-thesaurus both used by advanced classifier and ranker. The MTI universe is enriched with tools such as Unified Medical Language System (UMLS) aimed to augment, update and expand MTI vocabularies and standards. However, despite its complex structure and advanced AI technologies the latest comparative study by Chen (2023) revealed that MTI cannot yet be used as automated indexing implementation. The key problem is that the system exhibits inconsistencies in applying specificity principles with possible introduction of contradictions and biases in Medline. Consequently, librarians are advised to assess the changes introduced to index terms. Furthermore, Chen and colleagues recommended further assessment of MTI effectiveness and accuracy when the latter is used in searching for medical information or in semantic explores.

Another approach is designing AI-enabled indexing systems as frameworks using available open source AI tools in contrast to stand-alone closed systems as MTI (NLM) and MIA (NASA). This method offers more flexibility, because it utilizes open-source and popular tools, libraries and algorithms. In addition, open-source frameworks may get extended support and faster development from the communities. For example, the recently reported Annif framework (Ahmed, Mukhopadhyay, Mukhopadhyay, 2023) is based on Python and utilizes ready to apply Python routines – Term Frequency Inverse Document Frequency of records (TF-IDF) used to calculate relevance of words in a text and NLTK routine used to divides text into sentences. More importantly it utilizes the Neural Network of Ensemble (NNE) to overcome uncertainties discussed above by combining distinct base models. Nevertheless, the open-source frameworks may use different formats of thesaurus and metadata, so some additional tools and work may be needed to match the framework's vocabularies and meta-data with other vocabularies, e.g., with MeSH's vocabulary and metafiles.

AI in Acquisitions and Collection Development

In the process of acquisitions and collection development (ACD) librarians conduct specific tasks such as verification of bibliographic description, checking various available formats, etc. all under constraints of the library budgets. Under the presumption of "collection is owned by the library" the earlier attempts to automate ACD followed two paths. The first one used ES to assist librarians to "select the best and most relevant material for the library" (Das & Islam, 2021). The proposed systems aimed to provide advice based on matrix of answers they obtain from users. For instance, the Selection Advisor (an ES) inputs the users' answers from a questionnaire which covers six predefined categories: subject, intellectual content, potential use, relation to collection, bibliographic considerations, and language (Johnston & Weckert, 1990). Some other early systems also add questions about bibliographic data (e.g. local OPAC); contextual data such as library's policies and current finances such as library's budget. The second approach does not use ES for suggested acquisitions, but models the acquisition and content development process itself. For example, the Bibliographer's Workstation program reported in 1992 uses hypertext and models all four steps in the decision process of the collection development: identification, evaluation, selection/rejection and acquisition (Meador & Cline, 1991).

In the late 1990s, the architype of library collection(s) migrates from "owned" to "provision" model caused by the collective impact of expansion of network technologies that radically enlarged the accessibility of resources, digitalization on national, university and public holdings for access and safeguarding, makeover to network-based content, availability of digital full text databases and incorporation of formal criteria to evaluate the collection's quality. Consequently, in modern terms the library collection transformed from print based owned compendium to a widening assortment of resources, from print to online course modules, electronic books and textbooks, electronic journals and multimodal data sets. The variability in collections, existence of different formats and whole spectra of access modes increase the impact of collection management (synonym of collection development) which becomes central activity requiring routine in-loop tasks of dynamic curation, weeding, and prediction of the use of resources.

Curation and weeding are well defined in terms of descriptors so AI-assisted tools used are predominantly simple rule-based systems with suitable curation rulebook defined by library staff. In particular, the ES with decision tree were the most widely used solutions for that part of collection management process (Wagstaff & Liu, 2018), for instance, reported a weeding procedure in which they loop the list of predefined rules over collection, consulting librarians at each cycle until they reach the desired summary statistics.

In terms of prediction of resources used, the employed AI techniques sway away from rule-based systems toward Machine Learning approaches as reported by Silverstein & Shieber (1996). In particular majority of proposed systems utilize some type of supervised learning algorithms coupled with data mining techniques. The latter is typically used to discover hidden patterns and relevant information for resources usage which the former generates the actual prediction. For instance the DPA-LRBD model "specific to utilize data mining techniques in the context of the academic library to facilitate library administration" (Iqbal, Jamil, Ahmad, et al, 2020) uses deep neural network (DNN) coupled with support vector regressor (SVR) and random forest (RF) learning algorithms for collection management. Training is critical for accuracy so the authors trained their 2,211,413 total records and tweaked 78 parameters. For the latter the authors conducted 100, 300 and 500 epochs. The reported result was that DPA_LRBD achieved a success score (prediction vs actual) of 97% when more than 100 epochs were used.

From librarians' perspective the AI resulting milestones in the collection development process are: conducting data analytics reflecting the current specific needs of library patrons; applying strategies for maximizing the usage of available resources by identifying gaps in the collection and predicting new subject areas of interest based on data patterns; reaching out to faculty in order to involve them in the process (of collection development); enriching collection diversity by integrating different perspectives and ordering materials in underrepresented areas; enhancing order processing (automatically tracking order statuses, generating receipts, maintaining records of past transactions, etc.); developing methodologies for collection assessment and evaluation in order to most effectively use the library budget; developing metrics to evaluate what needs to be preserved. Obviously, partial or full automation of acquisitions and collection development process requires AI implementations which can learn from collection and patrons' requests and make reasonable predictions. ChatGPT offers enormous potential to libraries – it has the capabilities to automate aforementioned routine tasks leaving librarians free to work on strategies.

AI in Information Retrieval

Information retrieval systems (IRS) assist with retrieval, storage and representation of documents in various formats. Modern IRS applied in academic libraries are intervened with users' needs, users' feedback, documents' relevance and evaluation by librarians and patrons. Accordingly, the assessment of the effectiveness of particular IRS is done in the context of library services and is convolution of used technical solutions and non-technical metrics such as user's satisfaction, friendliness of IRS interface, or other applicable information science norms. All IRS loop versions of likelihood algorithms, depending on the type of IRS. Early IRS systems are using product of statistics (TF-IDF) or bag of words (BM25) models in which document is represented with terms (words and phrases). Depending on the IRS's architecture the collection of terms can be generated directly from the document or it can be obtained indirectly from embedded thesaurus and/or domain map. The inference mechanism practices numerical method coupled with term-weighting function(s). The commonly applied approach was to use statistical distribution of terms/keywords in a database and assign inter reliance value to each term. That methodology does not provide accuracy, because it either assumes that each keyword occurs independently and/or because of the assumptions in term-weight functions. In addition, because of the use of lexical only analysis, these systems cannot distinguish terms whose meaning depends on context. Furthermore, these systems will generate exclusive relation (two independent terms) for words which have the same meaning, but different lexical form.

The AI-enabled IRS systems' purpose is to improve IRS by replacing statistical methods with various ML algorithms at each step of IRS workflow. The applied AI technologies come from predictive and generative AI types. For instance, the reverse index generation can explore predictive AI in bibliometric modeling to calculate the "index term frequency distributions, indexing exhaustivity or term assignment, term co-occurrence frequency distributions, database and index growth, and more recently, the aspects of web-based IR such as frequency distributions of in links/ out links and document persistence" (Wolfram, 2016).

The documents' representations sway away from "terms" toward "topic" and with AI appearance to "language" model. For example, the early AI-enabled IRS reported by Strzalkowski, Perez-Carballo, & Martinescu (1996) roots a topic model. To generate "topic" this system applies clustering and parsing methods in order to group the words into topics. It then applies syntactic analyzer and subsequent fast parser aimed to extract certain type of phrases along with singe-word terms. Consequently, the semantic analyzer processes the semantic context and discovers similarity links between smaller subphrases. These similarity links are mapped into semantic relations (generalization, synonym, specialization etc.). The semantic relations are further used to transform user request captured by NLP driven module into a search query. All user requests are given in natural language and are processed by a NLP-enabled module which removes all indexes in requests which occur in unrelated contexts.

For topics model each "topic" is understood as characteristic hyperplane in multidimensional space of the document which must be separated as wide as possible. In other words, the IRS classifier should be able to distinguish clearly across planes and the classification should happen without external data input. These types of classifiers are called "wide margin" classifiers and are in a class of ML known as unsupervised learning algorithms. The classifier suitable for IRS which has the unsupervised learning abilities and can provide maximal gap separation is Supporting Vector Machine (SVM).

Another category of IRS uses language models (Ormeño, Mendoza, Valle., 2021). These IRS implementations consider each document as a language model, i.e., each document is believed to hold a mixture of topics. To conduct IR these systems, attempt to estimate the probability of generating a query from documents. The most widely used techniques are Latent Semantic Indexing (LSI) and probabilistic Latent Semantic Indexing (pLSI), (Deshmukh, Hegde, Lathi, 2012). However, as Wei discovered (Wei & Croft, 2006), the LSI and pLSI models tend to overfit due to their inconsistent semantics – these models utilize a set of individual parameters each linked explicitly to the training set.

In order to avoid the "garbage-in-garbage-out" problem, students/users should be able to formulate a correct query. Simultaneously they should understand the weaknesses and strengths of the particular IRS and be aware of possible biases. At the end of the search, they should be able to critically evaluate the output for meaningfulness and accuracy. The role of librarians in that process is to teach and guide students how to operate AI enabled IRS, to help cleaning the semantics of the problem, to help to design proper query and to convey AI literacy to patrons. That process when combined with increased effectiveness and accuracy of AI-driven IRS proliferates the collective learning and research, expands the interaction between users, fosters user-librarian communication and fuels interest in AI-enabled recommender systems (Dhelim, Aung, Ning, 2020).

AI in Reference Services

The nature of reference session guided by humans is identified as personalization of services and collaboration with the patron (Nardi & O'day, 1996). Early applications of AI in reference services used expert systems (Vickery et al., 1987). In the context of AI applications in reference services there are two interceding knowledge-based technologies: NLP for support of the direct communication with artificial agent, and some generative or predictive AI. The synergy of these technologies falls under the umbrella of Conversational AI as it was described above. Chatbots are instances of this cooperation, but they may have many alternative names such as conversation bots, conversational agents, chatterboxes, interactive bot, virtual talk bot, talk-bot and many others.

Chatbots are designed and tuned for specific application in which they are used. In the academic environment chatbots powered by state machines/finite automata have been used to help academic administration for long time, but recently they had been applied as teaching assistants for some classes (Peterson, 2020) and in library reference services.

There are two different classes of chatbots related to academic library reference services. The first class include pre-programmed implementations capable to answer simple general directional and predictable questions from their training scope. These chatbots are often called information retrieval chatbots. Typical examples are Amazon's Alexa, Echo and Apple's Siri virtual assistants. As reference tools these bots are suitable for routine tasks; they are typically easier to work with than a web site and are naturally remote service enabled. The abilities of preprogrammed bots are quite limited, but they still can support routine explorations based on user's input or they can be used to conduct multi-step explorations which could involve several searches under common goal. In addition, these bots can suggest help from a librarian when further guidance is needed. The second group includes bots driven by generative AI often named generative chatbots. These artificial agents are intended to provide human-like experience in face-to-face sessions. As reference tools they are intended to help resolve exploratory tasks containing complex searches. The most common platform used for that type of bot is ChatGPT. Despite its remarkable ability to generate new text, ChatGPT is not immune from errors, will propagate any bias defined in training sets, tends to be unbalanced towards web resources and does not support self-correction. In addition, the software works bad on nuances and does not provide citations of sources and may "invent" data ("software hallucination"). As shown in examples provided by Houston and colleagues (Houston & Corrado, 2023) these drawbacks may negatively affect any reference service employing ChatGPT.

The introduction of chatbots in libraries happened either a result of an academic institution's individual project or as coordinated effort from several parties such as student groups, college libraries and enterprises. The first "academic" AI-enabled chatbot in the United States was the Pixel project developed entirely with the use of the University of Nebraska Library's AIML language (Artificial Intelligence Mark-up Language) and uses open source PHP code (for web server) and SQL database. Pixel was designed to assist students and faculty to find information on the UNL web site (Allison, 2012). In Europe, Kornelia was the first chatbot settled for the public library. It was developed through joint efforts of several Swiss public libraries, student groups and companies (Dohrmann, Hügi, Scheurer, et. al., 2010).

The application of AI enabled chatbots is typically welcomed by users. As Kaushal and colleagues found in their study, "the stakeholders believe that incorporating chatbot with an existing library information system could deliver diverse services, which in turn would help in research and scholarly communication" (Kaushal & Yadav, 2022). The same authors pointed out users' concerns about privacy, intrusion by chatbots and even their hesitation "with respect to chatbots' comprehension of task complexity".

The common pitfalls with application of chatbots in reference is the patron's level of understanding of the nature and limitations of the chatbot itself. As the examples from CUNY Lehman College library show, some students were not clear about scope and abilities of the library's chatbot and confuse it with library provided chat (with a real librarian). That caused the library staff to change web links and tune the welcome messages to make clear that chatbot was *not* intended for deep research questions.

AI in Scholarly Communications

Bard and ChatGPT are popular instances of GenAI developed by Google and OpenAI. These chatbots are able to generate human-like text based on a given prompt and thus are another example of the powerful potential offered by generative AI. Consequently, most of the publishers today face the dilemma of identifying and, eventually, rejecting content written by these agents. In the realm of scholarly communications within academia, the use of AI can have both a positive and negative impact. It can accelerate formatting, text editing and even the peer review process and significantly reduce the cost of the editorial process. For instance, Elsevier alone employs more than one thousand technologists who are developing applications using ML and NLP

(Gabriel, 2019). The publisher transitioned from print to electronic to information solutions (P-E-S). ScienceDirect Topic Pages and Topics of Prominence are perfect illustrations of successful AI applications in scholarly communications. Along with highlighting the positive features, Gabriel emphasizes the need for monitoring and analyzing emerging AI scholarship. A very popular example is Grammarly, an AI assisted grammar and spellchecker that is used by a great number of students for improving their written English. On the negative side, the fact that ChatGPT can generate content raises issues of copyright and plagiarism, and emphasizes ethical concerns (Curtis, 2023). According to international jurisdictions in many countries an author must be a legal person, able to "give final approval to the version to be published" and to take responsibility and to guarantee the accuracy and integrity of the respective publication. Furthermore, chatbots don't have affiliations independent of their developers and can't be named as authors (Zielinski et al., 2023). An avalanche of sub-standard, low-quality online publications can lead to the substitution of human authors by machines and devaluation of their skills and expertise. It can jeopardize the quality of scholarly publishing and academia's authority in general and may even lead some to question the value of a college education. The accessibility of generative AI tools makes it easier to produce a poor-quality paper and consequently to compromise research integrity. In an ideal world, publishers should be able to detect LLM-written content. Of course, there are numerous software products, also AI based, that could solve that problem by identifying telltale signs such as fake references, etc., but the real issue is that such programs are still in their infancy and are prone to mistakenly attribute human-created content to machines (Conroy, 2023). Attempts have been made to regulate this grey area. A noteworthy White Paper, "Generative AI in Scholarly Communications: Ethical and Practical Guidelines for the use of generative AI in the publication process", a follow up document to "AI Ethics in Scholarly Communications", was recently published on the STM website. An appendix provides links to different publishers' policies and guidelines as well as recommended readings and resources.

AI LITERACY

The term AI literacy denotes "thinking in AI terms" which should describe the relation between AI and Society. AI literacy is associated with two separate concepts – the first is related to technology and the second is people. Accordingly, the definitions of AI literacy in literature vary greatly among researchers. Ridley & Pawlick-Potts (2021) define AI literacy as the relation of people to algorithmic thinking where the latter communicates computer and digital literacy. Per this view AI literacy cannot be seen as the direct successor of all preceding literacies such as digital literacy, computational literacy, scientific literacy and data literacy; rather, it is a new member of the literacy family which has inherited relations to some other members. The recent study from Ng et al. (2021) tries to conceptualize AI literacy and found that scholars define it either as: "know the basic functions of AI and how to use AI application", "applying AI knowledge, concepts and applications to different scenarios", "higher order thinking skills with AI applications" or "human centered considerations (ethics, safety etc.) with use of AI". Obviously, AI literacy cannot be precisely defined and should be explained as a broad convolution of three different quantities: knowledge about AI principles, ability to use AI in tools, services and applications, and ability to critically evaluate AI output. As Ng et al. pointed out, some authors also describe AI literacy as an extension of computer thinking (computer literacy) and therefore reformulate the above description as technical and conceptual understanding of AI, knowledge of techniques and strategies concerning AI, and dispositions when solving problems.

For academic libraries, there are two facets of AI literacy – librarians and students/patrons. From Ng's perspective, the AI literacy taxonomy described above could be very different for these distinct groups. For students AI literacy should boil down to knowledge and hands-on experience with knowledge bases in order to use them for problem solving. For librarians AI literacy emerges as a broad range of activities targeting proliferation of AI awareness for patrons and support for their AI skills development. In particular that could mean conducting hands-on seminars and workshops, presentations, creating LibGuides, teaching classes, etc. In practice however students typically navigate across the wide range of information sources (which use algorithms and AI) commonly available over the Internet. As a recent study of student experiences and perceptions in the era of algorithms shows (Head et al., 2020) the majority of students are capable to recognize the fact that information from algorithm driven sources is often ubiquitous and there are hidden layers that personalize results. In addition students deem that underlying algorithms may reinforce inequalities, may violate privacy by selling personal data to third party; such algorithms may collect data about users, and modify the content the particular user sees. Academic librarians should change the dynamics by making students partners while teaching AI literacy in order to better engage them in the learning process. That practical cooperative approach to AI literacy may lead students to critically examine the effects of AI algorithms and explore the social implications of AI in order to develop self-defense strategies.

In the scope of the first element of the above taxonomy, academic librarians need to understand AI on a conceptual level and to be able to convey that knowledge to students in a format of simple conceptually focused examples. For instance, librarians may use the simple display and its pixels to convey the concept of data representation depending on their knowledge of a particular AI product in the context of research and education tasks in addition to their ability to demonstrate various modes of software. Next, they could use their teaching skills and augment information literacy classes with examples and demonstrations of AI enabled application(s). Usually the most effective is the approach of hands-on collaborative project when the class discovers information needed to solve a problem. An important message to convey is that AI application(s) does not reason like a human; they do not have any doubts and when they make mistakes it is with confidence. Thus, it is different for predictive and generative type of AI application. Especially for generative AI the new output objects are similar to what was in the training set and thus is prone to any errors and/or biases available during the training. In order to express the concept of bias and limitation of AI, librarians can emphasize the fact that search engines have different level of adoption of AI, plus the fact that the underlying AI is of different design. Thus, by comparing and discussing the search results from a particular search engine (e.g., Google) to results from another one (students can be asked to conduct two searches with two different searching engines), with and without AI modules enabled, the librarians can demonstrate the importance of critical evaluation of the results by explaining incorrect answers (false hits) due to bias associated with generative AI and differences between generative and predictive AI.

The academic librarians do not develop code but they can take part in the development of AI-enabled library application via dedicated open shells. For example, the CUNY's Lehman College Library applied this approach and developed a chatbot using Ivy shell without doing any explicit programming at all (Ehrenpreis & DeLooper, 2022).

NEW ROLES OF LIBRARIANS IN THE REALM OF AI DRIVEN SERVICES: ISSUES AND CHALLENGES

In recent years, the re-definition of librarians' roles has become a frequent occurrence fueled by sequence of changes in the academic landscape – introduction of open science, introduction of citizen science, disruption of educational process by COVID-19, and lately the omnipresence of AI related research. Each of these events caused a re-definition of librarians' roles, but the outcomes invariably highlight the increased impact and importance of academic librarians in the education process. The successful journeys through constant changes were supported by librarians' pre-programmed qualifications and ability to learn and adapt, but the driving force was the focus on community service aimed to provide optimal and effective service to their respective community. The approach was to upgrade skills via collaborations with other parties achieving fast pace of growth to match the transformation's leap caused by the emerging new technologies.

As AI technologies mature overnight (the ChatGPT registered 1 million users within first five days of its existence), new skills and knowledge are needed. In this aspect the critical evaluation and conceptualization of new technologies with focus on library services were the first steps taken by librarians. Shared findings help librarians to recognize the value of new technologies as opportunities to strength their own abilities to provide innovations while keeping alive the human center of their services.

Librarians as Managers of Integrated Systems

Traditionally librarians' activities include information retrieval, handling metadata, cataloging, systematization and normalization. In the realm of emerging AI technologies, however, the fine line between information, data and knowledge become even more elusive. Many AI-enabled integrated library systems operate on a knowledge level. For instance, an intelligent IRS can exchange information with the user (i.e., it has information system abilities) and can make decisions. In their role as managers of integrated systems librarians are expected to demonstrate expertise and knowledge about operating these systems, the limitations of human-machine interface, the accuracy in context of input and possible pitfalls and shortcomings. Typically these skills are expected to be acquired by librarians "on-the-fly", but the new AI technologies require profound understanding of knowledge concepts and knowledge representation, inference logic, complex data structures, and programming. Thus, the challenge here is the conceptualization of modern AI concepts in formats accessible to librarians, so they could act as managers of particular AI-enabled library integrated systems.

Librarians as Prompt Mediators

The job of the prompt engineer was born from the reality of generative AI with the goal to pattern the model output and ensure meaningfulness of the response. IBM defines the qualification of the prompt engineer as "...familiarity with large language models, strong communication skills, the ability to explain technical concepts, programming expertise (particularly in Python) and a firm grasp of data structures and algorithms". One of the most common duties in the job descriptions of prompt engineers is associated with "tuning up" of generative ChatBots. Librarians can assist the process of tweaking the generative chatbot in its "human part" by communicating technical concepts in general terms and offer their communication skills. To do so librarians need to understand the concept of large language models and generative AI features and limitations. That aligns with descriptions of required additional skills and knowledge from librarians in relation with particular AI technology (Cox &

Mazumdar, 2022; Cox et al., 2019). As information professionals academic librarians can participate in prompt engineering education by teaching AI literacy classes which focus on AI and algorithm driven technologies. Some authors even describe prompt engineering librarian role as "similar to that of an information literacy or instructional librarian, but with a focus on artificial intelligence technologies" (Lund, 2023). However, as it was described above AI literacy is a convolution of several different quantities and thus has a scope beyond the extension of traditional information literacy.

Quite often the description of an AI-enabled library service blurs the different AI technologies used for that service. For example, chatbots are popular in library reference services, but the features of an information retrieval based chatbot and a generative chatbot are quite different. In addition, these two types of bots have different "human" appearances. Thus, it is important for academic librarians to be able to distinguish between different AI technologies; to understand the limitations of each technology; and to be able to generate/modify the query in order to get the matching answer. In the latter case, librarians are challenged to upkeep some of the functions of prompt engineers, but without the requisite education. In this respect, librarians should focus on serving their respective institutions, adding a human dimension to AI-enabled service in collaboration with their IT departments.

CONCLUSION

AI-enabled software systems applied in academic library services have a long history. The first AI-enabled systems in libraries date back more than twenty years ago and were rule based expert systems (developed in the late 1970s and mastered in the 1980s). Unfortunately, some early library tools were short lived and/or did not meet expectations. The analysis of reasons for their failures pointed out that the main cause was the incompatibility or immaturity of applied AI technology to the problem.

In the last decade, AI-enabled applications for libraries grew beyond rule-based expert systems toward generative and knowledge driven integrated systems, capable of using natural language processing for communication with patrons and which use extensive sets of machine learning algorithms. For librarians the AI revolution even closely connected to the digital revolution and presented a great set of new challenges requiring transformations of the roles of academic librarians. That included adding skills and knowledge needed to manage integrated AI systems, to take part in prompt-engineering as mediators in addition to obtaining conceptual understanding of new models and paradigms in AI. As stakeholders, librarians are called to serve their institutions by providing AI education to students/patrons on a conceptual level.

However, the biggest challenge has become the implementation and support of AI in libraries in a way where services stay in scope and definition of human centric AI – in other words, how to "humanize" AI in library services. In the AI revolution, librarians are guardians of the human aspect of academic libraries. Unconditionally, the use of AI in library services impacts the library support as a whole and is a part of transformations in both the educational process and research.

REFERENCES

Ahmed, M., Mukhopadhyay, M., & Mukhopadhyay, P. (2023). Automated Knowledge Organisation: AI/ML-based Subject Indexing System for Libraries. *DESIDOC Journal of Library and Information Technology*, *43*(1), 45–54. doi:10.14429/djlit.43.01.18619

Alberico, R. (2011). The future of expert systems and artificial intelligence technologies in. *The Application of Expert Systems in Libraries and Information Centres*, 194.

Allison, D. (2012). Chatbots in the library: Is it time? *Library Hi Tech*, *30*(1), 95–107. doi:10.1108/07378831211213238

Amram, T., Malamud, R. G., & Hollingsworth, C. (2023). Response to" From ChatGPT to CatGPT. *Information Technology and Libraries*, *42*(4). doi:10.5860/ital.v42i4.16983

Aronson, A. R., Mork, J. G., Gay, C. W., Humphrey, S. M., & Rogers, W. J. (2004). The NLM indexing initiative's medical text indexer. In *MEDINFO 2004* (pp. 268–272). IOS Press.

Asemi, A., & Asemi, A. (2018). Artificial Intelligence (AI) application in Library Systems in Iran: A taxonomy study. *Library Philosophy and Practice, 2.*

Balleste, R. (2002). The future of Artificial Intelligence in your virtual libraries. *Computers in Libraries*, *22*(9), 10–15.

Balleste, R. (2006). *Technology Trends in Law Libraries*. Law Librarianship for the Twenty-First Century.

Blackman, R. (2020). A practical guide to building ethical AI. *Harvard Business Review*, 15.

Brzustowicz, R. (2023). From ChatGPT to CatGPT: The implications of artificial intelligence on library cataloging. *Information Technology and Libraries*, *42*(3). doi:10.5860/ital.v42i3.16295

Butkovich, N. J., Taylor, K. L., Dent, S. H., & Moore, A. S. (2019). An expert system at the reference desk: Impressions from users. In *Expert Systems in Reference Services* (pp. 61–70). Routledge. doi:10.4324/9780429352539-5

Chen, E., Bullard, J., & Giustini, D. (2023). Automated indexing using NLM's Medical Text Indexer (MTI) compared to human indexing in Medline: A pilot study. *Journal of the Medical Library Association: JMLA*, *111*(3), 684–695. doi:10.5195/jmla.2023.1588 PMID:37483360

Conroy, G. (2023). How generative AI could disrupt scientific publishing. *Nature*, *622*(7982), 235. doi:10.1038/d41586-023-03144-w

Cox, A. M., Kennan, M. A., Lyon, L., Pinfield, S., & Sbaffi, L. (2019). Maturing research data services and the transformation of academic libraries. *The Journal of Documentation*, *75*(6), 1432–1462. doi:10.1108/JD-12-2018-0211

Cox, A. M., & Mazumdar, S. (2022). Defining artificial intelligence for librarians. *Journal of Librarianship and Information Science*, 09610006221142029.

Curtis, N. (2023). To ChatGPT or not to ChatGPT? The impact of artificial intelligence on academic publishing. *The Pediatric Infectious Disease Journal*, *42*(4), 275. doi:10.1097/INF.0000000000003852 PMID:36757192

Das, R. K., & Islam, M. S. U. (2021). Application of artificial intelligence and machine learning in libraries: a systematic review. *arXiv preprint arXiv:2112.04573*.

Davies, R., & James, B. (1984). Towards an expert system for cataloguing: Some experiments based on AACR2. *Program*, *18*(4), 283–297. doi:10.1108/eb046882

De Cremer, D., & Kasparov, G. (2021). AI should augment human intelligence, not replace it. *Harvard Business Review*, *18*, 1.

Deshmukh, A., Hegde, G., Lathi, R., & Govikarn, S. (2012, June). A literature survey on latent semantic indexing. In *International Conference on Computing* (p. 100). IEEE.

Dhelim, S., Aung, N., & Ning, H. (2020). Mining user interest based on personality-aware hybrid filtering in social networks. *Knowledge-Based Systems*, *206*, 106227. doi:10.1016/j.knosys.2020.106227

Dohrmann, E., Hügi, J., Scheurer, N., Trummer, A., Schneider, R., & Eggenberg, C. (2010). *Bridging the virtual and the physical space: Kornelia–a chatbot for public libraries.*

Ehrenpreis, M., & DeLooper, J. (2022). Implementing a chatbot on a library website. *Journal of Web Librarianship*, *16*(2), 120–142. doi:10.1080/19322909.2022.2060893

Ercegovac, Z., & Borko, H. (1992). Design and implementation of an experimental cataloging advisor-Mapper. *Information Processing & Management*, *28*(2), 241–257. doi:10.1016/0306-4573(92)90048-5

Filion, P., Moos, M., & Sands, G. (2023). Urban neoliberalism, smart city, and big tech: The aborted sidewalk labs Toronto experiment. *Journal of Urban Affairs*, *45*(9), 1625–1643. doi:10.1080/07352166.2022.2081171

Gabriel, A. (2019). Artificial intelligence in scholarly communications: An Elsevier case study. *Information Services & Use*, *39*(4), 319–333. doi:10.3233/ISU-190063

Generative AI in Scholarly Communications: Ethical and practical guidelines for the use of generative AI in the publication process. (2023, December 5). STM. https://www.stm-assoc.org/new-white-paper-launch-generative-ai-in-scholarly-communications/

Harisanty, D., Anna, N. E. V., Putri, T. E., Firdaus, A. A., & Noor Azizi, N. A. (2023). Is adopting artificial intelligence in libraries urgency or a buzzword? A systematic literature review. *Journal of Information Science*. doi:10.1177/01655515221141034

Head, A. J., Fister, B., & MacMillan, M. (2020). *Information Literacy in the Age of Algorithms: Student Experiences with News and Information, and the Need for Change*. Project Information Literacy.

Hjerppe, R., & Olander, B. (1989). Cataloging and expert systems: AACR2 as a knowledge base. *Journal of the American Society for Information Science*, *40*(1), 27–44. doi:10.1002/(SICI)1097-4571(198901)40:1<27::AID-ASI4>3.0.CO;2-R

Hodonu-Wusu, J. O. (2024). The rise of artificial intelligence in libraries: The ethical and equitable methodologies, and prospects for empowering library users. *AI and Ethics*, 1–11. doi:10.1007/s43681-024-00432-7

Houston, A. B., & Corrado, E. M. (2023). Embracing ChatGPT: Implications of Emergent Language Models for Academia and Libraries. *Technical Services Quarterly*, *40*(2), 76–91. doi:10.1080/07317131.2023.2187110

Iqbal, N., Jamil, F., Ahmad, S., & Kim, D. (2020). Toward effective planning and management using predictive analytics based on rental book data of academic libraries. *IEEE Access : Practical Innovations, Open Solutions*, *8*, 81978–81996. doi:10.1109/ACCESS.2020.2990765

Johnson, B. (2018). Libraries in the age of artificial intelligence. *Computers in Libraries*, *38*(1), 14–16.

Johnston, M., & Weckert, J. (1990). Selection advisor: An expert system for collection development. *Information Technology and Libraries*, *9*(3), 219.

Kaushal, V., & Yadav, R. (2022). The role of chatbots in academic libraries: An experience-based perspective. *Journal of the Australian Library and Information Association*, *71*(3), 215–232. doi:10.1080/24750158.2022.2106403

Lancaster, F. W., & Smith, L. C. (1990). *Artificial Intelligence and Expert Systems: Will They Change the Library?* Papers Presented at the Annual Clinic on Library Applications of Data Processing, Urbana, Illinois.

Lund, B. (2023). The prompt engineering librarian. *Library Hi Tech News*, *40*(8), 6–8. doi:10.1108/LHTN-10-2023-0189

Margetis, G., Ntoa, S., Antona, M., & Stephanidis, C. (2021). Human-centered design of artificial intelligence. Handbook of Human Factors and Ergonomics, 1085-1106.

Massis, B. (2018). Artificial intelligence arrives in the library. *Information and Learning Science*, *119*(7/8), 456–459. doi:10.1108/ILS-02-2018-0011

McCulloch, W. S., & Pitts, W. (1943). A logical calculus of the ideas immanent in nervous activity. *The Bulletin of Mathematical Biophysics*, *5*(4), 115–133. doi:10.1007/BF02478259

McDonald, J. D., & Levine-Clark, M. (Eds.). (2017). *Encyclopedia of Library and Information Sciences*. CRC Press. doi:10.1081/E-ELIS4

Meador, J. M., & Cline, L. S. (1991). *Collection Development in an Era of Networking: The Bibliographer's Workstation*.

Meng, C., Rombach, R., Gao, R., Kingma, D., Ermon, S., Ho, J., & Salimans, T. (2023). On distillation of guided diffusion models. In *Proceedings of the IEEE/CVF Conference on Computer Vision and Pattern Recognition* (pp. 14297-14306). IEEE.

Miao, Z. (2019). Investigation on human rights ethics in artificial intelligence researches with library literature analysis method. *The Electronic Library*, *37*(5), 914–926. doi:10.1108/EL-04-2019-0089

Mork, J. G., Jimeno-Yepes, A., & Aronson, A. R. (2013). The NLM Medical Text Indexer System for Indexing Biomedical Literature. *BioASQ@ CLEF, 1*.

Nardi, B. A., & O'Day, V. (1996). Intelligent agents: what we learned at the library.

Nayyer, K., & Rodriguez, M. (2022). Ethical implications of implicit bias in AI: Impact for academic libraries. Chicago: ACRL. In S.Hervieux & A.Wheatley (Eds.), The Rise of AI: Implications and applications of Artificial Intelligence in academic libraries (165-174). ACRL.

Ng, D. T. K., Leung, J. K. L., Chu, S. K. W., & Qiao, M. S. (2021). Conceptualizing AI literacy: An exploratory review. *Computers and Education: Artificial Intelligence*, *2*, 100041.

Nikolinakos, N. T. (2023). Ethical Principles for Trustworthy AI. In: EU Policy and Legal Framework for Artificial Intelligence, Robotics and Related Technologies - The AI Act. Springer. doi:10.1007/978-3-031-27953-9_3

Olmstadt, W. (2000). *Cataloging expert systems: Optimism and frustrated reality*.

Ormeño, P., Mendoza, M., & Valle, C. (2021). Topic models ensembles for ad-hoc information retrieval. *Information (Basel)*, *12*(9), 360. doi:10.3390/info12090360

Oyelude, A. A. (2017). What's trending in the library cybersphere–Recent conferences and posts focus on data and information literacy. *Library Hi Tech News*, *34*(6), 21–22. doi:10.1108/LHTN-06-2017-0040

Peterson, T. (2020). *Improve online learning and more with artificial intelligence*.

Porcel, C., López-Herrera, A. G., & Herrera-Viedma, E. (2009). A recommender system for research resources based on fuzzy linguistic modeling. *Expert Systems with Applications*, *36*(3), 5173–5183. doi:10.1016/j.eswa.2008.06.038

Ridley, M., & Pawlick-Potts, D. (2021). Algorithmic literacy and the role for libraries. *Information Technology and Libraries*, *40*(2). doi:10.6017/ital.v40i2.12963

Šauperl, A., & Saye, J. D. (2011). Pebbles for the mosaic of cataloging expertise: What do problems in expert systems for cataloging reveal about cataloging expertise? *Library Resources & Technical Services*, *43*(2), 78–94. doi:10.5860/lrts.43n2.78

Schmager, S., Pappas, I., & Vassilakopoulou, P. (2023, September). Defining Human-centered AI: a comprehensive review of HCAI literature. In *Proceedings of the Mediterranean Conference on Information Systems*. IEEE.

Silverstein, C., & Shieber, S. M. (1996). Predicting individual book use for off-site storage using decision trees. *The Library Quarterly*, *66*(3), 266–293. doi:10.1086/602885

Strzalkowski, T., Perez-Carballo, J., & Marinescu, M. (1996, April). Natural language information retrieval in digital libraries. In *Proceedings of the First ACM International Conference on Digital libraries* (pp. 117-125). ACM. 10.1145/226931.226954

Vickery, A., Brooks, H., Robinson, B., & Vickery, B. (1987). A reference and referral system using expert system techniques. *The Journal of Documentation*, *43*(1), 1–23. doi:10.1108/eb026798

Wagstaff, K. L., & Liu, G. Z. (2018). Automated classification to improve the efficiency of weeding library collections. *Journal of Academic Librarianship*, *44*(2), 238–247. doi:10.1016/j.acalib.2018.02.001

Wei, X., & Croft, W. B. (2006, August). LDA-based document models for ad-hoc retrieval. In *Proceedings of the 29th Annual International ACM SIGIR Conference on Research and Development in Information Retrieval* (pp. 178-185). ACM.

Wolfram, D. (2016, June). Bibliometrics, information retrieval and natural language processing: natural synergies to support digital library research. In *Proceedings of the Joint Workshop on Bibliometric-Enhanced Information Retrieval and Natural Language Processing for Digital Libraries (BIRNDL)* (pp. 6-13). ACM.

Wolfram, S. (2023). *What Is ChatGPT Doing... and Why Does It Work?* Stephen Wolfram Media.

Wu, J., Liang, C., Yang, H., & Giles, C. L. (2016, June). Citeseerx data: Semanticizing scholarly papers. In *Proceedings of the International Workshop on Semantic Big Data* (pp. 1-6). ACM.

Wu, J., Williams, K. M., Chen, H. H., Khabsa, M., Caragea, C., Tuarob, S., & Giles, C. L. (2015). Citeseerx: AI in a digital library search engine. *AI Magazine*, *36*(3), 35–48. doi:10.1609/aimag.v36i3.2601

Wu, X., Duan, R., & Ni, J. (2023). Unveiling security, privacy, and ethical concerns of chatgpt. *Journal of Information and Intelligence.*

Zielinski, C., Winker, M. A., Aggarwal, R., Ferris, L., Heinemann, M., Florencio, J., & Habibzadeh, F. (2023). WAME recommendations on chatbots and generative artificial intelligence in relation to scholarly publications. *Global Journal of Medicine & Public Health*, *12*(2). PMID:38089825

KEY TERMS AND DEFINITIONS:

AI Literacy: AI literacy cannot be precisely defined and should be explained as a broad convolution of: knowledge about AI principles, ability to use AI in tools, services and applications, and ability to critically evaluate AI output.

Artificial Intelligence in Libraries: That is a synergy between computing and psychology used to increase librarians' productivity, quality of services; quality of information yields and quality of communication with patrons.

Artificial Intelligence: Artificial intelligence (AI) is defined as intelligent performance expressed by artificial body usually a computer program.

Generative AI: A set of ML models that can generate new data, i.e., the output is object that look like the one on which model is trained; ChatGPT is the most popular instance.

Machine Learning: Machine Learning (ML) allows for the programming of the computers by using data instead of explicit instructions.

Chapter 3
Ethical Considerations and Privacy Concerns in AI-Enabled Libraries

Ali Kavak
https://orcid.org/0000-0001-5329-2420
Kırıkkale University, Turkey

ABSTRACT

The primary aim of this chapter is to discuss the ethical dilemmas and privacy concerns that the adoption of artificial intelligence technologies in libraries may bring.In particular, it addresses how artificial intelligence can be used in library services and the associated risks, such as bias, discrimination, lack of transparency, and violations of data privacy. Also explores how artificial intelligence systems can impact human-machine interaction and the potential for replacing library staff.

INTRODUCTION

Libraries are undergoing a significant transformation with the increasing integration of artificial intelligence (AI) technologies. AI-supported libraries offer numerous benefits, such as improved search capabilities, personalized recommendations, and enhanced user experiences. However, it is crucial to address the ethical issues and privacy concerns that arise from the implementation of these advanced systems. Ethical Issues

One of the main ethical concerns is the potential for bias in AI algorithms. These algorithms are trained on large datasets, which may include biased or discriminatory information. As a result, the recommendations and search results generated by AI

DOI: 10.4018/979-8-3693-1573-6.ch003

systems could perpetuate existing biases and inequalities. It is essential for libraries to ensure that their AI technologies are designed and developed in a way that mitigates bias and promotes fairness and inclusivity.

Another significant concern is the collection and use of user data. AI systems rely on vast amounts of data to operate effectively, including personal information about library users. Libraries must be transparent about how this data is collected, stored, and used, taking steps to protect user privacy. They should also obtain informed consent from users before collecting their data and provide options for users to opt out or limit data sharing.

As AI becomes increasingly integrated into libraries, it is crucial to navigate these ethical and privacy challenges carefully. Libraries should adopt robust policies and guidelines that promote fairness, transparency, and user privacy. By doing so, they can harness the power of AI while upholding the values of access, equality, and intellectual freedom that are at the core of library services.

Libraries have long been regarded as guardians of knowledge and information, ensuring equitable access for all. As AI becomes more prevalent in library services, it is essential to have open discussions about the ethical implications that arise. By doing so, we can ensure that these technologies are implemented responsibly and do not compromise user privacy or perpetuate discriminatory practices. Libraries have a unique role to play in fostering a fair and unbiased society, and this responsibility extends to the use of AI. As AI algorithms are trained on existing data, there is a risk of reinforcing biases present in that data. Library professionals must therefore actively engage in the development and deployment of AI systems, advocating for transparency and fairness throughout the process. Privacy concerns, too, demand our attention. Libraries must protect user data, ensuring that it is used solely for the purpose intended and not exploited for commercial gain. This can be achieved by adopting robust privacy policies, implementing secure data management practices, and regularly auditing AI systems for compliance with ethical guidelines. Through proactive engagement with these challenges, libraries can harness the transformative power of AI while upholding their core values of inclusivity, equity, and privacy.

The primary aim of this chapter is to discuss the ethical dilemmas and privacy concerns that the adoption of artificial intelligence technologies in libraries may bring. In particular, it addresses how artificial intelligence can be used in library services and the associated risks, such as bias, discrimination, lack of transparency, and violations of data privacy. Also explores how artificial intelligence systems can impact human-machine interaction and the potential for replacing library staff.

In the chapter that puts forward the ethical principles and best practices that libraries should consider when embracing artificial intelligence, concrete recommendations are provided to libraries on issues such as detecting and reducing biases in artificial intelligence systems, ensuring transparency and accountability, and safeguarding data security.

Data Security in Artificial Intelligence-Powered Libraries

Rapid advancements in AI technology are fundamentally reshaping libraries and information services. Libraries are harnessing the benefits and personalized information services offered by AI technology, but these developments also bring various information security threats. Particularly, the increasing prevalence of AI in education and information services has raised widespread ethical concerns. Protecting user data privacy has emerged as an urgent issue.

AI plays a pivotal role in the future industrial transformation by integrating numerous cutting-edge technologies and theoretical achievements. AI offers capabilities such as speech recognition, computer vision, and natural language processing through smart analytics. These capabilities enable data in information services to be intelligently scanned, scenarios to be generated, and fuzzy learning tasks to be automatically identified and addressed. Additionally, AI can perform complex tasks by simulating neural network operations, mimicking the functioning of the human brain. The application of AI in the field of librarianship can significantly enhance the efficiency and effectiveness of information services, effectively supporting users' information needs (Huang, 2023).

However, amidst this rapid technological progress, concerns about user data privacy and breaches of confidentiality have arisen as pressing ethical issues. Specifically, risks related to data leaks and unauthorized use of personal information have come to the forefront (Shazly et al., 2020) . Issues such as network fraud based on data traffic have also escalated. Moreover, inadequacies in privacy protection systems and monopolization of network technologies have highlighted the need for the examination of ethical risks posed by AI in terms of user data security (Dilmaghani et al., 2019).

One of the most critical data security concerns in AI-enabled libraries is finding a balance between automation and human involvement. While automation can streamline processes and enhance efficiency, it should not replace the valuable role that librarians play in curating information and providing personalized assistance to users. The implementation of AI should be viewed as a tool that augments human capabilities rather than a substitute for human expertise. Libraries must ensure that AI systems are designed to support and enhance the work of library professionals while still allowing for human intervention when necessary. To achieve this, it is crucial to adopt a user-centered approach, involve librarians in the design and development of AI systems, and provide adequate training to ensure their effective utilization (Oyelude, 2021).

While AI applications in libraries have the potential to increase efficiency, provide personalized services, and facilitate information access, it is crucial to implement these technologies responsibly and ethically. Firstly, although automation processes can allow librarians to focus on more complex tasks such as research support and user interaction, human participation and expertise remain indispensable (Cox & Mazumdar, 2022). AI should be positioned as a complement to human competencies. When offering personalized recommendations, the privacy of user data should be safeguarded with the utmost sensitivity, explicit consent should be obtained from users, and strict privacy protocols should be adhered to. To instill user trust, AI systems must be transparent in their decision-making processes, and the logic behind recommendations and actions should be explained. Bias risks should be considered in AI-based library systems, tested with diverse datasets, and subject to regular audits. Mechanisms for accountability regarding the potential harm from datasets should be established, and data security principles should be adopted with a focus on fairness, justice, and inclusivity. Librarians need continuous education on data security, collaboration with stakeholders, and regular evaluations of AI applications. When libraries embrace AI within a human-centered, responsible, fair, and transparent framework, they can safely harness the potential of these technologies while preserving the core values of the institution and its users (Jarrahi et. al., 2023).

The integration of AI applications within library settings, primarily for the purpose of gathering and analyzing user data to offer tailored recommendations and enhance services, raises pertinent concerns surrounding the safeguarding of individual privacy rights. In addressing these concerns, it becomes imperative for libraries to institute robust security measures characterized by the implementation of stringent encryption protocols, the acquisition of explicit and well-informed consent from users, and unwavering adherence to pertinent data protection regulations (Bradley, 2022). Furthermore, libraries should proactively formulate transparent policies delineating the parameters of user data utilization, storage, and retention, ensuring that these policies are communicated consistently to library patrons (Singley, 2020).

Particularly in the context of AI usage in information services, preserving user data privacy is of great importance, and recommendations should be made to address concerns regarding user data security (Huang, 2023). Furthermore, a profound examination of the relationship between AI and privacy is essential, emphasizing the necessity of safeguarding privacy rights even during the rise of AI technologies (Sifat, 2023). By assigning precedence to user privacy considerations and implementing AI practices that are steeped in ethics and responsibility, libraries can cultivate trust within their communities (Bradley, 2022) and make substantial contributions to the trajectory of AI characterized by ethics, reliability, and transparency (Singley, 2020).

The significance of user privacy, transparency, accountability, ethical considerations, and the continuous evolution in the integration of AI within library contexts is well-documented in existing research. Bubinger and Dinneen (2021) provides practical strategies for the advancement of ethical AI within library settings, while Coleman (2020) underscores the imperative for libraries to address biases when their collections are transformed into data. Breeding (2016) concentrates on the aspects of privacy and security within library systems, with a particular emphasis on web-based interactions with library patrons. Jaillant & Rees (2022) delves into the application of AI in digital archives and underscores the crucial role of trust, collaboration, and shared professional ethics in this domain. Collectively, these scholarly works underscore the need for libraries to prioritize user privacy by implementing robust encryption measures, anonymizing data, and securing explicit user consent for data collection and usage. Additionally, they underscore the significance of transparency in elucidating the ways in which user data is employed and in instituting mechanisms for user access, control, and removal of data.

In many studies, recommendations are made for the protection of user data in libraries, including secure storage measures, increasing education and awareness, promoting collaboration and knowledge sharing, regularly auditing data handling practices, compliance with data protection regulations, implementation of anonymization and encryption techniques, and the establishment of robust governance frameworks for safeguarding user data. Bradley (2022) emphasizes that libraries should engage with AI regulations and develop ethical frameworks to ensure trustworthy and transparent AI implementation. Chen et al. (2020) underscores the importance of privacy-preserving technologies in developing privacy-preserving AI systems. Bubinger and Dinneen (2021) suggests actionable approaches to promote ethical AI in libraries, including planning, evaluating, and auditing the ethics of AI-powered information services. Sturges et al. (2001) addresses concerns about user privacy in the digital library environment and highlights the necessity of creating guidelines to protect personal data. In summary, these studies emphasize the importance of implementing secure storage measures, increasing education and awareness, collaborating with experts, regularly auditing data handling practices, complying with data protection regulations, implementing anonymization and encryption techniques, and establishing strong governance frameworks to protect user data in libraries.

ETHICS IN ARTIFICIAL INTELLIGENCE-POWERED LIBRARIES

The increasing prevalence of AI and Machine Learning (ML) in libraries and information centers holds the promise of enhancing service delivery and efficiency. However, the utilization of these technologies also brings significant ethical challenges and risks. These risks encompass concerns related to bias and discrimination, privacy and security, the potential impact on employees through automation, and the absence of human interaction. When libraries and information centers employ these technologies, it is crucial to consider and address these risks and ethical challenges, ensuring that the use of these technologies aligns with the institution's values and mission (Mishra, 2023).

Technology possesses the potential for both positive utilization and potential misuse, a dichotomy that extends to the field of artificial intelligence (AI). Furthermore, the continuous advancement of AI technologies blurs the line between human and machine, often resulting in excessive anthropomorphism. This progression in AI technology has given rise to a new phenomenon known as the "digital divide," where technological advantages accrue more readily to certain socio-economic and geographical segments of society. The environmental repercussions of AI development remain a complex and incompletely understood matter. While official regulations in this domain remain limited, a multitude of independent international initiatives have been launched to delve into and address these and other ethical concerns (European Parliamentary Research Service [EPRS], 2020). Details regarding these initiatives are presented in Table 1 for reference.

Table 1. International ethical initiatives in artificial intelligence ethics

Initiative	Location	Key issues tackled
The Centre for Data Ethics and Innovation	United Kingdom	Delineating and rectifying deficiencies within our regulatory framework pertaining to AI data utilization, while optimizing the societal advantages derived from AI.
The Institute for Ethical AI & Machine Learning	United Kingdom	The Institute's objective is to enable individuals and entire nations to advance in AI development, guided by eight principles for responsible machine learning.
The Institute for Ethical Artificial Intelligence in Education	United Kingdom	Addressing the potential risks posed to young individuals and their education by the rapid expansion of new AI technology, and guaranteeing the ethical advancement of AI-driven educational technology (EdTech).
The Future of Life Institute	United States	Securing the advancement of AI for the betterment of humanity, emphasizing safety and addressing existential risks such as the autonomous arms race, human supervision of AI, and the potential hazards associated with highly advanced 'general/strong' or super-intelligent AI.
AI4All	United States	Fostering diversity and inclusivity within the realm of AI, with the aim of introducing underrepresented demographic groups to AI for the promotion of societal welfare and the greater good of humanity.
The Future Society	United States	The influence and regulatory framework of artificial intelligence with the overarching objective of advancing the welfare of society at large, encompassing policy analysis, consultative processes, collective knowledge, the orchestration of governance mechanisms, legal frameworks, and educational initiatives.
The AI Now Institute	United States	The advent of AI has ushered in a host of profound social implications, warranting a multifaceted examination in various domains.
The Institute of Electrical and Electronics Engineers (IEEE)	United States	Establishing societal and policy directives is imperative to maintain the human-centric nature of AI and intelligent systems, aligning them with humanity's core values and principles.
The Partnership on AI	United States	Exemplary guidelines for AI technologies encompass a comprehensive approach focusing on safety, equity, responsibility, transparency, labor and economic considerations, human-system collaboration, societal impact, and the advancement of the greater good.
The Association for Computing Machinery	United States	The research, development, and deployment of computers and networks should prioritize elements such as transparency, user-friendliness, security, inclusivity, accountability, and digital accessibility.
Special Interest Group on Artificial Intelligence (SIGAI), The Association for Computing Machinery	United States	Advocating for and bolstering the proliferation and implementation of AI principles and methodologies across the realm of computer science, as well as fostering AI education and disseminating research through diverse platforms.

Continued on folllowing page

Table 1. Continued

Initiative	Location	Key issues tackled
The European Robotics Platform (EUROP)	Europe	Unifying the European robotics and AI community with a strong industry-oriented approach, with a specific emphasis on enhancing competitiveness and fostering innovation.
euRobotics	Europe	Sustaining and amplifying European expertise and advancements in the fields of robotics, AI industrialization, and their economic repercussions.
The European Robotics Research Network (EURON)	Europe (Coordinator based in Sweden)	Coordinating research endeavors, facilitating educational programs and training initiatives, disseminating scholarly publications, convening conferences, fostering industrial collaborations, and nurturing international partnerships within the domain of robotics.
The Institute for Ethics in Artificial Intelligence	Germany	Prioritizing a human-centered approach to engineering and emphasizing the integration of cultural and social considerations in the context of rapid advancements in AI. This approach spans various fields, such as philosophy, ethics, sociology, and political science.
The Foundation for Responsible Robotics	The Netherlands	Enhancing the transparency, user-friendliness, security, inclusivity, accountability, and accessibility of computer systems and networks across the spectrum of research, development, and implementation.
AI4People	Belgium	Analyzing the societal ramifications of artificial intelligence and establishing the foundational principles, policies, and methodologies to construct a morally sound AI-centric society.
The Ethics and Governance of Artificial Intelligence Initiative	United States	Strives to guarantee that automation and machine learning technologies are investigated, created, and implemented in a manner that upholds societal ideals centered on equity, human self-governance, and ethical justice.
Saidot: Enabling responsible AI ecosystems	Finland	Assisting enterprises, governmental bodies, and institutions in establishing and implementing ethically sound AI ecosystems to furnish transparent, traceable, and dependable AI services.
The Personal Data Protection Law	Türkiye	It establishes principles for the lawful processing of personal data, data subject rights, and the obligations of data controllers and processors.
The Montréal Declaration	Canada	The conscientious advancement of AI, convening 400 stakeholders from diverse sectors of society to discern the ethical and moral quandaries, both immediate and enduring.
The UNI Global Union	Switzerland	Addressing workforce dislocation and ensuring transparency in the implementation of AI, robotics, data analytics, and machine learning within the work environment.
The Japanese Society for Artificial Intelligence (JSAI)	Japan	To guarantee the continued societal benefit of AI research and development, while upholding the principles of ethical and moral conduct in the pursuit of advancements in the field.

All of the initiatives listed in Table 1 acknowledge the need for ethical research, development, design, deployment, monitoring, and use of AI. However, each of them prioritizes different areas. These initiatives highlight a range of fundamental issues that can generally be categorized as follows:

- Human Rights and Well-being: The ethical considerations surrounding AI encompass its potential to either advance human rights and well-being, fostering autonomy and capabilities, or to introduce detrimental consequences that undermine human dignity.
- Emotional Harm: AI's impact on emotional development and mental health necessitates scrutiny, examining whether it can compromise or enhance these aspects.
- Accountability and Responsibility: Determining the appropriate parties responsible for AI systems and establishing accountability mechanisms for their actions is a critical concern.
- Security, Privacy, Accessibility, and Transparency: Ensuring AI's comprehensibility and transparency to society, while addressing security, privacy, and accessibility aspects, is a pivotal endeavor.
- Safety and Trust: Strategies to avert physical harm in the event of AI becoming untrustworthy are essential considerations.
- Social Harm and Social Justice: Designing and utilizing AI in an inclusive, impartial, and non-discriminatory manner is fundamental to fostering social harmony and justice.
- Economic Harm: The management of AI with adverse economic impacts on employment and opportunities, either through the displacement of human labor or the reduction in job quality and availability, necessitates careful consideration.
- Legality and Justice: Ensuring that AI and its data handling adhere to just, equitable, and lawful principles, subject to appropriate governance and regulation, is a fundamental concern. The question of whether AI should be granted 'personhood' status warrants examination.
- Control and Ethical Use – or Misuse – of AI: The identification and prevention of unethical AI applications is imperative. Ensuring that AI remains under complete human control, even as it evolves and learns, is a pivotal objective.
- Environmental Harm and Sustainability: The mitigation of potential environmental harm associated with AI's development and utilization requires strategic measures to promote sustainability in AI production.
- Informed Use: Measures to enhance public awareness, education, and information regarding AI usage and interaction are crucial for responsible AI deployment.

- Existential Risk: The prevention of an AI arms race and the proactive management and regulation of potential harm in advanced machine learning are vital concerns in ensuring responsible AI advancement.

The emergence of advanced AI poses profound ethical questions regarding the technology's potential benefits and risks to humanity. Core issues include human rights, well-being, accountability, transparency, privacy, security, safety, trust, inclusion, social justice, economic impacts, legality, governance, regulation, environmental sustainability, public education, existential risk mitigation, and the prevention of an AI arms race. Particular concerns involve emotional, mental and social harm; compensation for economic disruption; equitable and lawful data practices; effective oversight and controls to align AI with human values; and managing disruptive societal transitions. To actualize AI for social good, while proactively addressing dangers, multifaceted collaborative approaches are needed spanning computer science, engineering, ethics, law, policy, education and the humanities. Integrative frameworks must be developed to balance priorities including accessibility and transparency with privacy and security; foster public awareness and informed use of AI; implement inclusive and unbiased design; assign responsibility for harm; grant appropriate legal status and protections; enact governance safeguards against misuse; drive environmental stewardship; and ensure human control of increasingly capable AI systems. Through comprehensive ethics-based strategies, AI can be harnessed to enhance human empowerment while reducing risk. This will require nuanced understandings of complex challenges and context-specific applications of shared principles.

In general, these initiatives aim to identify and establish ethical frameworks and systems that prioritize human beneficence at the highest levels, focusing on delivering benefit to both human society and the environment, without placing these two goals in conflict. Additionally, they work to mitigate the risks and negative impacts associated with AI, with a specific focus on ensuring that AI is accountable and transparent (Chatila et al., 2018; Leikas et al., 2019).

Cox (2022), AI systems, underlines the need for clear policies and assessment techniques to ensure alignment with the priorities and needs of libraries. Jha (2023) engage in discussions regarding both the potential benefits of AI in library services and the barriers such as financial considerations, librarian attitudes, and technical skills that may impede its implementation. They emphasize the positive impact of AI on library operations and propose various applications that can be deployed without significant costs. Teredesai et al. (2020) focuses on the accountability of machine learning systems in healthcare and how this can be applied in different cultural contexts. Hoffmann et al. (2018) emphasizes the need to address the social and ethical implications of algorithms, including concepts such as justice, bias, transparency, accessibility, participation, and discrimination. Piano (2020) discusses ethical principles in machine learning and artificial intelligence, highlighting the need for improvement in applications related to justice, accuracy, accountability, and transparency. These articles collectively underscore the importance of addressing these ethical considerations in the development and deployment of artificial intelligence and machine learning systems.

In libraries and information centers, it is necessary to establish various ethical frameworks and principles concerning the use of artificial intelligence and machine learning, such as fairness, transparency, accountability, user autonomy, privacy, human oversight, and utility (Cox, 2022; Hoffmann et al., 2018; Jha, 2023; Mishra, 2023; Piano, 2020; Teredesai et al., 2020). These ethical guidelines and principles assist in adopting a responsible and ethical approach to developing and implementing AI and machine learning systems, taking into account the needs and interests of users. The fundamental components of these frameworks are as follows:

- Fairness: Libraries and information centers should design AI and machine learning systems to be unbiased and free from discrimination for all users. This includes diversifying the system by training it on various user data sets and regularly reviewing the system for bias and discrimination.
- Transparency: Libraries and information centers should ensure transparency in the operation of AI and machine learning systems by clearly conveying how they work, the data they use, and the decision-making processes. This not only builds trust but also helps identify potential issues and biases.
- Accountability: Libraries and information centers should assume responsibility by establishing clear policies and procedures for the use of these systems. This includes regular monitoring and evaluation of the systems and requires providing training and guidance to staff and stakeholders.
- User Autonomy: Libraries and information centers should respect user autonomy by allowing users to have control over their personal data and make informed decisions about how their data is used. This includes having clear and understandable privacy policies.
- Privacy: Libraries and information centers should collect and use personal data only for specific, legal purposes. Strong security measures are required to protect the data from unauthorized access and misuse.
- Human Oversight: Libraries and information centers should subject AI and machine learning systems to human oversight and intervention to ensure that decisions and actions align with library values and objectives. This involves creating clear procedures for situations where human intervention is necessary and providing training and support to personnel responsible for monitoring these systems.

- Utility: Libraries and information centers should design AI and machine learning systems to enhance the well-being of individuals and society. Priority should be given to user needs and interests.

These ethical frameworks and principles guide libraries and information centers in using AI and machine learning systems in a responsible and ethical manner that prioritizes the needs and interests of users and the broader community.

AI technologies have the potential to transform service delivery in libraries. However, the responsible and ethical use of AI is of critical importance. Therefore, international library associations are conducting significant research on the impact of AI on libraries and the ethical use of these technologies.

The "IFLA Statement on Libraries and Artificial Intelligence" guide, published by the International Federation of Library Associations and Institutions (IFLA) (2020), focuses on the ethical dimensions of using artificial intelligence in libraries and information centers. These specific areas are addressed under the following headings:

- Artificial intelligence has the potential to drive the transformation of library services, but this technology should be used with human oversight and ethical principles as its foundation. Libraries can collaborate with artificial intelligence researchers and developers to create ethical applications tailored to user needs.
- Libraries can organize artificial intelligence literacy programs to encourage their users to be informed about artificial intelligence and understand its societal impacts.
- Key ethical issues such as data privacy, AI bias, and transparency are essential considerations for libraries when utilizing artificial intelligence.
- Libraries can contribute to the responsible development of AI by participating in AI research, gaining expertise in data management and ethical use.
- Given the rapid evolution of AI technologies, it is important for library staff to undergo continuous training and regularly evaluate AI applications for effective and ethical use.
- Libraries should prioritize ethical principles such as transparency, accountability, continuous learning, and collaboration when adopting artificial intelligence.

This approach helps libraries maintain ethical principles while using AI technologies and providing better services to users. Furthermore, this approach enables libraries to keep pace with future information technologies while contributing to raising awareness within society about information technologies and their ethical and proper use. By emphasizing ethical considerations related to AI, libraries raise awareness among information users while also providing an opportunity to harness the potential benefits of AI technologies. In this way, libraries support the public's right to access information while fostering sensitivity to technological advancements and an ethical perspective.

Today, AI is rapidly transforming numerous sectors worldwide, and libraries are no exception. As library staff, understanding this swiftly evolving technology and grasping the associated ethical responsibilities is of paramount importance. Being equipped to assess the potential of AI to enhance library services, improve user experiences, and meet societal needs is crucial. In this context, the virtual course titled "AI Empowerment for Library Staff: Ethical, Equitable, and Engaging Solutions" organized by the American Library Association [ALA] (2023), aims to guide library professionals on these critical issues.

Through this course, participants will acquire the following skills:

- Fundamental Concepts: They will have the opportunity to develop a deep understanding of fundamental AI concepts, technologies, and real-world applications for libraries.
- Ethics and Equality: Participants will have the chance to explore ethical and equality-related aspects of using AI in library services.
- Design and Implementation: They will gain the ability to discover AI tools and platforms to plan, design, and deliver library services more effectively.
- Community Relations: Participants will learn about developing stronger community relations between library staff and local organizations, including members of systematically marginalized communities.
- Applied Project: They will have the opportunity to apply AI concepts and tools in a practical project aimed at addressing a real-world library issue, need, or opportunity.

Like many other fields in the information society, the use of AI in libraries is on the rise. AI applications, such as catalog analysis tools, systems that provide product recommendations to customers, and robotic reception services, are becoming more prevalent in libraries (Feng, 2021; Massis, 2018). However, such systems come with a multitude of ethical issues spanning from data collection to deployment. Ethical considerations such as bias, fairness, accountability, transparency, responsibility, and environmental impact need to be addressed meticulously (Bender et al., 2021; Slavkovik, 2020).

In response to these ethical challenges, various approaches have been adopted in scientific and public domains. These approaches range from general principles to comprehensive guidelines and cover the entire development cycle from conception to deployment. The primary goal of these approaches is not to guarantee the absence of ethical issues but rather to minimize them. In other words, these approaches aim to prevent or mitigate ethical concerns (Cihon et al., 2021; Naudé & Dimitri, 2021).

However, there is a shortage of such ethical guidance tailored specifically for libraries. Consequently, for libraries considering the use of AI or already implementing AI systems, it might be unclear how to assess or define the ethics of their own systems, taking into account these ethical concerns. This situation could become particularly critical when public institutions are required not only to address ethical but also legal aspects and potentially certify the ethics of their AI systems.

Privacy Concerns in Artificial Intelligence Libraries

Under this heading, we examine the challenges related to data protection in AI applications in libraries, best practices for handling user data in AI-supported library services, and compliance with relevant data protection laws and regulations. While harnessing the innovations brought by artificial intelligence, it is crucial to safeguard the privacy of user data. Adhering to principles such as data minimization, transparency, and purpose-specific limitations, as well as complying with data protection laws, contributes to the ethical implementation of AI. Libraries must earn the trust of users by adhering to best practices in data management.

As AI continues to reshape libraries, addressing the privacy concerns associated with the implementation of AI technologies is of paramount importance. While AI holds great potential for enhancing library services and improving user experiences, it also brings to the forefront significant questions related to data protection and privacy.

Libraries utilizing AI applications should transparently collect user data and obtain informed consent from users regarding how this data is collected, used, and shared. Whenever possible, data should be anonymized, or techniques like federated learning should be employed to prevent the centralization of sensitive information.

User data should be strictly used for its stated purposes and should not be shared more broadly without consent. Special care should be exercised when dealing with children's data. Staff members should be trained on privacy matters, and compliance with relevant legal frameworks such as GDPR (General Data Protection Regulation), UK GDPR (United Kingdom General Data Protection Regulation), HIPAA (Health Insurance Portability and Accountability Act), COPPA (Children's Online Privacy Protection Act) and KVKK (Personal Data Protection Law) is essential.

In essence, libraries must strike a balance between innovation and respecting user privacy. When implemented with care, AI can ethically enhance services. Continuous monitoring and review are of critical importance.

Data Protection in AI Library Applications

In Meurisch and Mühlhäuser (2021) study, the importance of comprehensive data protection approaches at various levels, including management, systems, and AI levels, in AI library applications is emphasized. This highlights that data protection is not merely a basic requirement but a serious need across these different levels. Jamieson and Salinas (2018) discusses how critical it is to preserve the privacy and confidentiality of human subjects in the digital age. This reflects a general awareness of the necessity for libraries to protect user data. Jones et al., (2020) focuses on ethical and practical privacy issues related to learning analytics applications in libraries. This draws attention to libraries' responsibilities in safeguarding user privacy when utilizing such technologies. Das and Islam (2021) provides a general overview of the implementation of artificial intelligence and machine learning in libraries, emphasizing the use of these technologies for data management, resource discovery, and user services. This enhances the overall understanding of how AI can offer potential advantages in libraries.

In the study by Xing et al. (2022), a comparative analysis of the perspectives on artificial intelligence privacy between Americans and Chinese is conducted. This research provides methodological guidance in examining the relationship between artificial intelligence and user privacy. Additionally, it offers guidance to governments in developing artificial intelligence regulations to protect privacy. In their study, Tait and Pierson (2022) emphasize the significance of the use of artificial intelligence and robots in libraries and information science due to their potential contribution to the digital transformation of information professions. Furthermore, the study addresses the challenges and opportunities in incorporating AI and robotics topics into LIS education.

Zhang et al. (2019) proposes an approach that encrypts user data to ensure anonymization and enhances query processing efficiency. Breeding (2015) emphasizes the necessity of encryption to protect sensitive data and discusses the privacy and security features of library automation systems. Breeding (2016) focuses on user privacy and measures to separate user information from borrowed materials in web-based library systems. Sturges et al. (2003) investigates user privacy in the digital library environment and underscores the importance of libraries having privacy policies and being prepared for data protection. In general, the documents highlight the need for robust data security measures, transparency in data collection and usage, anonymization techniques, and compliance with data protection regulations to ensure the protection of user data in AI library applications.

As seen from these studies, data protection is a prominent concern in the field of AI library applications. Transparency, informed consent, anonymization, and data minimization are stressed as essential for ensuring data protection in AI library applications. These elements signify that user privacy and data protection should be the fundamental principles to be upheld. As libraries continue to integrate AI algorithms for purposes like analyzing user behavior, providing resource recommendations, and tailoring services to individual preferences, the implementation of robust data protection measures becomes inevitable. In this context, the important considerations, based on the information obtained from relevant literature, can be listed as follows (Breeding, 2015; Das & Islam, 2021; Jamieson & Salinas, 2018; Jones et al., 2020; Meurisch & Mühlhäuser, 2021; Sturges et al., 2003; Xing et al., 2022):

- Data Security: Due to the sensitive nature of user information, libraries should implement robust security measures against unauthorized access or breaches. Using encryption techniques, access controls, and secure storage systems is crucial to protect user data from potential threats.
- Transparency and Consent: Libraries should be transparent with their users about the data they collect, how it will be used, and who can access it. Obtaining informed consent from users guarantees that they are aware of data processing activities and have the option to opt out.
- Anonymization and De-identification: Where possible, libraries should anonymize user data or remove identifiers to minimize the risk of re-identification. Techniques such as aggregation, pseudonym usage, or direct identifier removal can achieve this.
- Data Storage and Deletion: Libraries should establish clear data retention policies to ensure that user data is not stored longer than necessary. When data is no longer needed, it should be securely and permanently deleted to prevent potential misuse.
- Regulatory Compliance: Libraries should stay updated on relevant data protection laws and regulations such as GDPR. Compliance with these regulations ensures that user data is handled in a legal and ethical manner.
- Informed Consent: Libraries should obtain explicit consent from users before collecting and using their personal information. Transparent communication about how their data will be used can help build trust and empower users to make informed decisions about data sharing.
- Anonymization and Pseudonym Usage: To ensure privacy, libraries should anonymize user data or use pseudonyms whenever possible. By removing personal identifiers or replacing them with pseudonyms, libraries can reduce the risk of re-identification and protect user privacy.
- Data Minimization: Libraries should collect and store the minimum amount of data necessary for the intended purposes. Embracing the principle of data minimization can limit the potential impact of a data breach and reduce privacy risks associated with excessive user data storage.

From the perspective of libraries and information centers, ensuring the protection of user privacy is of paramount importance when evaluating the opportunities presented by AI applications. Libraries have begun to harness AI applications, such as analyzing user data to personalize services and provide resource recommendations. However, given the sensitivity of this data, it is essential to take security measures to prevent unauthorized access. Libraries should be transparent about their data processing activities and obtain informed consent from users. Data should be anonymized to the extent possible, and the accumulation of unnecessary data should be avoided.

In conclusion, even in the era of artificial intelligence, user trust remains indispensable for libraries. Therefore, the utmost care and priority should be given to data protection. An approach grounded in respect for user rights will enable libraries to make the most of artificial intelligence while ensuring user privacy.

Best Practices for Handling and Securing User Data in AI-Enabled Library Services

In AI-assisted library services, the processing and security of user data are of great importance. Several sources provide important insights on this topic.

Fortier (2015) emphasizes the importance of raising awareness about the evaluation of tracking practices that library websites use to monitor visitor behaviors and how these tracking practices can potentially jeopardize user privacy. Also highlights the necessity for librarians to provide digital literacy education to help users protect their privacy. Jones et al. (2020) provides a detailed examination of the ethical and practical privacy issues related to learning analytics applications in libraries. In this context, asserts that user privacy and data protection are top priorities in libraries.

Ardagna (2006) stresses the significance of data processing policies that allow users to control how their personal information is disclosed and used. These policies enable users to have more control over their data. Bubinger and Dinneen (2021) discusses the ethical management of AI-supported information systems and the need for planning, evaluating, and overseeing this process. Points out the requirement to promote ethical AI applications in libraries and provide practical guidance.

Hwang and Hanson (2021) offers an in-depth discussion on the necessity for libraries to engage in learning analytics and the ethical development and implementation of these systems. Libraries have the potential to understand user behaviors, improve access to resources, and enhance services using learning analytics tools. However, it is emphasized that user privacy and ethical considerations should play a crucial role in this process. Emphasizes the importance of integrating user privacy and data ethics principles when designing learning analytics systems in libraries.

Ziyue and Ya (2020) focuses on the importance of establishing privacy protection mechanisms when developing smart library services. These mechanisms should regulate the collection and use of users' personal data while ensuring privacy protection. Libraries should prioritize user privacy and effectively implement privacy protection measures when developing such smart services.

Jones et al. (2020), in a different context, concentrates on the ethical and practical privacy concerns related to learning analytics applications in libraries. Libraries have the capacity to monitor and analyze user behavior using learning analytics tools. However, underscores the importance of considering user privacy and ethical concerns when processing this data. Recommends that libraries approach such applications within an ethical framework and safeguard user privacy rights.

Butters (2007) focuses on privacy concerns associated with RFID systems in libraries. While RFID technology is used for tracking and managing resources in libraries, it is essential to protect users' personal data during this process. Highlights the need for secure systems and awareness of privacy risks. Libraries should consider user privacy concerns and ethically implement RFID technology.

These articles collectively emphasize the crucial point that libraries need to focus on user privacy and ethical considerations when using AI-based technologies and data analytics tools. Protecting user privacy, embracing data ethics principles, and implementing reliable privacy mechanisms can help libraries sustain and develop their information services in a sustainable and ethical manner.

In general, these articles emphasize the need for privacy and highlight the importance of regular data audits and secure data sharing practices. They also stress the need to empower users in protecting their privacy, particularly in the context of AI-supported library services. This approach underscores the complexity of the measures required to ensure user privacy and data protection, providing libraries with a framework in this regard.

As highlighted in these discussions, some guiding principles to consider when addressing privacy concerns in AI-based library services include:

- Privacy by Design: Libraries should incorporate privacy considerations into the design and development of AI systems from the outset. By embedding privacy features and security measures into the architecture, libraries can ensure that user data is protected throughout the system's entire lifecycle.
- Regular Data Audits: Regular audits of data storage and processing practices can help libraries identify potential vulnerabilities or risks to user privacy. These audits should assess data retention policies, access controls, and data sharing practices for compliance with privacy regulations.
- Secure Data Sharing: When collaborating with external partners or sharing data with third-party vendors, libraries should create clear contracts outlining data protection requirements and security measures. Selecting trustworthy

partners with a commitment to privacy and robust security measures is crucial.

- User Empowerment: Libraries should empower users by providing them with control over their personal data. This may include offering users the option to view, edit, delete, or restrict the use of their data within AI-supported library services.
- Data Minimization: Libraries should collect and store only the minimum amount of personal information necessary for a specific purpose. This helps safeguard user privacy by avoiding unnecessary data accumulation. For example, for verifying that a user has borrowed a book, storing basic information like their name and the book's ID may be sufficient.
- Encryption: Libraries should encrypt sensitive data and adopt secure transmission protocols. Encryption, especially during data storage and transmission, ensures that user information remains protected. For instance, sensitive information such as records of books borrowed by users should be encrypted.
- Staff Training: Regular data privacy training for library staff is essential. Staff should have the necessary skills to handle and protect user data correctly and adhere to data privacy policies. Training should cover compliance with data privacy regulations and preparedness for potential security breaches.
- Data Breach Preparedness: Libraries should establish and regularly test plans for what to do in the event of a data breach. This facilitates a quick and effective response in the event of a data breach, including notifying relevant parties and initiating remediation processes.
- Privacy Impact Assessments: Before deploying new AI systems or technologies, libraries should conduct privacy impact assessments. These assessments address questions such as what data will be collected, how it will be used, and the impact on user privacy. Privacy impact assessments help design privacy from the start and identify potential risks, particularly when implementing new technologies.

The establishment of mechanisms to protect library user privacy has become a complex issue in light of the rapid development of information technology. In this process, while the seamless sharing of user data across different platforms and industries offers significant advantages, it also raises concerns regarding privacy protection. Striking a balance between the opportunities presented by smart services and user privacy is crucial and requires a comprehensive approach. One of the most fundamental challenges in this regard is ensuring user privacy and security.

From the perspective of smart services, user privacy is subject to policy guidance and regulatory oversight. This topic represents a potential source of conflict among library stakeholders, including library staff and management, users, and third-party organizations. Therefore, the background of policy principles and technology applications is of paramount importance in understanding and managing mechanisms for protecting user privacy.

When examining this framework, it consists of a macro-level background, core elements, and service control layers. Specifically, this framework can be divided into three main modules, as depicted in Figure 1. These modules provide a useful guide for libraries in taking steps to protect user privacy and shaping the management of this process.

Figure 1. Framework for protecting user privacy in artificial intelligence-powered smart library service applications
(Ziyue & Ya, 2020)

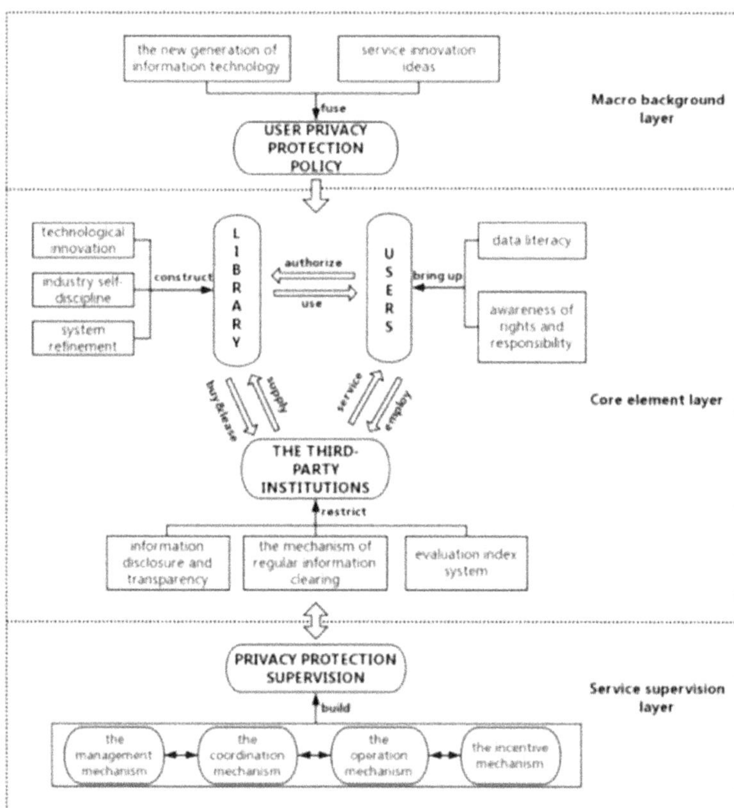

The framework in Figure 1 consists of three main layers: macro background, core elements, and service supervision. The macro background layer highlights the role of information technology and innovative service concepts in shaping privacy policies. Technological advancements and new ideas drive policy formulation. The core element layer involves three key stakeholders: libraries, users, and third-party organizations. Libraries must select qualified third parties and adhere to laws. The service supervision layer emphasizes the need for comprehensive oversight mechanisms for user privacy protection. This includes management, coordination, operation, and incentives. Library associations often oversee the management and coordination of privacy protection policies. They formulate rules, regulations and industry guidance. The coordination mechanism balances the perspectives of different stakeholders in the supervision system. The operation mechanism takes a holistic approach to privacy protection, influenced by coordination and incentives. The incentive mechanism acts as a driving force for the operation mechanism.

Overall, the framework underscores the complex, multi-layered effort required by libraries to develop effective policies that safeguard user privacy in the context of evolving technologies and service concepts.

Compliance With Relevant Data Protection Laws and Regulations

In addition to implementing best practices, libraries must also ensure compliance with relevant data protection laws and regulations. Libraries should closely monitor and adhere to national and local data protection and privacy laws in the countries where they operate.

For example, in Turkey, the fundamental law for the protection of personal data is the Personal Data Protection Law (KVKK). The KVKK regulates various aspects of personal data processing, storage, and transfer. Libraries in Turkey should adopt a data protection policy in compliance with KVKK and conduct data processing activities within the framework of KVKK. Libraries operating within the European Union must comply with the General Data Protection Regulation (GDPR) concerning the collection, processing, and storage of personal data. Libraries in the United Kingdom are subject to data protection regulations under the UK GDPR. Libraries in Australia should adhere to privacy laws concerning data protection. Libraries serving users in California must comply with user rights and data protection regulations specified in the California Consumer Privacy Act (CCPA). In India, the Personal Data Protection Law regulates the collection, storage, and use of personal data. Libraries in India should act in accordance with this law. In Brazil, the General Data Protection Law (LGPD) is in place. Libraries in Brazil should take data protection measures in line with LGPD and, in case of data breaches, report them within the mandatory 72-hour timeframe.The Personal Data Protection Act in Singapore regulates the use of personal data for both the public and private sectors. Libraries in Singapore must also comply with this law (Jeske et al., 2016; Pauletto, 2021; The Law on Protection of Personal Data, 2016; Tikkinen-Piri et al., 2018; Tzanou, 2020).

Additionally, other national and local libraries should be informed about national or local laws related to data protection and privacy in their regions. By staying up-to-date with legal requirements and implementing appropriate measures, libraries can demonstrate their commitment to protecting user privacy and ensure compliance with applicable regulations.

There are numerous studies emphasizing the critical importance of privacy and protection of personal data in libraries. These studies generally highlight the need for libraries to raise more awareness on these issues and to comply with relevant data protection laws in their respective countries. Based on this data, there is also an evident need for libraries to review and update their data protection policies.

Eroğlu and Çakmak (2020) focuses on academic libraries in Turkey, aiming to identify awareness and perception gaps among library managers regarding the privacy of personal data. This study examines how prepared academic libraries in Turkey are regarding the privacy of personal data and offers recommendations to increase awareness among library managers. It underscores the necessity for libraries to provide better protection for personal data.

Bogosavljević (2019) addresses the protection of personal data in documents and highlights the need for higher security in computer systems, as well as the establishment of laws and regulations. This study emphasizes the importance of more effective protection of personal data in library computer systems and suggests that laws and regulations should set specific data protection standards.

Lemos and Passos (2020) investigates the application of the General Data Protection Law (GDPL) in Brazil to libraries and underscores the necessity of compliance with the law to ensure privacy in Brazilian libraries. This study mentions that Brazilian libraries must adhere to GDPL and emphasizes the need for libraries to protect the personal data of users more effectively by complying with this law.

Noh (2014) investigates initiatives to educate public librarians on the importance of user privacy issues, aiming to provide librarians with an educational program in this regard, reduce privacy violations, and measure the effects of the educational program.

Sturges et al. (2001; 2003) discusses user privacy in the context of digital libraries, expressing concerns about the impact of current technical and legal developments on privacy and the need for guidelines on privacy issues for information professionals. This study highlights the importance of user privacy in digital libraries and the need for information professionals to be vigilant in the face of rapidly changing legal and technical developments in this field.

As artificial intelligence technologies become more prevalent in libraries, addressing privacy concerns is paramount. Libraries must prioritize data protection, follow best practices for handling user data, and comply with relevant data protection laws and regulations. This way, libraries can strike a balance between leveraging the benefits of artificial intelligence and safeguarding user privacy, allowing them to thrive successfully in the rapidly changing information landscape.

DISCUSSION

This study provides a comprehensive examination of the significant ethical and privacy issues arising from the integration of AI in libraries. As AI-enabled systems become more prevalent, upholding core values like fairness, transparency, accountability, and privacy is imperative. The attached study makes several salient recommendations, such as regular algorithmic audits to detect bias, obtaining informed consent from users, implementing privacy and security protections, and establishing oversight procedures.

Zhang et al. (2021), emphasizes the increasing interest in the field of artificial intelligence ethics by providing information on the fundamental elements of AI ethics and the current landscape. Bubinger and Dinneen (2021), highlights the need for practical guidance to promote ethical AI in libraries and suggests approaches that can be adapted from other contexts. Bradley (2022) emphasizes the opportunities for libraries to contribute to the development of ethical frameworks by researching AI regulations in libraries. Kennedy (2019) underscores the importance of considering the ethical implications of AI in research libraries. Wojcik et al. (2021) emphasize the importance of conducting a profound ethical assessment before the implementation of augmented intelligence in libraries, underscoring the significance of considering the ethical and social implications of such technologies. Dixon (2008) emphasizes the growing concerns about digital authentication and access management in libraries, particularly regarding the privacy, identifiability, and disclosure of user-related data, underscoring the importance of data and information security. These studies highlight the significance of supporting core values such as justice, transparency, accountability, and privacy in the integration of AI into libraries and provide recommendations to achieve these goals.

Additional research also stresses the need for ethical AI principles tailored to libraries. For instance, Breeding (2016) advises creating AI codes of ethics centered on beneficence, justice, human control, transparency, and accountability. Hoffmann et al. (2018) suggests participatory design processes that engage library stakeholders in formulating ethical AI policies. Ong (2021) proposes an ethical framework for evaluating the consequences of affectively-aware AI, emphasizing the responsibilities of AI developers and operators. LaBrie and Steinke (2019) discusses the need for an ethical audit framework for AI algorithms to ensure they do no harm and address biases. Bui and Noble (2020) argues for a moral framework of justice in AI, emphasizing the importance of interrogating power structures and addressing inequalities. These papers collectively support the idea that libraries can benefit from adopting ethical frameworks to guide the assessment and adoption of AI systems.

Regarding privacy, techniques like data minimization, anonymization, and encryption are widely endorsed (Bradley, 2022; Breeding, 2016). Bradley (2022) recommends managing data ethically through purpose limitations, access controls, consent, and de-identification. Breeding (2016) advises separating patron data from usage data and leveraging authentication methods like proxy servers to preserve anonymity. Such measures allow AI utilization while safeguarding privacy.

Additionally, ongoing education for library professionals on AI ethics is vital (Hoffmann et. al., 2018). Topics like bias mitigation, transparency requirements, regulatory compliance, and re-identification risks should be covered. Libraries can also contribute to AI literacy in their communities through public programming and instructional initiatives.

In essence, libraries must be proactive in developing ethical frameworks, policies, and tools tailored to AI systems. Participatory design processes, impact assessments, bias audits, and human oversight mechanisms can align AI with library values. Prioritizing privacy and security in data practices is equally important. With diligence and collaboration, libraries can implement AI ethically and responsibly.

CONCLUSION

This comprehensive chapter examines the significant ethical considerations and privacy concerns that arise with the increasing integration of AI technologies in libraries. As highlighted throughout the study, AI-enabled libraries can provide transformative benefits such as enhanced search capabilities, personalized recommendations, and improved user experiences. However, the responsible and ethical implementation of these advanced technologies is imperative.

The chapter emphasizes that core ethical principles of fairness, transparency, accountability, user autonomy and privacy must be upheld when AI systems are adopted in libraries. Measures to reduce algorithmic bias, ensure explainability of decisions, establish accountability frameworks, obtain informed consent from users, and safeguard data privacy are crucial. The potential risks of automating certain tasks, displacing library professionals, and decreasing human interaction must also be evaluated.

Furthermore, the chapter stresses the paramount importance of protecting user privacy and complying with relevant data protection laws when processing the significant amounts of user data needed to train and operate AI systems. Best practices highlighted include implementing privacy and security by design, collecting only necessary data, anonymization techniques, encryption, access controls, staff training, and regulatory compliance. Regular audits, privacy impact assessments before deployment, and user empowerment are also advised.

The necessity for continuous education of library staff on AI ethics and active engagement of libraries in AI research is emphasized. By collaborating with developers and researchers, tailored ethical AI applications can be created for libraries. In addition, libraries can contribute to responsible AI advancement in society through literacy initiatives and expertise sharing.

The ethical and privacy issues brought about by artificial intelligence applications in libraries require comprehensive solutions to ensure the responsible and respectful adoption of these technologies. Researchers and practitioners are provided with some recommendations in this regard. Researchers should focus on developing ethical AI frameworks and tools tailored to libraries, while practitioners should update policies and procedures in light of this guidance. Interdisciplinary collaboration and ongoing review will help protect library values while harnessing the power of artificial intelligence.

For Researchers:

- Conduct studies on algorithm auditing methods and bias detection in AI systems tailored for library applications. This can help identify discrimination risks.
- Develop techniques for libraries to collect consent from users in an informed, accessible and ethical manner before gathering data to train AI algorithms. Studies on innovative consent mechanisms can guide libraries.
- Research strategies for libraries to transparently communicate how user data is employed in AI systems, providing explanations without compromising privacy or disclosing trade secrets. Explainability methods should be explored.
- Investigate approaches for evaluating whether particular AI applications are appropriate and constructive for deployment in libraries, considering ethical obligations. Create AI impact assessment frameworks.
- Develop educational resources and training guidelines to assist libraries in keeping professionals updated on AI ethics, privacy measures, and emerging best practices. The creation of such materials can promote competency.

For Practitioners:

- Formulate comprehensive policies and update existing ones to address ethical AI system development, privacy protection, informed consent, and regulatory compliance. Checklists can help guide policy creation.
- Conduct privacy impact assessments before deploying new AI technologies, evaluating data practices, legal compliance, security controls, and potential risks. Take corrective actions to address identified issues.
- Provide ongoing training to library staff on AI ethics, privacy, consent requirements, and security topics. Ensure competency in policy implementation and compliance.
- When collaborating with external AI developers, institute contractual clauses mandating ethics principles, privacy protections, and transparency. Require evidence of accountability measures.
- Establish mechanisms for human oversight and monitoring of AI system outputs to identify problems early, minimize harms, and enable course correction. Document procedures for human intervention.
- Develop explanatory materials for library users regarding any AI systems employed, the user benefits, the data gathered, and their privacy rights. Transparency builds trust.
- Continuously audit AI systems and associated data practices to identify biases, ensure responsible usage, and address new security vulnerabilities. Adjust policies and controls accordingly.

Regularly reviewing the ethics and privacy implications of AI systems and taking proactive measures to address them will assist libraries in navigating these technologies responsibly. A diligent, human-centric approach can enable AI's advantages while safeguarding library values.

In conclusion, this chapter provides libraries with comprehensive insights and guidance regarding the multifaceted ethical and privacy challenges accompanying AI integration. By proactively addressing these concerns through ethical frameworks, transparency, user empowerment, staff training, and technological safeguards, libraries can harness the promise of AI to transform services while upholding their duty to patrons and society. Although AI introduces complex considerations, its tremendous potential can be realized through a human-centric approach rooted in library values.

REFERENCES

American Library Association [ALA]. (2023). *AI Empowerment for Library Staff: Ethical, Equitable, and Engaging Solutions*. ALA. https://elearning.ala.org/local/catalog/view/product.php?productid=940

Ardagna, C. A., De Capitani di Vimercati, S., & Samarati, P. (2006). Enhancing user privacy through data handling policies. In *Data and Applications Security XX: 20th Annual IFIP WG 11.3 Working Conference on Data and Applications Security, Sophia Antipolis, France, July 31-August 2, 2006. Proceedings 20* (pp. 224-236). Springer Berlin Heidelberg. https://link.springer.com/chapter/10.1007/11805588_16

Bender, E. M., Gebru, T., McMillan-Major, A., & Shmitchell, S. (2021, March). On the Dangers of Stochastic Parrots: Can Language Models Be Too Big? In *FAccT '21: Proceedings of the 2021 ACM Conference on Fairness, Accountability, and Transparency* (pp. 610–623). ACM. https://dl.acm.org/doi/abs/10.1145/3442188.3445922

Bogosavljević, M (2019). Protection of personal data in documents: Application of the law on personal data protection in serbia and abroad. *Moderna arhivistika* 2(1), 106–15. http://dx.doi.org/. doi:10.54356/MA/2019/GHKV7413

Bradley, F. (2022). Representation of libraries in artificial intelligence regulations and implications for ethics and practice. *Journal of the Australian Library and Information Association*, *71*(3), 189–200. doi:10.1080/24750158.2022.2101911

Breeding, M. (2015). Smarter Libraries through Technology: Protecting the Privacy of Library Patrons. *Smart Libraries Newsletter, 35*. https://journals.ala.org/index.php/sln/issue/download/261/19

Breeding, M. (2016). *Privacy and security for library systems*. ALA TechSource. https://journals.ala.org/index.php/ltr/issue/viewFile/549/303

Bubinger, H., & Dinneen, J. D. (2021). Actionable approaches to promote ethical AI in libraries. *Proceedings of the Association for Information Science and Technology*, *58*(1), 682–684. doi:10.1002/pra2.528

Bui, M., & Noble, S. U. (2020). We're missing a moral framework of justice in artificial intelligence. *The Oxford handbook of ethics of AI*, 163-179. https://books.google.com/books

Butters, A. (2007). RFID systems, standards and privacy within libraries. *The Electronic Library*, *25*(4), 430–439. doi:10.1108/02640470710779844

Chatila, R., Firth-Butterfield, K., & Havens, J. C. (2018). Ethically aligned design: A vision for prioritizing human well-being with autonomous and intelligent systems (version 2). *University of southern California Los Angeles*. https://apps.dtic.mil/sti/citations/AD1170922

Chen, H., Hussain, S. U., Boemer, F., Stapf, E., Sadeghi, A. R., Koushanfar, F., & Cammarota, R. (2020, July). Developing privacy-preserving AI systems: The lessons learned. In *2020 57th ACM/IEEE Design Automation Conference (DAC)* (pp. 1-4). IEEE. 10.1109/DAC18072.2020.9218662

Cihon, P., Kleinaltenkamp, M. J., Schuett, J., & Baum, S. D. (2021). AI Certification: Advancing Ethical Practice by Reducing Information Asymmetries. *IEEE Transactions on Technology and Society*, *2*(4), 200–209. doi:10.1109/TTS.2021.3077595

Coleman, C. N. (2020). Managing bias when library collections become data. *International Journal of Librarianship*, *5*(1), 8–19. doi:10.23974/ijol.2020.vol5.1.162

Cox, A. (2022). *The rise of AI: implications and applications of artificial intelligence in academic libraries (ACRL publications in librarianship, no. 78)* (S. Hervieux & A. Wheatley, Eds.). Association of College and Research Libraries. doi:10.1080/24750158.2022.2103917

Cox, A. M., & Mazumdar, S. (2022). Defining artificial intelligence for librarians. *Journal of Librarianship and Information Science*, *22*, 1–11. doi:10.1177/09610006221142029

Das, R. K., & Islam, M. S. U. (2021). Application of artificial intelligence and machine learning in libraries: a systematic review. *arXiv preprint arXiv:2112.04573.* https://doi.org/ doi:10.48550/arXiv.2112.04573

Dilmaghani, S., Brust, M. R., Danoy, G., Cassagnes, N., Pecero, J., & Bouvry, P. (2019, December). Privacy and security of big data in AI systems: A research and standards perspective. In *2019 IEEE International Conference on Big Data (Big Data)* (pp. 5737-5743). IEEE. 10.1109/BigData47090.2019.9006283

Dixon, P. (2008). Ethical issues implicit in library authentication and access management: Risks and best practices. *Journal of Library Administration*, *47*(3-4), 141–162. doi:10.1080/01930820802186480

Eroğlu, Ş., & Çakmak, T. (2020). Personal data perceptions and privacy in Turkish academic libraries: An evaluation for administrations. *Journal of Academic Librarianship*, *46*(6), 102251. doi:10.1016/j.acalib.2020.102251

European Parliamentary Research Service [EPRS]. (2020). The ethics of artificial intelligence: Issues and initiatives. *Panel for the Future of Science and Technology.* EPRS. https://www.europarl.europa.eu/stoa

Feng, W. (2021). The Applications of Artificial Intelligence in Reading Promotion in Chinese University Libraries. *Diversity, Divergence, Dialogue - iConference 2021, 16th International Conference on Information,* Beijing, China. https://www.ideals.illinois.edu/handle/2142/109662

Fortier, A., & Burkell, J. (2015). Hidden online surveillance: What librarians should know to protect their own privacy and that of their patrons. *Information Technology and Libraries*, *34*(3), 59–72. doi:10.6017/ital.v34i3.5495

Hoffmann, A. L., Roberts, S. T., Wolf, C. T., & Wood, S. (2018). Beyond fairness, accountability, and transparency in the ethics of algorithms: Contributions and perspectives from LIS. *Proceedings of the Association for Information Science and Technology*, *55*(1), 694–696. doi:10.1002/pra2.2018.14505501084

Huang, L. (2023). Ethics of artificial intelligence in education: Student privacy and data protection. *Science Insights Education Frontiers*, *16*(2), 2577–2587. doi:10.15354/sief.23.re202

Hwang, S. Y., & Hanson, M. (2021). Learning analytics and privacy: A library perspective. *Internet Reference Services Quarterly*, *25*(3), 69–72. doi:10.1080/10875301.2021.1946456

International Federation of Library Associations and Institutions [IFLA]. (2020). *IFLA statement on libraries and artificial intelligence.* IFLA Publications. https://repository.ifla.org/handle/123456789/1646

Jaillant, L., & Rees, A. (2023). Applying AI to digital archives: Trust, collaboration and shared professional ethics. *Digital Scholarship in the Humanities*, *38*(2), 571–585. doi:10.1093/llc/fqac073

Jamieson, T., & Salinas, G. (2018). Protecting human subjects in the digital age: Issues and best practices of data protection. *Survey Practice*, *11*(2), 1–10. https://digitalcommons.unomaha.edu/emergencyservicespublications/1/. doi:10.29115/SP-2018-0028 PMID:37201036

Jarrahi, M. H., Askay, D., Eshraghi, A., & Smith, P. (2023). Artificial intelligence and knowledge management: A partnership between human and AI. *Business Horizons*, *66*(1), 87–99. doi:10.1016/j.bushor.2022.03.002

Jeske, M., Intahchomphoo, C., Landriault, E., & Bioni, B. R. (2016). The intersection of freedom of information, privacy legislation and library services in Canadian jurisdictions. *Legal Information Management*, *16*(1), 14–21. doi:10.1017/S1472669616000050

Jha, S. K. (2023). Application of artificial intelligence in libraries and information centers services: Prospects and challenges. *Library Hi Tech News*, *40*(7), 1–5. doi:10.1108/LHTN-06-2023-0102

Jones, K. M. L., Briney, K. A., Goben, A., Salo, D., Asher, A., & Perry, M. R. (2020). A Comprehensive Primer to Library Learning Analytics Practices, Initiatives, and Privacy Issues. *College & Research Libraries*, *81*(3), 570–591. https://ssrn.com/abstract=3567955. doi:10.5860/crl.81.3.570

Kennedy, M. L. (2019). What do artificial intelligence (AI) and ethics of AI mean in the context of research libraries. *Research Library Issues, 299*, 3-13. https://publications.arl.org/18nm1db/

LaBrie, R. C., & Steinke, G. (2019). Towards a framework for ethical audits of AI algorithms. In *Ethical Audits of AI Algorithms*. https://scholar.archive.org/work/wv7pfbs3uve5xegh336ffeeuta/access/wayback/https://aisel.aisnet.org/cgi/viewcontent.cgi?article=1398&context=amcis2019

Leikas, J., Koivisto, R., & Gotcheva, N. (2019). Ethical framework for designing autonomous intelligent systems. *Journal of Open Innovation*, *5*(1), 18. doi:10.3390/joitmc5010018

Lemos, A. N. L. E., & Passos, E. (2020). A adequação das bibliotecas à Lei Geral de Proteção de Dados. *Cadernos de Informação Jurídica (Cajur), 7*(1), 85-103. http://cajur.com.br/index.php/cajur/article/view/265

Massis, B. (2018). Artificial intelligence arrives in the library. *Information and Learning Science*, *119*(7/8), 456–459. doi:10.1108/ILS-02-2018-0011

Meurisch, C., & Mühlhäuser, M. (2021). Data protection in AI services: A survey. *ACM Computing Surveys*, *54*(2), 1–38. doi:10.1145/3440754

Mishra, S. (2023). Ethical ımplications of artificial ıntelligence and machine learning in libraries and ınformation centers: a frameworks, challenges, and best practices. *Library Philosophy and Practice (e-journal)*. https://digitalcommons.unl.edu/libphilprac/7753

NaudéW.DimitriN. (2021). Public procurement and ınnovation for human-centered artificial ıntelligence. IZA Discussion (Paper No. 14021), https://ssrn.com/abstract=3762891

Noh, Y. (2014). Digital library user privacy: Changing librarian viewpoints through education. *Library Hi Tech*, *32*(2), 300–317. doi:10.1108/LHT-08-2013-0103

Numarasi, K. (2016). The Law on Protection of Personal Data. *T.C. Resmi Gazete (Official Gazette of the Republic of Turkey)* (number: 29677) https://www.mevzuat.gov.tr/MevzuatMetin/1.5.6698.pdf

Ong, D. C. (2021, September). An ethical framework for guiding the development of affectively-aware artificial intelligence. In *2021 9th International Conference on Affective Computing and Intelligent Interaction (ACII)* (pp. 1-8). IEEE. 10.1109/ACII52823.2021.9597441

Oyelude, A. A. (2021). AI and libraries: Trends and projections. *Library Hi Tech News*, *38*(10), 1–4. doi:10.1108/LHTN-10-2021-0079

Pauletto, C. (2021). Options towards a global standard for the protection of individuals with regard to the processing of personal data. *Computer Law & Security Report*, *40*, 105433. doi:10.1016/j.clsr.2020.105433

Piano, S. (2020). Ethical principles in machine learning and artificial intelligence: Cases from the field and possible ways forward. *Humanities & Social Sciences Communications*, *7*(1), 1–7. https://www.nature.com/articles/s41599-020-0501-9. doi:10.1057/s41599-020-0501-9

Shazly, H., Ferraro, A., & Bennet, K. (2020, November). Ethical Concerns: An overview of Artificial Intelligence System Development and Life Cycle. In *2020 IEEE International Symposium on Technology and Society (ISTAS)* (pp. 33-42). IEEE. 10.1109/ISTAS50296.2020.9462201

SifatI. (2023). Artificial Intelligence as an Institution: Impacts, Integration Strategies, and Policy Directions (August 18, 2023). Available at SSRN: https://ssrn.com/abstract=4545403 doi:10.2139/ssrn.4545403

Singley, E. (2020). A holistic approach to user privacy in academic libraries. *Journal of Academic Librarianship*, *46*(3), 102151. doi:10.1016/j.acalib.2020.102151

Slavkovik, M. (2020, November). Teaching AI Ethics: Observations and Challenges. In *Norsk IKT-konferanse for forskning og utdanning,* (4). https://hdl.handle.net/11250/2764233

Sturges, P., Davies, E., Dearnley, J., Iliffe, U., Iliffe, U., Oppenheim, C., & Hardy, R. (2003). User privacy in the digital library environment: An investigation of policies and preparedness. *Library Management*, *24*(1/2), 44–50. doi:10.1108/01435120310454502

Sturges, P., Teng, V., & Iliffe, U. (2001). User privacy in the digital library environment: A matter of concern for information professionals. *Library Management, 22*(8/9), 364–370. doi:10.1108/01435120110406309

Tait, E., & Pierson, C. M. (2022). Artificial intelligence and robots in libraries: Opportunities in LIS curriculum for preparing the librarians of tomorrow. *Journal of the Australian Library and Information Association, 71*(3), 256–274. doi:10.1080/24750158.2022.2081111

Teredesai, A., Ahmad, M. A., & Eckert, C. (2020). *Fairness, Accountability, Transparency in AI at Scale: Lessons from National Programs, School of Engineering and Technology Publications*. Digital Commons. https://digitalcommons.tacoma.uw.edu/tech_pub/394/

Tikkinen-Piri, C., Rohunen, A., & Markkula, J. (2018). EU General Data Protection Regulation: Changes and implications for personal data collecting companies. *Computer Law & Security Report, 34*(1), 134–153. doi:10.1016/j.clsr.2017.05.015

Tzanou, M. (Ed.). (2020). *Personal data protection and legal developments in the European Union*. IGI Global. https://www.igi-global.com/publish/ doi:10.4018/978-1-5225-9489-5

Wojcik, M. (2021). Augmented intelligence technology. The ethical and practical problems of its implementation in libraries. *Library Hi Tech, 39*(2), 435–447. doi:10.1108/LHT-02-2020-0043

Xing, Y., He, W., Zhang, J., & Cao, G. (2022). AI Privacy Opinions between US and Chinese People. *Journal of Computer Information Systems, 63*(3), 492–506. doi:10.1080/08874417.2022.2079107

Zhang, Y., Wu, M., Tian, G. Y., Zhang, G., & Lu, J. (2021). Ethics and privacy of artificial intelligence: Understandings from bibliometrics. *Knowledge-Based Systems, 222*, 106994. doi:10.1016/j.knosys.2021.106994

Ziyue, X., & Ya, C. (2020, August). The Research on User Privacy Protection of library Intelligent Service. In *2020 International Symposium on Computer Engineering and Intelligent Communications (ISCEIC)* (pp. 200-205). IEEE. 10.1109/ISCEIC51027.2020.00050

KEY TERMS AND DEFINITIONS

AI Ethics: The study of the ethical implications of artificial intelligence systems, providing frameworks and principles to ensure the responsible and beneficial development and use of AI that respects human values.

Algorithmic Bias: Systematic and repeatable errors in a computer system that create unfair outcomes, stemming from biases in the algorithm's design and training data. Addressing biases in AI algorithms used by libraries is crucial to prevent discrimination.

Anonymization: The process of removing personally identifiable information from datasets to protect privacy. Anonymizing user data helps mitigate re-identification risks when training AI algorithms.

Artificial Intelligence (AI): The simulation of human intelligence in machines that are programmed to think like humans and mimic their actions. AI systems can perform tasks such as learning, reasoning, problem-solving, perception, and prediction. In libraries, AI can be used for applications like cataloging, user recommendations, and enhancing search capabilities.

Data Privacy: The right of individuals to control what information about themselves is collected and how it is used. Libraries must safeguard user data privacy and security when employing AI systems that utilize this data.

Encryption: Encoding information in such a way that only authorized parties can access it. Encrypting sensitive user data provides protection against unauthorized access, especially during transmission and storage.

Informed Consent: Obtaining a user's permission before collecting or processing their personal data, with full transparency about how the data will be used. Ensuring informed consent is key to ethical AI usage in libraries.

Machine Learning (ML): A subset of artificial intelligence where algorithms are programmed to learn from data and improve themselves over time without explicit programming. Machine learning models can detect patterns in data and make predictions. Libraries can leverage ML for tasks like personalized book recommendations based on borrowing history.

Transparency: In the context of AI systems, transparency involves clearly communicating how the system works, the data used for training, and the logic behind algorithmic decisions. AI transparency allows identification of potential biases and builds user trust.

Chapter 4
Cyber Sentinels:
Exploring the Cybersecurity Awareness of Indian Library Professionals

Subhajit Panda
https://orcid.org/0000-0002-1578-1159
Chandigarh University, India

Navkiran Kaur
Punjabi University, India

ABSTRACT

Libraries in this digital era of information dissemination serve as crucial hubs for accessing information and resources, making cybersecurity awareness among library professionals paramount. This chapter delves into the crucial realm of cybersecurity awareness in library environments, emphasizing its multifaceted nature, including data security, privacy, and threat mitigation. Real-world consequences of inadequate awareness underscore the urgency of addressing this issue. It explores the spectrum of cyber threats libraries face, emphasizing the pivotal role of cultivating cybersecurity awareness among librarians. Strategies for enhancing library cybersecurity are presented, recognizing its pivotal role in safeguarding valuable digital resources. Using surveys and comprehensive analysis, it provides insights into the cybersecurity awareness of Indian library professionals, examining their expertise, threat awareness, and influencing factors, revealing essential areas for improvement and further research.

DOI: 10.4018/979-8-3693-1573-6.ch004

INTRODUCTION

In today's digital landscape, libraries have become vibrant centers providing a plethora of digital services, encompassing everything from online databases to virtual programs (LISEDUNETWORK, 2019). Nevertheless, this digital transformation also exposes libraries to cybersecurity threats. To effectively tackle these challenges, libraries must give paramount importance to cybersecurity awareness, institute robust security measures, fortify their systems, collaborate with partners, and remain vigilant about emerging threats (Adakawa et al., 2020). This proactive stance is imperative for safeguarding systems, data, and patron privacy, thereby allowing libraries to fulfill their mission securely (Kim, 2016b).

In India, library professionals often lack adequate cybersecurity awareness, posing risks to the security and privacy of stored and transmitted data. This study aims to assess the current state of cybersecurity awareness among Indian library professionals, identify knowledge gaps, and provide a basis for policy development and initiatives to enhance awareness.

This research explores factors contributing to cybersecurity awareness, including demographics, education, and training. The study addresses questions about IT expertise levels among Indian library professionals, their cybersecurity awareness, and the factors influencing their awareness levels. The study's findings will benefit library professionals, policymakers, and stakeholders concerned with cybersecurity in the digital age. Elevating cybersecurity awareness among Indian library professionals is crucial to secure sensitive data and create a trustworthy digital environment for library users.

LITERATURE REVIEW

Cybersecurity awareness in libraries is a critical topic in today's digital age, where the protection of sensitive information and digital resources is paramount. This literature review synthesizes findings from eleven articles that explore various aspects of cybersecurity awareness in libraries, highlighting the main findings and identifying gaps in research.

Kim's (2016a) article emphasized the importance of libraries advocating for online privacy amidst the challenges of balancing cybersecurity, usability, and privacy. It highlighted incidents like security breaches, network vulnerabilities, and phishing scams, illustrating the tension between security and usability, such as CAPTCHAs causing accessibility issues. The article addressed the conflict between cybersecurity and privacy, citing mass surveillance and potential threats like the FBI's request for a backdoor app. It urged libraries, known for safeguarding intellectual freedom, to support online privacy through initiatives like the Library Freedom Project, emphasizing privacy's role in human autonomy, free expression, and free association in the digital age. Dark et al. (2018) addressed the challenges related to cybersecurity education and workforce development. They stressed the necessity of a cybersecurity digital library (DL) to tackle these challenges. The authors introduced CLARK, a prototype curriculum management platform that hosts cybersecurity learning objects, as a valuable tool for the cybersecurity education community. Ajie (2019) turned the spotlight on cyber security in Nigerian academic libraries, discussing the rising incidence of cybercrime and its economic and security implications. The paper examined the effectiveness of electronic security systems in these libraries, addressing various threats and proposing cybersecurity measures. It underscored the importance of implementing security measures to improve the situation in academic libraries.

Ngwum et al. (2020) embarked on an exploration of digital library security and proposed a novel model for evaluating digital library security. They identified core security criteria and requirements for digital libraries and assessed the model's effectiveness using the CLARK cybersecurity curriculum digital library. The results indicated that the model was effective in evaluating security requirements. Mamun et al. (2021) delved into the growing significance of cyber security awareness in Bangladesh in response to increased technology usage and cyber threats. The article underscored the lack of awareness among citizens and organizations and called for reinforced cyber security policies and procedures. It provided recommendations to enhance awareness and strengthen cyber security in the region. Taylor et al. (2022) addressed the global cybersecurity crisis and the need for accessible, high-quality cybersecurity curriculum in academic institutions. They discussed the CLARK cybersecurity curriculum resource library and highlighted its role as a living digital library. The paper examined existing cybersecurity repositories and factors influencing digital library success, ultimately presenting CLARK as a multifaceted solution to meet critical demands in cybersecurity education.

Alhaif's (2023) study delved into cybersecurity awareness among information specialists in Saudi university libraries. It aimed to assess the level of cybersecurity awareness, necessary competencies, training needs, and differences in awareness based on gender, years of experience, and training courses attended. The study revealed a high degree of cybersecurity awareness among information specialists in Saudi university libraries, with statistically significant differences observed in relation to gender, experience, and training courses. Aregbesola and Nwaolise (2023) shifted the focus to the challenges faced by academic libraries in developing countries when it comes to cybersecurity for safeguarding digital collections. They emphasized the long-term benefits of prioritizing cybersecurity, including building trust among users, fostering collaboration among institutions, and providing a secure environment for academic research. The paper offered guidelines and insights to enhance cybersecurity practices in academic libraries, ensuring the protection of digital collections and the mitigation of cyber threats. Igbinovia and Ishola (2023) delved into the realm of cyber security in university libraries in Nigeria and its implications for Library and Information Science education. The study found that librarians possessed moderate knowledge of cyber security, and university libraries were exposed to various cyber threats. Challenges included the disposition of library management towards cyber security and poor password management. The study emphasized the need for cyber security education in library schools and the willingness of librarians to learn about it. Kont (2023) directed attention towards the cyber security awareness of Estonian library staff. The study employed an online survey and the Human Aspects of Information Security questionnaire to gauge knowledge, attitudes, and behavior related to cyber security. The findings indicated a good level of cyber security awareness among library employees, although specific areas, such as device usage and incident prevention and handling, required more attention. Sinha (2023) explored the intersection of the metaverse and cybersecurity in a digital library context. The case study focused on ensuring the security of the library's metaverse, encompassing authentication protocols, encryption, and firewalls. The authors discussed potential risks and challenges associated with the metaverse and emphasized the importance of effective cybersecurity measures in mitigating these risks. The study underscored the necessity of cybersecurity in virtual shared spaces to ensure secure access to information.

While these reviewed articles offer valuable insights into various facets of cybersecurity awareness in libraries, a significant research gap exists concerning the assessment of the effectiveness of cybersecurity awareness programs within library settings. While the majority of the literature concentrates on understanding awareness levels, challenges, and the imperative need for education, empirical research evaluating the tangible impact of awareness initiatives and training programs on the cybersecurity practices of library professionals is notably scarce. In light of this gap, the present research not only endeavors to provide a comprehensive overview of cybersecurity in libraries and assess the awareness levels among Indian library professionals but also endeavors to gauge their actual expertise in identifying cyber threats and effectively responding to cyberattacks. Furthermore, it seeks to analyze the influencing factors that shape cybersecurity awareness in this context.

STUDY OBJECTIVES

The main objectives of the study are to,

i) Define and emphasize the significance of cybersecurity & cybersecurity awareness.
ii) Explore the multifaceted nature of cybersecurity.
iii) Highlight real-world consequences of inadequate cybersecurity awareness.
iv) Identify and analyze cyber threats faced by libraries.
v) Stress the importance of cultivating cybersecurity awareness among librarians.
vi) Outline strategies for enhancing library cybersecurity.
vii) Assess cybersecurity awareness among Indian library professionals by focusing on their expertise, threat awareness, and influencing factors.
viii) Propose future research directions in library cybersecurity.

UNDERSTANDING CYBERSECURITY & CYBERSECURITY AWARENESS

What is Cybersecurity?

In 2009, the International Telecommunication Union (ITU) defined cybersecurity in its report "Recommendation ITU-T X.1205" as "*Cybersecurity is the collection of tools, policies, security concepts, security safeguards, guidelines, risk management approaches, actions, training, best practices, assurance and technologies that can be used to protect the cyber environment and organization and user's assets.*"

The Committee on National Security Systems (CNSS) (2010) simply described cybersecurity as "*the ability to protect or defend the use of cyberspace from cyber-attacks.*"

The Oxford Online Dictionary (2014) provides the meaning of cybersecurity as "*the state of being protected against the criminal or unauthorized use of electronic data, or the measures taken to achieve this.*"

According to Khurana (2017), "*Cyber security is generally the techniques set to protect the cyber environment of the user. This environment includes the user themselves, the devices, networks, applications, all softwares etc.*"

While, in the context of library environments, cybersecurity can be defined as: "the comprehensive framework encompassing tools, policies, security concepts, safeguards, guidelines, risk management strategies, actions, training, best practices, assurance measures, and technologies that are specifically tailored to protect digital assets, sensitive information, and digital resources within the library's digital ecosystem. It includes measures to defend against cyber threats and unauthorized access while ensuring the confidentiality, integrity, and availability of digital data and services, ultimately safeguarding the library's mission to provide secure access to information and protect patron privacy in the digital age".

Defining Cybersecurity Awareness and Its Significance

Cybersecurity awareness refers to the level of understanding, knowledge, and consciousness individuals or organizations possess regarding the various aspects of cybersecurity (mimecast, n.d.). It encompasses a wide spectrum of competencies, from recognizing potential cyber threats to adopting secure practices, and from understanding the consequences of security breaches to being able to respond effectively in case of a cyber incident (Alzubaidi, 2021). Following are some notable significance of cybersecurity awareness (Spanning Cloud Apps, 2022):

Thwarting Cyber Threats

Cybersecurity awareness is the first line of defense against a multitude of cyber threats, including malware, phishing, ransomware, and social engineering attacks. Understanding these threats empowers individuals and organizations to proactively protect their digital assets.

Data Privacy

In an era of pervasive data collection and sharing, awareness of cybersecurity is crucial to safeguarding personal and sensitive information. Being aware of privacy risks and protective measures helps in preserving data confidentiality.

Preventing Financial Loss

Cyberattacks can result in substantial financial losses for individuals and organizations. A high level of cybersecurity awareness can help identify potential scams or fraudulent activities, preventing financial damage.

Protecting Reputation

Security breaches can tarnish an individual's or organization's reputation. Cybersecurity awareness enables swift response and damage control in the event of an incident, preserving trust and credibility.

Legal and Regulatory Compliance

Many regions and industries have enacted stringent data protection and cybersecurity regulations. Awareness is essential for compliance with these laws, avoiding legal repercussions.

Ensuring Business Continuity

For organizations, being aware of cybersecurity risks is vital for business continuity. Understanding the potential disruptions that cyber incidents can cause allows for better planning and resilience.

National Security

On a larger scale, cybersecurity awareness contributes to national security. A populace that is educated about cyber threats can help thwart cyberattacks that may have implications for a country's security.

So, cybersecurity awareness is not merely a buzzword but a fundamental necessity in the digital age. It equips individuals and organizations with the knowledge and tools needed to protect themselves from cyber threats, safeguard data, and mitigate potential damages. Its significance extends beyond personal or organizational interests, encompassing broader societal and national security implications.

The Multifaceted Nature of Cybersecurity

Cybersecurity is a complex and multifaceted discipline that spans various dimensions, each crucial in its own right. Fredrick Chang (2012), former Director of Research at the National Security Agency in the United States discusses the multidisciplinary nature of cybersecurity: "*A science of cybersecurity offers many opportunities for advances based on a multidisciplinary approach, because, after all, cybersecurity is fundamentally about an adversarial engagement. Humans must defend machines that are attacked by other humans using machines. So, in addition to the critical traditional fields of computer science, electrical engineering, and mathematics, perspectives from other fields are needed*" (Craigen et al., 2014).

The concept of cybersecurity goes beyond the mere protection of computer systems and networks and encompasses a comprehensive approach that includes (CybSafe, 2019):

Data Security

At its core, cybersecurity is about safeguarding data. This involves implementing measures to ensure data integrity, confidentiality, and availability. Data security encompasses encryption, access controls, and secure data storage practices to prevent unauthorized access, alteration, or loss of critical information.

Privacy Protection

Privacy is an integral part of cybersecurity, especially in an age where personal information is frequently collected and shared online. Cybersecurity efforts extend to respecting individual privacy rights by establishing robust privacy policies, consent mechanisms, and anonymization techniques to protect personal data from misuse or exposure.

Threat Mitigation

Cyber threats come in various forms, including malware, phishing, ransomware, and advanced persistent threats. Cybersecurity aims to proactively identify, assess, and mitigate these threats. This involves deploying intrusion detection systems, firewalls, and antivirus software, as well as continually monitoring for suspicious activities to respond promptly to potential breaches.

Incident Response

Even with preventive measures, cybersecurity acknowledges that incidents may occur. Therefore, it includes developing effective incident response plans and strategies to minimize damage, recover from attacks, and learn from security breaches to prevent future occurrences.

Education and Awareness

Cybersecurity is not solely a technical concern. It also entails educating individuals and organizations about cyber risks and best practices. Raising awareness is critical to empowering users to make informed decisions, recognize potential threats, and practice safe online behaviors.

Legal and Regulatory Compliance

Compliance with cybersecurity laws and regulations is essential. Organizations must adhere to industry-specific and regional cybersecurity standards and report data breaches as required by law. Compliance is a key aspect of managing cyber risk.

Security Culture

Building a security-conscious culture within an organization is a vital component of cybersecurity. It involves fostering a mindset where security is everyone's responsibility, from top management down to every employee, and integrating security into organizational processes and decision-making.

Continuous Monitoring and Adaptation

Cyber threats are constantly evolving. Effective cybersecurity requires continuous monitoring of systems and networks, staying informed about emerging threats, and adapting security measures accordingly.

INTRODUCING CYBERSECURITY IN LIBRARIES

Cybersecurity awareness in libraries is a critical step towards safeguarding sensitive information, protecting patron privacy, and ensuring the integrity of digital resources. In today's digital age, libraries serve as hubs for information access, making them potential targets for cyber threats. By prioritizing cybersecurity, libraries can establish a secure digital environment, educate patrons and staff about safe online practices, and play a pivotal role in promoting digital literacy and privacy protection. This introduction lays the foundation for a proactive approach to addressing cybersecurity challenges within the library profession (IFLA, 2022).

Cyber Threats in Libraries

Cyber threats in libraries are a growing concern due to the increasing digitalization of library services and the vast amount of sensitive information they handle. Libraries are not immune to cyberattacks, and they face various threats that can compromise data security, patron privacy, and operational integrity. Here are some notable cybersecurity threats libraries should be aware of:

Phishing Attacks

Cybercriminals send deceptive emails that appear legitimate to library staff or patrons. These emails often contain malicious links or attachments designed to steal login credentials, personal information, or distribute malware. Libraries may be targeted for their user databases or staff access (Gillis, 2020).

Ransomware

Ransomware attacks can encrypt a library's data and demand a ransom for decryption keys. If successful, these attacks can disrupt library operations, compromise patron data, and lead to financial losses (Beaman et al., 2021).

Data Breaches

Libraries store a wealth of sensitive information, including patron records, circulation history, and personally identifiable information (PII). Data breaches can result from cyberattacks, insider threats, or insecure data handling practices, exposing patrons to identity theft and other risks (Froehlich, 2022).

Insider Threats

Malicious or negligent employees, contractors, or volunteers can pose a significant cybersecurity risk. They may intentionally or unintentionally compromise library systems, steal data, or misuse privileged access (Web Master, 2022).

Weak Passwords

Libraries often use various software systems, and weak or reused passwords can make these systems vulnerable to unauthorized access. Cybercriminals may use brute force attacks to crack passwords or exploit password-sharing among library staff (Hanna, 2021).

Outdated Software and Systems

Failure to regularly update and patch software and systems can leave libraries susceptible to known vulnerabilities. Cybercriminals can exploit these weaknesses to gain unauthorized access or distribute malware (Gondek, n.d.).

Denial-of-Service (DoS) Attacks

DoS attacks can disrupt library services by overwhelming servers or network resources with a flood of traffic. This can render library websites, online catalogs, and digital resources inaccessible to patrons (Gu & Liu, 2012).

Social Engineering

Cybercriminals use social engineering techniques to manipulate library staff or patrons into revealing sensitive information or performing actions that compromise security. Social engineering tactics can include pretexting, baiting, or tailgating (Imperva, 2019).

Unsecured Wi-Fi Networks

Libraries often offer public Wi-Fi access, which can be exploited by attackers to intercept data traffic, launch man-in-the-middle attacks, or distribute malware to unsuspecting patrons.

Third-Party Vulnerabilities

Libraries may rely on third-party vendors for software and services. If these vendors experience data breaches or vulnerabilities, it can indirectly impact the security of library systems and patron data.

Importance of Cybersecurity Awareness Among Librarians

Cybersecurity awareness among librarians is of paramount importance in today's digital age (Farid et al., 2023). Librarians play a critical role in safeguarding sensitive information, ensuring the integrity of digital resources, and promoting patron privacy (Anday et al., 2012). Here are several reasons highlighting the significance of cybersecurity awareness among librarians (Khan et al., 2021):

Protection of Patron Data

Libraries store a vast amount of patron data, including personal information, borrowing history, and research preferences. Cybersecurity awareness ensures that librarians take appropriate measures to protect this sensitive data from unauthorized access or data breaches.

Preservation of Patron Privacy

Librarians are stewards of patron privacy rights. A strong understanding of cybersecurity helps librarians maintain the confidentiality of patron records, reading habits, and online interactions, which is essential to uphold intellectual freedom.

Defending Against Cyberattacks

Librarians must be prepared to defend library systems and networks against cyberattacks. Awareness of common attack vectors, such as phishing and malware, enables librarians to recognize and mitigate threats before they lead to data breaches or system disruptions.

Promoting Safe Internet Use

Libraries often provide public internet access. Cybersecurity-aware librarians can educate patrons about safe online practices, such as using secure connections and avoiding suspicious websites, to protect them from cyber threats.

Resource Integrity

Libraries offer digital resources, databases, and e-books. Cybersecurity awareness helps librarians ensure the integrity of these resources by preventing unauthorized access, piracy, or tampering.

Cybersecurity Education

Librarians serve as educators, and their knowledge extends to cybersecurity. By staying informed and promoting cybersecurity awareness, librarians can help patrons, especially students and researchers, develop digital literacy and protect themselves online.

Library Operations

Cyberattacks can disrupt library operations, affecting services, catalog access, and resource availability. Librarians with cybersecurity awareness can implement measures to maintain continuity during such incidents and ensure minimal disruption.

Compliance with Regulations

Libraries are subject to data protection and privacy regulations. Cybersecurity awareness helps librarians adhere to these regulations, avoid potential legal issues, and protect the library's reputation.

Preventing Identity Theft

Libraries often require personal information for registration and access to services. Cybersecurity-aware librarians can help prevent identity theft by securing this information and educating patrons on the risks.

Crisis Management

In the event of a cybersecurity incident, librarians need to respond swiftly and effectively. Cybersecurity awareness ensures that they are prepared to manage and mitigate the consequences of an attack.

Professional Development

As technology evolves, ongoing cybersecurity training is essential for librarians to stay current with emerging threats and best practices. Cybersecurity awareness supports their professional development and the ability to adapt to changing digital landscapes.

Public Trust

A library's reputation for security and trustworthiness is essential. Cybersecurity awareness helps maintain public trust by demonstrating a commitment to protecting patron data and privacy.

Overall, cybersecurity awareness is crucial for librarians to fulfill their roles as guardians of information, promoters of digital literacy, and protectors of patron rights. By staying informed about cybersecurity risks and best practices, librarians can create a safe and secure digital environment for library users and uphold the values of privacy and intellectual freedom.

How to Make a Library Cybersecure?

Securing a library's digital environment is crucial to protect sensitive information, patron privacy, and maintain the integrity of digital resources (Suqri & Fatuyi, 2012). Here are step-by-step recommendations to make a library cybersecure:

Conduct a Cybersecurity Assessment

- Start by assessing the current state of cybersecurity within the library.

- Identify potential vulnerabilities, such as outdated software, weak passwords, or insufficient network protection.
- Determine the library's specific cybersecurity needs and risks.

Establish a Cybersecurity Policy

- Develop a comprehensive cybersecurity policy tailored to the library's requirements.
- Clearly define roles and responsibilities for staff members regarding cybersecurity.
- Ensure that the policy complies with relevant regulations and standards.

Educate Staff and Patrons

- Provide cybersecurity training and awareness programs for library staff.
- Educate patrons about safe online practices, privacy protection, and the risks of cyber threats.
- Offer workshops and resources to enhance digital literacy.

Implement Strong Access Controls

- Enforce strong password policies, requiring complex passwords and regular changes.
- Implement multi-factor authentication (MFA) for staff accessing sensitive systems.
- Restrict access to sensitive data and systems on a need-to-know basis.

Regularly Update Software and Systems

- Keep all software, including operating systems, antivirus, and applications, up to date with security patches.
- Use a vulnerability management system to identify and address software vulnerabilities promptly.

Secure the Network

- Employ firewalls and intrusion detection/prevention systems to safeguard the network.
- Segregate the network to isolate sensitive data and critical systems from public or less secure networks.

Backup and Disaster Recovery

- Implement regular data backups, including offsite and cloud backups.
- Develop a disaster recovery plan to ensure data can be restored in case of a cyber incident.

Regularly Monitor and Audit

- Continuously monitor network traffic and systems for signs of unauthorized access or suspicious activities.
- Conduct regular cybersecurity audits to assess the effectiveness of security measures.

Incident Response Plan

- Develop a detailed incident response plan that outlines procedures for handling cyber incidents.
- Train staff on how to respond to incidents promptly and effectively.

Collaborate with Cybersecurity Experts

- Seek partnerships with cybersecurity professionals or organizations to stay informed about emerging threats and best practices.
- Consider hiring or consulting with cybersecurity experts for in-depth assessments and recommendations.

Data Encryption

- Encrypt sensitive data both in transit and at rest to protect it from unauthorized access.
- Utilize secure communication protocols for data transmission.

Regular Security Awareness Training

- Continuously educate staff and patrons about cybersecurity threats and best practices.
- Keep everyone informed about the evolving threat landscape.

Patch Management

- Establish a systematic process for applying security patches and updates to all systems and software.
- Prioritize critical updates and patches that address known vulnerabilities.

Third-Party Vendor Security

- Evaluate and monitor the cybersecurity practices of third-party vendors providing software or services to the library.
- Ensure that vendors meet cybersecurity standards and guidelines.

Regularly Test Security Measures

- Conduct penetration testing and vulnerability assessments to identify weaknesses in the library's cybersecurity defenses.
- Use the findings to make improvements and updates.

Stay Informed

- Stay up-to-date with cybersecurity trends, threats, and best practices through industry publications, conferences, and cybersecurity news sources.

Budget for Cybersecurity

- Allocate resources and budget specifically for cybersecurity initiatives and enhancements.

By following these step-by-step recommendations, libraries can significantly enhance their cybersecurity posture, reduce the risk of cyber incidents, and protect both their patrons and their valuable digital assets.

AWARENESS OF INDIAN LIBRARY PROFESSIONALS ABOUT CYBERSECURITY: A SHORT SURVEY

Methodology

To evaluate the awareness level of Library Professionals about cybersecurity, a short survey was conducted with the assistance of an online questionnaire created using Google Forms (available at: https://forms.gle/m6LmLut1qQ3PAKS28). The survey was distributed among the target groups in both online and printed formats, as required. The questionnaire encompassed three sections, addressing respondents' levels of expertise, awareness of cyber threats, and the factors influencing cybersecurity awareness.

Identifying the Sample

The survey spanned approximately 10 months, from October 1, 2022, to August 15, 2023, and was distributed to over 400 targeted sample groups of Library Professionals. Of these, 277 individuals participated in the survey, resulting in a response rate of 69.25%. This survey included participants from various regions across India, and a thorough follow-up was conducted three times during the survey period to ensure maximum data completeness.

Response Analysis and Discussion

Respondents' Level of Expertise

The assessment of respondents' level of expertise is a critical aspect of understanding their readiness and capabilities in navigating the digital landscape. This evaluation allows for the gauge of their proficiency in using technology, handling software applications, and comprehending IT-related concepts. Assessing their expertise enables the tailoring of educational initiatives and support systems to bridge knowledge gaps and empower individuals to make informed decisions in the digital age.

Table 1. Competence level in respondents' level of expertise

SN	Expertise	Competence Level (N=277)			
		None (n%)	Basic (n%)	Working (n%)	Advance (n%)
1	Downloading and Installing Software	0 (0.00%)	12 (4.33%)	228 (82.31%)	37 (13.36%)
2	Hardware/Software Maintenance and Problem Determination	0 (0.00%)	28 (10.11%)	219 (79.06%)	30 (10.83%)
3	Taking Back-up, Handling Removable Storage	0 (0.00%)	17 (6.14%)	205 (74.01%)	55 (19.86%)
4	Navigating Between Computer Programs	5 (1.81%)	33 (11.91%)	211 (76.17%)	28 (10.11%)
5	Use Advanced Programming (Knowledge of Hardware/ Software Architecture to Design and Build Software)	148 (53.43%)	52 (18.77%)	64 (23.10%)	13 (4.69%)
6	Knowledge of Using Open Source Codes and Troubleshooting of Codes	26 (9.39%)	66 (23.83%)	160 (57.76%)	25 (9.03%)
7	Good in Networking (LAN Administration, Network Design, Network Security, and Network Management)	10 (3,61%)	28 (10.11%)	218 (78.70%)	29 (10.47%)
8	Good in Different Programming Languages (Visual Basic, Java, C#, C, C++, SQL, etc)	127 (45.85%)	73 (26.35%)	56 (20.22%)	21 (7.58%)

The survey questionnaire assesses eight competencies commonly required at the respondents' level within a library environment. Analysis of the responses reveals that the majority of respondents demonstrate a working-level competence in six out of the eight competencies, while for the remaining two, the majority of respondents indicate a complete lack of expertise.

Furthermore, in a more in-depth examination, it becomes evident that respondents exhibit the highest level of expertise in downloading and installing software, with 82.31% displaying a working-level proficiency and 13.36% demonstrating an advanced level of competence. On the other hand, respondents show the most advanced level of proficiency in taking backups and handling removable storage, with 19.86% exhibiting this level of expertise.

However, the responses also highlight a significant gap in expertise when it comes to advanced programming or different levels of programming languages, with respondents indicating very little to no expertise in these areas.

Awareness of Cyber Threats

Libraries face various cybersecurity threats in the digital era that can jeopardize the security of their digital resources. To ensure the safety of their digital services, libraries must be aware of potential threats. Some common cyber threats that libraries may encounter during digital service provision include:

- *Malware Attacks:* Malware attacks, encompassing viruses, Trojans, ransomware, and various delivery methods, pose a common threat to libraries.
- *Packet Sniffing:* Packet sniffing, an interception technique for network data, can be exploited by cybercriminals to steal sensitive information like passwords or credit card numbers.
- *Spear-Phishing:* Spear-phishing, a targeted email scam, aims to deceive library employees into disclosing sensitive data or activating malware-infected links, underscoring the importance of training and awareness programs for recognition and prevention.
- *External Hacking:* External hacking entails unauthorized attempts to access library systems from outside the organization, necessitating the implementation of robust access controls, firewalls, and security measures for protection.
- *Input Injection:* Input injection attacks, where malicious code is inserted to exploit vulnerabilities for unauthorized system access, necessitate libraries to implement security testing and code review processes for detection and remediation.
- *Weak Audit Trail:* A weak audit trail poses cybersecurity risks by hindering the detection and investigation of security incidents.
- *Denial of Service (DoS):* Denial of Service attacks involve overwhelming a system with traffic in order to make it unavailable to users.
- *Social Engineering:* Social engineering is a tactic used by cybercriminals to manipulate library employees into divulging sensitive information or performing actions that are harmful to the organization.
- *Insider Threats:* Insider threats are risks that come from within an organization, such as employees or contractors who have access to sensitive information.
- *Advanced Persistent Threats (APTs):* Advanced Persistent Threats (APTs) are long-term, targeted attacks that are designed to gain access to an organization's systems and remain undetected for an extended period.

Out of 277 only 77 respondents seems to have some sense of advance programming knowledge and selected for the next stage of the survey.

Table 2. Awareness of cyber threats among library professionals

SN	Cyber Threats	Awareness Level (N=77)			
		Unaware (n%)	**Aware (n%)**	**Witness (n%)**	**Practically Handle (n%)**
1	Malware Attacks	0 (0.00%)	23 (29.87%)	50 (64.94%)	14 (18.18%)
2	Packet Sniffing	2 (2.60%)	65 (84.42%)	10 (12.99%)	0 (0.00%)
3	Spear-Phishing	0 (0.00%)	33 (42.86%)	38 (49.35%)	6 (7.79%)
4	External Hacking	0 (0.00%)	56 (72.73%)	13 (16.88%)	8 (10.39%)
5	Input Injection	5 (6.49%)	51 (66.23%)	17 (22.08%)	4 (5.19%)
6	Weak Audit Trail	0 (0.00%)	13 (16.88%)	64 (83.12%)	0 (0.00%)
7	Denial of Service (DoS)	0 (0.00%)	30 (38.96%)	12 (15.58%)	35 (45.45%)
8	Social Engineering	0 (0.00%)	68 (88.31%)	9 (11.69%)	0 (0.00%)
9	Insider Threats	2 (2.60%)	9 (11.69)	10 (12.99%)	54 (70.13%)
10	Advanced Persistent Threats (APTs)	0 (0.00%)	18 (23.38%)	46 (59.74%)	13 (16.88%)

The survey questionnaire includes ten common cyber threats in library environments. Analysis of responses reveals that while the majority of respondents are aware of or have witnessed such threats in their libraries, very few have practical experience in handling them.

Furthermore, a closer examination reveals that among these threats, the majority of respondents are aware of packet sniffing (84.42%), have witnessed weak audit trails (83.12%), and have practical experience with insider threats (70.13%). However, a small percentage of respondents are unaware of any of these threats.

It is noteworthy that despite awareness and practical exposure to these cyber threats in library environments, respondents often do not handle them independently. This underscores the reliance of library personnel in India on technical staff, such as IT professionals, due to a lack of proficient technical skills.

Influenced Factors of Cybersecurity Awareness

Several factors can contribute to the level of awareness of library professionals about cybersecurity. Here are a few examples:

- *Demographics:* Cybersecurity awareness among library professionals can vary based on age, gender, and experience, with younger individuals typically more tech-savvy, while older professionals may require additional training to stay updated on evolving technologies and threats.
- *Education:* Library professionals' education and training levels can impact their cybersecurity awareness, with higher education often correlating with a better understanding of cybersecurity concepts, while those with less formal education may require additional training to enhance their skills.
- *Training:* The level and type of training significantly affect library professionals' cybersecurity awareness, with specialized cybersecurity training enhancing awareness, while ongoing professional development keeps them updated on evolving threats and best practices.
- *Organizational Culture:* The culture of an organization can also impact the level of cybersecurity awareness among library professionals. If an organization prioritizes cybersecurity and provides training and resources to support it, professionals are more likely to have a higher level of awareness.
- *Type of Library:* The library type where a professional works can affect their cybersecurity awareness; those in defense libraries often have higher awareness due to sensitive data, while those in public or academic libraries may have lower awareness due to less exposure to sensitive information.
- *Access to Information:* Library professionals who have access to cybersecurity information and resources, such as cybersecurity policies, guidelines, and training materials, are more likely to have a higher level of awareness.
- *Technical skills:* The level of technical skills and knowledge of library professionals can also impact their awareness of cybersecurity. Professionals with a strong technical background are likely to have a better understanding of cybersecurity concepts and practices.
- *Attitude towards Technology:* Library professionals' attitudes toward technology can influence their cybersecurity awareness, with tech-savvy individuals typically having higher awareness levels, while those less comfortable with technology may require additional training and support to enhance their skills.
- *Prior Experience:* Prior experience with cybersecurity incidents, such as a data breach, can also impact the level of awareness among library professionals.

Those who have experienced such incidents may be more aware of the risks and consequences of cybersecurity threats.

- *Communication and Collaboration:* Effective communication and collaboration among library professionals can positively impact cybersecurity awareness, as those who engage in regular interaction with peers are more inclined to exchange information and best practices related to cybersecurity, ultimately enhancing their awareness of the issue.

Table 3. Factors influenced the cybersecurity awareness of library professionals

SN	Factors	Response (N=277)				
		Strongly Agree (n%)	Agree (n%)	Neutral (n%)	Disagree (n%)	Strongly Disagree (n%)
1	Demographics	56 (20.22%)	125 (45.13%)	89 (32.13%)	5 (1.81%)	2 (0.72%)
2	Education	173 (62.45%)	86 (31.05%)	16 (5.78%)	2 (0.72%)	0 (0.00%)
3	Training	260 (93.86%)	13 (4.69%)	0 (0.00%)	4 (1.44%)	0 (0.00%)
4	Organizational Culture	59 (21.30%)	168 (60.65%)	21 (7.58%)	22 (7.94%)	7 (2.53%)
5	Types of Library	203 (73.29%)	50 (18.05%)	14 (5.05%)	8 (2.89%)	2 (0.72%)
6	Access to Information	30 (10.83%)	107 (38.63%)	124 (44.77%)	13 (4.69%)	3 (1.08%)
7	Technical Skills	244 (88.09%)	31 (11.19%)	2 (0.72%)	0 (0.00%)	0 (0.00%)
8	Attitude Towards Technology	186 (67.15%)	60 (21.66%)	29 (10.47%)	2 (0.72%)	0 (0.00%)
9	Prior Experience	134 (48.38%)	57 (20.58%)	75 (27.08%)	8 (2.89%)	3 (1.08%)
10	Communication and Collaboration	20 (7.22%)	47 (16.97%)	92 (33.21%)	106 (38.27%)	12 (4.33%)

The survey questionnaire encompasses ten factors that influence the cybersecurity awareness of library professionals in various effective ways. Analysis of responses reveals that the majority of respondents strongly agree that factors such as education (62.45%), training (93.86%), library types (73.29%), technical skills (88.09%), attitude towards technology (67.15%), and prior experience (48.38%) significantly impact the cybersecurity awareness of library professionals. Respondents also agree that demographics (45.13%) and organizational culture (60.65%) greatly influence cybersecurity awareness. However, regarding the factor of access to information, the majority of respondents choose to remain neutral (44.77%), while for the factor of communication and collaboration, most respondents disagree (38.27%).

SUMMARY OF THE CHAPTER

Theoretical Part

The theoretical section of this chapter begins by delving into the concept of cybersecurity awareness. It defines the term and highlights its crucial significance in the digital age. The multifaceted nature of cybersecurity, encompassing data security, privacy, and threat mitigation, is discussed, along with real-world consequences that underscore the importance of adequate awareness.

Additionally, the chapter introduces the topic of cybersecurity in libraries. It outlines the various cyber threats libraries face, emphasizing the importance of awareness among librarians. Furthermore, it provides insights into the measures required to make libraries cybersecure, ensuring the protection of valuable digital resources.

Survey Section

The survey methodology for assessing cybersecurity awareness among Library Professionals utilized Google Forms and encompassed three sections: evaluating expertise, measuring awareness of cyber threats, and identifying influencing factors. Over 10 months, the survey reached sufficient targeted groups, resulting in a commendable 69.25% response rate. Geographical diversity was ensured through comprehensive follow-ups.

The response analysis focuses on three areas:

- *Respondents' Expertise:* Most respondents display working-level competence in six out of eight competencies, excelling in downloading and installing software. However, expertise in advanced programming is limited.
- *Cyber Threat Awareness:* A significant proportion of respondents are aware of cybersecurity threats in libraries, such as packet sniffing, weak audit trails, and insider threats. Yet, practical experience in handling them is limited, leading to reliance on IT professionals.
- *Influencing Factors on Cybersecurity Awareness:* Factors like education, training, library types, technical skills, attitude towards technology, and prior

experience significantly influence cybersecurity awareness. Demographics and organizational culture also play roles. However, access to information receives a neutral response, and communication and collaboration are met with disagreement by most respondents.

FUTURE DIRECTIONS FOR RESEARCH

As the digital landscape continues to evolve and cybersecurity threats become more sophisticated, there are several promising directions for future research in the realm of cybersecurity within library environments:

Cybersecurity Education and Training

Investigate innovative approaches to cybersecurity education and training tailored specifically for library professionals. This research should explore effective pedagogical methods, the development of specialized curricula, and the integration of cybersecurity awareness into library science programs.

Behavioral Aspects of Cybersecurity

Delve deeper into the behavioral aspects of cybersecurity awareness and practices among library professionals. Research could focus on understanding the psychology behind decision-making related to cybersecurity, including risk perception and the influence of organizational culture.

Cyber Threat Intelligence

Explore the utilization of cyber threat intelligence within library settings. Investigate the feasibility of libraries establishing their threat intelligence sharing mechanisms and examine how libraries can collaborate to enhance collective cybersecurity efforts.

Privacy and Data Protection

Given libraries' role as custodians of vast amounts of sensitive user data, research should emphasize privacy protection and data security. Investigate advanced encryption techniques, data anonymization methods, and privacy-preserving technologies that can safeguard user information.

Emerging Technologies

Examine the implications of emerging technologies such as artificial intelligence, blockchain, and Internet of Things (IoT) on library cybersecurity. Assess potential threats and vulnerabilities associated with these technologies and develop proactive security strategies.

Cross-Sector Collaboration

Foster research collaborations between libraries, academia, government agencies, and industry partners to create a holistic approach to cybersecurity. Investigate best practices for sharing threat intelligence and experiences across sectors.

Policy and Compliance

Explore the development of cybersecurity policies and compliance frameworks tailored to the library environment. Analyze the impact of regulatory changes and compliance requirements on libraries and their ability to protect user data.

Incident Response and Recovery

Investigate effective incident response and recovery strategies for libraries. Develop comprehensive incident response plans, including protocols for data breach notification, and assess the readiness of library professionals to handle cybersecurity incidents.

Awareness Campaigns

Evaluate the effectiveness of cybersecurity awareness campaigns within library settings. Measure the impact of training programs, workshops, and awareness initiatives on the behavior and practices of library professionals.

International Collaboration

Promote international collaboration in library cybersecurity research to facilitate the exchange of knowledge and best practices across borders. Investigate how libraries in different regions can benefit from shared experiences and global threat intelligence.

By pursuing research in these directions, the field of cybersecurity in library environments can advance, ensuring that libraries remain resilient against evolving threats and continue to provide secure digital services to their users. These future research endeavors will play a crucial role in safeguarding the invaluable information and resources entrusted to libraries in the digital age.

CONCLUSION

In the age of digital information dissemination and related cyber threats, library professionals have assumed a multifaceted role that extends beyond traditional library functions. Their responsibilities encompass managing digital resources, safeguarding data, and educating users about cybersecurity. Librarians also contribute to policy development, incident response, and advocacy for privacy and digital literacy. This evolving role reflects the critical importance of cybersecurity in preserving and providing secure access to digital information in modern libraries.

This chapter explores the crucial realm of cybersecurity awareness in library environments, emphasizing its multifaceted nature, including data protection, privacy, and threat mitigation. The real-world implications of inadequate awareness underscore the urgency of this issue. We delve into the cyber threats libraries confront and underscore the pivotal role of cybersecurity awareness among librarians. We present strategies to enhance library cybersecurity, recognizing its significance in safeguarding valuable digital resources. The survey methodology, sample identification, and analysis provide insights into the cybersecurity awareness of Indian library professionals, examining their expertise, threat awareness, and influencing factors, revealing essential areas for improvement.

As we navigate the digital age, the importance of cybersecurity awareness in libraries cannot be overstated. Equipping library professionals with the knowledge and skills to protect against evolving threats is imperative. This chapter serves as a foundational step toward establishing a more secure and resilient library ecosystem, highlighting the ongoing need for research and action in the field of cybersecurity awareness.

REFERENCES

Adakawa, M. I., Al-hassan, Z. M., & Auyo, M. A. (2020). Now and Future of Libraries: the Necessity to Equip Librarians with Cybersecurity Skills. In *Management of Library and Information Centers in the Era of Global Insecurity*. https://www.researchgate.net/publication/346967054

Ajie, I. (2019). A Review of Trends and Issues of Cybersecurity in Academic Libraries. *Library Philosophy and Practice (E-Journal)*, 1–20. https://digitalcommons.unl.edu/libphilprac/2523

Alhaif, A. M. (2023). Training Needs of Information Specialists at Saudi Universities Libraries to Achieve Cybersecurity Requirements. *International Journal of Education and Information Technologies*, *17*, 38–50. doi:10.46300/9109.2023.17.5

Alzubaidi, A. (2021). Measuring the level of cyber-security awareness for cybercrime in Saudi Arabia. *Heliyon*, *7*(1), e06016. doi:10.1016/j.heliyon.2021.e06016 PMID:33537477

Anday, A., Francese, E., Huurdeman, H. C., Yılmaz, M., & Zengenene, D. (2012). Information Security Issues in a Digital Library Environment: A Literature Review. *Bilgi Dünyası*, *13*(1), 117–137. doi:10.15612/BD.2012.171

Aregbesola, A., & Nwaolise, E. (2023). Securing Digital Collections: Cyber Security Best Practices for Academic Libraries in Developing Countries. *Library Philosophy and Practice (E-Journal)*, 1–13. https://digitalcommons.unl.edu/libphilprac/7822

Beaman, C., Barkworth, A., Akande, T. D., Hakak, S., & Khan, M. K. (2021). Ransomware: Recent advances, analysis, challenges and future research directions. *Computers & Security*, *111*(1), 102490. doi:10.1016/j.cose.2021.102490 PMID:34602684

Brown, C. (2020, October 27). *How can library and information services protect people against cyber attacks?* https://www.vable.com/blog/cyber-security-what-your-library-needs-to-know

Committee on National Security Systems (CNSS). (2010). *National Information Assurance Glossary. CNSS Instruction No. 4009*. CNSS. http://www.ncix.gov/publications/policy/docs/CNSSI_4009.pdf

Craigen, D., Thibault, N. D., & Purse, R. (2014). Defining Cybersecurity [Review of *Defining Cybersecurity*]. *Technology Innovation Management Review*, 13–21. https://www.researchgate.net/publication/267631801

CybSafe. (2019, April 23). *7 reasons why security awareness training is important*. CybSafe. https://www.cybsafe.com/blog/7-reasons-why-security-awareness-training-is-important/

Dark, M., Kaza, S., & Taylor, B. (2018). CLARK – The Cybersecurity Labs and Resource Knowledge-base – A Living Digital Library. *2018 USENIX Workshop on Advances in Security Education, ASE 2018, Co-Located with USENIX Security 2018*. Unsenix. https://www.usenix.org/conference/ase18/presentation/dark

Farid, G., Warraich, N. F., & Iftikhar, S. (2023). Digital information security management policy in academic libraries: A systematic review (2010–2022). *Journal of Information Science*. doi:10.1177/01655515231160026

Froehlich, A. (2022, July). *What is a data breach?* SearchSecurity. https://www.techtarget.com/searchsecurity/definition/data-breach

Gillis, A. (2020, May). *What is Phishing? How it Works and How to Prevent it.* SearchSecurity. https://www.techtarget.com/searchsecurity/definition/phishing

Gondek, C. (n.d.). *The Cybersecurity Risks of Using Outdated Software.* https://originstamp.com/blog/the-cybersecurity-risks-of-using-outdated-software/

Gu, Q., & Liu, P. (2012). Denial of Service Attacks. In Handbook of Computer Networks (pp. 454–468). Springer. doi:10.1002/9781118256107.ch29

Hanna, K. T. (2021, September). *What is a brute-force attack? - Definition from TechTarget*. SearchSecurity. https://www.techtarget.com/searchsecurity/definition/brute-force-cracking

IFLA. (2022). *IFLA Statement on Cybersecurity* (pp. 1–5). IFLA. https://repository.ifla.org/bitstream/123456789/1912/1/IFLA%20Statement%20on%20Cybersecurity.pdf

Igbinovia, M. O., & Ishola, B. C. (2023). Cyber security in university libraries and implication for library and information science education in Nigeria. *Digital Library Perspectives*, *39*(3), 248–266. doi:10.1108/DLP-11-2022-0089

Imperva. (2019). *What is Social Engineering | Attack Techniques & Prevention Methods*. Learning Center. https://www.imperva.com/learn/application-security/social-engineering-attack/

International Telecommunication Union (ITU). (2009). *X.1205: Overview of cybersecurity*. ITU. https://www.itu.int/rec/T-REC-X.1205-200804-I/en

Khan, A., Ibrahim, M., & Hussain, A. (2021). An exploratory prioritization of factors affecting current state of information security in Pakistani university libraries. *International Journal of Information Management Data Insights*, *1*(2), 100015. doi:10.1016/j.jjimei.2021.100015

Khurana, S. (2017). A Review Paper on Cyber Security. [IJERT]. *International Journal of Engineering Research & Technology (Ahmedabad)*, *5*(23). doi:10.17577/IJERTCONV5IS23011

Kim, B. (2016a). Cybersecurity and digital surveillance versus usability and privacy1: Why libraries need to advocate for online privacy. *College & Research Libraries News*, *77*(9), 442–451. doi:10.5860/crln.77.9.9553

Kim, B. (2016b, August 24). *Keeping Up With... Cybersecurity, Usability, and Privacy*. Association of College & Research Libraries (ACRL). https://www.ala.org/acrl/publications/keeping_up_with/cybersecurity

Kont, K.-R. (2023). Libraries and cyber security: the importance of the human factor in preventing cyber attacks. *Library Hi Tech News*. doi:10.1108/LHTN-03-2023-0036

Lisedunetwork. (2019, September 26). *Library and Information Services*. Library & Information Science Network. https://www.lisedunetwork.com/library-and-information-services/

Mamun, A. A., Ibrahim, J. B., & Mostofa, S. M. (2021). Cyber Security Awareness in Bangladesh: An Overview of Challenges and Strategies. *International Journal of Computer Science and Information Technology Research*, *9*(1), 88–94. https://www.researchpublish.com/upload/book/paperpdf-1611555745.pdf

Mimecast. (n.d.). *What is Cyber Awareness Training?* Mimecast. https://www.mimecast.com/content/cyber-security-awareness-training/#:~:text=Cyber%20awareness%20refers%20to%20the

Ngwum, N. I., Raina, S., Aguon, S., Taylor, B., & Kaza, S. (2020). A Model for Security Evaluation of Digital Libraries: A Case Study on a Cybersecurity Curriculum Library. *Journal of the Colloquium for Information Systems Security Education*, *7*(1), 1–12. https://www.researchgate.net/publication/344357576

Oxford University Press. (2014). Cybersecurity | Meaning of Cybersecurity by Lexico. In *Oxford Online Dictionary*. Oxford Press. http://www.oxforddictionaries.com/definition/english/Cybersecurity

Rashid, M. H. A. (2023, September 10). *Role of Libraries in Promoting Information Literacy and Critical Thinking Skills in the Digital Age*. Library & Information Management. https://limbd.org/role-of-libraries-in-promoting-information-literacy-and-critical-thinking-skills-in-the-digital-age/

Sinha, K. (2023). The Metaverse and Digital Libraries. In B. Holland (Ed.), Handbook of Research on Advancements of Contactless Technology and Service Innovation in Library and Information Science (pp. 1–22). IGI Global. doi:10.4018/978-1-6684-7693-2.ch001

Spanning Cloud Apps. (2022, June 30). *Cybersecurity Awareness: Definition, Importance & More*. Spanning. https://spanning.com/blog/cybersecurity-awareness/

Suqri, M. N. A., & Fatuyi, E. A. (2012). Information Security and Privacy in Digital Libraries: Challenges, Opportunities and Prospects. *International Journal of Digital Library Systems, 3*(4), 54–61. https://www.researchgate.net/publication/260174707

Taylor, B., Kaza, S., & Dark, M. (2022). Designing a Cybersecurity Curriculum Library: Best Practices from Digital Library Research. In K.-K. R. Choo, T. Morris, G. Peterson, & E. Imsand (Eds.), *National Cyber Summit (NCS) Research Track 2021. NCS 2021. Lecture Notes in Networks and Systems* (pp. 47–59). Springer. doi:10.1007/978-3-030-84614-5_5

Web Master. (2022, June 9). *What Is an Insider Threat? Malicious vs. Negligent Threats*. Vera. https://www.vera.com/intellectual-property-protection/insider-threat/

Yusuf, R. A., & Awoyemi, O. O. (2022). Cyber Security and Its Implication on Library Users' Privacy. *Owena Journal of Library and Information Science*, *9*(1), 1–13.

KEY TERMS AND DEFINITIONS

Cyber Threats: In library, cyber threats refer to various malicious actions and risks, such as cyberattacks, data breaches, malware, phishing, and ransomware, targeting digital assets, patron information, and library services. Countermeasures are essential to safeguard digital resources and ensure uninterrupted access to information.

Cybersecurity Awareness: Cybersecurity awareness in the library context refers to the understanding, knowledge, and vigilance of library professionals and users regarding the potential cyber threats and risks that digital information and systems face. It involves recognizing the importance of cybersecurity, staying informed about evolving threats, and adopting best practices to protect digital resources, user privacy, and data integrity within the library environment.

Cybersecurity: Cybersecurity in the library involves a comprehensive approach to safeguarding digital assets and sensitive information. It encompasses strategies, policies, and technologies aimed at preventing, detecting, and mitigating cyber threats, ensuring the integrity, confidentiality, and availability of digital resources while promoting user privacy and trust in the library's digital ecosystem.

Information Security: Information security in the library context involves policies, practices, and technologies aimed at protecting digital information, ensuring confidentiality, integrity, and availability. It safeguards against unauthorized access, data breaches, and cyber threats, maintaining trust in digital environments.

Threat Mitigation: Threat mitigation in the library involves the strategic and proactive efforts to identify, assess, and reduce potential risks and hazards that could compromise the security and integrity of digital information, systems, and resources within a library environment. It encompasses a range of preventive measures, policies, and actions aimed at minimizing the impact of cyber threats, ensuring the continuity of library services, and safeguarding patrons' privacy and data.

Chapter 5 Challenges and Barriers to Integrating AI in Library Environments

Sanchita Ghosh
Brainware University, India

Amitava Podder
Brainware University, India

Piyal Roy
Brainware University, India

Bitan Roy
Brainware University, India

Saptarshi Kumar Sarkar
Brainware University, India

ABSTRACT

Modern libraries involving AI present improved productivity, user experiences, and resource management. Responsible AI approaches are crucial because of ethical factors including algorithmic biases and patron data privacy. Organizational barriers provide serious difficulties that necessitate strategic ways for successful implementation. The integration scenario includes budget limits and expenditures related to AI technologies. Adoption of AI is made more complicated by regulatory factors, such as adherence to data protection laws and potential legal ramifications. Through the synthesis of extant research, this article offers a thorough comprehension of these intricate challenges. Technical, ethical, organizational, financial, and regulatory aspects provides insightful information for researchers, politicians, and librarians. In order to promote responsible AI integration in libraries and optimize the advantages of emerging technologies, the evaluation seeks to provide guidance for future strategies, policies, and decision-making procedures.

DOI: 10.4018/979-8-3693-1573-6.ch005

INTRODUCTION

In the contemporary landscape of libraries, the integration of AI stands as a transformative force, reshaping traditional functions and services. This introduction sets the stage for exploring the increasing pervasiveness of AI in modern libraries and its profound implications for the field. In recent years, the adoption of AI technologies in libraries has gained momentum, marking a departure from conventional practices. Libraries, once primarily engaged in manual cataloguing and information retrieval, are now at the forefront of embracing AI to usher in a new era of efficiency, enhanced user experiences, and optimized resource management (Cox et al. 2019). This shift reflects a fundamental change in the role of libraries, positioning them as dynamic hubs at the intersection of information, technology, and user engagement.

The integration of AI in libraries offers multifaceted advantages, with automation, data analysis, and improved decision-making processes standing out as key benefits (Okunlaya et al. 2022). Automation streamlines routine tasks, freeing up valuable time for librarians to focus on user interactions and specialized services. Data analysis empowers libraries to derive actionable insights from vast datasets, informing collection development and resource optimization. Improved decision-making processes, driven by AI algorithms, contribute to more effective and user-centric library services.

As libraries evolve into information hubs in the digital age, the profound impact of AI becomes increasingly evident. The intersection of AI and library services is not merely a technological advancement; it represents a paradigm shift that demands attention from librarians, researchers, and policymakers. Understanding the implications and potential of AI in libraries is not only a necessity but also a strategic imperative for those navigating the evolving landscape of information management.

Brief Overview of the Increasing Role of AI in Modern Libraries

In the contemporary landscape of modern libraries, the role of AI has undergone a significant expansion, transcended routine tasks and permeated various facets of library operations. AI technologies, notably natural language processing (NLP), machine learning, and data analytics, play a pivotal role in reshaping the traditional functions of libraries (Rodríguez et al. 2021). These technologies are instrumental in automating mundane tasks that were historically time-consuming for librarians, such as cataloguing and circulation processes. Automation liberates valuable time and resources, enabling librarians to shift their focus from repetitive tasks to more strategic endeavours, such as user engagement and the provision of specialized services.

Moreover, the integration of AI in modern libraries extends beyond mere automation. AI-driven recommendation systems represent a key application, contributing to the personalization of user experiences within the library ecosystem. By leveraging machine learning algorithms, these systems analyse user behaviours, preferences, and historical data to generate tailored recommendations. This functionality is particularly valuable in the context of vast digital collections, where users can benefit from more efficient and targeted discovery of relevant resources (Rodríguez et al. 2021). The increasing role of AI in modern libraries is not merely a technological upgrade but a transformative shift that optimizes library workflows and enhances the quality of services offered to users. Librarians, empowered by AI technologies, find themselves better equipped to navigate the evolving information landscape and meet the diverse needs of library patrons.

Importance of Understanding Challenges and Barriers for Successful Integration

The integration of AI into modern libraries is a transformative endeavour that holds immense potential. However, acknowledging and comprehending the challenges and barriers associated with this paradigm shift is crucial for ensuring the successful implementation of AI technologies. Technical challenges, such as issues related to system compatibility and data quality, are formidable hurdles that demand attention. Ensuring seamless integration requires addressing compatibility issues with existing library systems, which may vary in their technological infrastructure. Moreover, the quality and standardization of data become paramount to the accurate functioning of AI algorithms. Incomplete or inconsistent data can compromise the effectiveness of AI applications, emphasizing the need for meticulous data management practices.

Ethical considerations add another layer of complexity to AI integration. The protection of patron data is a critical ethical concern, requiring libraries to adhere to data protection regulations and implement robust privacy measures (Slatter et al. 2013). Furthermore, algorithmic biases pose ethical challenges, as AI systems may inadvertently perpetuate biases present in training data. Recognizing and mitigating these biases is essential to ensure fair and equitable AI outcomes in library services. Understanding these challenges goes beyond mere acknowledgment—it is a prerequisite for librarians, researchers, and policymakers to navigate the complexities of AI integration successfully. By recognizing the technical challenges, stakeholders can devise strategies to address system compatibility issues and enhance data quality. Ethical considerations, on the other hand, call for a thoughtful and responsible approach to AI implementation, ensuring that patron data is safeguarded, and AI algorithms are free from biases. In essence, a comprehensive understanding of challenges and barriers positions libraries to make informed decisions, adopt effective strategies, and implement responsible practices, ultimately maximizing the benefits of AI integration while safeguarding ethical principles and technical robustness.

Purpose and Scope of the Review Paper

The purpose of this review paper is to conduct a systematic examination and analysis of the challenges and barriers that impede the effective integration of AI in modern library environments. Through the synthesis of existing literature, the review aims to offer a comprehensive understanding of the multifaceted issues faced by libraries when adopting AI technologies. The scope of this review paper is broad and encompasses various dimensions of challenges and barriers associated with AI integration in libraries. The review addresses technical challenges such as system compatibility, data quality, and scalability. It delves into ethical considerations, including patron data protection and algorithmic biases (Mehra, 2018; Dawson, 2021). Furthermore, the review explores organizational barriers, such as resistance to change and the lack of AI expertise among library staff.

The financial landscape is also considered, with a focus on costs associated with AI implementation and budget constraints (Slatter et al. 2013). Additionally, the regulatory landscape is addressed, emphasizing compliance with data protection regulations and legal implications of AI use in libraries (Mehra, 2018; Dawson, 2021). Through an in-depth exploration of these dimensions, the paper seeks to contribute valuable insights to inform future strategies, policies, and decision-making processes related to AI integration in libraries. By systematically analysing the challenges and barriers, the review paper aims to provide a knowledge base that can guide libraries in navigating the complexities of AI adoption, fostering responsible practices, and maximizing the benefits of AI technologies.

LITERATURE REVIEW

In delving into the literature review section of the extensive paper addressing the "Challenges and Barriers to Integrating AI in Library Environments," a meticulous examination of existing research and scholarly works unveils a rich tapestry of insights. This segment serves as a crucial foundation for comprehending the historical evolution, pivotal applications, success narratives, and formidable challenges intertwined with the integration of AI in the intricate realm of libraries. Commencing with a historical perspective (2.1), the review illuminates the transformative journey of library technologies, elucidating the incremental steps from early automation through integrated library systems (ILS) to the integration of sophisticated AI technologies. The pioneering role of ILS is underscored with citations from (Bawden et al. 2018), delineating the foundational automation of routine tasks such as cataloguing, circulation, and acquisitions. This historical narrative sets the stage for the subsequent sections, portraying a vivid landscape of AI's evolution within the library domain.

Transitioning seamlessly to the exploration of key AI applications (2.2), the literature review meticulously dissects the diversified operational aspects enhanced by AI technologies in library environments. It unveils the prominence of AI-driven recommendation systems in optimizing user experiences, citing Luo & Jiang (2021), thereby underscoring the role of data-driven personalization in resource discoverability and user engagement. Navigating through natural language processing (NLP) and machine learning applications, elucidated by (Xie et al. 2016) and (Kastrin et al. 2023) respectively, the review paints a comprehensive picture of how AI algorithms contribute to interactive user assistance, automation of collection development, and improved knowledge organization systems. The integration of AI in metadata enrichment, as highlighted by Lee & Kim (2019), emerges as a critical application facilitating enhanced resource discovery through algorithm-assisted metadata extraction. The subsequent section on success stories and best practices in AI integration (2.3) accentuates real-world examples, providing tangible evidence of libraries that have successfully harnessed AI technologies. The exemplary case study of the Library of Congress serves as a beacon, showcasing the effective implementation of machine learning algorithms to classify and organize digital images, as outlined in the literature (Library of Congress, 2022). This real-world illustration not only reinforces theoretical concepts but also extracts practical strategies employed to surmount challenges in AI integration, contributing valuable insights for libraries contemplating similar endeavours. Best practices, underscored by (Archer et al. 2021) and Buckland (2020), add a layer of pragmatic guidance, emphasizing comprehensive staff training, continuous monitoring, and collaborative efforts between librarians, technologists, and stakeholders.

As the literature review transcends these sections, a coherent narrative emerges, weaving together the historical trajectory, multifaceted applications, and tangible successes of AI integration in library environments. The citations act as guiding stars, grounding the exploration in the authoritative voices of scholars and practitioners. This collective scholarly tapestry not only illuminates the evolving landscape of AI in libraries but also lays the groundwork for navigating the intricate challenges discussed in subsequent sections. The literature review, thus, stands as a testament to the wealth of knowledge available and paves the way for a deeper understanding of the complexities and potentials entwined with the integration of AI in contemporary library settings.

Historical Perspective on the Evolution of AI in Libraries

The historical evolution of AI in libraries unfolds as a transformative journey, offering valuable insights into the changing landscape of library technologies. In the early stages, libraries embarked on automation endeavours primarily through the implementation of integrated library systems (ILS). These systems, emerging in the latter half of the 20th century, laid the groundwork for the computerization of fundamental library functions such as cataloguing, circulation, and acquisitions (Bawden et al. 2018). The integration of ILS represented a crucial first step toward leveraging technology to streamline routine tasks and improve operational efficiency. This phase marked a departure from the traditional automation of tasks towards more sophisticated methods for information retrieval and user interaction (Souchet et al. 2023). Expert systems, characterized by rule-based decision-making, allowed libraries to explore advanced approaches to managing and disseminating information.

AI evolution in libraries has led to the adoption of advanced technologies like natural language processing, machine learning, and semantics. These innovations have improved search functionality, personalized recommendations, and knowledge organization. Machine learning algorithms enable libraries to understand user preferences and deliver tailored content. The historical context of AI in libraries is crucial for understanding the incremental steps towards enhancing efficiency and providing user-friendly services. This historical perspective helps envision future trajectories and potential innovations in the dynamic intersection of AI and library environments.

Key AI Applications in Library Environments

AI applications in libraries have revolutionized functionality and user-centric services. These include recommendation systems, natural language processing, and machine learning. These systems use machine learning algorithms to analyse user behaviour and preferences, providing personalized recommendations for library resources. This optimizes the discovery process, enhancing user satisfaction and engagement. This shift towards user-centric library services allows users to efficiently navigate vast digital collections and discover relevant content.

Natural Language Processing (NLP)

NLP plays a pivotal role in AI applications within library environments. Libraries have deployed chatbots equipped with NLP capabilities to provide interactive user assistance and support. These chatbots enhance user engagement by offering real-time, conversational interactions, assisting users with queries, and facilitating a seamless information-seeking process (Xie et al. 2016). The integration of NLP contributes to a more accessible and user-friendly library environment, breaking down language barriers and simplifying the user experience.

Machine Learning for Collection Development

Machine learning algorithms have become instrumental in automating collection development processes. Libraries leverage these algorithms to analyse user demand patterns and emerging trends, optimizing collection curation. By understanding user preferences and predicting future demands, libraries can strategically acquire, organize, and manage their collections to meet the evolving needs of their user base (Mattern, 2020). This application not only enhances operational efficiency but also ensures that libraries stay attuned to the dynamic information landscape.

Metadata Enrichment

AI integration in libraries improves resource discovery by extracting and enhancing metadata. These algorithms analyze and augment metadata associated with library resources, enhancing information accuracy and richness. This enhances resource organization and retrieval, improving library collections' accessibility. As libraries adopt AI applications, it's crucial to assess their impact on user experiences, information access, and operations. This understanding helps librarians make informed decisions, tailor services, and innovate in response to technological advancements.

Success Stories and Best Practices in AI Integration

The Library of Congress in the US successfully implemented machine learning algorithms to classify and organize a vast collection of digital images, enhancing accessibility and discoverability of digital assets. This case demonstrates how AI can be leveraged to enhance resource organization and user access. Best practices in AI integration include comprehensive staff training, ongoing training programs, and continuous monitoring and evaluation of AI systems to address potential biases or limitations during operation. These practices demonstrate the potential of AI in enhancing library settings and resource organization.

This proactive approach ensures responsible and ethical use of AI in library services. Collaborative efforts between librarians, technologists, and stakeholders are also recognized as a critical component of successful AI integration (Xie et al. 2016). Such collaborations foster a multidisciplinary approach, combining the expertise of library professionals with technological know-how, ensuring that AI implementations align with the specific needs and goals of the library.The success stories and best practices of AI initiatives in libraries serve as benchmarks for other libraries, enabling them to tailor best practices to their specific contexts and objectives, providing a foundation for navigating the challenges and opportunities of AI integration.

TYPES OF CHALLENGES

The integration of AI into library systems presents challenges like compatibility, data quality, scalability, and performance. Libraries must plan for these by considering growth, investing in hardware upgrades, and implementing ethical measures like data protection and transparency. They must also address staff resistance due to job security concerns or fear of technology replacing human roles. To overcome these, libraries should prioritize effective communication, tailor training programs, cultivate an adaptive organizational culture, invest in staff development programs, and adopt a forward-thinking approach, viewing AI as an enabler rather than a threat.

Technical Challenges

The integration of AI into library systems presents challenges such as compatibility, data quality, scalability, and performance. Compatibility involves aligning AI solutions with diverse library systems, while data quality and standardization are crucial for effective AI utilization. Metadata standards enhance consistency and interoperability. Scalability and performance concerns arise when AI algorithms' computational demands exceed available resources. Libraries must strategically plan for these challenges, considering the growth of services and collections, and investing in hardware upgrades, cloud-based solutions, and parallel processing technologies. By addressing these challenges, AI can enhance efficiency and responsiveness in library services.

Compatibility Issues With Existing Library Systems

The integration of AI into library environments is a complex task due to compatibility issues with existing systems. Libraries rely on ILS, databases, and digital repositories for various operations. The integration process must be precise to avoid disruptions and maintain the integrity of existing structures, especially in complex ecosystems where AI applications may compromise their effectiveness. (García et al. 2021) emphasize the need for careful consideration during the integration process to mitigate compatibility challenges. Successful integration requires a deep understanding of the intricacies of each existing system within a library. This involves addressing issues related to data formats, communication protocols, and system architectures to create a seamless interface between AI applications and the library's technological infrastructure.

The compatibility challenge underscores the importance of developing standardized approaches and protocols for AI integration in libraries. Establishing interoperability standards ensures that AI solutions can seamlessly interface with diverse library systems, promoting a cohesive technological environment. This challenge is not only technical but also strategic, requiring a comprehensive understanding of the library's technological landscape and a thoughtful approach to integration. As libraries navigate this technical challenge, it becomes imperative to leverage collaborative efforts between librarians, IT professionals, and AI specialists. The multidisciplinary collaboration ensures a holistic approach to addressing compatibility issues, aligning technological strategies with the overarching goals of the library. In conclusion, compatibility issues with existing library systems pose a formidable technical challenge in the integration of AI into library environments. The resolution of this challenge demands a nuanced understanding of diverse library systems, meticulous planning, and collaborative efforts to ensure that the introduction of AI enhances rather than disrupts the established workflows and functionalities.

Data Quality and Standardization

Implementing AI in libraries is intricately linked to the challenges of data quality and standardization, presenting significant hurdles to successful integration. Libraries, as custodians of vast and diverse datasets, must grapple with the inherent complexities of ensuring the quality, consistency, and standardization of their accumulated data for effective AI utilization (Mattern, 2020).The wealth of data within libraries encompasses diverse formats, structures, and sources, ranging from catalogue entries and user interactions to digital archives. (Kastrin et al. 2023) underscores the critical role of data quality in the successful integration of AI, emphasizing that inconsistent or incomplete data can compromise the accuracy of AI algorithms. Poor data quality can lead to erroneous outputs, ultimately hindering the potential benefits that AI technologies can offer to library services and operations.

Addressing data quality challenges requires a multi-faceted approach. Librarians and information professionals must implement robust data governance strategies to ensure the reliability and accuracy of the data used by AI systems. This involves establishing data quality standards, validating data at the point of entry, and implementing regular data cleansing processes to rectify inconsistencies (Xie et al. 2016). Standardizing data formats and structures is equally crucial. Libraries often manage data from diverse sources, and the lack of standardized formats can impede the interoperability of AI applications with existing library systems. Developing and adhering to data standards ensures that AI algorithms can effectively process and analyze information, contributing to more accurate and reliable outcomes (Rodríguez et al. 2021).

Furthermore, the incorporation of metadata standards plays a pivotal role in data standardization efforts. Metadata provides essential contextual information about library resources, and adhering to established metadata standards enhances the consistency and interoperability of data used by AI applications (Lee & Kim, 2019). In conclusion, data quality and standardization are formidable challenges that must be addressed for the successful integration of AI in libraries. By prioritizing data governance, establishing standards, and leveraging metadata conventions, libraries can enhance the reliability of their datasets, ensuring that AI technologies operate on high-quality, standardized information, thereby maximizing their impact on library services.

Scalability and Performance Concerns

Integrating AI into library environments brings forth inherent challenges, particularly concerning scalability and performance. The dynamic nature of libraries, with the potential for scaling up services and expanding digital collections, demands that AI systems exhibit the capability to handle increased workloads efficiently (Zeng et al. 2023). The scalability challenge centres on the ability of AI applications to adapt and perform optimally as libraries grow and evolve. Luo and Jiang (2021) highlight that scalability concerns arise when the computational demands of AI outstrip the available resources. This is particularly crucial as libraries strive to enhance their services, accommodate growing user bases, and manage expanding digital repositories.

Performance concerns further underscore the need for careful consideration in AI implementation. Libraries rely on responsive and efficient systems to meet user expectations. The computational demands of AI algorithms, especially in resource-intensive tasks such as natural language processing and machine learning, can impact the overall responsiveness of library services (Mattern, 2020). Achieving a balance between the computational requirements of AI applications and the available resources is imperative for ensuring optimal performance.

To address scalability and performance concerns, libraries must engage in strategic planning and resource allocation. This involves assessing the computational capabilities of existing infrastructure, understanding the potential growth trajectory of library services, and proactively planning for the scalability requirements of AI systems. Additionally, investing in hardware upgrades, cloud-based solutions, and parallel processing technologies can contribute to enhancing the scalability and performance of AI applications in libraries (Archer et al. 2021). Moreover, the choice of AI algorithms and models plays a crucial role in addressing scalability and performance challenges. Libraries must select algorithms that align with the available computational resources and can efficiently handle varying workloads without compromising performance (Rodríguez et al. 2021). In conclusion, scalability and performance concerns are integral challenges in the integration of AI into library environments. Libraries must adopt a forward-thinking approach, considering the potential growth of services and collections, while strategically planning for the computational demands of AI systems. By addressing these challenges, libraries can ensure that AI technologies contribute to, rather than hinder, the efficiency and responsiveness of their services.

Ethical and Privacy Challenges

The integration of AI in library environments presents ethical challenges, especially in protecting patron data and ensuring fairness in AI algorithms. Libraries must establish robust mechanisms for data protection, adhere to ethical standards, and promote transparency in data processing practices. Addressing bias in AI algorithms requires curating and pre-processing data, monitoring AI systems regularly, and ensuring transparency in decision-making processes. Collaborative efforts between librarians, data scientists, and stakeholders are crucial for ethical AI implementation. Libraries must implement ethical guidelines, establish accountability mechanisms, and foster ongoing education to ensure AI-driven decisions align with ethical values.

Patron Data Protection and Privacy Concerns

The integration of AI in library environments introduces ethical challenges, particularly in the realm of patron data protection and privacy. Libraries, as custodians of sensitive information about their users, face the responsibility of safeguarding patron data during the implementation of AI systems (Mehra, 2018).

Libraries accumulate and manage a wealth of patron data, including borrowing history, user preferences, and potentially personally identifiable information. The utilization of AI in library operations, such as personalized recommendation systems or data analytics, may involve the processing and analysis of this sensitive data. Patron data protection becomes a critical consideration to prevent unauthorized access, misuse, or breaches that could compromise the privacy of library users.

(Mehra,2018) emphasizes the paramount importance of establishing robust mechanisms for patron data protection. Libraries must adhere to ethical standards and legal frameworks, such as data protection regulations and privacy laws, to ensure the responsible and secure handling of patron information. This includes implementing encryption protocols, access controls, and data anonymization techniques to mitigate the risks associated with the processing of personal data.

Privacy concerns in AI integration extend beyond legal compliance. Libraries must also consider the ethical implications of data usage and algorithmic decision-making. Transparency in how AI algorithms operate and make recommendations is crucial for building trust with patrons (Slatter et al. 2013). Libraries should communicate clearly about the purposes of data collection, the types of data processed, and the measures in place to protect patron privacy.

To navigate these challenges, librarians must stay informed about evolving privacy regulations, ethical guidelines, and best practices in AI ethics. Regular audits and assessments of AI systems can help identify and address potential vulnerabilities in patron data protection, reinforcing the commitment to ethical AI practices (Archer et al. 2021). In conclusion, patron data protection and privacy concerns are paramount ethical considerations in the integration of AI in libraries. By establishing robust safeguards, adhering to legal frameworks, and promoting transparency in data processing practices, libraries can uphold the trust of their patrons while harnessing the benefits of AI technologies.

Bias and Fairness in AI Algorithms

The deployment of AI in library environments presents a significant ethical challenge due to potential biases in the training data. These biases can manifest in various forms, such as racial, gender, or socioeconomic inequalities. Libraries must address these biases to uphold equity and fairness in library services. Mitigating bias in AI algorithms requires careful curating and pre-processing of training data, as well as careful monitoring of the algorithms to prevent inadvertently reinforcing existing social disparities.

Ongoing monitoring of AI systems is another crucial element in addressing bias. Regular audits and evaluations of algorithmic outputs can help identify and rectify instances of bias that may arise during system operation (Slatter et al. 2013). Transparency in the decision-making processes of AI algorithms is equally important, allowing libraries to understand and rectify biases that may emerge during algorithmic decision-making. Librarians and AI developers must engage in continuous education and training to stay informed about the ethical considerations surrounding bias and fairness in AI. To ensure fairness in AI implementation, libraries must be aware of emerging best practices, ethical guidelines, and tools for assessing bias in algorithms. Collaborative efforts between librarians, data scientists, and stakeholders are crucial for a comprehensive approach. By curating training data, implementing transparency measures, and fostering diverse collaborations, libraries can navigate challenges and promote equitable and just library services.

Ethical Considerations in Decision-Making Processes

The use of AI in library decision-making raises ethical concerns, particularly regarding transparency and accountability. AI algorithms influence resource allocation, recommendations, and user interactions, raising concerns about the ethical implications of automated processes. Ensuring transparency in AI-driven decision-making is crucial, as it can erode trust and make it difficult to assess the fairness and validity of algorithmic decisions.

Libraries must grapple with the accountability of AI systems for their decisions. The complexity of AI algorithms, especially in machine learning, can make it challenging to pinpoint responsibility when decisions lead to unintended consequences or biases (Xie et al. 2016). Establishing clear lines of accountability and mechanisms for addressing the impacts of AI decisions is essential for responsible The text emphasizes the need for ethical guidelines and frameworks in AI governance in libraries, prioritizing fairness, transparency, and user privacy. Libraries should establish policies that align with ethical principles, and ongoing ethical training for librarians and stakeholders is crucial. This awareness empowers professionals to make informed decisions, address biases, and advocate for responsible AI practices.

Collaboration between libraries, AI developers, and ethicists becomes essential for navigating the ethical landscape of AI-driven decision-making. Engaging in interdisciplinary dialogues ensures a comprehensive understanding of the ethical challenges and fosters the development of solutions that prioritize ethical considerations. In conclusion, ethical considerations in AI decision-making processes pose significant challenges for libraries. Prioritizing transparency, establishing accountability mechanisms, implementing ethical guidelines, and fostering ongoing education are crucial steps toward ensuring that AI-driven decisions align with the ethical values and principles upheld by libraries.

Organizational and Cultural Challenges

The integration of AI in library environments faces challenges like job security concerns and fear of technology replacing human roles. To overcome these, libraries should prioritize communication, tailor training programs, cultivate an adaptive organizational culture, invest in staff development, and adopt a forward-thinking approach, viewing AI as an enabler rather than a threat.

Resistance to Change Among Library Staff

The integration of AI into library environments brings forth organizational challenges, with one of the prominent issues being the resistance to change among library staff. The introduction of AI technologies often necessitates a fundamental shift in workflows, job roles, and responsibilities, leading to apprehension and resistance among staff members (Xie et al. 2016). Resistance to change is a common phenomenon in organizational settings, and libraries are no exception. Staff members may be concerned about job security, fear of technology replacing human roles, or simply discomfort with adopting new technologies. This resistance can hinder the successful implementation of AI, limiting its potential benefits for library services and operations.

To overcome resistance to AI integration in library staff, effective communication is crucial. It should clearly explain the rationale behind AI, its alignment with the library's mission, and its positive impact on staff and patrons. Open and transparent communication reduces uncertainty and promotes a shared understanding of organizational goals. Training programs should be tailored to staff needs, enhancing confidence and empowering them to contribute meaningfully to the integration process. A long-term strategy is to foster a culture of adaptability within the library, involving staff in the implementation journey and celebrating small successes.

(Buckland, 2020) emphasizes that libraries must acknowledge the emotional and psychological aspects of change and be responsive to the concerns of staff members. This includes providing ongoing support, addressing individual challenges, and actively involving staff in decision-making processes related to AI implementation. In conclusion, resistance to change among library staff poses a significant organizational challenge in the integration of AI. By prioritizing effective communication, tailored training programs, and the cultivation of an adaptive organizational culture, libraries can overcome resistance and foster a collaborative environment conducive to the successful implementation of AI technologies.

Lack of AI Expertise and Training

A notable organizational challenge in the integration of AI into libraries revolves around the lack of expertise and training among library staff. The intricate nature of AI technologies may leave staff members without the necessary skills to comprehend, implement, and maintain AI systems effectively (Rodríguez et al. 2021).Libraries, traditionally focused on manual cataloguing and information retrieval, may not have the in-house expertise required for the adoption of AI. This deficiency in knowledge and skills can impede the library's ability to harness the full potential of AI technologies for enhancing services and operations.

To address the lack of AI expertise, strategic investment in staff development programs is needed. These programs should equip library professionals with the necessary knowledge to understand AI concepts, choose appropriate technologies, and integrate AI into workflows. Continuous learning and upskilling are crucial to stay updated on AI trends. Collaborative learning environments, such as workshops, peer mentoring, and partnerships with external experts, can enhance the learning experience and foster a supportive community within the library.

Libraries may also explore external training resources, including online courses, certifications, and workshops offered by reputable institutions and organizations specializing in AI education (Xie et al. 2016). This external training can supplement in-house programs and provide staff with diverse perspectives on AI applications in libraries. Furthermore, libraries should consider cultivating a culture that values and promotes continuous learning. Recognizing and rewarding staff members who actively engage in AI training and development initiatives can incentivize a proactive approach to building AI expertise within the organization. In conclusion, addressing the lack of AI expertise and training is crucial for successful AI integration in libraries. By investing in comprehensive staff development programs, fostering collaborative learning environments, and promoting a culture of continuous learning, libraries can empower their staff to navigate the complexities of AI technologies and leverage them for improved library services.

Cultural Shift Towards Embracing AI Technologies

Libraries are facing challenges in embracing AI technologies due to their crucial role in information management. This transformation requires a culture that values innovation, experimentation, and continuous learning. Libraries need to shift from traditional practices to a forward-thinking approach, viewing AI as an enabler rather than a threat. This aligns with the broader digital transformation in libraries, which requires adapting to technological advancements, including AI, to remain relevant in the digital age. Libraries must adopt AI for efficiency but also imbue ethical values in its use. This requires a commitment to responsible AI practices, ensuring ethical considerations guide decision-making processes. Training and education are essential for libraries to adapt and thrive in this new digital landscape. programs, as advocated by (Archer et al. 2021), play a pivotal role in fostering this cultural shift. Staff members need to be equipped with the skills and knowledge to navigate the evolving technological landscape, and a culture of continuous learning supports this ongoing development. In conclusion, the cultural shift towards embracing AI technologies is foundational for successful integration in libraries. By instilling a culture of innovation, adaptability, and ethical responsibility, libraries can create an environment where AI is seamlessly integrated into existing practices, enhancing overall library services.

BARRIERS TO INTEGRATION

The integration of AI in libraries faces financial and regulatory challenges, including the need for significant investments in hardware, software, and personnel. To overcome these, libraries should strategically plan and allocate resources, engage in strategic partnerships, and explore alternative funding sources. They must also ensure data protection, adopt privacy-by-design principles, and establish clear policies. To overcome concerns like job displacement and privacy invasion, libraries should adopt a user-centric approach, involving active engagement, education, and transparent communication. Advocacy campaigns, workshops, and feedback sessions can help demystify AI and alleviate concerns.

Financial Barriers

The integration of AI in libraries faces financial challenges due to the need for significant investments in hardware, software, and personnel. To overcome these constraints, libraries must strategically plan and allocate resources, consider potential return on investment, engage in strategic partnerships, explore shared resources, joint initiatives, and explore alternative funding sources like grants and sponsorships.

Costs Associated With Implementing AI Solutions

Financial barriers are a significant obstacle to the integration of AI in libraries, as it requires significant investments in hardware, software, and specialized personnel. Libraries often operate within constrained budgets, which can lead to challenges in allocating funds for AI technology procurement and implementation. The costs include initial investment, ongoing maintenance, updates, and potential system expansions. Libraries must strategically plan and allocate resources for AI integration, including purchasing AI algorithms, acquiring computational resources, and investing in staff training programs. The specialized nature of AI expertise also adds to the financial burden. Smaller libraries or those with limited budgets face even greater challenges. To overcome these financial barriers, libraries should engage in strategic planning, including a comprehensive cost-benefit analysis, and collaborate with external partners, shared resources, and grant opportunities. In conclusion, strategic planning, careful budgeting, and collaborative models are crucial for overcoming these financial barriers and ensuring sustainable AI integration in library environments.

Budget Constraints and Resource Allocation

Budget constraints pose additional challenges to the financial barriers hindering the integration of AI in libraries. Libraries typically operate within fixed budgets, leaving limited flexibility for substantial investments in emerging technologies (Slatter et al. 2013).

The challenge lies in aligning the financial resources available with the costs associated with AI implementation. Anderson (2019) emphasizes the need for libraries to navigate these constraints strategically, considering the diverse expenses involved in AI integration, including hardware, software, personnel, and ongoing maintenance costs. Libraries must engage in strategic budgeting to allocate funds efficiently, prioritizing areas that yield the maximum impact on library services and operations. The allocation of resources becomes a delicate balancing act, requiring careful consideration of AI's potential benefits against existing budgetary constraints (Xie et al. 2016).

Resource allocation extends beyond financial considerations to include human resources. Anderson (2019) notes that libraries must assess staffing needs for successful AI integration. This may involve reallocating existing staff or hiring new personnel with specialized AI expertise. However, such decisions must be made within the confines of budgetary limitations. Strategic partnerships and collaborations with external entities, as suggested by (Archer et al. 2021), can be instrumental in overcoming budget constraints. Libraries can explore shared resources, joint initiatives, or collaborative funding opportunities to pool financial resources and collectively invest in AI technologies. Moreover, libraries may seek alternative funding sources, such as grants and sponsorships, to supplement their budgets for AI integration (Xie et al. 2016). Applying for grants that specifically support technology initiatives or collaborating with industry partners can provide additional financial support for AI projects. In conclusion, budget constraints exacerbate the financial barriers to AI integration in libraries. Strategic budgeting, efficient resource allocation, and exploring collaborative funding opportunities are essential strategies for libraries to navigate these constraints and successfully embark on AI initiatives.

Regulatory Barriers

The integration of AI in libraries faces regulatory challenges, especially in compliance with data protection regulations. Libraries must ensure the protection of patron data, implement robust security measures, and obtain explicit consent for data processing. They must adopt privacy-by-design principles and establish clear policies for handling patron data. Engaging legal experts or consultants can help navigate these barriers. Additionally, the integration of AI introduces complex legal implications, including intellectual property, copyright, and liability. Libraries must clarify legal guidelines regarding AI-generated content, liability, and ethical AI use, and stay updated on existing regulations to ensure ongoing compliance.

Compliance With Data Protection Regulations

The integration of AI in libraries faces regulatory barriers due to the need to comply with data protection regulations. Libraries are responsible for safeguarding patron data and must strike a balance between harnessing AI's capabilities and upholding user privacy rights. The General Data Protection Regulation (GDPR) in Europe and similar global regulations impose strict requirements on data collection, processing, and storage. Libraries must ensure their AI applications comply with these regulations to prevent unauthorized access, data breaches, or misuse of patron information. This requires robust security measures, transparent data practices, and explicit user consent for data processing activities.

Furthermore, libraries need to establish clear policies and procedures for handling patron data in the context of AI integration. This includes defining data retention periods, providing transparent information to users about AI-driven processes, and offering mechanisms for patrons to exercise their rights over their personal data (Xie et al. 2016). To navigate these regulatory barriers, libraries may benefit from engaging legal experts or consultants with expertise in data protection laws. Collaborating with professionals can aid in interpreting and applying regulations effectively, ensuring that AI applications align with the legal requirements governing patron privacy. In conclusion, compliance with data protection regulations is a critical regulatory barrier in AI integration for libraries. Navigating this challenge requires a nuanced understanding of the legal landscape, the implementation of robust privacy measures, and proactive efforts to align AI practices with data protection standards.

Legal and Policy Implications of AI Use in Libraries

The integration of AI in libraries presents complex legal and policy challenges, including intellectual property, copyright, and liability. Libraries must navigate these issues to ensure ethical and responsible AI use. Intellectual property and copyright issues arise from AI-generated content, which raises questions about ownership, authorship, and copyright laws. Libraries must clarify legal guidelines for AI-generated content, respecting copyright regulations while fostering innovation. Liability and accountability issues arise from AI-generated decisions, such as automated recommendations or resource allocations. Libraries must establish clear policies to ensure accuracy and fairness of AI outcomes. Ethical and responsible AI use is also crucial, with explicit policies guiding the ethical deployment of AI technologies. Libraries must stay abreast of existing regulations governing AI use, ensuring ongoing compliance through regular reviews and updates. Developing clear policies and legal guidelines is essential for libraries to navigate these challenges and ensure responsible AI practices.

User Acceptance Barriers

The integration of AI in libraries faces significant barriers due to concerns like job displacement, privacy invasion, and perceived erosion of human touch. To overcome these, libraries should adopt a user-centric approach, involving active engagement, education, and transparent communication. Advocacy campaigns, workshops, and feedback sessions can help demystify AI, clarify its benefits, and alleviate concerns. Involving users in design and decision-making fosters ownership and empowerment. Effective communication strategies, including transparent explanations and collaboration between librarians, technologists, and users, are crucial for creating an open environment and building trust.

User Apprehension and Concerns

The successful integration of AI in libraries is hindered by user acceptance, which can stem from concerns about job displacement, privacy invasion, and the erosion of human touch. These concerns can impact users' willingness to engage with AI-driven systems, hindering their adoption and effectiveness. To address these concerns, libraries should communicate the complementary nature of AI, emphasizing that its implementation is intended to augment rather than replace human roles. Privacy invasion is another concern, especially in sensitive patron data. Libraries should implement transparent data practices, robust security measures, and clear communication to ensure users' privacy is a top priority. The perceived erosion of human touch in library services can also contribute to user apprehension. To address these concerns, libraries should adopt a user-centric approach, involving active engagement, education, and transparent communication. This approach can help dispel concerns and foster a sense of ownership and empowerment in AI implementations.

Communication Strategies for Promoting AI Acceptance

In the integration of AI in libraries, effective communication strategies emerge as pivotal tools for fostering user acceptance. Libraries, cognizant of the apprehensions and concerns users may harbor, must employ transparent communication to elucidate the benefits of AI, allay fears, and actively involve users in the decision-making process (Xie et al. 2016).

Buckland (2020) emphasizes that communication is not merely about disseminating information but establishing a dialogue with the library community. Collaborative efforts between librarians, technologists, and users are crucial in creating an environment of openness and trust. Libraries can conduct user education programs, workshops, and informational sessions to demystify AI technologies, providing users with a clear understanding of how AI enhances library services without compromising human-centric values. User involvement in decision-making processes, as advocated by (García et al. 2021), not only enhances transparency but also empowers users to contribute to the development and implementation of AI initiatives. Soliciting user feedback, preferences, and concerns ensures that AI technologies align with user expectations, fostering a sense of ownership within the library community. Furthermore, libraries can employ targeted communication strategies to address specific concerns. For instance, in addressing fears of job displacement, libraries can communicate that AI is intended to complement, rather than replace, human roles, as highlighted by Anderson (2019). Clear and honest communication about the collaborative nature of human-AI interactions can alleviate concerns about a perceived erosion of the human touch in library services (Xie et al. 2016).

Continuous and bidirectional communication channels, including user feedback mechanisms and avenues for questions and clarifications, contribute to building a culture of trust. (Archer et al. 2021) underscores the importance of feedback loops in AI integration, allowing libraries to adapt their strategies based on user experiences and concerns. In conclusion, communication strategies play a central role in promoting user acceptance of AI in libraries. Transparent communication, collaboration, user involvement, and targeted strategies are essential components of an effective communication approach, fostering a positive perception of AI technologies within the library community.

CASE STUDIES

The Library of Congress and Singapore National Library Board have successfully integrated AI into their collections, enhancing accessibility and discoverability. The Library of Congress used machine learning algorithms to digitize images, while the Singapore NLB used AI-driven recommendation systems to offer personalized recommendations. Both libraries emphasize the importance of strategic planning, collaboration, and continuous evaluation in integrating AI. The dynamic nature of AI integration necessitates libraries to adapt their approaches based on user feedback and assessment. These case studies provide valuable insights for libraries considering AI adoption in their libraries.

Examine Real-World Examples of Libraries Overcoming Challenges

The Library of Congress in the United States successfully integrated AI into its digital collection, overcoming challenges in digitizing and organizing its vast collection of images. By utilizing machine learning algorithms, the library was able to classify and organize digital images, a process that would have been labor-intensive and time-consuming if done manually. This approach improved accessibility and discoverability of the digital image collection, enhancing user experience. This case study provides valuable insights into how libraries can strategically use AI to address specific challenges and showcases the potential of AI to enhance the curation and accessibility of vast and diverse collections. It serves as an inspiring example for others seeking to enhance their operations through innovative technology.

Highlight Successful AI Integration Stories: The Singapore National Library Board

A compelling success story in AI integration unfolds at the Singapore National Library Board (NLB), showcasing the transformative impact of AI technologies on library services and user experiences.

Context of the Success Story

The Singapore NLB recognized the potential of AI to enhance user engagement and resource discoverability in its library services. Faced with the challenge of providing personalized recommendations to a diverse user base, the NLB sought innovative solutions through AI integration.

Strategies Employed

The NLB strategically implemented AI-driven recommendation systems, harnessing the power of machine learning algorithms. These systems analyzed user behavior, preferences, and historical data to offer personalized recommendations for resources within the library's vast collections.

Outcomes and Impact

The implementation of AI-driven recommendation systems led to a notable improvement in resource discoverability and user satisfaction. Users experienced a more tailored and efficient exploration of library resources, contributing to an overall enhanced library experience.

Insights Gained

The success story of the Singapore NLB provides valuable insights into the practical benefits of AI integration in library settings. By leveraging AI for personalized recommendations, the NLB not only addressed a specific challenge but also demonstrated the potential of AI to significantly impact user engagement and satisfaction.

This success story serves as an exemplary case of how libraries can strategically adopt AI technologies to improve user services and meet evolving demands. The NLB's experience highlights the positive outcomes achievable through thoughtful AI integration, offering inspiration for other libraries seeking to enhance their services through innovative technological solutions.

Extracting Lessons Learned and Key Takeaways From AI Integration Case Studies

The examination of case studies involving the Library of Congress and the Singapore National Library Board (NLB) yields valuable lessons and key takeaways for the successful integration of AI in library environments.

Strategic Planning and Alignment

One of the primary lessons learned is the significance of strategic planning and alignment with organizational goals. Both the Library of Congress and the Singapore NLB strategically integrated AI technologies to specifically address challenges and enhance user services. This strategic approach ensured that AI initiatives were purposeful and directly contributed to the fulfilment of organizational objectives[1].

Collaboration and Interdisciplinary Efforts

Collaboration emerges as a key takeaway, emphasizing the need for interdisciplinary efforts. The Library of Congress case study underscores the importance of collaboration between librarians, technologists, and stakeholders (Xie et al. 2016).

Successful AI integration requires a collective effort, leveraging the expertise of diverse professionals to ensure comprehensive and effective implementation.

Continuous Evaluation and Adaptation

The case of the Singapore NLB highlights the crucial role of continuous evaluation and adaptation. The NLB's success in AI-driven personalization is attributed to its commitment to monitoring and refining AI systems to meet evolving user needs This emphasizes the dynamic nature of AI integration, requiring libraries to adapt their approaches based on ongoing assessment and user feedback.

These case studies collectively underscore the importance of strategic foresight, collaboration, and adaptability in the successful integration of AI in library environments. They provide valuable insights for libraries seeking to embark on similar initiatives, offering a roadmap for effective and purposeful AI adoption.

RECOMMENDATIONS FOR FUTURE INTEGRATION

To integrate AI in libraries, they should invest in interoperable solutions, prioritize data quality, and mitigate scalability concerns with cloud-based solutions. Ethical AI practices should be established, including patron data protection, privacy guidelines, fairness in algorithms, and stakeholder involvement. Libraries should also develop clear mechanisms for data protection, bias detection, and engage stakeholders in AI technology development. To foster organizational readiness and cultural change, libraries should address resistance to change, overcome AI expertise gaps, and embrace AI technologies. Clear communication of AI benefits, staff training programs, and ongoing professional development are essential steps in fostering a culture that values innovation and continuous learning.

Strategies for Addressing Technical Challenges

Effectively addressing the technical challenges associated with AI integration in libraries requires a strategic approach encompassing interoperability, data quality, and scalability. Several recommended strategies emerge from the literature.

1. To ensure seamless integration with existing library systems, it is advisable for libraries to invest in interoperable AI solutions (Rodríguez et al. 2021). Interoperability fosters compatibility, allowing AI applications to interface with diverse library systems without causing disruptions to established workflows.

This approach promotes a cohesive and integrated technological ecosystem within the library.

2. Prioritize Data Quality and Standardization:

Addressing challenges related to data quality and standardization is paramount for the successful implementation of AI in libraries. Regular audits and data governance practices should be prioritized to ensure the accuracy and consistency of the data being utilized (Mattern, 2020). Establishing robust protocols for data validation and cleansing enhances the reliability of AI algorithms, contributing to more accurate and meaningful outcomes.

3. Mitigate Scalability Concerns with Cloud-Based Solutions:

Scalability and performance concerns can be effectively mitigated by adopting cloud-based AI solutions. Cloud computing offers flexible resources based on demand, allowing libraries to scale their AI applications efficiently as services or collections expand (Zeng et al. 2023). This strategy enables libraries to optimize computational resources, ensuring optimal performance and responsiveness of AI systems. These strategies offer a comprehensive framework for libraries to navigate and overcome technical challenges, ensuring a smooth and effective integration of AI technologies into their operations.

Frameworks for Ensuring Ethical AI Practices in Libraries

The ethical integration of AI in libraries necessitates the establishment and implementation of robust frameworks. Libraries can adopt several key strategies to ensure ethical AI practices.

Patron Data Protection and Privacy Guidelines

To safeguard patron data and privacy, libraries should develop and adhere to clear guidelines (Mehra, 2018). Emphasizing compliance with data protection regulations is critical in ensuring that AI applications handle sensitive user information responsibly. By establishing robust mechanisms for data protection, libraries can build trust with their patrons and uphold ethical standards.

Fairness and Transparency in AI Algorithms

Prioritizing fairness and transparency in AI algorithms is paramount. Implementation of bias detection mechanisms and regular audits of algorithmic outputs are essential steps to identify and address potential biases (Bartolome et al. 2022)Libraries must actively strive to eliminate discriminatory outcomes and ensure equitable access to resources and services for all users.

Stakeholder Involvement in Ethical Decision-Making

The adoption of ethical decision-making frameworks is crucial, emphasizing the involvement of stakeholders in the development and deployment of AI technologies (Slatter et al. 2013). Collaborative efforts between librarians, technologists, and other stakeholders can contribute to the creation of ethical guidelines that consider diverse perspectives and potential implications. This approach fosters a collective commitment to responsible AI practices. These frameworks provide a comprehensive approach to ensuring ethical AI practices in libraries, promoting transparency, fairness, and stakeholder involvement in the development and deployment of AI technologies.

Approaches to Fostering Organizational Readiness and Cultural Change

To successfully foster organizational readiness and cultural change for AI integration, libraries can implement a range of strategies addressing resistance, expertise, and cultural shift.

Addressing Resistance to Change

Libraries can combat staff resistance through effective change management strategies. Clear communication of the benefits of AI integration, coupled with staff training programs, creates a foundation for overcoming apprehension (Xie et al. 2016). Establishing a supportive environment that encourages experimentation and learning helps staff adapt to the evolving landscape of AI technologies.

Overcoming Lack of AI Expertise and Training

To tackle the lack of AI expertise, libraries should invest in ongoing professional development for staff (Rodríguez et al. 2021). Collaborating with external training providers and offering in-house workshops contribute to building AI literacy.

Ensuring that library staff are well-versed in AI technologies enables them to actively participate in and contribute to the successful implementation of AI initiatives.

Fostering a Cultural Shift Towards Embracing AI Technologies

Leadership support plays a pivotal role in fostering a cultural shift towards embracing AI technologies. Cultivating a culture that values innovation, experimentation, and continuous learning is essential for creating an environment where AI is seen as an enabler rather than a threat (Xie et al. 2016). Leadership should actively promote a mindset that embraces change and positions AI as a valuable tool in advancing library services.These approaches provide a comprehensive strategy for libraries to foster organizational readiness and cultural change, addressing resistance, building expertise, and cultivating a culture that embraces AI technologies.

CONCLUSION

This review paper discusses the challenges and barriers associated with the integration of AI in library environments. Technical issues include compatibility issues, data quality concerns, and scalability issues, emphasizing the need for robust technical solutions. Ethical and privacy concerns, such as patron data protection and biases in AI algorithms, require clear ethical guidelines and frameworks. Organizational and cultural challenges include resistance to change, lack of AI expertise, and a need for cultural shift. Overcoming these requires effective change management, continuous staff training, and fostering a culture of innovation and adaptability. The paper emphasizes the importance of collaborative efforts, involving various stakeholders, to overcome these challenges. Libraries should actively participate in ongoing research, experimentation, and knowledge sharing to remain at the forefront of technological advancements. By fostering a culture of continuous learning and collaboration, libraries can position themselves as leaders in harnessing AI technologies to meet the ever-evolving needs of their communities.

Summary of Key Challenges and Barriers Discussed

In summary, this review paper has thoroughly examined the multifaceted challenges and barriers associated with the integration of AI in library environments. The technical challenges highlighted include compatibility issues with existing systems, data quality concerns, and scalability issues (García et al. 2021) These challenges emphasize the need for robust technical solutions and strategies to ensure seamless AI integration within diverse library infrastructures. Ethical and privacy challenges, explored in-depth, underscore the importance of responsible AI practices. Concerns related to patron data protection, biases in AI algorithms, and ethical decision-making processes demand careful consideration to uphold user privacy and ethical standards (Archer et al. 2021). Addressing these challenges requires the establishment of clear ethical guidelines and frameworks, emphasizing transparency and fairness.

Organizational and cultural challenges, including resistance to change, lack of AI expertise, and the need for a cultural shift, highlight the human aspects of AI integration. Overcoming these challenges involves effective change management, continuous staff training, and fostering a culture that embraces innovation and adaptability (Buckland, 2020; (García et al. 2021)). The success of AI integration is contingent on organizational readiness and a proactive approach to cultural transformation. Through this comprehensive analysis, the review paper contributes valuable insights to the ongoing discourse on AI integration in libraries. The identified challenges serve as crucial considerations for librarians, researchers, and policymakers, emphasizing the importance of addressing technical, ethical, and organizational aspects to ensure the successful incorporation of AI technologies in library environments.

Emphasis on the Importance of Collaborative Efforts

The exploration of challenges in AI integration across libraries underscores a recurring theme—the pivotal role of collaborative efforts. Overcoming the multifaceted challenges necessitates the collective expertise and engagement of various stakeholders, including librarians, technologists, and policymakers. Collaborative initiatives form a cornerstone for a holistic approach, facilitating the exchange of ideas, experiences, and best practices (Buckland, 2020; Anderson, 2019).

Libraries stand to gain immensely from shared knowledge and resources, creating a collaborative environment that contributes to the development of effective strategies for successful AI integration. Buckland (2020) emphasizes the need for libraries to transcend individual silos and foster interdisciplinary collaboration, recognizing that the challenges of AI integration require diverse perspectives and skill sets. Anderson (2019) echoes this sentiment, highlighting the importance of breaking down organizational barriers through collaboration.

Call to Action for the Continued Exploration and Integration of AI in Library Environments

As the review paper unfolds potential solutions and future directions, it issues a resounding call to action for the continued exploration and integration of AI in library environments. Rather than viewing challenges as insurmountable obstacles, the call to action positions them as catalysts for innovation and improvement. Libraries are encouraged to actively participate in ongoing research, experimentation, and knowledge sharing to remain at the forefront of technological advancements (Rodríguez et al. 2021).

In the swiftly evolving landscape of information and technology, libraries emerge as dynamic hubs of knowledge. The call to action accentuates the imperative for libraries to adopt a proactive, adaptable, and visionary stance in their approach to AI integration. By fostering a culture of continuous learning and collaboration, libraries can position themselves as leaders, harnessing AI technologies to meet the ever-evolving needs of their communities.

REFERENCES

Archer, L., Godec, S., Calabrese Barton, A., Dawson, E., Mau, A., & Patel, U. (2021). Changing the field: A Bourdieusian analysis of educational practices that support equitable outcomes among minoritized youth on two informal science learning programs. *Science Education*, *105*(1), 166–203. doi:10.1002/sce.21602 PMID:34588711

Bartolomé, J., & Garaizar, P. (2022). Design and Validation of a Novel Tool to Assess Citizens' Netiquette and Information and Data Literacy Using Interactive Simulations. *Sustainability (Basel)*, *14*(6), 3392. doi:10.3390/su14063392

Bawden, D., & Robinson, L. (2018). The dark side of information: Overload, anxiety and other paradoxes and pathologies. *Journal of Information Science*, *44*(6), 745–747.

Chen, Y., & Yan, F. (2016). Centuries of sociology in millions of books. *The Sociological Review*, *64*(4), 872–893. doi:10.1111/1467-954X.12399

Cox, A. M., Pinfield, S., & Rutter, S. (2019). The intelligent library: Thought leaders' views on the likely impact of artificial intelligence on academic libraries. *Library Hi Tech*, *37*(3), 418–435. doi:10.1108/LHT-08-2018-0105

J., & Kim, Y. (2019). Automated metadata extraction and enrichment for digital libraries: A survey. Journal of Information Science, 45(6), 715–734.

Kastrin, A., & Hristovski, D. (2021). Scientometric analysis and knowledge mapping of literature-based discovery (1986–2020). *Scientometrics*, *126*(2), 1415–1451. doi:10.1007/s11192-020-03811-z

Okunlaya, R. O., Syed Abdullah, N., & Alias, R. A. (2022). Artificial intelligence (AI) library services innovative conceptual framework for the digital transformation of university education. *Library Hi Tech*, *40*(6), 1869–1892. doi:10.1108/LHT-07-2021-0242

Panda, S., & Chakravarty, R. (2022). Adapting intelligent information services in libraries: A case of smart AI chatbots. *Library Hi Tech News*, *39*(1), 12–15. doi:10.1108/LHTN-11-2021-0081

Rodriguez, S., & Mune, C. (2022). Uncoding library chatbots: Deploying a new virtual reference tool at the San Jose State University library. *RSR. Reference Services Review*, *50*(3/4), 392–405. doi:10.1108/RSR-05-2022-0020

Rodríguez-García, M. Á., García-Sánchez, F., & Valencia-García, R. (2021). Knowledge-based system for crop pests and diseases recognition. *Electronics (Basel)*, *10*(8), 905. doi:10.3390/electronics10080905

Saeidnia, H. R. (2023). Ethical artificial intelligence (AI): Confronting bias and discrimination in the library and information industry. *Library Hi Tech News*. Advance online publication. doi:10.1108/LHTN-10-2023-0182

Safder, I., Hassan, S. U., Visvizi, A., Noraset, T., Nawaz, R., & Tuarob, S. (2020). Deep learning-based extraction of algorithmic metadata in full-text scholarly documents. *Information Processing & Management*, *57*(6), 102269. doi:10.1016/j.ipm.2020.102269

Shreiner, T. L., & Dykes, B. M. (2021). Visualizing the teaching of data visualizations in social studies: A study of teachers' data literacy practices, beliefs, and knowledge. *Theory and Research in Social Education*, *49*(2), 262–306. doi:10.1080/00933104.2020.1850382

Slatter, D., & Howard, Z. (2013). A place to make, hack, and learn: Makerspaces in Australian public libraries. *The Australian Library Journal*, *62*(4), 272–284. doi:10.1080/00049670.2013.853335

Souchet, A. D., Lourdeaux, D., Burkhardt, J. M., & Hancock, P. A. (2023). Design guidelines for limiting and eliminating virtual reality-induced symptoms and effects at work: A comprehensive, factor-oriented review. [Lee]. *Frontiers in Psychology*, *14*, 1161932. doi:10.3389/fpsyg.2023.1161932 PMID:37359863

Xie, I., & Matusiak, K. (2016). *Discover digital libraries: Theory and practice*. Elsevier.

Zeng, J., Cao, S., Chen, Y., Pan, P., & Cai, Y. (2023). Measuring the interdisciplinary characteristics of Chinese research in library and information science based on knowledge elements. *Aslib Journal of Information Management*, *75*(3), 589–617. doi:10.1108/AJIM-03-2022-0130

ENDNOTE

1 Singapore National Library Board. (2021). AI in Libraries: Transforming User Experiences. Retrieved from https://www.nlb.gov.sg/AI

Chapter 6
Innovation Characteristics Considered by Top World Universities' Librarians Adopting AI:
Insights From Rogers' Diffusion of Innovations

Daniel Tomiuk
Université du Québec à Montréal, Canada

Cataldo Zuccaro
Université du Québec à Montréal, Canada

Aslı Gül Öncel
https://orcid.org/0000-0001-8740-7361
Galatasaray University, Turkey

Michel Plaisent
Université du Québec à Montréal, Canada

Younes Benslimane
York University, Canada

Prosper Bernard
Université du Québec à Montréal, Canada

ABSTRACT

This chapter aims to present to the readers the point of view of the managers of the world top universities' libraries as compiled by topuniversityranking.com. After an introduction presenting the special relevance of the academic libraries and the importance of the respondents, an analysis of data is conducted to verify the application of Rogers theory in the special context of AI. The survey used the standard scales from the theory and applies them to the introduction to AI, after qualifying

DOI: 10.4018/979-8-3693-1573-6.ch006

respondents in terms of knowledge. The theory explains the adoption by using five factors affecting innovation: relative advantage, compatibility, compatibility, complexity, trialability, and observability. Since AI is a relatively new technology in many libraries, a better understanding of the leaders will be beneficial.

INTRODUCTION

Research carried out by PwC indicates that artificial intelligence (AI) is projected to boost the global Gross Domestic Product (GDP) by as much as 14% by the year 2030. PwC anticipates that AI will contribute approximately $15.7 trillion to the worldwide economy by the close of 2030 (PwC Report, 2023). As per a report by Goldman Sachs released in July 2023, it is anticipated that artificial intelligence (AI) will drive a yearly increase of 7% in the Gross Domestic Product (GDP) until the year 2033 (Goldman Sachs Report, 2023).

Furthermore, the IMF's January 2024 report reveals that artificial intelligence is anticipated to have a profound impact on the business landscape (IMF, 2024). It highlights that AI is expected to influence nearly 40% of global employment. This revelation is reinforced by economists' findings in recent years.

Developed economies are projected to feel the impacts of artificial intelligence sooner than developing ones. This is attributed to the fact that the employment structures in developed nations are predominantly cognitive in nature.

Libraries have undergone many revolutions in a short period of time due to the push of technology, from the card system to the integrated library systems, the cloud, and the Web 3.0 (de Leon, Flores & Alomo, 2024). The latest frontier in this technological progression is Artificial Intelligence (AI), namely natural language processing (Zhang & Lu, 2021), gaining prominence in just a few years due to ChatGPT. AI, heralded as a disruptive technology, is projected to reach a market value 16 trillion in a few years (Kelly et al, 2023). According to the findings of the IMF 2024 report, it is highly probable that the transition process of libraries in developed countries to artificial intelligence will outpace that of developing countries.

Most studies of AI in library settings have focused on the perception of librarians and very few have investigated the actual adoption of AI applications. Research indicates that approximately 25% of librarians incorporate AI applications in their work (Winkler & Kiszla, 2022; Yoon et al. 2022), with one study revealing an even smaller percentage (8%) actively utilizing AI in their libraries (Hervieux & Wheatley, 2021). Additionally, systematic review examining AI-supported library services concluded that libraries were slow in adopting AI to support the services they provide (Harisanty, 2023). Collectively, these findings suggest a relatively low adoption rate of AI in libraries, at least at that time when their data was collected in 2022, which in the rapidly evolving realm of AI, can seem like an eternity ago.

Furthermore, this limited number of studies failed to employ any well-established theoretical framework or inferential statistics to explain possible differences between librarians who have adopted AI and those who have not. Instead, they simply attributed that decision to poor awareness of the potential of AI in improving library operations (Hervieux & Wheatley, 2021) or to differences in encountered challenges, such as the lack of funding, AI's developmental stage, and lack of leadership support (Huang, 2022).

A better approach for explaining the difference between I adopters and non-adopters among librarians would entail using the five factors of Rogers' Diffusion of Innovations theory (Rogers, 1962, 1983). In this context, AI applications would be considered as innovations - namely, relative advantage, compatibility, complexity, trialability, and observability - could serve to capture the key characteristics of these innovations. Utilizing this theory, librarians' perceptions of these AI characteristics could help provide important insights into the divergence in adoption rates and patterns. To the best of our knowledge, this approach has not been used in the context AI in library settings.

FOUNDATIONS

The Use of AI in Libraries and Applications

AI is expected to be used for customers, librarians, and management of libraries (Asemi & Asemi, 2022).

Some authors have made significant contributions in this area:

- Cox (2019) conducted interviews with 33 librarians, educators, and IT experts, highlighting various applications of AI in library settings. These applications ranged from back-office operations and the automation of clerical tasks to facilitating user requests and aiding in management support.
- Huang (2022) administered a questionnaire to Taiwanese librarians, yielding 472 valid responses. Participants detailed the applications they had implemented, and the issues and challenges posed by their implementation, notably citing funding shortages and inadequate technical support as primary obstacles. Among the initial applications adopted, natural language processing and virtual librarian reference (chatbots) emerged as the most frequent. Common challenges mentioned were information security/privacy concerns, incorporating library core values and funding and costs.

- de Leon (2024) provides an overview of the main benefits anticipated from AI in libraries and its services. These benefits include improving users' search experiences, personalizing recommendations and services to individual users, automating routine tasks to enable librarians to focus on more complex tasks, helping in the preservation of library collections, and providing continuous service availability with the help of virtual assistants and chatbots to answer basic reference inquiries.
- Lund et al. (2020) conducted an electronic survey answered by 236 librarians affiliated with the International Federation of Library Associations' Information Technology and Academic and Research Libraries listservs. Their aim was to categorize users in relation to their adoption styles. While results aligned with expectations, there was a noted bias toward early adoption. This was likely due to certain members of the list possessing greater expertise in IT than the general population.

Roger's Theory of the Diffusion of Innovations

"Three factors influence the adoption of innovation in organizations. They are individual characteristics (leadership attitude toward change), internal characteristics of the organizational structure (centralization, complexity, interconnectedness, number of employee and organizational slack), and external characteristics (system openness) of the organization" (Amini and Jahanbakhsh Javid, 2023, p 1221). However, the primary theoretical framework for understanding the introduction of innovation remains Rogers' theory of the diffusion of technologies, initially formulated in 1962 and revisited by the author in 1983. This theory has been widely applied across various domains, from marketing to medicine, and of course technology. According to Rogers, adoption is conceptualized as "the process by which an innovation is communicated through certain channels over time among the members of a social system. It is a special type of communication in that the messages are concerned with new ideas" (Rogers, 2003, p.5).

Mo et al. (2021) apply four factors of Rogers theory to explain the willingness of individuals to receive a new vaccine: (1) Attributes of the innovation, namely its perceived effectiveness; (2) communication channel, namely social media; (3) characteristics of the adopters, namely its degree of openness to innovation; and (4) the structure of the social system. In another study, Pinho (2021) analyzed 631 valid responses from Portuguese higher education students. The author found Diffusion of Innovation theory to be useful in explaining the acceptance of e-learning.

Questioning the reluctance of lecturers to introduce technology in the classroom despite its known benefits, Goh & Sigala (2020) employed Rogers' theory to explain the rate of adoption and provides three (3) useful examples:

a) For compatibility, they suggest that lecturers accustomed to social media will adopt ICT in class earlier, because it aligns with their values and culture;
b) As for trialability, they mention the need of resources to experiment adequately until becoming comfortable with the technology; and
c) In terms of observability, they emphasize student satisfaction as a measurable indicator.

Lee (2004) applied Rogers' innovation-diffusion model to examine nurses' attitudes toward the implementation of a computerized care plan system. The research took place at the respiratory intensive care units situated within a medical center located in northern Taiwan. The analysis was structured around the five (5) features of the implementation decision outlined in Rogers' model. Each stage was examined with respect to specific aspects: for relative advantage, the potential to save paper; for compatibility, an improved evaluation process; for complexity, the usability of the system; for trialability, the availability of nursing-related materials; and for observability, the recording of assessments and outcomes. The findings suggest that Rogers' model effectively captures nurses' behaviours as they navigate the adoption of workplace innovations.

Scott et al's (2008) conducted a study involving 153 physicians in Alberta, Canada. The participating physicians were provided with The Healthy Heart Kit (HHK) survey, which serves as a risk management and patient education resource aimed at preventing cardiovascular disease and promoting cardiovascular health. The findings revealed that the utilization of the HHK was correlated with the intention to use the HHK, relative advantage, and years of experience. Additionally, physicians' intention to use the HHK was also significantly associated with the relative advantage and the observability of the benefits provided by the HHK.

The main constructs of Rogers' theory encompass the following:

a) Innovation: Refers to a new process, product or service. Innovations range from marginal to more disruptive improvements. For example, the transition from analog to digital technology was an innovation during its time but the transformation from telephones to mobile phones represented a more disruptive innovation.
b) Adapters: The theory distinguishes among five (5) types of adaptors: innovators (2.5%), early adaptors (13.5%), early majority (34%), late majority (34%), and laggers (16%).
c) Communication channels: Refer to the formal and informal communications within organizations or society.
d) Time: The process of innovation adoption and diffusion involves a transition from one state to another, which occurs over time and through communications.

e) Social system: Refers to the network of internal and external influences that shape the dissemination of information and opinions.
f) Stages: Adoption is a multi-stage process. It begins by awareness, followed by persuasion, which leads to a decision and consequent implementation, and finally confirmation of the innovation's value and its enduring presence.
g) Characteristics: The attributes/factors relevant for a decision of adapting and implementing an innovation. These include relative advantage of the innovation, its compatibility with the actual situation, equipment, core values, the level of complexity of the innovation, the observability of its results and the opportunity to trial the innovation or experience it in action. All these are considered collectively, one possibly compensating for another. For example, significant relative advantage may offset a lack of compatibility or high complexity. Among the factors above, relative advantage, compatibility, and complexity are believed to be the most influential in determining adoption rate (Tornatzky and Fleischer, 1990).

Characteristics of the Decision to Implement

Relative Advantage

Roger's theory centers on the user's perspective of what constitutes an innovation (Amini and Jahanbakhsh Javid, 2023). He defines relative advantage as the extent to which an innovation is perceived as superior to the idea it replaces. When looking at the initial cost of innovation, it can be said that relative advantage reflects economic profitability. Here, the initial cost of the innovation plays a pivotal role in its diffusion. Factors such as saving time and reducing discomfort are among the sub-dimensions of relative advantage. In a study about exclusive breastfeeding in Africa, Oyelana et al. (2021) distinguish between participants' perspective on relative advantage (such as babies' safety and milk availability) and the objective advantage of milk sharing, as evaluated by experts.

When one looks at technological developments, there is a very high probability of adoption of products that provide a much more significant improvement compared to existing systems. Consider notebooks (laptop computers) compared to desktops. The former's advantage lies in its portability, facilitating use anywhere. A study by Min et al. (2021) on tourists' use of Uber, users evaluate Uber's advantages over traditional methods in terms of perceived ease of use and usefulness. This evaluative approach can be extended to other characteristics of Rogers' theory.

Compatibility

Rogers' concept of compatibility is defined as to the extent to which the innovation aligns with the values, experiences, and needs of potential adopters. It can be said that if any product is developed and compatible with the lifestyle and beliefs of the consumer, that product has a higher chance of being accepted. For example, a consumer concerned about climate change would be inclined to adopt an energy source that generates fewer carbon emissions. This consumer prefers to utilize a new solar panel that aligns with her environmental values all while meeting her home's energy needs. This exemplifies Rogers' compatibility factor.

In a study by Nordhoff et al. (2021), the authors found a significant positive correlation between compatibility and the intention to use driverless shuttles when individuals perceived them as harmonious with their daily routines. Overall, this indicates that innovations are more likely to be embraced when they seamlessly integrate into users' established practices and preferences.

Level of Complexity

Rogers (1983) describes complexity as the extent to which an innovation is perceived as relatively challenging to comprehend and utilize. This situation occurs especially with technological products. As a result of a new update in computer programs, if this new program is not user-friendly, there is a high probability that the product will not be adopted (Miranda et al., 2016). In a study on e-learning, Sakala and Chigona (2020) found that students are willing to adopt a tool despite its complexity if they perceive it as useful. This suggests that while complexity may pose a barrier to adoption, perceived usefulness can mitigate resistance among users.

Observability

Observability is the degree to which the innovation delivers tangible outcomes or benefits. If observable positive outcomes result from the implementation of an innovation, then that innovation is more likely to be adopted. It is said that in the absence of observation, the diffusion of innovation will take more time (Joo et al., 2014). For instance, consider someone purchasing an electric car not only for personal reasons but also to showcase their environmental consciousness, thereby making the benefits of the innovation visibly evident.

Trialability

This is the degree to which the innovation allows for testing or experimentation before a decision to adopt is finalized (Rogers, 1983). When consumers or companies can trial an innovation, they are more inclined to do so when the associated costs or risks are minimal. For example, offering users a free trial version of a statistical software for a limited period enables them to become acquainted with the software, thus increasing the likelihood of them purchasing it. Liu et al (2019) found a positive correlation between the perceived benefits and the acceptance of a road test with driverless vehicles.

RESEARCH DESIGN AND DATA COLLECTION

To gain deeper insights into the extent of AI adoption within academic libraries, we devised a study using a cross-sectional methodology, utilizing a web survey link distributed via email invitations.

Population and Sample

Our study focused on the top 1403 universities globally, as per the 2023 QS World University Rankings. We opted for this ranking due to its extensive history and transparent methodology, making it a preferred choice over other rankings. Any discrepancies between this ranking and others were not a concern, particularly as these rankings tend to converge for institutions ranked within the top 1000 or 1500. Variations are more noticeable among lower-ranked institutions, which were not central to our study objectives. Consequently, although differences between ranking systems do exist, these were not expected to significantly impact our findings, given our focus on sampling from the highest-rated universities.

Choosing to study academic libraries helped mitigate the variability observed in "conventional" libraries, which often exhibit differences in funding, clientele, and mission focus. Moreover, academic libraries were deemed particularly significant due to their direct ties to research, rendering them more inclined to adopt AI to address urgent demands and effectively access up-to-date information. The list of universities encompassed institutions from over 100 countries, with only a surprising 14% representing American universities. Notably, the top universities were concentrated in countries with the largest economies, such as the United States, UK, China mainland, Japan, Russia, Germany, India, Italy, South Korea, Australia, and Brazil, collectively accounting for 50% of the highest-rated institutions.

The compilation of academic libraries was meticulously conducted by a research assistant who visited each university website. From there, the assistant accessed the library's homepage and gathered pertinent information, including the name and email address of the library director or a designated customer service representative. If the director's name was identified, it was directly included in the list for personalized addressing. When it was another person, the mention "to transmit to the direction" was used instead of the director's name. This method aimed to maximize engagement with library leadership.

During the codification process, a variety of titles were encountered namely, VP, Director, head, Chief, etc. Therefore, we decided to use the generic term "director" given that it was deemed appropriate for consistency and clarity.

Questionnaire

Our survey instrument consists of 19 items designed to tap into the five key characteristics of innovation as outlined in Rogers' theory (1962, 1983): Relative Advantage (5 items), Compatibility (3 items), Complexity (4 items), Observability (4 items), and Trialability (3 items). Each question is presented in Likert scale format, ranging from 1 (strongly disagree) to 5 (strongly agree). While wider scales, such as 7- or 9-point scales are generally preferred for comprehensive analysis, we opted for a 5-point scale to facilitate ease of response, particularly for respondents using mobile phones. The instrument was refined following Moore and Benbasat's (1991) and subsequently adapted by Benslimane and Yang (2008) to suit the specific context of our study.

A separate series of questions were used to gather data on the respondent's awareness of AI, their attitudes toward AI (as discussed by Wheatley & Hervieux, 2019), and the extent of AI technology implementation (in accordance with studies by Huang, 2022; Oyelude, 2021). The questionnaire concluded with questions pertained to socio-demographic details concerning both the respondent and their library.

Respondents

From the 1403 individuals invited to participate, we received 106 responses, constituting a response rate of 7.6%. Given the responsibilities and demanding roles held by the study's targeted participants, this response rate is nevertheless commendable. Because our respondents were affiliated with prestigious universities, we feel that our study prioritized quality of response over quantity.

Our respondents were relatively young given their burden of responsibility. Among them, 61% hold directorial roles, while others bear titles such as Chief Library Officer, Dean of the Library, Assistant Provost for Educational Resources and Information, and University Librarian. Regarding their career stage, 1.4% were aged 40 years or younger, 29.5% fell between the ages of 41 and 50, 40% were aged between 51 and 60, and the remaining 19% were over 60. They managed an average of 82.46 employees with considerable variability (standard deviation of 77), and a median of 60. The mode was 30, with the highest number of managed employees being 528. The distribution of gender across different university sizes is detailed in table 1 below.

Table 1. Distribution of gender among the sizes of universities

Distribution Chi 2= 1.919 sig=.751	Small	Medium	Large	Total
Count females	6	28	21	55
% of females across size	11%	51%	38%	100%
% of females within a given size	67%	48%	55%	52%
Count males	3	29	17	49
% of males across size	6%	59%	35%	100%
% of males within a given size	33%	50%	45%	47%
Count total	9	58	38	105
% of respondents across size	9%	55%	36%	100%
% of respondents within a given size	100%	100%	100%	100%

An almost equal proportion of women (52.4%) and men (46.7%) answered the questionnaire. Most respondents came from medium-sized universities (55.2%) or large universities (36.2%), with a small percentage from small universities (8.6%). Chi-square statistics ($\chi^2 = 1.919$, $p = .751$) indicate that the distribution of men and women is not associated with the size of the university.

DATA ANALYSIS

Examination of Factors of Decision About Innovation Decision

Rogers' theory identifies five factors that influence the decision-making process regarding the adoption and implementation of a new technology. Below, we present this study's participant perspectives across these five factors. Each of these factors underwent assessment using varying numbers of items (ranging from 3 to 5). The following sections and tables showing a 5-point Likert scale (where 1=Strongly disagree, 2=Disagree, 3=Neutral, 4=Agree, and 5=Strongly agree) along with abbreviations such as s.d. (for standard deviation) and med (for median).

Within these tables, readers will find response frequencies for all items used to measure their corresponding factor, alongside aggregated measures (i.e., averages for each factor) pertaining to the median, the mean and the standard deviation. These were obtained by summing all items scores for each factor and dividing by the total number of items.

Relative Advantage

Relative advantage has a strong influence when deciding to implement a new technology, albeit requiring consideration of other factors. The following table presents the perceptions of respondents about the relative advantage of AI on their work.

Table 2. Perceptions of the relative advantage of AI applications

Perception of AI application benefits	1	2	3	4	5	Med.	Mean	s.d.
help to accomplish tasks more quickly			12%	57%	31%	4	4.19	0.634
improve the quality of work		2%	18%	60%	20%	4	3.98	0.676
make it easier to do job		4%	15%	58%	23%	4	4	0.734
enhance our effectiveness on the job			19%	59%	22%	4	4.03	0.642
give greater control over job	4%	16%	42%	25%	13%	3	3.28	1.014
Relative advantage						3.8	3.88	0.546

Results indicate that overall, a vast majority of respondents (74%) either *agree* (response option 4 on the Likert scale) or *strongly agree* (response option 5) that AI can bring a relative advantage (= 52% + 22%).

Table 2 also indicates that only a minority of respondents fail to recognize the benefits of AI, particularly concerning job control (relative advantage – item 5). It is possible that the existing scale may not be adequate for measuring relative advantage in the case of AI technology. Nevertheless, there could be other reasons why respondents might not recognize the benefits of AI in providing greater control over their job.

First, some may not fully understand how AI works and its potential benefits. This lack of understanding can lead to skepticism/reluctance to recognize the benefits of AI and embrace it for their work (Ångström et al., 2023).

Second, change can be daunting for many employees. Introducing AI into the workplace may be perceived as a threat to job security or autonomy. Some individuals may resist AI technologies out of fear that they will be replaced or that AI will alter the nature of their organizational roles (Jussupow et al., 2022).

Third, employees may have negative perceptions regarding AI (Brougham & Haar, 2018). This may include concerns about privacy, data security, or the potential for AI to make mistakes. For many, these concerns can overshadow any perceived benefits associated with greater job control. Fourth, employee perception regarding AI can be influenced by organizational culture and leadership attitudes toward AI adoption (Badghish & Soomro, 2024). An organization that doesn't effectively communicate AI benefits to its employees and fails to provide adequate training and support, employees may be less likely to recognize its potential advantages. Finally, employees may have their own personal biases (either positive or negative) when it comes to AI. Some may prefer traditional methods of working and resist AI, while others may be more open to innovation (Sindermann et al., 2021).

To verify if opinions significantly deviated from the neutral point (3), a one-sample t-test was performed. The test yielded a value of $t=16.379$, with a two-sided p-value $<.001$, indicating statistical significance. It follows that the perception of AI as offering adopters a relative advantage is statistically significant.

Compatibility

While a technology may offer a relative advantage, its successful implementation cannot be assumed without thorough evaluation and potential adaptation. In other terms, new technology is never adopted into a social void. Social factors influence how individuals, groups and communities perceive, accept, and use a new technology. In the context of our study, *compatibility* refers to the degree a new AI application aligns with the organization's culture, existing values, behaviours, and other technologies.

Table 3. Perception of the compatibility of AI applications

Using AI	1	2	3	4	5	Med	Mean	s.d.
compatible with all aspects of work	6%	29%	32%	27%	7%	3	3	1.03
fits well with the way we like to work	2%	18%	37%	35%	9%	3	3.3	0.928
fits into our work style	3%	19%	39%	31%	8%	3	3.22	0.94
Compatibility						3.33	3.18	0.858

According to the results in Table 3, more respondents than not report that AI aligns well with the culture, values, behaviours, etc. surrounding their work. Overall, 39% (31% + 8%) of respondents either *agree* or *strongly agree* that AI is compatible with their work. Overall, more respondents have positive views regarding compatibility as those who hold negative ones. Data shows that 34% (27% + 7%) of the respondents *agree* or *strongly agree* that using AI was compatible with all aspects of work (compatibility - item 1) while 35% (6% + 29%) believe the opposite. As for item 2 (compatibility), 44% (35% + 9%) report that they *agree* or *strongly agree* that AI fits with the way they like to work compared to 20% who either *disagree* or *strongly disagree*. For item 3 (compatibility), 39% of respondents *agree* or *strongly agree* that AI fits into their work style, which was on par with the number of respondents who chose the neutral point on the Likert-scale indicating a position of neither agreement nor disagreement with the statement.

Overall, a considerable number of respondents (36%, on average across all three items) choose the neutral point for compatibility. There may be several reasons for this. Some respondents may simply have limited experience or exposure to AI technology in their workplace (Lund & Wang, 2023). Without sufficient familiarity with a technology, it is possible that respondents feel uncertain about whether AI aligns or not with their work style. Others may have mixed or conflicting feelings influencing their perception of AI's compatibility with their work style. For instance, some may recognize the potential benefits of AI but may also have concerns about AI's impact on their job security. Such respondents may choose the neutral option on the Likert scale to reflect that uncertainty. Arguably, whether an employee feels that AI is compatible with his/her work may depend on the role and tasks associated with that work (Stieglitz et al., 2021). For repetitive tasks or data analysis, AI may be perceived as more compatible. The same can be said of jobs having routine processes that can benefit from AI and automation. Conversely, AI may be seen as much less compatible for tasks that require creativity, critical thinking, or human interaction, as employees may perceive AI as unable to replicate such aspects effectively.

A one-sample t-test was performed to verify if the opinions were different from the neutral point 3. The test yields a value of 2.183, two-sided p=.031. Despite the modest difference, the statistical analysis confirms the significance of the variance between perceptions of compatibility and the neutral point. Our analysis reveals that, while AI is generally perceived as compatible, there are notable discrepancies in individual assessments.

Complexity

The relative simplicity or complexity of the technology also plays an important role in the diffusion of innovation. The simpler an innovation, the faster its diffusion. The table below illustrates the perspectives of respondents on this matter.

Table 4. Perceptions of the relative complexity level of AI applications

AI applications	1	2	3	4	5	Med	Mean	s.d.
are easy to understand	8%	33%	31%	25%	4%	3	2.84	1
are easy to implement	4%	44%	40%	11%	2%	3	2.63	0.8
are easy to use		10%	41%	44%	5%	3	3.43	0.743
are easy to learn		18%	35%	43%	5%	3	3.34	0.827
Complexity level						3	3.05	0.653

Results in Table 4 show that respondents perceive AI technology as generally difficult to implement and complex to understand (i.e., "how it works") but relatively easy to learn and use. Implementing AI can be challenging for several reasons.

First, AI can involve complex algorithms, data processing techniques, and machine learning. Successful implementation requires specialized knowledge and expertise in areas such as data science, programming, and artificial intelligence. This kind of knowhow may be lacking in many organizations (Jöhnk et al., 2021).

Second, AI algorithms need large amounts of high-quality data for training purposes to make accurate predictions or adequate decisions. However, many organizations face challenges in collecting data, organizing and accessing the data, ensuring its quality, and managing data privacy and security concerns. Developing effective data strategies has important challenges such as data silos and decentralized data which makes it a difficult task (Claussen, 2023).

Third, AI must also be integrated with existing systems, software, and processes. This can become complex and time-consuming. AI integration into an existing IT infrastructure can become hindered by technological compatibility issues, legacy systems, and technical constraints (Singh & Adhikari, 2023).

Fourth, successful AI implementation requires significant resources. This includes financial investment in technology, technical expertise, training, and time. Smaller organizations often struggle in finding sufficient resources for AI initiatives (Makarius et al., 2020). Larger organizations may also face challenges which can include coordination efforts across several departments and teams.

Fifth, the successful introduction of AI technologies into the workplace often requires changes (Brunnbauer, 2023). This may occur in terms of workflows, job roles, and organizational processes. Moreover, resistance to change and lack of training can seriously impede the successful adoption and utilization of AI solutions (Ryan et al., 2022). Sixth, AI implementation may require ethical and regulatory considerations (Reddy, 2023; Ryan et al., 2022) due to concerns of data privacy, transparency, and accountability to ensure compliance with applicable laws and regulations when implementing AI solutions. Finally, although AI is eliciting increasing attention from organizations, it is still in its infancy (Mac Aonghusa & Michie, 2020). In parallel, the shortage of AI talent can be partially attributed to the fact that AI is still in its early stages of development and adoption. It is very likely that the shortage of experienced AI talent will persist for some time, given the growing global demand for AI and the limited supply of professionals with the necessary expertise.

Our analyses also indicate that understanding and keeping pace with AI is a challenge for organizations. This is likely attributable to several factors such as the complexity of various AI which encompasses a range of technologies, including machine learning, natural language processing (NLP), and robotics. Understanding the algorithms and various applications of AI can be complex, especially for non-technical organizational stakeholders. This is further accentuated by the rapid pace of innovation of AI and a lack of in-house expertise. New algorithms, techniques, and applications continue to be developed. Without access to skilled professionals who can explain, develop and implement AI solutions, organizations will continue to struggle.

A one-sample t-test was performed to verify if the opinions were different from the neutral point 3. The test yields a value of t=.747, two-sided p=.457. It follows that the perception of respondents is not statistically different from the neutral point and that opinions are divergent or that the respondents are undecided about this aspect.

Observability

Observability is an important factor to consider understanding the diffusion of innovation. The main questions are related to the visibility of the benefits. Is it possible to see them either inside or outside the organization. Table 5 below presents the perceptions of respondents regarding this factor.

Table 5. Perception of observability

	1	2	3	4	5	Med	Mean	s.d.
It is easy to tell others about the results of implementing AI	2%	14%	33%	42%	9%	4	3.41	0.91
We can communicate to others the consequence of implementing AI	1%	8%	27%	55%	10%	4	3.65	0.796
The results of implementing AI are (can be) apparent to us	1%	7%	35%	51%%	7%	4	3.55	0.759
It would be easy to explain why implementing AI may or not be beneficial	3%	11%	31%	48	7%	4	3.44	0.887
Observability					2	3.5	3.5	0.632

According to Rogers' diffusion of innovations theory, observability is the extent to which the results/benefits of adopting AI are visible or observable to others. It indicates how easily employees can perceive the advantages or outcomes of using AI. This factor impacts their decision regarding AI adoption. In general, observability scores are high with most respondents (57.3% = 49.0% + 8.3%) indicating they *agree* or *strongly agree* that the benefits of AI are readily observable.

A one-sample t-test was performed to verify if the opinions were different from the neutral point 3. The test yields a value of t=8.259, two-sided p<.001). It follows that the perception of the observability is statistically significant and that respondents perceive favorably the observability when it comes to AI.

Trialability

Trialability pertains to the ability to partially test AI (i.e., through a pilot test) before fully implementing it or experimenting with it in a different context/location. Table 6 below presents the perceptions of respondents in this regard.

Table 6. Perceptions of the trialability

	1	2	3	4	5	Med	mean	s.d.
having a great deal of opportunity to try various AI apps	13%	28%	50%	6%	9%	3	2.9	1.178
being able to try various AI apps before deciding to implement	11%	22%	33%	29%	5%	3	2.93	1.077
having experienced AI apps on a trial basis to see their capacities	14%	19%	18%	39%	10%	3	3.12	1.231
Trialability						3	2.96	0.995

A one-sample t-test was performed to verify if the opinions were significantly different from the neutral point 3. The test yields a value of t=-.365, two-sided p=.716. It follows that there is no statistical difference between the perceptions of respondents with the neutral point.

General Considerations

An overview of the perceptions of respondents about the factors potentially influencing the implementation of AI suggests that:

a. AI is perceived as a relative advantage (t=16.379, two-sided p<.001)
b. AI is perceived as compatible (2.183, two-sided p=.031)
c. AI is not perceived being complex or simple (t=.747, two-sided p=.457)
d. AI is perceived as observable (t=8.259, two-sided p<.001)

e. AI is not perceived as easily triable (t=-.365, two-sided p=.716)

In conclusion, except for the relative advantage perceived, where the respondents in general clearly indicated their perception about the relative advantage of AI, and in a lesser manner the observability of the results, the respondents did not indicate their perception or did not have a clear opinion.

The Role of Knowledge and Experience

A detailed examination was performed among respondents to compute the number of applications installed in their library. The following table presents the distribution of the usage of applications in terms of number, which measure does not consider the daily frequency of usage, the importance of the usage, etc.

Table 7. Distribution of the quantitative usage of applications

Number of applications	Frequency	Percent	Valid Percent	Cumul Percent
0	40	38%	44%	44%
1	19	18%	21%	65%
2	11	10%	12%	77%
3	12	11%	13%	90%
4	4	4%	4%	95%
5	3	3%	3%	98%
6	1	1%	1%	99%
7	1	1%	1%	100%
Total	91	86%	100%	
System	15	14%		
Total	106	100%		

Results indicate that 40 (44%) respondents did not have any application either already implemented or in the process of being implemented contrary to 51 (56%) who do. Among those who have implemented an AI application the vast majority (90%) have 3 or fewer applications, the maximum being 7.

A t-test was used to compare the perceptions of those who have a deeper knowledge of AI applications either because they already implemented some or are in the process of doing so. The table below compares the user and no user of the application. It appears in the table below that those using avec a higher score on all five factors despite only three being statistically significative as can be seen in the table below:

Table 8. Impact of experience with AI application on perceptions

	Not using :mean, std. dev. (n)	Using mean std. dev. (n)	t	2-sided p
Relative advantage	3.69, 0.056 (40)	4.02, 0.051 (50)	-2.917	0.004
Compatibility	2.91, 0.078 (40)	3.40, 0.810 (48)	-2.852	0.005
Complexity level	2.89, 0.052 (40)	3.08, 0.073 (51)	-1.453	0.15
Observability	3.34, 0.064 (40)	3.55, 0.570 (49)	-1.569	0.12
Trialability	2.72, 0.093 (39)	3.16, 0.980 (48)	-2.147	0.035

To verify this possibility a correlation was computed between the five factors and the self-assessment of the familiarity with the concept of AI. Surprisingly in neither case (all respondents or user respondents only), there was a statistically significant relationship between the factors and familiarity. Being familiar with the concept is not sufficient to deal with the innovation process.

The Attitude Toward AI

A correlation was computed between attitude toward AI and Knowledge about it. For all respondents, the r=.317, sig=.001, n=104 while for AI users the correlation is r=.443, sig=0.001, n=49. In both cases, the relationship is statistically significant. This result will be useful to vendors to convince potential customers by first providing a better understanding of the concepts.

Two series of correlations were computed to determine if the attitude was or was not related to the factors of diffusion: with all respondents and with only the users. They provide sensibly the same results, as can be seen in the table below:

Table 9. Correlation between attitude and factors of diffusion of innovation

factor (r, 2-tailed sig, n)	**all respondents**	**users only**
Relative advantage	**r=.519 sig=.001 (101)**	**r=.400 sig=.005 (48)**
Compatibility	**r=.442 sig= .001 (101)**	**r=.518 sig=.001 (46)**
Complexity level	r=.172 sig=.082 (103)	r=.244 sig=.090 (49)
Observability	**r=.417 sig=.001 (102)**	**r=.433 sig=.002 (47)**
Trialability	r=.172 sig =.088 (100)	r=.106 sig=.484 (46)

CONCLUSION, RECOMMENDATIONS, AND FUTURE RESEARCH

This paper presents a study on the perception of the managers of the libraries of the top of the world's best universities. The authors are very grateful to these important persons for agreeing to share their opinions about AI which proves how crucial is the topic for now and for the coming years. From their responses, our results show that relative advantage permitted by AI is the most recognized factor among respondents, followed by compatibility concern and observability. The results were very similar from actual or coming users with non-users of AI. The familiarity was shown to be unrelated to the factors, but the attitude is related to knowledge of the concepts of AI. Consequently, the vendors of AI solutions should pay attention to providing sufficient information to generate a positive attitude toward AY which in turn can into a better perception of the relative advantage, the compatibility, and the observability factors. Despite the knowledge to draw from this study, the reader must notice the relatively small number of respondents among the 1400 universities answered the questionnaire. These universities are the best ones and then not representative of the set of all world universities. They probably benefit from better funding, the support of more technicians, and a culture of innovation. The decision to use a questionnaire comes with the limitations of information richness compared to interviews.

IMPLICATION AND POLICY RECOMMENDATIONS

AI presents significant opportunities for libraries to evolve and enhance their services in various ways. This includes streamlining, improving, and enhancing library operations, analytical capabilities, user experiences, and customer service (Subaveerapandiyan, 2023). AI can automate librarians' routine tasks such as inventory management, cataloging, and circulation. AI algorithms can easily and quickly analyze the content of library materials (text, images, and audio) to extract relevant metadata (author names, titles, publication dates, subjects, keywords). Automated metadata generation accelerates the cataloging of new materials and ensures better consistency and accuracy across the library's collections. It also makes new materials available to patrons sooner than before.

AI-driven technologies also help digitize print materials and convert these into searchable digital copies of print materials using optical character recognition (OCR) improving accessibility to patrons (both on- and offline). This can be particularly useful to patrons with disabilities by providing easier access to library resources. AI-powered translation tools can also translate written materials (i.e., books, articles, manuscripts, and documents) from one language to another using machine learning algorithms and natural language processing (NLP). This allows the creation of multilingual catalogs, enabling patrons from various linguistic backgrounds to search for and access library resources in their preferred language which further improves accessibility.

Morevoer, AI promises significant enhancements in analytic capabilities in libraries (Litsey and Mauldin, 2018; Xu, 2023). AI offers insights into patron behavior (e.g., borrowing patterns, search queries, and content consumption habits). This helps libraries tailor their collections and services to better meet patrons' evolving needs and preferences. AI-powered recommendation systems can analyze patron data to generate personalized recommendations for relevant materials based on patrons' interests and usage patterns. Such systems can also help patrons discover new content and encourage exploration of the library's collections. AI also helps libraries anticipate future trends and demands through predictive analytics. AI algorithms can forecast future usage patterns and trends, which helps libraries optimize resource allocation, plan for collection growth, and anticipate user needs.

Finally, AI improves customer service and patrons' overall experience. Virtual assistants and chatbots can handle basic patron inquiries (e.g., library hours, location, and general information about services and collections) which helps reduce the volume of inquiries that staff need to address personally. Moreover, chatbots and virtual assistants can provide such services round-the-clock, 24/7, even when library staff are not available.

To fully realize AI's potential, here are some measures that should be implemented:

Raising awareness and improved education among librarians about the potential benefits of AI adoption. This can be achieved in various ways such as develop training programs and workshops focused on AI technologies and their applications in library settings (from the fundamentals to specific AI platforms). Creating online resources can also help. This can include webinars, tutorials, and guides that provide easily accessible and up-to-date information about AI technologies and their benefits.

In parallel, library administrators and decision-makers should also ***allocate sufficient resources and provide strong leadership support***. This can help to facilitate the integration of AI applications into library operations as well as advocating for organizational buy-in and commitment toward AI-innovation. Libraries should conduct a thorough assessment of required resources and funding. Conducting a cost-benefit analysis to evaluate the potential return on investment (ROI) should consider many factors such as upfront costs when acquiring AI applications, ongoing operational expenses, and the potential benefits and savings associated with AI implementation (i.e., improved efficiency, enhanced user experiences, and cost savings from automation). Training and education should also be a priority. For instance, funds can be made available for librarians to attend conferences, seminars, and webinars focused on AI can provide valuable insights from industry experts, case studies of successful AI implementations in libraries, and networking opportunities to share knowledge and experiences.

Given the high variability in the costs of AI-solutions, libraries should consider ***adopting AI solutions at a pace that they can afford and effectively manage***. AI encompass a wide range of applications, tools, and platforms. There are open-source AI solutions freely available, allowing libraries to access and deploy them without significant financial burden (e.g., ChatGPT). Other AI solutions are offered under licensing agreements or subscription models. Fees may add up quickly as they are paid based on factors such as usage, number of users, or level of service. Rushing into AI adoption without careful consideration of a library's needs, resources, and capabilities can lead to inefficiencies, implementation challenges, and setbacks. Gradual adoption should also be considered. It can help libraries prioritize high-impact AI applications to address immediate needs, minimize risk and resource constraints, and help stay aligned with strategic goals. Importantly, gradual adoption helps to gain experience and expertise in AI which then makes for smoother integration of AI solutions in the future. Conducting pilot tests can also be an effective implementation strategy. These involve implementing AI on a smaller scale, within a controlled environment or a solution with limited scope. This is then followed up by performance, usability, and suitability evaluations, ahead of broader deployment. Overall, gradual and smaller-scale pilot implementations can help in demonstrating AI's potential value, functionality, and benefits within the library context. They can also help build confidence among stakeholders, justify further investment, and pave the way to broader adoption of AI-solutions.

Libraries should prioritize ***understanding the perspectives and attitudes of users (employees and both current and potential patrons) towards AI***. This can allow libraries to tailor AI-powered services that better align with user expectations, preferences, and comfort levels, ensuring a positive user experience. This can also help to identify potential barriers to adoption and develop strategies to address them through education, training, and support. Furthermore, user feedback (both librarians' and patrons') can be useful for iterative and continuous improvement and refinement of AI-powered services.

Libraries should also ***undertake an impact assessment*** which includes how AI adoption can affect services, user experiences, and organizational structure and outcomes. This involves evaluating how AI technologies may disrupt traditional library functions and workflows. Libraries should identify strategies that mitigate potential challenges given that AI adoption in libraries is best seen as a disruptive technology. It introduces new capabilities and functionalities that fundamentally transform how libraries deliver services. AI also changes how users interact with library resources and services. Furthermore, AI disrupts traditional roles within libraries. Most tasks once performed manually (e.g., cataloging, metadata management, reference assistance) are likely to become automated or "augmented" in some

FUTURE RESEARCH DIRECTIONS

This chapter is an initial exploration into the introduction of innovation within academic libraries. Further studies are needed in key areas, namely:

This chapter reports on a cross-sectional analysis with a relatively limited number of respondents, primarily due to budgetary constraints. Subsequent studies should be conducted with a larger sample size and with the support of the Association of Librarians to ensure a broader representativity of results.

Furthermore, our study specifically targeted the top 1400 universities. We assumed they would be early adopters of AI in their operations. However, to validate this assumption against realities in the field, it is essential to expand the study population to include all academic libraries initially, and subsequently, all types of libraries, including municipal and town libraries.

While this study primarily delved into aspects from Rogers' theory, we intentionally omitted certain dimensions from the questionnaire for the sake of brevity to reduce respondent fatigue and improve response rates. Nevertheless, these other facets merit empirical exploration. This includes early adopters' characteristics, preferred communication channels in different contexts, different implementation timelines for various AI applications, whether there is an influence of the social system in public versus private libraries, and the challenges that emerge in gradual and multi-stage implementation and deployment processes.

Several potential future research directions can also be identified. This includes investigating specific barriers to AI adoption in libraries which could involve qualitative research methods such as interviews or focus groups (with staff and patrons) to gain deeper insights into the factors influencing AI adoption. Comparative analyses could also be conducted across different types of libraries to examine specific factors influencing their adoption decisions which could provide a more nuanced understanding of how organizational context shapes AI adoption decisions in libraries. Longitudinal studies can also be conducted to track changes in AI adoption rates and perceptions over time. This could help identify evolving challenges and opportunities, and how learning from previous AI implementations affects future decisions and implementations. It would also help assess the long-term impact of AI technologies on library practices and services offered to patrons. Finally, cross-cultural differences in AI adoption could be examined. This could be among librarians and patrons from different countries and regions. Studies could explore how cultural norms, values, and institutional contexts influence AI perceptions and adoption decisions in libraries which would provide a more comprehensive understanding of global AI adoption trends.

REFERENCES

Amini, M., & Jahanbakhsh Javid, N. (2023). A Multi-Perspective Framework Established on Diffusion of Innovation (DOI) Theory and Technology, Organization and Environment (TOE) Framework Toward Supply Chain Management System Based on Cloud Computing Technology for Small and Medium Enterprises. *International Journal of Information Technology and Innovation Adoption*, *11*, 1217–1234.

Benslimane, Y., & Yang, Z. (2008, December). Project management trends in IS development: A study of the IT sector in China. In *2008 IEEE International Conference on Industrial Engineering and Engineering Management* (pp. 1759-1763). IEEE. 10.1109/IEEM.2008.4738174

Boden, M. (1987). Artificial intelligence: Cannibal or missionary? *AI & Society*, *1*(1), 17–23. doi:10.1007/BF01905886

de Leon, L. C. R., Flores, L. V., & Alomo, A. R. L. (2024). Artificial Intelligence and Filipino Academic Librarians: Perceptions, Challenges and Opportunities. *Journal of the Australian Library and Information Association*, 1-18.

Goh, E., & Sigala, M. (2020). Integrating Information & Communication Technologies (ICT) into classroom instruction: Teaching tips for hospitality educators from a diffusion of innovation approach. *Journal of Teaching in Travel & Tourism*, *20*(2), 156–165. doi:10.1080/15313220.2020.1740636

Harisanty, D., Variant Anna, N. E., Eranti Putri, T., Firdaus, A. A., & Noor Azizi, N. (2023). Is Adopting Artificial Intelligence in Libraries Urgency or a Buzzword? *Journal of Information Science*, 1–12. doi:10.1177/01655515221141034

Hervieux, S., & Wheatley, A. (2021). Perceptions of Artificial Intelligence: A Survey of Academic Librarians in Canada and the United States. *Journal of Academic Librarianship*, *47*(1), 102270. doi:10.1016/j.acalib.2020.102270

Huang, Y.-H. (2022, July). Exploring the Implementation of Artificial Intelligence Applications among Academic Libraries in Taiwan. *Library Hi Tech.*. doi:10.1108/LHT-03-2022-0159

IMF-International Monetary Fund. (2024). *Gen-AI: Artificial Intelligence and the Future of Work. IMF Staff Discussion Notes.* IMF. https://www.imf.org/en/Publications/Staff-Discussion-Notes/Issues/2024/01/14/Gen-AI-Artificial-Intelligence-and-the-Future-of-Work-542379?cid=bl-com-SDNEA2024001

Joo., Y. J., Lim, K. Y., ve Lim, E. (2014). Investigating the structural relationship among perceived innovation attributes, intention to use and actual use of mobile learning in an online university in South Korea. *Australasian Journal of Educational Technology, 30*(4), 427–439.

Kelly, S., Kaye, S.-A., & Oviedo-Trespalacios, O. (2023). What Factors Contribute to the Acceptance of Artificial Intelligence? A Systemic Review. *Telematics and Informatics*, *77*, 101925. doi:10.1016/j.tele.2022.101925

Lee, T.-T. (2004). Nurses' adoption of technology: Application of Rogers' innovation-diffusion model. *Applied Nursing Research, 17*(4), 231-238. doi:10.1016/j.apnr.2004.09.001

Litsey, Y., & Mauldin, W. (2018). Knowing What the Patron Wants: Using Predictive Analytics to Transform Library Decision Making. *Journal of Academic Librarianship*, *44*(1), 140–144. doi:10.1016/j.acalib.2017.09.004

Liu, P., Xu, Z., & Zhao, X. (2019). Road tests of self-driving vehicles: Affective and cognitive pathways in acceptance formation. *Transportation Research Part A, Policy and Practice*, *124*, 354–369. doi:10.1016/j.tra.2019.04.004

Lund, B. D., Omame, I., Tijani, S., & Agbaji, D. (2020). Perceptions toward artificial intelligence among academic library employees and alignment with the diffusion of innovations' adopter categories. *College & Research Libraries*, *81*(5), 865. doi:10.5860/crl.81.5.865

Min, S., So, K. K. F., & Jeong, M. (2021). Consumer adoption of the Uber mobile application: Insights from diffusion of innovation theory and technology acceptance model. In *Future of tourism marketing* (pp. 2–15). Routledge. doi:10.4324/9781003176039-2

Miranda, M. Q., & Farias, J. S. (2016). Technology Adoption in Diffusion of Innovations Perspective: Introduction of an ERP System in a Non-Profit Organization. *RAI Revista de Administração e Inovação, 13*, 48-57.

Mo, P. K. H., Luo, S., Wang, S., Zhao, J., Zhang, G., Li, L., Li, L., Xie, L., & Lau, J. T. (2021). Intention to receive the COVID-19 vaccination in China: Application of the diffusion of innovations theory and the moderating role of openness to experience. *Vaccines*, *9*(2), 129. doi:10.3390/vaccines9020129 PMID:33562894

Moore, G. C., & Benbasat, I. (1991). Development of an instrument to measure the perceptions of adopting an information technology innovation. *Information Systems Research*, *2*(3), 192–222. doi:10.1287/isre.2.3.192

Nordhoff, S., Malmsten, V., van Arem, B., Liu, P., & Happee, R. (2021). A structural equation modeling approach for the acceptance of driverless automated shuttles based on constructs from the Unified Theory of Acceptance and Use of Technology and the Diffusion of Innovation Theory. *Transportation Research Part F: Traffic Psychology and Behaviour*, *78*, 58–73. doi:10.1016/j.trf.2021.01.001

Oyelana, O., Kamanzi, J., & Richter, S. (2021). A critical look at exclusive breastfeeding in Africa: Through the lens of diffusion of innovation theory. *International Journal of Africa Nursing Sciences*, *14*, 100267. doi:10.1016/j.ijans.2020.100267

Pinho, C., Franco, M., & Mendes, L. (2021). Application of innovation diffusion theory to the E-learning process: Higher education context. *Education and Information Technologies*, *26*(1), 421–440. doi:10.1007/s10639-020-10269-2

Rogers, E. M. (1983). *Diffusion of innovations* (3rd ed.). Free Press of Glencoe.

Sakala, L. C., & Chigona, W. (2020). How lecturers neutralize resistance to the implementation of learning management systems in higher education. [Springer US.]. *Journal of Computing in Higher Education*, *32*(2), 365–388. doi:10.1007/s12528-019-09238-7

Scott, S. D., Plotnikoff, R. C., Karunamuni, N., Bize, R., & Rodgers, W. (2008). Factors influencing the adoption of an innovation: An examination of the uptake of the Canadian Heart Health Kit (HHK). *Implementation Science : IS*, *3*(1), 41. doi:10.1186/1748-5908-3-41 PMID:18831766

Subaveerapandiyan, A. (2023). Application of Artificial Intelligence (AI) In Libraries and Its Impact on Library Operations Review. *Library Philosophy and Practice (e-journal), 7828*. https://digitalcommons.unl.edu/libphilprac/7828

Tornatzky, L. G., & Fleischer, M. (1990). *The Processes of Technological Innovation*. Lexington Books.

Winkler, B., & Kiszla, P. (2022). Views of Academic Library Directors on Artificial Intelligence: A Representative Survey in Hungary. *New Review of Academic Librarianship*, *28*(3), 256–278. doi:10.1080/13614533.2021.1930076

Xu, Z. (2023). *Research on the application of artificial intelligence in the library sector. International Conference on Artificial Intelligence and Computer Engineering (ICAICE 2022)*, Wuhan, China. 10.1117/12.2671477

Yoon, J. W., Andrews, J. E., & Ward, H. L. (2022). Perceptions on Adopting Artificial Intelligence and Related Technologies in Libraries: Public and Academic Librarians in North America. *Library Hi Tech, 40*(6), 1893–1915. doi:10.1108/LHT-07-2021-0229

Zhang, C., & Lu, Y. (2021). Study on artificial intelligence: The state of the art and future prospects. *Journal of Industrial Information Integration, 23*, 100224. doi:10.1016/j.jii.2021.100224

KEY TERMS AND DEFINITIONS

Champion: A natural leader in the organization (or in society) bringing and selling the idea of innovation through the business. They are described as proactive, generous, ambitious, innovative, daring, rebellious, energetic, passionate, feeling others with their energy, taking initiatives without waiting for permission, and clear and convincing advocates of change.

Chatbot: A natural language application capable of mimicking human conversation, in several languages, with voice or text input and providing three types of answers: rule-based (expert system, advanced FAQ) AI trained, and generative (ChatGPT, for example)

ChatGPT: Acronym of Chat Generative Pre-trained Transformer, it is a generative chatbot, created by the enterprise OpenAI, capable of producing coherent and personalized answers from access to a large set of data previously used to train it.

Creativity: Is the manifestation of the production of a new object or process, the propriety of what has been thought to form a new (original) item hopefully useful (worthwhile. It can be an idea, an artistic manifestation (like song poetry, or choreography), a theory a new process, or an object. Creating is different than making, the necessary step to become an innovation.

Culture of Innovation: The global environment put in place by organizations or resulting from its history that favors new creative thinking and its application, despite the potential risks associated; it is recognizable by active opportunity management, the curiosity of members, their style of communication, the collectiveness vision and the presence of a transformational leadership

Disruptive Innovation: An innovation so different from the previous product/service/process using advanced techniques over existing ones and offering so many other advantages: cheaper, simplified, smaller, more friendly, and accessible to more people than the previous items becomes obsolete. The smartphone Apple is such a disruptive innovation over the simple phone or camera, the word processing software over the typewriter, the DVD over the floppy disks, Powerpoint over the retro-projector in classrooms.

Innovation: The practical result of introducing in the public space (for example a commercial market) the result of a creative idea (product or service), realized through research and development into a physical object, idea, or process, increasing the effectiveness of the previous incarnation of this innovation by some quality like lower cost, durability, speed, personalization, etc. The digitalization of telephone lines over analog is an example of such an innovation. Innovation can be incremental (for example a speed improvement of CPU), Architectural (2G, 3G, 4G, 5G phone networks), or Breakthru disruptive (from mainframe to PC, ChatGPT).

Chapter 7
The Application of Artificial Intelligence for Reference Purposes in Academic Libraries

Elisha Mupaikwa
https://orcid.org/0000-0002-0313-7139
National University of Science and Technology, Zimbabwe

ABSTRACT

Artificial intelligence has played an important role in reference services for academic libraries. This chapter reviews 40 journal articles published between 2000 and 2023. It reports that artificial intelligence technologies of machine learning, robots, and natural language processing have all played an important role in providing personalised services in information literacy, sentiment analysis, information retrieval and recommendations on library materials. In addition, the review reported an increased usage of ChatGPT among academics and reference librarians in academic libraries. The review generally showed a limited adoption of artificial intelligence for reference purposes in the developing world due to several limitations such as lack of knowledge and skills, lack of finance and limited infrastructure among these institutions.

DOI: 10.4018/979-8-3693-1573-6.ch007

INTRODUCTION

Although libraries are typically associated with the collection, management, preservation, and dissemination of printed materials, technological advancements have revolutionized a number of the services that libraries have historically provided. However, traditional libraries now confront difficulties that have rendered traditional books outdated and library instructions meaningless due to the quick technological advancements of the web and the internet. Additionally, information literacy courses are now part of the curriculum, bridging the gap between theory and practice. Meanwhile, technology has taken over some traditional library functions, meaning that desk-reference library services may soon become obsolete as virtual reference services take their place. One of the main library departments that has been impacted by these technological advancements is the reference services division. Through the integration of these technologies into their regular services, artificial intelligence has the potential to revolutionize reference services in academic libraries. Academic library reference librarians must employ technology to give the information and literacy skills that today's "netgen" generation of users require. They cannot remain static or traditional in their services or outreach to users (Musangi, 2015). Today's academic library patrons and technological advancements have altered the physical layout and operations of libraries, which affects the delivery of information as these institutions work to reinvent their offerings to better meet the requirements and expectations of their patrons. Libraries no longer have to be concerned about geographic restrictions while providing reference services to their clients. Reference services have four basic objectives, according to Tyckoson (2011): educating users, providing informational answers to queries, recommending resources, and promoting library services.

Accessing physical library collections in many traditional libraries requires laborious manual labour. However, in recent years, advances in AI-related machine learning technologies have made it easier for library staff and patrons to locate books, locate digital content on the web, and locate and retrieve it from institutional repositories and databases. Convolutional Neural Networks (CNN) and Recurrent Neural Networks (RNN), which have shown success in text identification and recognition, have been used to do this (Yang et al, 2016). According to Singh (2019), it can be difficult for readers to find books in a library with a wide selection of volumes. For this reason, technologies like RFID and AI are becoming more and more relevant in libraries. As libraries' features evolve, shaped by the always-shifting requirements and characteristics of the communities they serve, certain changes are highly pertinent and are even reflected in the terminology used to designate different types of libraries. In such circumstances, academic libraries have always looked for innovative approaches to provide their users with efficient service in ever-evolving settings. These days, reference services have a special place among libraries, offering personalised and quick service to readers on a subject that piques their interest.

BACKGROUND

Diverse authors have provided varying definitions of AI. According to Hervieux and Wheatley (2021), as AI is still a relatively new topic in library and information science, there isn't a single, widely recognised definition of the term. What unites these definitions, though, is the recognition that the field of AI as a whole aims to create computer systems that simulate human behaviour and intelligence when addressing problems. The majority of the literature concurs that any system claiming to be artificially intelligent needs to have the following qualities:

i) Thinking humanely;
ii) Thinking rationally;
iii) Acting humanely; and
iv) Acting rationally.

The fields of medicine, engineering and manufacturing, health, education, agriculture, information systems, and the broader discipline of information science are the main fields that emerged as having been researched and benefited from various experimental AI projects and innovations. However, it appears that no single field has dominated AI innovations and research on AI acceptance. Although the use of AI in these different disciplines dates back to the 1960s, there has been a noticeable upsurge in use and interest in these technologies since the turn of the twenty-first century. However, a great deal of study has been done on new AI advancements and their applications by academics from a variety of fields and disciplines.

While some universities have made attempts to create and implement AI-based solutions for the wide application discipline of library and information science, information literacy and reference services have recently dominated discussions on the use of AI in academic libraries. From these discussions, Zhang and Lu (2021) state that massive data, methods for pattern recognition, machine learning, natural language processing, advancements in computing hardware, computer vision, and machine learning are some of the general major drivers of artificial intelligence. These AI-related motivators have given rise to experimental initiatives in robotics, expert systems, machine learning, and decision support systems. According to Kumar and Sheshandri (2019), neural networks, fuzzy logic, image processing, NLP, speech recognition, and robotics have all been used in these AI-based initiatives. This has caused improvements in ordinary library and information services duties like cataloguing, indexing, collection development, reference services, and circulations to emerge in the field of library and information science.

In the industrialized world, libraries in the US, Canada, and Australia are among those that have employed artificial intelligence (AI); in the developing world, however, certain libraries in South Africa and Nigeria appear to have embraced AI across a range of library tasks. However, Hervieux and Wheatley (2021) note that while user interest in using AI has increased, there has been little progress made in developing AI systems to serve library tasks. In the developed world, on the other hand, academic libraries report using AI at a low rate. The majority of respondents in libraries in both Canada and the US (77%) stated that they used AI in their personal lives, whereas fewer respondents (60%) said they used AI as virtual assistants—although these respondents also brought up privacy and ethical concerns. These 27 universities are listed in Table 1 below, with 15 of them being in Canada and 12 of them being in the United States of America. Wheatley and Hervieux (2019) conducted an environmental scan on academic libraries that had incorporated AI into their websites in both countries.

Table 1. Canadian and USA academic libraries with web-based AI

Canadian Universities	American Universities
University of Alberta; University of British Columbia; University of Calgary; Dalhousie University; Université Laval; University of Manitoba; McGill University; McMaster University; Université de Montréal; University of Ottawa; Queen's University; University of Saskatchewan; University of Toronto; University of Waterloo; Western University;	Stanford University; Massachusetts Institute of Technology; California Institute of Technology; Harvard University; Princeton University; Yale University; University of Chicago; John Hopkins University; University of Pennsylvania; University of California, Berkeley; University of Rhode Island; University of Oklahoma;

Of the 27 universities investigated, 56% of these were Canadian universities that reported having integrated AI into their library websites while 44% were from the USA.

There isn't much literature available in African libraries regarding reference services. According to Luo (2015), the only two nations where published research on library reference services could be found were South Africa and Nigeria. However, there appears to be less use of AI in university libraries generally in underdeveloped countries. For instance, Oyetola et al. (2023) bemoan the lack of AI deployment in university libraries in Nigeria, despite extensive research on the topic. This is despite the technology's promise to enhance library services. Then, Oyetola et al.

(2023) advised Nigerian academic libraries to adopt AI tools like chatbots, barcodes, RFIDs, and robots to provide high-quality services, especially to re-establish their relevance in the communities and re-establish a connection with its remote users.

Das and Islam (2021) claim that artificial intelligence (AI) has several applications in academic libraries. Several machine learning (ML) approaches, including logic regression, KNN, and AdaBoost, have been extensively employed in collection management to generate metadata, find resources, and acquire books. SVM and association rules, user ratings, book recommendations, bibliographic data, recommender systems, and recommender systems have all been used for circulation. Furthermore, various ML and AI methods like pattern recognition have been applied. For collection discovery and search analysis, deep learning, neural network methods, and convolutional neural networks have also been utilized. Especially emphasizing reference services, the adoption of AI in academic libraries has had a significant impact on information searching and discovery, information literacy, and reference services, according to Cox et al. (2019). One innovation used to support reference services in academic libraries was chatbots, or virtual assistants that answered patrons' questions. Take the University of California's Alexa, for instance, which can accurately search the library's catalogue and find answers to frequently asked questions (Hervieux and Wheatley, 2021). Expert systems are among the AI-driven technologies that could be employed; Adejo and Misau (2021) reported on this case in Nigerian academic libraries, where robotics, natural language processing, and pattern recognition were used to achieve this.

Gundakanakanal and Kaddipujar (2019) list expert systems, natural language processing, robotics, machine learning, and pattern recognition as the several fields of artificial intelligence that aim to mimic human intellect in problem-solving. Expert systems are seen as the auxiliary reference librarian, according to Gundakanal and Kaddipujar (2019), who also state that reference services are the main activity that libraries seek out. Natural language processing has been used to improve indexing so that relevant papers are more precisely retrieved, as well as to search OPAC and obtain reliable information.

Researchers are paying more attention to how AI might be used for reference, even if the majority of studies indicate that AI usage in academic libraries has increased. Alongside this, academic libraries have begun using AI tools more frequently for reference. According to a Tella (2023) global survey, the developed world appears to be adopting AI for reference purposes more than the developing world. Of the 64 countries surveyed, China, Canada, and the USA were the top adopters of AI for reference purposes in academic libraries, while Africa had the fewest adopters, with only South Africa and Nigeria contributing each university among the adopters of AI for reference purposes, as shown in Table 2 below.

Table 2. Libraries using AI for reference purposes

University Using AI for Reference Purposes	Country
University of Punjab	Pakistan
Kingdom University	Bahrain
University of Malaya; National University of Malaysia Raffles University; Asia Pacific University of Technology & Innovation; Multimedia University, Cyberjaya Campus MMU.	Malaysia
Flinders University China; The University of Nottingham Ningbo China; Tsinghua University; Jiao Tong University Chinese University of Hong Kong; Peking University Harbin Institute of Technology; Zhejiang University Hong Kong University of Sci and Tech; Wuhan University Xidian University; Xi'an Beihang University City of University of Hong Kong; Beijing Institute of Technology	China
University of Alberta; University of British Columbia University of Calgary; Dalhousie University Université Laval; University of Manitoba McGill University; McMaster University Université de Montréal; University of Ottawa Queen's University; University of Saskatchewan University of Toronto; University of Waterloo Western University	Canada
Stanford University; Massachusetts Institute of Technology California Institute of Technology; Harvard University Princeton University; Yale University; University of Chicago Johns Hopkins University; University of Pennsylvania University of California Berkeley; University of Oklahoma University of Rhode Island; University of Nebraska	USA
University of Pretoria, SA	South Africa
University of Lagos	Nigeria
University of Sheffield; Northumbria University Newcastle University; University of Strathclyde University of East London; University of Hull Keele University, Bournemouth University Kent University; Anglia Ruskin University University of Bedfordshire; Aston Villa University	UK

Virtual reference services, reader advisory librarians, chat services, virtual storytellers, text translation, and material location were the main functions these technologies performed for reference services (Tella, 2023). Researchers like Okpokwasili (2019) in Nigeria suggested libraries employ AI in academic libraries since it enhances services and user satisfaction with libraries matching users' needs. This is especially true in poorer nations where AI adoption is being used for reference reasons. Notwithstanding these suggestions and the widespread recognition in studies of the beneficial effects AI has had on academic libraries, there is less evidence that library managers in the various demographic segments of the globalized knowledge society value AI. Thus, the purpose of this chapter is to examine the many applications of artificial intelligence in reference services within academic libraries. This is due to the generalization of recent material on AI's use in reference services. An analysis of the use of AI in particular reference services fields helps library personnel gain a solid grasp and respect for AI. The chapter begins by classifying academic library reference services. It then discusses the various ways that artificial intelligence is applied to these services, as well as the various technologies that academic libraries use to provide reference services. The chapter also dedicates a special section to ChatGPT in recognition of the substantial study that has been done on the topic.

METHODOLOGY

This chapter is a review of literature from journal articles selected from Google Scholar, Taylor and Francis, JSTOR, ScienceDirect and PubMed. Inclusion criteria: Publications between 2000 and 2023 were selected for the review and the key search terms that were used were "Artificial intelligence in academic libraries", "Artificial intelligence for reference purposes", "Chatbots in academic libraries", "chatbots for reference purposes", and "Machine learning for reference purposes".

Categorising Reference Services

The term "reference service" covers a wide range of tasks related to providing individualised help to library patrons, such as bibliographic training, liaison work, and selection. Reference service, according to, also denotes a direct encounter between a librarian and a user, which happens in certain physical service locations, usually the reference desk. This means that users approach reference librarians with concerns ranging from straightforward directions to intricate instructional inquiries. It is an interactive environment focused on physical service locations, typically a reference desk in the library. This model's typical flaw is that it works best for directed queries, handling difficult and in-depth ones quickly and superficially because other users in line discourage discussion aimed at answering the user's query (Musangi, 2015). a distinct reference service model that separates basic question-and-answer from complex or in-depth service by splitting the reference desk into two or more service points. In actual use, this concept has an "information desk" manned by paraprofessionals who screen out straightforward directions and forward other reference queries to licensed librarians. Establishing an information desk and a research consultation service office is another strategy in this model. The information desk gives library users quick answers, directions, and referrals to librarians when needed, while the research consultation service office is typically manned by librarians-answers more involved, lengthy queries (Reih, 1999). Numerous scholars have argued for a radical overhaul of reference services. Today's library patrons want reference services to be provided in a manner that meets their expectations since they are conducting informational research online through Google and electronic journals, and interacting with reference librarians via text messaging, instant messenger services, and email. Over the years, trends have shifted away from static reference services, where patrons wait at a desk for assistance, to a more blended, mobile, and adaptable model of helping patrons," according to Dempsey (2011). The expectations and behaviour of patrons seeking information are evolving as a result of developments in communication technologies. As a result, users want reference services to be reflective of their information-seeking habits and to provide them with the option to retrieve information through recognizable channels. The work environment for reference librarians has changed due to technological advancements since customers now want more help with electronic information sources than they do with print, and librarians are spending more time learning new skills. The shift to digital reference through the integration of communication technology is one of the most significant recent trends in reference services. Digital/virtual reference services enable librarians to assist users in obtaining information in a virtual setting through a variety of channels, including chat and email, according to Zanin-Yost (2004). According to Dempsey (2011), any library looking to rethink how they offer reference services to their patrons must consider offering virtual reference services. Library reference services must transition to an easily navigable digital reference environment if they are to meet the evolving expectations of users regarding their information needs.

The way academic libraries classify their reference services has undergone numerous changes. Kartz (2001), for instance, divides reference services into direct and indirect categories. Two additional categories are assigned to direct reference services. First, reference and information services, which include helping people find material directly and second, official and informal advice on how to use libraries and information centres. The selection of materials required for reference services and reference administration, or the planning and management of reference services, are the two components that make up indirect reference services. Kartz (2001) offers an additional classification of information and reference services. Reference information services are categorized under this classification as responsive information services, or services that are offered in response to a particular demand that the user has expressed. Information services offered in advance of a need are referred to as anticipatory information services, which make up the second category. Passive information services, often referred to as responsive information services, are offered in response to user requests; requests can be made in person, over the phone, by email, or through correspondence. Reference librarians are educated to provide individualized assistance to customers in all of these settings, helping them access information in a variety of formats such as books, articles, and digital resources. Another classification of reference services is given by Ashikuzzaman (2022), who defines them as either ready reference services or long-range reference services. To meet customers' information demands quickly and effectively, ready-reference services typically offer factual information such as definitions and statistics of in-depth analysis. Conversely, long-range reference services offer comprehensive research and support to users with specialized or sophisticated information demands. Databases, eBooks, and other online resources are some of the digital resources that users may try to access at the library (Ashikuzzaman, 2022). Generally speaking, though, reference services in university libraries cover a wide range of tasks, such as community outreach, research support, technology assistance, information literacy, reference desk services, reader advisory services, and information retrieval. Libraries now require the services because of the following roles they have played:

i) Supporting academic success through facilitating the pursuit of knowledge
ii) Meeting the diverse information needs of users
iii) Assisting users navigate information resources
iv) Facilitating research excellence for academic staff and students
v) Promoting information literacy across a wide range of users
vi) Facilitating access to specialised collections
vii) Assisting users with technology integration
viii) Providing interdisciplinary and collaborative research support across faculties
ix) Preparing students for future careers

AI Systems and Their Applications in Reference Services

Machine Learning Models and Machine Learning in Library Reference Services

A collection of artificial intelligence (AI) technologies known as "machine learning" allows computer systems to learn from past experiences, such as data observations, and adapt their behaviour to better complete tasks (Nguyen et al., 2019). The term "machine learning" refers to a variety of techniques that let computers learn from data without having to be specifically programmed to produce a certain result. ML algorithms, which can be broadly classified as "supervised" and "unsupervised" approaches, employ statistical models to find patterns in data. ML applications are useful tools for decision-making because of their ability to find patterns in big datasets for intelligent decision-making while forecasting the future and creating links between items. While unsupervised approaches can broaden our perspectives by discovering new connections in data, supervised machine-learning techniques directly benefit from human experience and input (Cordell, 2020). There exists a range of semi-supervised machine learning approaches that aim to combine human experience with computational serendipity, situated between the extremes of supervised and unsupervised learning. To make judgments about unlabeled data, supervised machine learning uses labelled training data. Machine learning is the process of applying statistical models and techniques to massive, both organized and unstructured datasets to extract useful insights and find patterns within the data. In a general machine learning application, the steps include data collection and preparation, model and parameter selection, training, performance evaluation, and selection of relevant features or variables for the ML algorithm (Cox and Mazumdar, 20022).

Web crawlers and other data-collecting techniques can be aided by machine learning to increase service accessibility for library patrons. Reference services have employed them to gather information from both homogeneous and heterogeneous sources to comprehend user patterns of library usage and to utilize this knowledge to distribute library customers with information that is specifically relevant to them. As a result, related items may now be grouped and text from digital resources can be found more easily (Cordell, 2022). Furthermore, the technologies have improved the way people are presented with information. Neural networks, for instance, are used to associate data from different sources, enabling visualisations that let people browse collections based on visual resemblance. A project using convolutional neural networks from Yale's DH lab is one of many instances of services; it enables users to investigate photographs that share similarities in more detail (Cordell, 2022). In addition, the Central Institute of Technology Kokrajhar (CLCITK) has employed neural networks, Random forests, and support vector machines to predict book availability (Daimari et al., 2021). Furthermore, the use of ML in academic libraries has enhanced access to information, helped researchers appropriately track material about their research topics, and made recommendations regarding research topics that still require further investigation (Harisanty et al., 2022). Librarians can forecast and anticipate the requirements of their patrons by analyzing past data regarding how they have used the library. Although these might be reference service consumers, this is useful when deciding on collection development and acquisition. Libraries can forecast the demands of their patrons by analyzing past data regarding usage patterns. Nonetheless, there are often contexts in which academic libraries use their electronic resources. Because of this, machine learning technologies are becoming powerful instruments for comprehending users' context and language usage. Therefore, the application of ML makes it possible to create reference systems that support context awareness in helping users find the information they require.

Context-aware library systems identify users and tailor services to meet their unique needs, concentrating on research demands based on usage patterns (Noh, 2913). According to Noh (2023), context awareness can be studied by breaking the topic down into 5W1H (Who, What, Where, When, How, and Why). Artificial intelligence systems can comprehend the meaning behind words in text sequences thanks to machine learning techniques for natural language processing.

Chatbots

Software programs known as chatbots are created to mimic human conversations through text or audio. In recent times, chatbots have become a vital tool for businesses to communicate with customers in natural language via messaging apps, web portals, mobile applications, and phone calls, among other digital platforms (Panda and Chakravarty, 2021). Panda and Chakravarty (2021) state that a carefully thought-out and constructed chatbot will:

i) Examine conversational data already in existence to determine the kinds of questions individuals ask
ii) ii) Evaluate appropriate responses to those inquiries by use of a training procedure
iii) Use NLP and machine learning to understand the context and improve future response times to those questions.

Chatbots are categorized based on the services they give; task-oriented chatbots are made to offer services in a certain domain context, whereas chit-chat bots are made to converse with users. However, according to NiBen et al. (2022), three different kinds of chatbots are mutually incompatible in terms of their features and designs: advisory (medium-term), persistent partners (permanent engagement with users and interdependence), and temporary supporters (short-term one-off). Aslam (2023) has classified chatbot technology into several categories, including machine learning, deep learning, elaboration livelihood models (ELM), natural language processing (NLP), and natural language understanding (NLU) models (such as ChatGPT). Nonetheless, due to their capacity to comprehend spoken languages, decipher the semantic meaning of user input, and identify morphemes, natural language processing (NLP) algorithms have been an essential component in the development of chatbot technology. These algorithms provide chatbots with the ability to behave like humans, resulting in a chat system or interface that is easy to use. These technologies are also referred to as hybrid chatbots, rule-based chatbots, and self-learning chatbots. Chatbots that operate on rules react to queries in a predetermined manner. Because conversations follow a flowchart, fewer subjects are veering but quicker resolutions. Conversely, self-learning chatbots are made to learn from their user interactions and gradually enhance their performance. Chatbots that are hybrids incorporate elements of self-learning and rule-based approaches. They may employ rules to identify specific user information types and generate relevant responses. However, they may also employ machine learning to enhance their functionality over time and adjust to changing customer demands (Adetayo, 2023). Early chatbots used in academic libraries were renowned for giving users in reference services instant feedback. As chatbots for information bases or FAQs, they are widely utilized (Adetayo, 2023).

Despite general declines in library use of reference services (Feldman et al., 2018), chat inquiries have generally been strong (Côté et al., 2016; Fan et al., 2017). There are more chat queries when proactive chat options are used (Epstein, 2018; Fan et al., 2017). In most libraries nowadays, chat is a well-liked method for asking reference queries (Lapidus et al., 2020). These chatbots have often been text-based input/output devices that have been trained to respond to a predetermined list of straightforward queries. Many organizations have included these within their library websites, although occasionally they have been integrated into social media platforms. The dynamic operating environment that today defines the academic library setting is the reason these have failed (Mukherjee and Patra, 2023). Yan and Zhao (2023) claim that chatbot use has expanded across a range of domains. To offer quick reference services, these have primarily been integrated into reference services offered through library websites in librarianship. These bots can now provide recommendations, assist with simple research questions, and provide information about policies, services, and other matters related to libraries thanks to this integration (Mukherjee and Patra, 2023). They have been employed as virtual assistants to suggest books to researchers and library patrons. As a result of these technologies' ongoing evolution, customers can now engage with reference services around the clock thanks to their adoption of machine learning algorithms that autonomously learn their needs. With the advent of virtual reference services during the COVID-19 pandemic, these technologies have gained even more significance. One of these technologies is ChatGPT, which offers consumers a personalized solution to their questions in place of conversational agents.

Academic libraries are increasingly using chatbots as conversational agents to supplement reference services. For instance, a survey conducted in 2010 by Rubin and Chen among academic libraries in Canada revealed that, even in the largest academic libraries, conversational agents were nonexistent before 2010. Moreover, certain universities, like the University of Western Ontario, relied on text-based services, including the Intelli Response-developed instant answer agent "Ask Western Library services," for reference needs. Rubin and Chen (2010) state that automated virtual reference services, virtual reader advice services, virtual conversational club hosts, virtual book club hosts, and virtual storytellers are examples of other conversational agents in use. One of these Canadian innovations is ADELE, which tracks student inquiries and activities and provides feedback that highlights the key components of the assignment. Since about 2010, research has indicated that academic libraries in developing nations have been utilizing AI more frequently. A survey conducted by Guy et al. (2023) among Canadian university libraries revealed that just two of the libraries employed chatbots for reference services. However, 73.58% of the libraries that Guy et al. (2023) looked into used live chat services that allowed users to text library staff. These services included LibraryH3LP, Libchat from Sringshare, AskAway, and Tawk.to, Zendesk, Facebook Messenger, SkylerAL Live!, and Ivy.ai, though some of the latter were not well-liked by librarians. Nonetheless, interactive FAQs are typically employed as chatbots, where users submit keywords and receive recommendations for pages that might address their questions (Guy et al., 2023).

Several chatbots are being employed at different libraries right now. For instance, the University of Hamburg Library System produced Stella in 2004, and libraries in Germany started creating chatbots in the middle of the 2000s. This robot could respond to any kind of input inquiry in the library and answer queries twenty-four hours a day, seven days a week (McNeal and NewYear, 2013). INA appeared on the Hamburg Bookhalls website in 2006, Askademicus in the Dortmund College of Technology library in 2005, and Kornelia in the Kornhaus libraries in Bern, Germany are a few more instances of chatbot usage in German libraries (McNeal and NewYear, 2013). Due to decreased funding for public libraries, the Emma chatbot was created in 2009 at Mentor Public Library using the AI markup language. From 2009 to 2012, 36,000 library patrons asked common reference inquiries and received immediate answers from the robot about the library. If the robot was unable to provide an answer, it would use the terms from the user's response to simulate a reference interview and point the user toward the online resources available through the library. Using AIML metadata and Pandorabots hosting service, Emma was changed into a free, open-source service named Infotabby in 2012 (Vincze, 2017). Stanford University uses the Beacon robot as a digital assistant that can respond to inquiries about the library (Weigert, 2020). To facilitate users' book searches, the University of Oklahoma developed Bizzy in 2017. Because it can respond to queries using plain language instead of a structured search, this modifies earlier search procedures (Weigert, 2020).

While Mukherjee and Patra (2023) claim that chatbots have become more popular worldwide as a result of advancements in machine learning algorithms for pattern matching and artificial intelligence's mark-up languages, these advancements appear to have benefited only the developing world, where their use has expanded. Research generally agrees that libraries' adoption of chatbots has been driven primarily by the need to improve user experience. However, chatbots have not been widely used for reference purposes in many developing nations of Africa and Asia, such as India, Nigeria, South Africa, and Zimbabwe (Kausha and Yadav, 2022).

There is now potential for service improvement and innovation development due to the employment of chatbots as reference aids in academic libraries. According to Tella (2020), reference service robots have made it easier for patrons to access and retrieve information on their own in libraries, giving librarians more time to attend to other crucial information services and the changing demands of their patrons. This is feasible as, in their capacity as conversational agents, they can be employed in virtual reference services to simulate the in-person communication that distinguishes physical reference services. Furthermore, these technologies have been employed as virtual storytellers and for reader advisory services. According to Das and Islam (2011), chatbots that operate in libraries and use data for training could benefit in understanding the needs of library patrons. Rubin and Chen (2010), on the other hand, contend that when conversational agents are used in Canadian university libraries, they should be used to supplement in-person communication rather than to replace it. On a library website, chatbots can serve as a marketing tool for reference services, introducing users to a range of resources and services offered by the library. This is particularly effective if a connection is made between the chatbots and other resources. Additionally, they boost the community's awareness of the library and its usage of the website (Vincze, 2017).

ChatGPT

Several Generative Pre-trained Transformers (GPT) have been created to help deliver the appropriate information at the appropriate moment. Academic libraries and postsecondary educational establishments have acquired these GPTs. ChatGPT is a tool for information collection that can collect and process large amounts of data from various sources, including websites (a process known as web scraping) and other media platforms like social media. This data is used to determine market trends, analyze sentiment, and gain insights into user behaviour (Aithal and Aithal, 2023). In addition, ChatGPT offers a platform for assisting with reference services via natural language processing (NLP). This enables it to analyze and interpret unstructured data, including text and audio recordings, making it useful for obtaining information from qualitative and consumer feedback surveys. Additionally, chatbots have been used for data mining, which involves searching through large datasets for specific information like keywords or trends to help library users with literature reviews. They have also been used to provide customer service, perform citation searches to help researchers find more sources related to a given topic or author, check references for accuracy and completeness, and retrieve information. According to Lund and Wang (2023), the implementation of ChatGPT in academic libraries has resulted in enhanced productivity, better information accessibility, reader-specific personalized content, and greater researcher collaboration. ChatGPT is important because it improves searching, finding, referencing, and information services in libraries. However, some academics have noted its shortcomings in terms of metadata creation and cataloguing, and others have voiced concerns about ChatGPT's ethical implications. However, according to published research, ChatGPT's broader lawsuits in libraries have been filed for:

i) Reaching out and communicating with others;
ii) making accommodations for people with disabilities;
iii) offering book recommendations or requirements;
iv) iv) transforming language;
v) v) encouraging involvement and promotion;
vi) vi) searching through catalogues; and
vii) and vii) developing a collection.

Aithal and Aithal (2023) list several examples of these GPTs and these are:

i) ROBERT: created for text classification and language modelling by Facebook AI Research
ii) CTRL: Created by Salesforce to generate and complete text
iii) XLNet: Created by Google and Carnegie Mellon University to handle lengthy text sequences for text summarization and classification
iv) BERT (Bidirectional Encoder Representation from Transformers): Its ability to comprehend word context in a sequence makes it valuable for sentiment analysis and natural language comprehension.
v) T5: carries out natural language tasks like text translation, summarization, and answering questions
vi) GTP1: Created by Open AI to produce logical text and respond to queries. The GPT2 is more powerful than this.
vii) GPT2: It was also created by OpenAI and produces grammatically sound and coherent answers to a variety of requests, such as text completion, translation, and summarization.
viii) GT3: created by OpenAI, it has a range of capacities for finding the appropriate information and producing replies that resemble those of a human being in response to a variety of cues, such as summarizing, translating, and text completion.

Expert Systems in Library Reference Services

An expert system is another AI-based tool that academic libraries have utilized to offer customized reference services. This is a reference to a knowledge-based system that stands in for a human expert and provides guidance and expert opinion on choices and resolutions to specific problems. Expert systems are helpful in reference services because they help users find materials and information by asking what kind of information they need and then presenting that information in the format that best suits their needs (Singh et al., 1996).

Numerous librarian expert systems have been created to assist users, provide answers to straightforward reference queries, and clarify the findings. Expert system implementation in academic libraries has a lengthy history, having begun with multiple library automation programs in the 1960s. Among these projects were Shelpro by Drabenmstott and other partners, and CLOD-x and CUTT-x by Salvic and Jobrica in 1994 and 1996, respectively. In addition to these, earlier at the University of Chicago, Berkerly REFSEARCH produced several innovations for book retrieval and specific bibliographic inquiries answered, and another was developed to address problems regarding topic qualification. Additional systems developed were the Online Reference System (ORS) at Bowling Green State University in North Carolina, the Reference Librarian Enhancement System (REFFLES1) at the University of California and Los Angeles, a prototype reference system called DISTREF at Charles Sturt University in Australia to support students enrolled in distance education, and the Patient Information Assistant for Information Retrieval at the University of Austin (De Silva, 1999).

Robots

According to Tella (2020), telepresence robots, which enable students to approach a robot under the supervision of a librarian with questions they might be embarrassed to ask, are among the robot-based technologies that have been used to supplement disk-reference services. These technologies also offer virtual content that ensures anonymity for library users. However, humanoid robots have been employed to mimic human behaviour in engaging dialogues, narrating tales, and instructing users, making them useful resources for information literacy at university libraries (Tella, 2020). Research indicates that the implementation of humanoid robots has enhanced reference services and enabled users to receive assistance (Emiri, 2023). For instance, Emiri (2023) revealed that 8.2% of the libraries in Southern Nigeria had robots, and 40.6% of them had chatbots that they utilized for a range of functions, including reference services. Robots in the Pepper project, which was introduced in 2014 as a library assistant to assist patrons and library personnel, are among the projects that have been implemented at the Technical University of Applied Sciences in Wildau (Stahl, Mohnke and Seeliger, 2018).

Natural Language Processing in Library Reference Services

The interdisciplinary field of natural language processing pertains to computers' capacity to identify and comprehend human language in written forms (Zheng and Lu, 2021). Zhang and Lu (2021) have classified natural language processing (NLP) into seven distinct areas. These include machine translation, information retrieval, text mining, grammatical and semantic analysis, information extraction, question-and-answer systems, and dialogue systems. NLP in library and information science refers to the application of AI and ML methods for data processing and analysis to enhance library services. Reference services are one of the main services that could profit from the application of NLP. These technologies can classify questions that are frequently aimed at library reference services and route them to the appropriate departments within the library. Libraries can manage enormous datasets and provide standardized interfaces through the use of categorization techniques.

Uses of AI in Reference Services

Sentiment Analysis and Reference Services in Academic Libraries

The study of sentiment analysis, also known as opinion mining, has expanded within the field of product marketing. It has also recently drawn interest from LIS practitioners and researchers. Opinion mining, or sentiment analysis, is a method for gleaning viewpoints and feelings from user feedback. Text mining and machine learning algorithms for natural language are applied in web-based contexts. According to Khaiser, Saad, and Mason (2023), these technologies frequently resulted in a 20% increase in the accuracy of identifying users' emotions and sentiments. Sentiment analysis is frequently used in information literacy instruction for academic libraries, and these establishments have discovered that it stimulates new ideas, enhanced offerings, and customized services for library patrons. According to Coddera, Romero, and Moya (2017), sentiment analysis has been applied to commercial apps such as IBM Watson, Google Cloud, and Microsoft Azure. These systems have been able to accurately analyze sentiments with 89–90% accuracy by utilizing artificial intelligence neural networks and deep learning techniques. In a similar vein, other programs or APIs, such as Vader or Meanin Cloud Concepnet, likewise demonstrated an equivalent degree of opinion mining accuracy.

Text Mining

According to Arshad et al. (2020), text mining is the method and technology used to search through massive amounts of unstructured and unclassified data and information in the form of text written in natural language to find, retrieve, and extract high-quality, meaningful, and purposeful information. Text mining has been used to examine how libraries use social media to promote their resources and services. This has had a significant impact on how libraries engage with their patrons, strengthening their bonds with them (Al-Daihani and Abrahams, 2015). Information extraction, topic tracking, summarization, classification, clustering, idea linking, information visualisation, and question answering are some of the text mining applications for libraries (Al-Daihani and Abrahams, 2015). According to Arshad et al. (2020), text-mining applications for academic libraries' reference services include:

i) Identifying and specifying particular documents;
ii) Improving predicted accuracy;
iii) Automatic text categorization;
iv) Extracting meaning; and
v) Extracting specific information.

Dixon et al. (2010) state that among the most difficult jobs on academic library websites that have been determined by text mining algorithms are discovering journal articles and journal titles. One proposed by Tang et al. (2008) called ArnetMiner is one of several text-mining experimental projects that have been implemented in academic libraries. Its goals were to model the entire academic network, extract and mine academic social networks, extract researcher profile data from the web, integrate publication data from existing digital libraries into the network, and provide search services for academic work.

Recommender Systems

Recommender systems are software tools and methods that provide relevant recommendations for consumers based on their preferences for certain goods and items. These systems offer consumers a customized experience by allowing them to filter, rate, and select alternatives that may be of interest to them as output. Over the years, there has been a steady increase in research on recommender systems and their applications, especially in the areas of book, document, image, movie, music, retail, and TV show recommendations. Numerous data mining approaches, including association rules, clustering, decision trees, k-nearest neighbour, link analysis, neural networks, regression analysis, and other heuristic methods, have been used by these systems (Park et al., 2012). Recommender systems offer suggestions for goods and services to users based on machine learning algorithms. As an illustration, consider book suggestions made with support vector machines (SVM) and association rules (Das and Islam, 2021).

AI-driven recommender systems have become increasingly important to academic libraries' reference services. Recommender systems have gained popularity in academic libraries as methods for assessing and screening vast volumes of data and enhancing user services. Libraries have employed various recommender systems to leverage various open-source software tools, such as Xiao and Gao's (2020) monograph selection. By selectively providing users with information on recent acquisitions based on their search history and patterns, their use in academic libraries has greatly enhanced access to intellectual materials for academic staff and students. Furthermore, recommendation algorithms generate user profiles based on the ontology of research concerns and suggest papers viewed by persons who are similar to the user (Aguilar, Valdivizo-Diaz, and Riofrio, 2017).

Data Mining (DM) and Information Retrieval

According to Harisanty et al. (2023), artificial intelligence (AI) has enhanced academic libraries' information access by surfacing frequently used search items automatically, discovering documents quickly and precisely, and enhancing search engine usability through voice or text inputs. Academic libraries have been using various digital technologies for information retrieval. DM with AI methods has been one of these technologies. Data mining, which is defined as a knowledge discovery technique that works with huge organized and unstructured information to find hidden patterns, is crucial to academic libraries' reference services. Academic libraries have employed data mining integrated with AI technologies to find hidden patterns and rules, clusters, classifications, research subject identification, social network analysis, and forecast and display models. Khademizadeh and Rafienagab (2023) discovered through their research of the literature that the main use of DM in academic libraries had been to uncover hidden patterns and norms, which were then followed by forecasting future trends. Library administrators can enhance user satisfaction by identifying trends in the use of electronic resources by analyzing data gathered from web portals, library websites, and circulation figures. Librarians may manage and comprehend users and their information demands by using data mining to analyse users' usage habits. This kind of information is useful when disseminating information selectively in web-based contexts using RSS feeds.

Siguenza-Guzman et al. (2015) found that the data mining functions of clustering, association, classification, and regression had been helpful in academic libraries, especially in studying usage behaviour, collection development, and usability of websites and online services. This was in their review of the applications of DM in academic libraries. All of these library service functional domains are characteristics of virtual reference services, which are currently powered by AI. AI applications in libraries seek to improve the retrieval of related articles, their rating, and dissemination to users upon request by using association rules to find associations between items in a database. By segmenting no established clusters, clustering algorithms are utilized to find unexpected trends when training of pre-specified records is not available. This makes it possible for academic libraries to provide specialized reference services to certain users and groups according to their individual information needs based on search patterns and usage habits. Neural networks, k-nearest means algorithms, classification, and analysis are often utilized tools for clustering (Siguenza-Guzmana et al., 2015). However, classification algorithms are used to find patterns when there are predetermined criteria for grouping variables. Neural networks, decision trees, and if-then-else rules are a few examples of tools utilized in this process. Regression statistical techniques include linear regression and logic regression, which map data into practical situations to identify recurring patterns.

Information Literacy

Tella (2022) states that the new information literacy curriculum in Nigeria should cover topics such as 5G, IoT, AI, ML, cloud computing, blockchain, cybersecurity, virtual and augmented reality, and robotics. Numerous models of information literacy have been put to the test as a foundation for instruction and as a means of encouraging information literacy in academic institutions where decision-making necessitates highly technical and refined knowledge (Tella, 2022). Some of these approaches have been developed in response to shortcomings in the conventional information literacy models and instructional programs found in academic libraries.

Since students' use of generative AI has gained attention recently, librarians have been urged to enhance existing information literacy programs and redesign them to appeal more to millennials, who make up the majority of library patrons in academic libraries worldwide. However, calls for the responsible and ethical use of these new and potentially disruptive technologies, particularly in the areas of research and information literacy in academic libraries, must go hand in hand with the transformation of information literacy in academic libraries and the adoption of innovations like AI, among them ChatGPT.

Users and scholars at academic libraries have received information literacy training via ChatGPT, among other reference activities. Information literacy encompasses social ethics and information awareness as well as the knowledge and abilities of information and technology, as well as the capacity to apply it for learning, collaboration, communication, and problem-solving (Shi et al., 2023). Information literacy is the capacity to identify information needs, locate it, and apply it wisely (Akakpo, 2023). According to a Gardijam (2023) study conducted in Croatia, ChatGPT was incorporated into the LIS curriculum and used for information literacy training. Technological developments have made it possible to integrate what Muraszkiew (2019) refers to as a “troika” of AI, IoT, and 5G internet, which work in tandem and complement one another to support information services. According to the report, IoT, AI, and 5G have enhanced one another’s abilities to change academic libraries’ information and educational offerings, especially their reference services. The usage of the internet and web-based services has made it necessary for libraries to train patrons in information literacy, and AI and its related troika have played a big part in this. Nonetheless, reference services in educational institutions are frequently the responsibility of teachers and ICT technologists, and in certain institutions, there have been disagreements about who should provide users with information literacy training and library teaching.

Technology like artificial intelligence (AI) has been discovered to be useful in teaching California State University students who Manuel (2008) refers to as Generation Y (Millennials). The way that this generation of users seeks information has evolved from that of previous generations using libraries; they now favour web and internet services that are characterized by big data, the Internet of Things, and 5G technology. These AI-enabled information literacy skills allow libraries to analyze student learning behaviour. For instance, Chinese universities’ Shi (2023) model, which used these techniques to forecast learning behaviour, was found to have an accuracy value of 92.50%, which helped them modify their ways of instruction. According to Tella (2022), one of the cutting-edge technologies utilized to provide information literacy in the United States is the usage of humanoid robots in the Roanoke County Public Library. Tella (2022) recommended the integration of artificial intelligence (AI) into reference services, namely information literacy, despite noting that none of the university libraries under his investigation had used AI for reference purposes.

CHALLENGES

Several challenges have been identified as hindrances to the usage of AI in academic libraries, specifically for reference purposes. According to Cox, Pinfield and Rutter(2018), these challenges include resource limitations, lack of finance and inadequate infrastructure among academic libraries. From a review by Tella(2022), some challenges that faced libraries in their efforts to use AI for reference purposes were the quality of intelligence generated by the systems, linguistics styles that sometimes can not adapt to the human conversational styles, threats to privacy and threats to intellectual freedom, bias and cost. Other challenges also included a lack of experts, poor networks, poor training, lack of innovation and limited knowledge about the technology. Additionally, academic libraries and educational institutions have been advised to use ChatGPT with caution for instructional methods and reference purposes. However, Adetayo (2023) lists several obstacles that academic libraries must overcome to successfully implement this technology, including lost jobs, improper use of the technology, imprecise query responses, and limited comprehension. University libraries hold vast volumes of data and information, much of which is pricey and user-specific with varying access levels, according to Khaushal and Yadav (2022). Libraries have been hesitant to adopt chatbot technology because of the unavoidable difficulties with system limitations, privacy regulations, and user acceptability, which pose several hazards. Wang et al. (2019) define perceived risk as having two main components: losses (the seriousness of the consequences) and uncertainty (the possibility of unfavourable outcomes) (Khaushal and Yadav, 2022).

CONCLUSION

There is a general acknowledgement that the use of AI for reference purposes in academic libraries helps libraries improve their services and provides personalised support to library users. This has benefited researchers, the student population and academics in general. However, from the results of the review, fewer than anticipated academic libraries have integrated AI into reference services. There have been several challenges that have hindered these institutions from harnessing AI for reference purposes and the key challenges that emerge are lack of funding particularly in the developing world, lack of skills and competence in the design and development of AI solutions for reference purposes and lack of knowledge among library managers on the potential benefits that academic libraries may realise from the use of AI in reference services. Chatbot adoption in academic libraries began in the mid-2000s although researchers have expressed concern at the cost, sustainability and technical limitations among institutions (Yan and Zhao, 2023).

REFERENCES

Adejo, A. A & Misau, A.Y.(2021), Application of artificial intelligence in academic libraries in Nigeria. *Library philosophy and practice(e-journal), 6639.*

Adetayo, A. J. (2023). Artificial intelligence chatbots in academic libraries: The rise of ChatGPT. *Library Hi Tech News*, *3*(3), 18–21. doi:10.1108/LHTN-01-2023-0007

Aguilar, I., Valdivizo-Diaz, P., & Riofrio, G. (2017). (2017). A general framework for intelligent recommender systems. *Applied Computing and Informatics, 13*(2), 147–160. doi:10.1016/j.aci.2016.08.002

Aithal, S & Aithal, P.S (2023). *Effects of AI-based ChatGPT on Higher Education libraries.*

Akakpo, M. G. (2023, November 09). Skilled for the Future: Information Literacy for AI Use by University Students in Africa and the Role of Librarians. *Internet Reference Services Quarterly*. doi:10.1080/10875301.2023.2280566

Al-Daihani, S. M & Abrahams, A. (2015). A text mining analysis of academic libraries tweets. *The Journal of Academic Librarianship, 42(2016), 135-143.*

Arshad, M., Khan, A., Ahmed, P. & Shah, N.A(2020). *Next-Generation Data.*

Ashikuzzaman, M. D (2022). *Reference services of the library and its types.*

Aslam, F. (2023). The impact of artificial intelligence on chatbot technology: a study of the current advancements and leading innovations. *European Journal of Technology.*

Cordell, R. (2022). *Machine learning + libraries. A report on the state of the field.* Library of Congress.

Corredera, A., Romero, M., & Moya, J. M. (2017). Affective computing for smart operations: A survey and comparative analysis of the available tools, libraries and web services. *International Journal of Innovative and Applied Research, 5*(9).

Cox, A. M., & Mazumdar, S. (2022). Defining artificial intelligence for librarians. *Journal of Librarianship and Information Science*. doi:10.1177/09610006221142029

Cox, A. M., Pinfield, S., & Rutter, S. (2018). The intelligent library Thought leaders' views on the likely impact of artificial intelligence on academic libraries. *Library Hi Tech, 37*(3), 418–435. doi:10.1108/LHT-08-2018-0105

De Silva, S. M. (1997). A review of expert systems in library and information science. *Malaysian Journal of Library and Information Science*, 2(2), 57–92.

Dempsey, M. (2011). Blending the trends: A holistic approach to reference services. *Public Services Quarterly*, 7(1/2), 3–17. doi:10.1080/15228959.2011.572769

Dixon, L., Duncan, C., Fegan, J. C., Mandernach, M., & Warlick, S. E. (2010, Winter). Finding articles and journals via Google Scholar, journal portals and link resolvers: Usability study results. *Reference and User Services Quarterly, 50*(2), 170–181. doi:10.5860/rusq.50n2.170

Ehrenpreis, M., & DeLooper, J. P. (2022). *Implementing a chatbot on a library website*. CUNNY Academic Works. Publications and Research. doi:10.1080/19322909.2022.2060893

Emiri, O. T. (2023). *Adoption and utilisation of artificial intelligence by librarians in university libraries in Southern Nigeria. Library Philosophy and Practice (e-Journal)*. Libraries at the University of Nebraska.

Epstein, M. (2018). That thing is so annoying: How proactive chat helps us reach more users. *College & Research Libraries News*, *79*(8), 436. doi:10.5860/crln.79.8.436

Fan, S. C., Fought, R. L., & Gahn, P. C. (2017). Adding a feature: Can a pop-up chat Does the box enhance virtual reference services? *Medical Reference Services Quarterly*, *36*(3), 220–228. doi:10.1080/02763869.2017.1332143 PMID:28714818

Feldman, J. D., Lopez, E., Gaspard, C. S., Barton, K. D., & Barcenes, L. F. III. (2018). Making it work for everyone: An evolving reference service. *Medical Reference Services Quarterly*, *37*(1), 10–18. doi:10.1080/02763869.2018.1404381 PMID:29327989

Gundakanakanal, S. S., & Kaddipujar, M. (2019). Intelligent libraries: New horizons with artificial intelligence. *Journal of Information Management and Educational Technology*, *3*(2&3).

Guy, J., Pival, P. R., Lewis, C. J., & Groome, K. (2023). *Reference chatbots in Canadian academic libraries*. Information Technology and Librarians. doi:10.5860/ital.v42i4.16511

Harisanty, D., Anna, N. E., Putri, T. E., & Firdaus, A. A. (2023). Leaders, practitioners and scientists awareness of artificial intelligence in libraries: A pilot study. *Library Hi Tech*.

Katz, W. A. (2001). *Introduction to Reference Works. 2vols*. McGraw-Hill.

Kaushal, V., & Yadav, R. (2022). The Role of Chatbots in Academic Libraries: An Experience-based Perspective. *Journal of The Australian Library and Information Association*, *71*(3), 215–232. doi:10.1080/24750158.2022.2106403

Khaiser, F. K., Saad, A., & Mason, C. (2023). Sentiment analysis of students' feedback on institutional facilities using text-based classification and natural language processing (NLP). *Journal of Language and Communication*, *10*(1), 101–111. doi:10.47836/jlc.10.01.06

Kumar, V. & Sheshandri, K. (2019). Application of artificial intelligence in academic libraries.

Lapidusa, M., Bond, I., Wentza, E., King, S. B., & Mahnken, S. S. (2020). Measuring the quality of reference services provided by paraprofessionals at an academic library. *Journal of Academic Librarianship*, *46*(5), 102198. doi:10.1016/j.acalib.2020.102198

Lund, B. D., & Wang, T. (2023). Chatting about ChatGTPT: How may artificial intelligence impact on academia and libraries. *Library Hi Tech News*. doi:10.1108/LHTN-01-2023-0009

Luo, L., & Buer, V. B. (2015). Reference service evaluation at an African academic library: The user perspective. *Library Review*, *64*(8/9), 552–566. doi:10.1108/LR-04-2015-0046

Manuel, K. (2002). Teaching Information Literacy to Generation. *Journal of Library Administration*, *36*(1-2), 1–2, 195–217. doi:10.1300/J111v36n01_12

McNeal, M., & Newyear, D. (2013). Introducing chatbots in libraries, Streamlining Information Services Using Chatbots (Library TechnologyReports). ALATechSource, Chicago, IL.

Muraszkiewcz, M. (2019). The synergetic impact of artificial intelligence, the Internet of Things and 5G on information literacy and education. *ZIN*, *57*(2), 7–22.

Musangi, P, S. (2015). Redefining reference services in academic libraries: A critical review. *An International Peer Reviewed Bilingual E-Journal of Library And Information Science, 2*(04).

Nißen, M., Selimi, D., Janssen, A., Cardona, D. R., Breitner, M. H., Kowatsch, T., & von Wangenheim, F. (2022). See you soon again, chatbot. A design taxonomy to characterise user-chatbot relationships with different time horizons. *Computers in Human Behavior*, *107043*(127), 107043. doi:10.1016/j.chb.2021.107043

Noh, Y. (2013). A study on the next-generation digital library using context awareness technology. *Library High Tech.31*(2).

Okpokwasili, N. (2019). *Artificial Intelligence in Libraries and Users Satisfaction in Higher Institutions in Nigeria. International Journal of Research in Informative Science Application & Techniques*. IJRISAT.

Oyetoloa, S.O., Oladokun, D.D., Maxwell, C. E., & Akor, S.O. (2023). *Artificial intelligence in the library: gauging the potential application and implications for contemporary library services in Nigeria.*

Panda, S & Chakravarty. (2021). Implementing conversational AI in libraries: A practical approach. In *Impact of COVID-19 in academic institutions,* 124-145. Springer.

Park, D. H., Kim, H. K., Choi, I. Y., & Kim, J. K. (2012). A literature review and classification of recommender systems research. *Expert Systems with Applications*, *39*(11), 10059–10072. doi:10.1016/j.eswa.2012.02.038

Rieh, S. Y. (1999). Changing reference service environment: A review of perspective from managers, librarians and users. *Journal of Academic Librarianship*, *25*(3), 178–186. doi:10.1016/S0099-1333(99)80197-9

Shi, Y., Sun, F., Zuo, H. & Peng, F. (2023). Analysis of Learning Behavior Characteristics and Prediction of Learning Effect for Improving College Students' Information Literacy Based on Machine Learning. *IEEE Education Society section*. IEEE.

Siguenza-Guzman, L., Saquicela, V., Avila-Ordóñez, E., Vandewalle, J., & Cattrysse, D. (2015). Literature Review of Data Mining Applications in Academic Libraries. *Journal of Academic Librarianship*, *41*(4), 499–510. doi:10.1016/j.acalib.2015.06.007

Singh, B. (2019). SIS: Smart identify systems for library books. *International Journal for Modern Trends in Science and Technology*, *5*(11).

Singh, D. K., Singh, B. K., & Dube, Y. P. (1996). Expert Systems and their Application in Library and Information Systems. *DESIDOC Bulletin of Information Technology*, *16*(4), 9–12. doi:10.14429/dbit.16.4.3272

Stahl, B., Mohnke, J., & Seeliger, F. (2018). Roboter ante portas? About the deployment of a humanoid robot into a library. *Proceedings of the IATUL, Conference Paper 6*. Research Gate.

Tang, J., Zhang, J., Yao, L., Li, J., Zhang, L., & Su, Z. (2008). *ArnetMiner: Extraction and Mining of Academic Social Networks*. KDD'08, Las Vegas, Nevada, USA.

Tella, A. (2020). Robots are coming to libraries: Are libraries ready to accommodate them? *Library Hi Tech News*, *2*(8), 13–17. doi:10.1108/LHTN-05-2020-0047

Tella, A. (2022). Teaching information literacy in Nigerian universities using advanced technologies. *Regional Journal of Information and Knowledge Management*, *7*(2), 38–53.

Tella, A. (2023). Application of Artificial Intelligence for Reference Services in Academic Libraries: A Global Overview through a Systematic Review of Literature. *Journal of Library Resource Sharing*, *32*(1-5), 11–26. doi:10.1080/26915979.2023.2281668

Tyckoson, D. A. (2011). Issues and trends in the management of reference services: A historical perspective. *Journal of Library Administration*, *51*(3), 259–278. doi:10.1080/01930826.2011.556936

Vincze, J. (2017). Virtual reference librarians (chatbots). *Library Hi Tech News*, *34*(4), 5–8. doi:10.1108/LHTN-03-2017-0016

Viyakuma, S., & Sheshadri, K. N. (2019). Applications of artificial intelligence in academic libraries. *International Journal on Computer Science and Engineering*, *7*(16).

Wallace, N., & Feeney, M. (2018). An Introduction to Text Mining: How Libraries Can Support Digital Scholars. [QQML]. *Qualitative and Quantitative Methods in Libraries*, *7*, 23–30.

Wang, Y., Gu, J., Wang, S., & Wang, J. (2019). Understanding consumers' willingness to use ridesharing services: The roles of perceived value and perceived risk. *Transportation Research Part C, Emerging Technologies*, *105*, 504–519. doi:10.1016/j.trc.2019.05.044

Weigert, V. (2020). *Chatbots in libraries.* Library Services. https://libraryservices.jiscinvolve.org/wp/2020/09/chatbots-in-libraries/

Xiao, J., & Gao, W. (2020). Connecting the Dots: Reader Ratings, Bibliographic Data, and Machine-Learning Algorithms for Monograph Selection. *The Serials Librarian*, *78*(1-4), 1–4, 117–122. doi:10.1080/0361526X.2020.1707599

Yan, R., & Zhao, X. (2023). Chatbots in libraries. A systematic literature review. *Education for information,* Research Gate.

Zanin-Yost, A. (2004). Digital reference: What the past has taught us and what the future will hold. *Library Philosophy & Practice*, *7*(1), 1–16.

Zhang, C., & Lu, Y. (2021). Study on artificial intelligence. The state and future prospects. *Journal of Industrial Information Integration*, *23*, 23. doi:10.1016/j.jii.2021.100224

Chapter 8
Optimizing Library Services Through the Integration of Artificial Intelligence Tools and Techniques

Mandira Bairagi
https://orcid.org/0009-0008-0855-6253
Rashtrasant Tukadoji Maharaj Nagpur University, India

Shalini Ramdas Lihitkar
https://orcid.org/0009-0005-1479-490X
Rashtrasant Tukadoji Maharaj Nagpur University, India

ABSTRACT

The use of artificial intelligence (AI) has transformed several industries, including research and education. Due to relevance and global competitiveness, in the present scenario incorporation of artificial intelligence in library workflow is inevitable. Libraries are changing in the age of information explosions to keep up with technological improvements and provide access to the greatest information while avoiding obstacles. This chapter provides a thorough description of the use of artificial intelligence (AI) tools and techniques in distinct sections of Library management and services. Creating devices that can imagine and work like humanoid brains is the aim of artificial intelligence. Artificial intelligence integration has the potential to improve library space intelligence and eliminate physical obstacles. The chapter offers a complete grasp of how AI could alter library infrastructure and services in the future, leading to better outcomes for readers, educators, researchers, and students.

DOI: 10.4018/979-8-3693-1573-6.ch008

INTRODUCTION

The modern world is greatly impacted by technologies and individuals, radically changing our behaviors, emotions, thoughts, and ways of interacting and communicating. Rapid and significant technical breakthroughs are changing teaching and learning approaches at the same time, which is gradually changing the nature of education. Artificial intelligence (AI) is a discipline devoted to solving problems related to human cognition, and it has a remarkable impact on education.

The industry currently refers to the rapidly developing artificial intelligence (AI) technology as the fourth industrial revolution **(Park, 2017)**. In 1956, the official proposal of artificial intelligence was made at an academic meeting in Dartmouth, USA. Additionally, this symposium was acknowledged as a milestone in the development of artificial intelligence worldwide **(McCarthy, 2019)**. The fields of computer science, control science, information science, cognitive science, neuroscience, euro physiology, psychology, linguistics, and brain science have all contributed to the development of artificial intelligence as a comprehensive field. Its main goals are to imitate human intelligence activities, advance the science of human intelligence, and research the creation of intelligent computers or systems. Three categories of artificial intelligence exist: behaviorism, connectionism, and symbolism. Symbolism is a type of intelligent simulation that mimics intelligent human behavior using logical reasoning **(Pence, 2014)**. The learning algorithm and connection mechanism between one neural network and another are the fundamental idea of connectionism. Perceptual-action control and cybernetic theory underpin behaviorism. Problem solving, natural language processing, artificial neural networks, genetic algorithms, expert systems, knowledge engineering, artificial life, deep learning, intelligent control, etc. are now the most popular technical domains in artificial intelligence research **(Haibin, 2016)**.

There are four distinct phases in the evolution of artificial intelligence from 1956 to the present **(Kunying, 2017)**. In the realm of artificial intelligence research, a diverse array of technologies is explored, ranging from expert systems such as flight tracking and medical diagnostics, to natural language processing, exemplified by speech recognition and automatic speech output. Additionally, neural networks play a crucial role, particularly in pattern recognition systems for tasks such as face, character, and handwriting recognition. Furthermore, robots, encompassing industrial and consulting variants, are also integral components of this field's investigation. A few academics further categorize artificial intelligence into the following fields: machine learning, robotics, computer vision, natural language processing, cognition and reasoning, and gaming ethics **(Warwick, 2011)**.

There are numerous classification schemes and a fairly broad definition of artificial intelligence. Artificial intelligence can be classified into three categories based on its overall level: weak artificial intelligence, which is only good in certain areas, strong artificial intelligence, which is comparable to human intelligence, and super artificial intelligence, which is superior to human intelligence overall. Humans have mastered weak artificial intelligence, but strong artificial intelligence has not yet been achieved **(Hongwei, 2018)**, according to the total level of artificial intelligence progress.

Both educators and students use artificial intelligence (AI) applications in education (AIEd) on a large scale these days. These AIEd solutions improve education in conventional classrooms and workplaces by fusing AI with a number of learning sciences, including education, psychology, linguistics, and neuroscience. The primary goal is to push and encourage the development of efficient, adaptable, and personalized AI-driven educational apps **(Chen, 2020)**

In the era of information explosions libraries are also evolving and accommodate with technological advancements and access best information by avoiding various barriers which is required to face. To manage a smart library, various software and tools are using to complete the routine library practices along with introducing new services. RFID technology, the Internet of Things, big data, cloud computing, artificial intelligence, and other cutting-edge technologies are used to deliver the best and most intelligent library services.

In present scenario Artificial Intelligence have a great role in every part of society development. Librarian also can use the advantages of technology in various library work as well as special services. Expert Systems (ES) for cataloguing and searching facility, Natural Language Processing (NLP) for conversation, Speech recognition for virtual assistants, Robotics for reference services are few example where library can successfully use the benefits of intelligent system.

Artificial intelligence (AI) is pervasive in contemporary technology and has great promise for updating, improving, and enhancing a wide range of digital applications. Virtual assistants are one area that academics have frequently been less concerned about, although AI has the potential to disrupt librarianship on several fronts. As mobile usage overtakes other internet access trends, librarians need to be aware of the technical constraints that their clients must deal with.

The Applications of AI technology in modern libraries and the many AI tools that can be used to library services will be discussed in the paper that follows in addition; it will address the positive, negative and ethical issues of implementing AI in libraries and speculate on future applications of AI in modern libraries.

1.1 The characteristics of modern AI benefited libraries are:

(1) The modern library uses cutting edge technologies such and other AI tools to achieve the natural incorporations of patrons and libraries.

(2) Patrons may associate with the same platform, which tracks and gathers user information and personal needs to offer consumers comprehensive, humanized services.
(3) The rate of labor and raw material can be decreased, and library resources can be developed and used rationally with the help of a modern technology enhanced library.
(4) Patrons especially scholars can be complete their task related to library speedily without any hassle.

OBJECTIVES

1. Evaluate AI technology's user experience and efficiency in library workflows.
2. Examining potential future applications and artificial intelligence developments to expand

Library capabilities.

3. Assessing advantage and integration challenges of AI in library operations.
4. Considering the ethical consequences and issues of AI-powered utility tools for libraries.

Redefining Libraries in the Era of AI

Artificial intelligence has a growing impact on how smart phones and the mobile internet are used **(Llanasas 2020)**. Artificial Intelligence has been utilized for improving gadget efficiency, removing glare from images, searching images, and streamlining facial recognition. AI-driven virtual assistants like Siri, which are excellent at speech recognition and internet searches, are also a common component of modern smart phones. The emergence of voice-activated Internet access on smart phones has contributed to the growth of the mobile internet by facilitating users with a convenient, quick, and easy method to obtain information. Users now expect more from libraries in terms of service availability. A variety of data retrieval techniques were flourished to manage the enormous resources stored in libraries and enable users to access it as the amount of information contained inside escalated. Due to the rapid increase in information creation in recent years, to make it easier to find and get items from the library's collection, automated and intelligence-based search systems have been created and implemented., whether they are electronic or paper-based.

People's interactions with information are being redefined by the changes brought about by the mobile internet. When using a smart phone, people are more likely to look for information quickly and specifically than to conduct in-depth research. Because small screens are constrained, more attention is paid to the first few search results. Compared to desktop computer searches, which presently account for around 60% of all searches, patrons concentrate more time on the web pages that come from mobile searches. The way people search is also changing as a result of the growing popularity of virtual assistants like Apple's Siri, Microsoft's Cortana, Amazon's Alexa, and Google Assistant. A recent poll found that over half of youngsters and adults use voice search on a daily basis **(Granitzki 2017)**.

Librarians may demonstrate advanced AI-based search strategies to consumers even with little funding because they have access to free resources. Machine learning has led to the emergence of a new type of literature search software called literature mapping tools (like Research Rabbit or Connected Papers). These programs can produce literature maps that show the connections between earlier, later, and related works when initially seeded with a few relevant important articles. Some of these apps even go so far as to identify other articles that might be of interest and keep track of the literature to recommend relevant articles as they come out.

HARNESSING ARTIFICIAL INTELLIGENCE (AI) FOR ENHANCED LIBRARY MANAGEMENT AND SERVICE OPTIMIZATION

Expert System (ES)

Software designed to offer expert opinions, suggestions, or solutions to certain issues is known as an expert system. Knowledge bases, inference engines, and user interfaces are some of the components that make up expert systems. The knowledge base is used for storage and cataloging process of making collections that exist in digital library, while the inference engine is used to search the detail collection that available in digital libraries such as the ability to work like an expert **(Diviyana et al., 2015)**. By using AI expert systems, library can enhance the accuracy and relevance of search results, helping patrons quickly find the information they need within the library's collection.

Expert systems have a great deal of promise to improve quality and productivity in library operations. These systems are vital for reference services because they teach students how to use references properly, recommend pertinent sources for certain queries, and act as an electronic resource for information specialists and reference librarians. This system includes a thorough comprehension of the reference process, topic-specific information retrieval, and efficient user interaction with the library. Artificial intelligence-based cataloging is currently being automated through two methods: integration with electronic publishing systems and human-machine interfaces. It is not easy to translate AACR2 into the organized rules required for the Expert System to function. With encouraging results, expert systems are being applied in a number of scenarios for library classification:

Coal SORT is a conceptual browser that consists of a frame-based semantic network and software that allows users to navigate the conceptual structure. In the same way, EP-X is a hierarchical frame-based semantic concept network system.

To automatically classify texts, BIOSIS makes use of a knowledgebase. AI applications can use the organized and useful representations of information provided by the indexing languages. Periodic indexing is being done through the development of expert systems. Based on the data supplied by the indexer, these systems are able to draw conclusions and allocate pertinent subdivisions in accordance with those conclusions. The library's Expert System in Acquisition is yet another essential component. Building electronic collections involves the participation of library users, whose counsel and assistance should be sought out at every stage.

Natural Language Processing (NLP)

The computer can interpret questions and answers by using natural language processing to identify the major ideas in each query. The aim is to create and construct a machine that analyzes and produces human-readable language. A wide range of applications are made possible by NLP tools, such as sentiment analysis, language translation, text summarization, and chat bots. These tools have greatly improved the ability to understand and generate human technology. One may initially associate the word NLP with the ability to write or speak in full sentences, process the request through a machine, and then speak.

NLP is applicable in numerous fields of study. Applying this to the study of libraries and information science, and more especially to the process of searching databases like online public access catalogs (OPAC), one can see that indexing is the foundation of document retrieval. "The aim of indexing is to increase precision, the portion of the retrieved documents that are relevant; and recall, the proportion of relevant documents that are retrieved".

It's possible that library users won't realize how vague their search terms are. When natural language is used for Dialog database searches, library users can do direct searches without the help of information professionals. When utilizing an electronic library catalog, a user could want the catalog to comprehend an entire phrase, such as "Find all your sources which contain a mention of natural language processing for the use of Library and information science." The benefit of having a human librarian is that they may serve as a go-between for the machine and the library user because they are skilled in natural language and search and query. Furthermore, some URLs are case-sensitive. Natural language access to the website might be feasible in the future. To fully utilize this new technology, library users must learn how to use a computer.

While early prototypes of Natural Language Inference systems were less capable of handling the complexity of human language, their use has limitations. These artificial intelligence (AI) systems are becoming more advanced. It's debatable if they will ever fully convey the nuances that are particular to human-to-human communication. But more and more commercial applications are making use of scripted and predictable interactions for informational, assistive, social, and instructional purposes. Although there is still a long way to go before conversational bots can provide a fully authentic conversational experience, the potential applications for libraries are undoubtedly fascinating.

Robotics

As a subfield of machine learning, robotics focuses on improving motor and cognitive abilities. Mechanical human beings, robots are automated entities that carry out tasks under direct human control or through pre-programmed instructions using different approaches to artificial reasoning. Artificial intelligence (AI)-powered chatbots can be included into library websites and applications to provide consumers with rapid assistance. Chatbots can answer frequently asked questions, make suggestions, help with basic research requests, or give instructions on how to use a library.

These days, robots are being created to do book retrieval and shelving tasks in libraries. Through a web interface, the improved robotic library system allows users to easily access off-site printed library resources whenever they need them. BookBot technology uses an automated library catalog to make it simple for patrons to request and obtain books. These volumes are then transported to the specified location for user distribution, either within or outside the library.

Libraries are adopting wireless, handheld RFID scanners and readers to swiftly scan their holdings and produce reports on misplaced or missing books. Libraries are also incorporating RFID tags into their collections. Additionally, robots are designed to perform a multitude of tasks within the library setting, ranging from shelving books to retrieving them. The Westport Library in Connecticut recently purchased two robots to help teach patrons and student's computer programming and coding abilities. An artificially intelligent library catalogue was produced by two Aberystwyth University students.

Murphy, 2015 states that the de Young Fine Arts museum in San Francisco purchased two virtual presence robots so that disabled visitors could tour the museum from a distance. A visitor can use the microphone, voice, camera, and screen on a BeamPros robot to engage with other visitors after logging in with it on their computer at home or at work. Robots and artificial intelligence enhance the effectiveness and efficiency of library operations and improve user engagement in libraries, museums, and archival centers.

Recommendation Systems

AI-powered recommendation systems can help library patrons locate new books, articles, or other materials based on their interests and past selections. These technologies enhance surfing and promote exploration by analyzing user activity and providing suitable material recommendations.

In recent times, recommender systems have become highly common on the internet. Several news platforms have posters that say things like, "People who liked this article also liked that one." The objective is to personalize the website's navigation. As the area has developed over time, the concept of a recommender system has changed. **Resnick and Varian (1997)** provide the most well-known description of a recommender system, defining it as a system that can analyze user preferences for certain objects and suggest items that the user might find interesting.

More recently, recommender systems have been given a boost in user pleasure and experience due to the application of various AI algorithms. Artificial intelligence makes preferable recommendations than conventional approaches. Recommender systems have entered a new phase as a result, offering more sophisticated insights into the links between people and things, displaying more complicated data visualizations, and uncovering extensive information in contextual, virtual, demographic, and textural data.

Intelligent Personal Assistants (IPAs)

The intelligent service module's ultimate purpose is to offer ubiquitous active services to library patrons. To do this, it leverages internet technology to create a hybrid online and offline environment that gives users access to a wide range of resources. As previously said, the future of intelligent digital library services will center on active service. The intelligent service module is capable of integrating user-generated data from both the network and the physical library environment, finishing the information screening process and completing the active push to users through intelligent recommendation.

The intelligent service module significantly raises the quality of the library's services by constructing an intelligent perception space for users through a variety of methods, such as automatic perception, embedded situations, and semantic correlation. Intelligent search, intelligent consulting, intelligent space, and intelligent learning are just a few of the individualized services that consumers can receive from the intelligent service module.

With the advent of the huge internet revolution, a new paradigm of communication between humans and machines has emerged (**Santos et al., 2018**). Users that engage in this type of speech-based engagement can virtually converse with another person. The Voice Assistant, also known as the Intelligent Personal Assistant, has gained popularity as a method of human-computer interaction as a result of the recent advancements in Artificial Intelligence and Speech Recognition technology **(Zhang, et al., 2018).**

The IPAs can be a particularly useful tool for persons who are unable to use a keyboard or monitor because of their busy hands and eyes **(Nielsen, 2003)**. In these circumstances, it is more practicable to deploy IPAs with voice recognition capabilities as they would give consumers a more natural person-to-person contact and human-like entity.

Types of Virtual AI Assistants

AI Chatbots. A Computer programs that employ artificial intelligence (AI) to interact with customers via text-based user interfaces on messaging apps, social media sites, and websites. These conversational agents answer questions, aid clients, and carry on conversations in their capacity as virtual assistants. Artificial intelligence (AI) chatbots use machine learning (ML) and natural language processing (NLP) algorithms to learn from human interactions and improve their responses over time.

Conversational Agents. Using both speech and text interfaces, conversational agents allow virtual assistants to have conversations that resemble those of a human, going beyond text-based interactions. Artificial intelligence (AI) systems that are intelligent are designed to recognize complex language patterns, infer user intents, and provide replies that are appropriate for the given context. Conversational AI is included into virtual assistants to improve their skills and provide a more rational and organic user experience.

AI Virtual Assistant. These dependable virtual assistants possess multi-platform and multi-device capabilities and excel in a wide array of duties. Artificial intelligence (AI) virtual assistants are voice-activated, natural language-speaking chatbots that link to several services and apps to provide seamless information access, scheduling, and control over smart home devices. AI virtual assistants like Apple Siri and Amazon Alexa are well-known examples.

Leading Virtual Assistant Technologies and Devices

- **Siri.** With iOS, iPadOS, watchOS, macOS, and tvOS devices, Apple provides its voice-activated personal virtual assistant. It uses voice recognition technology driven by artificial intelligence.
- **Cortana.** Microsoft's personal productivity assistant, leverages the Bing search engine for a number of activities, such as responding to user inquiries and creating reminders.
- **Copilot.** The latest version of the Windows OS comes with an AI assistant called Copilot that may be utilized with any Windows application or program. It offers a chatbot driven by artificial intelligence that imitates a standard Windows user experience.
- **Google Assistant.** This virtual voice assistant software was developed by Google for Android smart phones. Google Assistant may be used to plan events and alarms, play games, adjust hardware preferences, and respond to queries on the user's device.
- **Amazon Alexa.** Alexa is a cloud-based speech service that is accessible on over 100 million Amazon devices and devices made by third parties. It is mostly used through Amazon's line of hands-free speakers, known as Amazon Echo. Users can activate Alexa by calling out the wake word. When the device is ready to accept a command, a light will indicate to the user that Alexa is ready to take it. Common commands include "play pop music" and "what is the weather today." Moreover, Alexa will have access to generative AI with
- **Samsung's Bixby.** Samsung's virtual AI assistant works with various smart refrigerators in addition to mobile devices. Bixby may be used for a number of things, including as reading news articles, scheduling meetings, sending texts, and getting location-specific weather information.
- **Mycroft AI Platform.** The first voice assistant available as an open source project is called Mycroft, and it works with desktop computers, cars, and even Raspberry Pis. The main objective is to make any device into a smart personal assistant by providing voice control.

Text Summarization

Text summaries of books, papers, and other large materials can be automatically generated by AI. This can be useful for people who want to quickly understand a piece of writing without reading it in every detail.

In this present study we are trying to explore the use of AI technology in modern library as well as usage of AI-driven tools for upgrading the skill and speed up work of library patrons especially research scholar and academicians. Library can helps educators and scholars identify relevant software tools concerning the application of AI for educational purposes.

Typically, the first step in any scientific research process is to review the state of the art, which can entail reading a large number of papers (**Bhatia et al., 2012**). By expediting the study process, automatically synthesizing scientific publications would aid researchers in their investigation. Because scientific papers have a distinctive structure and include citation phrases, their automatic summarization is different from that of generic literature. The majority of useful data in scientific publications is displayed as tables, figures, and pseudo code for algorithms. However, a general text does not typically have these features. Consequently, in order to improve the quality of the generated summary and produce ad hoc automatic summarizers, a number of strategies that take into account the unique structure of a scientific paper were put forward.

Data Analytics

To identify trends, patterns, and user behavior, AI algorithms can analyze library data. With the help of this information, librarians can improve collection development, identify popular materials, or improve user experience, among other data-driven choices.

Libraries can better analyze user behavior, provide new services, and enhance existing ones by utilizing data analytics. Libraries produce a great deal of data from their operations, and analytics offers a methodical approach to using this data to make decisions. Libraries may use big data, research data management, the Internet of Things (IoT), and Geographic Information Systems (GIS) to improve their services and show stakeholders how relevant they are by utilizing tools like R for data analytics and visualization. Additionally, libraries can employ data analytics to carry out tasks like statistical inference, regression modeling, retrieval system comparison, data visualization, report production, and prediction, all of which help them to finally demonstrate their value to users and parent companies. Additionally, the application of analytics in libraries offers chances to work in fields like workflow for data analytics, RDM, GIS, and IoT **(Tiwari, A., 2018)**

In general, data analytics is necessary for libraries to better serve their patrons, adjust to the growing volume of data and information, and show stakeholders how valuable they are.

Big Data Used to Improve Discoverability

An AI-powered indexing tool in academic libraries can help users discover new sources of information from a variety of fields by automatically assigning keywords based on concepts it finds in a document through content analysis. They are able to locate more specific and accurate data as a result, supporting their research.

As the ACRL notes, "academic librarians have been integrating AI technology into their collections and using it to enhance discoverability."

To do this, they use artificial intelligence (AI) to improve the metadata for photographs, publications, and theses. This has significantly boosted the caliber of academic collections. Artificial Intelligence (AI) is proven to be a disruptive force in the quickly changing academic library landscape, with numerous benefits to improve cost-effectiveness, operational efficiency, and service efficacy. By using state-of-the-art AI-powered library service platforms, libraries are able to automate workflows and transform collection management for environmentally conscious and progressive practices.

Challenges arise with Artificial Intelligence (AI) and Big Data, particularly when working with huge and dynamic datasets in multiple formats. Librarians looking for relevant information share the belief that big data analytics can help organizations get valuable insights into customer behavior. Using AI to filter various data sources and build smart pipelines that provide reliable, high-quality data to visualization dashboards is the main goal. This makes it easier to evaluate library performance in a timely and transparent manner, which helps to decide what items to add to or remove from the library and helps to find the best content providers.

The surge of structured and unstructured information, known as Big Data, extends beyond libraries and is characterized not only by volume but also by the speed of processing and the multitude of formats **(Pence 2014).** Recent discussions have expanded the dimensions of Big Data to include veracity, value, and variability. Across disciplines and industries, reliance on the analysis of Big Data sources is growing, as emphasized by Clive Humby's comparison of data to the "New Oil" in 2006 (2020). However, for this analogy to hold true, raw data must be appropriately formatted, contextualized, and accessible in a timely manner, a process where AI agents play a vital role. Access to high-quality structured data is crucial for academic researchers and modern companies alike.

Libraries and librarians are already pivotal resources for potential Big Data users. Even modest academic libraries subscribing to numerous databases serve as gateways to proprietary, open access databases, and government data. Librarians assist users in identifying suitable databases and navigating their nuances. While libraries should ideally function as digital data centers for campuses, the trend of users accessing resources remotely or feeling self-sufficient challenges this role.

AI agents emerge as a solution, offering user support anytime, anywhere via smart phones or computers.

Big Data and artificial intelligence complement each other. Cloud data warehouses have mitigated previous challenges in processing Big Data. AI agents assist users in identifying databases, formatting queries, ranking search results, and determining search scope within databases. In the overwhelming sea of data, AI agents become invaluable. To stay relevant in modern research, librarians must expand their support for Big Data resources.

AI technologies are becoming more commonplace in libraries over time, bridging the gap between technology and custom and bringing about important advances. While most librarians have been reluctant to adopt information technologies in the past, some are actively working to develop the skills required to use AI technology in their jobs.Top of Form

1. **User Services Transformation:** The introduction of AI is causing a paradigm shift in academic libraries, which have historically placed a strong emphasis on providing trustworthy and customized services. User relationships are changing as a result of AI-powered chatbots, which are skilled at delivering information quickly and individually. Programming, interlibrary loans, circulation, collection development, and reference are examples of services that are always changing in response to user needs and new technological advancements. In order to meet the changing needs of their patrons for text-based interactions and round-the-clock support, libraries are embracing AI and developing creative programs that instruct users on how to use new AI capabilities safely and effectively. The incorporation of artificial intelligence technology into circulation services is improving the accessibility of digitally native objects. Not only can personalized recommendations enhance user experience, but they also protect sensitive data by drawing on past searches and borrowing patterns of the user.
2. **Focus on AI and Data Literacy:** As information literacy has developed, it has also included data literacy and AI literacy. Libraries play a vital role in developing these essential skills, enabling users to confidently navigate an AI-dependent society. While AI literacy includes knowing the rationale, limitations, possible impacts, and goal of AI, data literacy focuses on thinking critically about data. Libraries are essential for promoting AI literacy because they give users the tools they need to interact with AI processes and tools.
3. **Analytics Revolution:** Libraries used to rely solely on static data for analysis, which was a laborious process that produced out-of-date and useless information. By identifying trends almost instantly, the integration of AI with library analytics is transforming this methodology. AI-generated insights can

be used by librarians to improve library services through effective planning and administration.

The Use of AI is Changing the Role of Librarians and Has Several Significant Implications

1. **Content Indexing Enhancement**: By recognizing concepts and allocating pertinent keywords, AI techniques raise the consistency and caliber of content indexing. Automation surpasses human capacities and supports librarians in their work by accelerating the discovery of new material across disciplines. In comparison, manual indexing approaches are less multidisciplinary and take a lot of time.
2. **Efficient Document Matching**: Artificial intelligence processes documents faster and more accurately than humans. Researchers and libraries can get knowledge more quickly when publications are properly indexed, which makes it possible to identify similarities and differences between them quickly.
3. **Citation System Transformation**: When analysing researcher networks, AI algorithms offer a more sophisticated understanding than conventional citation systems. AI algorithms go beyond the constraints of popularity-based citation systems by concentrating on the content of papers, providing better mapping of the research environment and assessments of the literature.
4. **Advances in Content Summarization**: Artificial intelligence (AI) technologies contribute to improved information accessibility by supporting extractive and abstractive summarization. Information consumption is made easier by automatic content summarizing, which decreases the requirement for human involvement.
5. **Improved Service Quality:** By offering resources and unambiguous responses, chatbots driven by AI improve the consumer experience. Librarians can focus on more difficult work by automating repetitive requests, which could lead to an extension of library service hours.
6. **Future Impact Factor Assessment:** By analyzing arguments and cross-referencing with other studies, future AI algorithms may assess the standard of scientific study. This change places more emphasis on trustworthy and proven findings than it does on readership numbers.
7. **Operational Efficiency Boost**: By reducing costs and improving service efficacy, AI helps to boost operational efficiency. Cutting-edge library service platforms maximize collection analysis, visualization, and preservation when combined with machine learning.

Tools Which are Used to Apply AI Technologies for Educational and Library Purposes

AI tools can be incredibly valuable for students, academicians and scholars across various disciplines. Academic libraries have significantly increased their digital offerings in recent years, not only to include electronic books and journal articles but also to enable the discovery and usage of software applications. Despite the fact that some academic librarians may claim they lack a basic understanding of AI or that they are unqualified to speak on the topic, they have probably been interacting with AI through the various software programs they support.

These days, citation management programs serve as a hook to get users back to the library and librarian for assistance, as fewer people visit the library and many believe they can access reliable, high-quality content online. Product designers can learn a lot from librarians about how effectively their products function with databases licensed by libraries. They can also get feedback from user interactions and regular testing of new features and iterations of the product. The librarian's worth to the institution does grow when they become experts in using and utilizing these programs to support the researchers, faculty, and students of the library.

AI Tools for Academia and Research

1. **Research Rabbit** (https://www.researchrabbit.ai)

Using Research Rabbit, a "citation-based literature mapping tool," users can contribute one or more papers (seed papers) to the text corpus. The application will locate related papers and display, on network maps, the relationships between the seed papers and related publications. Users of Research Rabbit must register for an account in order to set up notifications, and the service is free.

2. **Puzzle Labs** (https://www.puzzlelabs.ai/)

It is a user-driven glossary powered by AI. Puzzle Labs can assist us in structuring data into knowledge-filled treasure troves that will pique the interest and encourage learning in our visitors of all ages.

3. **Scite** (https://scite.ai/assistant)

Discovering and assessing scientific papers with Smart Citations is made easier with the award-winning scite platform. With the use of Smart Citations, which describe the citation's context and classify the citations according to whether they support or refute the cited claim, users can easily understand how a scientific publication has been cited. This helps Librarians to provide accurate, credible answers that patrons can depend on.

Features

- Evaluate the credibility of a paper by analyzing its citations and identify any retractions or corrections.
- Identify potential collaborators or competitors in your research area by analyzing their citation networks.
- Track the impact of your own research by monitoring its citation metrics.

4. Open Read (https://www.openread.academy/)

Open Read is an AI-powered interactive platform that offers users a thorough and user-friendly method for arranging, interacting with, and evaluating different types of literature, including papers, journals, and research materials. The platform has many features, like Paper Espresso, which helps academics save time by digesting documents and producing literature reviews, and a Q&A system that answers queries about studies quickly.

The AI technology of the platform eliminates the need for laborious reading by extracting statistics, formulas, tables, and other crucial facts from research articles. Additionally, Open Read has a robust note-taking system that makes taking notes more efficient by organizing, linking, and back linking notes in various contexts so that they are easier to access when needed.

5. **Cohesive** (https://cohesive.so/)

Creating, honing, editing, and publishing excellent writing without having to worry too much about prompts is possible with Cohesive, an AI editor. For YouTube videos, Instagram captions, Facebook posts, content rephrasing, story creation, and much more, you may write scripts.

6. **Consensus** (https://consensus.app/)

Librarians can give patrons information supported by peer-reviewed research by using consensus. By doing this, the knowledge exchanged is guaranteed to be accurate and credible, enhancing public confidence in the library as a reliable source. It helps to conduct the effective research. It aggregates findings directly from scientific studies.

7. **Lateral** (https://www.lateral.io/)

Lateral AI is an online application that can help you read articles up to ten times faster by reading, finding, organizing, and sharing your research in one location. This robust instrument boasts an easy-to-use interface that streamlines the research process, even given its intricate nature.

Librarians can work together and exchange expertise with other information specialists through Lateral. This encourages a community-driven strategy that keeps libraries creative and improves research capacities.

8. **End Note** (https://endnote.com/)

End Note automates citation management for librarians, saving time and effort when researching programs, grants, and other projects. Accurate citations also ensure information shared is properly attributed.

End Note can import references in four different ways:

1. Enter them into a template (last resort, mostly for elusive references unavailable online, such as personal correspondence, websites, and maps).
2. The best approach is a direct export from a database.
3. Use End Note as a database and catalog search engine.
4. Do a database search, save the results to your desktop, and then utilize EndNote's import function.

AI Tools to Enhance Patron Experiences

1. **Botsonic** (https://writesonic.com/botsonic)

Chatbots allow librarians to be in two places at once! By training a bot with our library's knowledge, we extend our personal assistance beyond the front desk. Patrons can get quick answers around the clock to basic questions, freeing up librarians to tackle more complex research needs.

2. **Quick Chat** (https://www.quickchat.ai/)

A library chatbot can handle basic inquiries, freeing up librarians to focus on in-depth research and personalized assistance. AI chatbots provide patrons with around-the-clock access to information, improving the self-service experience.

3. **Copyscape** (https://www.copyscape.com/)

Librarians can use Copyscape to ensure library materials are original and do not contain plagiarized content. This protects the library's integrity and sets a good example for patrons.

Copyscape offers two more potent professional solutions to stop content theft and fraud in addition to a free plagiarism checker for locating copies of your web pages online. Better plagiarism detection than the free version is offered by Copyscape Premium, which also offers a ton of other features including batch search, private index, case tracking, uploading PDF and Word files, originality checks via copy and paste, an API, and WordPress connection.

Through automatic daily or weekly web scanning and email notifications when new copies of your content are discovered, Copy sentry offers complete protection for your website. A free tool to compare two online pages or articles, a thorough guide about plagiarism, and free plagiarism warning banners for your website are all provided by Copyscape.

AI Tools to Accelerate Productivity for Librarian

1. **MEM** (https://get.mem.ai/)

An AI assistant can be a librarian's secret weapon! With MEM's help, we can juggle a million tasks, remember every detail, and make the most of each precious minute. This means we have more time to devote to helping patrons directly.

2. **Dante** (https://dante-ai.com/)

Before anything is printed, librarians can work with an AI editor to remove typos, consistency issues, and other mistakes. We may present a positive picture of our institutions by producing polished, error-free, and professional library communications with Dante's assistance. Instead of typing, speak with Dante AI, and get voice responses.

3. **AndiSearch** (https://andisearch.com/)

An intelligent search assistant can help librarians efficiently navigate the vast amount of information needed to answer complex patron questions. AI-guided research expedites the discovery of relevant resources and knowledge.

Andi is a precise, ad-free, and privacy-focused artificial intelligence chatbot. It makes use of a novel kind of search engine that combines real-time data, semantic search technology, and generative AI. Andi provides you with answers instead of simply links; it's like conversing with an intelligent buddy.

4. **Chat PDF** (https://www.chatpdf.com/)

Without having to read the entire research report, librarians can rapidly summarize it using ChatPDF. This helps patrons receive timely, pertinent information to support their job while also saving time. By posting a relevant PDF, anyone can ask questions they may have.

5. **Perplexity AI** (https://www.perplexity.ai/)

Perplexity AI can assist librarians in staying up to date with the latest research trends. This ensures library resources incorporate current knowledge and information to meet patrons' evolving needs.

6. **Audio Pen** (https://audiopen.ai/)

AudioPen can transcribe audio recordings for librarians, saving time and effort. This makes spoken content like interviews, lectures, and oral histories searchable and accessible for patrons. Recording ourselves with the app feels natural and it quickly summaries and transcribes what we say. When we are on the go and just have access to our phones, or when we are not in the mood to open our laptops, the web app has come in quite handy.

7. **Cataloging.ai** (https://in.linkedin.com/company/cataloging-ai)

Cataloging.ai can generate metadata for library items, saving librarians from the tedious task of manual data entry. This frees up time for more valuable tasks that directly serve patrons.

Create, arrange, and update product catalogs in e-commerce with the use of catalog artificial intelligence (AI). Beyond simple automation, though, is its functionality. Product data is also analyzed, categorized, and improved with the use of machine learning algorithms. Using catalog AI can provide a number of major advantages, including:

1. Teams will have less work to do, freeing them up to concentrate on more strategically important parts of the company.
2. The manual cataloging technique has very high possibilities for human mistake where as in automation chances are minimal.
3. Individualized suggestions produced by AI systems after examining the preferences and interactions of users.

4. The provision of highly personalized offerings has resulted in an enhanced user experience and subsequently increased conversion rates. The provision of highly personalized offerings has resulted in an enhanced user experience and subsequently increased conversion rates.

8. Flixier (https://flixier.com/)

Flixier can transcribe audio/video materials for librarians, making the content searchable, shareable, and accessible. This allows spoken content to reach and benefit a wider audience. Video, picture, sound, transition, auto-subtitle, and much more can all have text added to them. Furthermore, don't need to download or install any software to quickly trim, clip, or crop videos. Regardless of skill level, produce high-quality material quickly. To fulfill the demands of all users, Flixier blends a robust UI with pre-made drag and drop capabilities.

9. **Quillbot** (https://quillbot.com/)

Librarians are only as good as the words we put on the page. Quillbot helps ensure our writing is clear, concise, and correct - whether it's for signage, newsletters, or grant proposals. Well-crafted communications help us effectively engage and inform our patrons.

KEY FEATURES

Content summary, plagiarism detection, and grammatical check. Thus, scholars, essayists, and authors can reap significant advantages from Quillbot AI. It can take a lot of effort to produce professional, high-quality material. Quillbot uses AI to speed up the process by providing one-click solutions and real-time writing advice. It is also less expensive because it is an all-in-one solution that eliminates the need to buy several instruments.

10. **Grammarly** (https://www.grammarly.com/)

Writing for clients is a librarian's daily task. Grammarly ensures that writing is well-edited and businesslike. It increases customer confidence that they can rely on the information it provides by getting rid of embarrassing errors. It's a free Grammar checker.

AI Tools to Aid Marketing and Promotions for Librarians

1. **Fable Fiesta** (https://fablefiesta.com/)

Storytelling is magic, and Fable Fiesta can help librarians weave spells that cast imagination on our youngest patrons. With AI assistance, we can create captivating characters and worlds that will spark children's creativity and love of reading. It is excellent AI story and script generator, dynamic character and world builder as well as intelligent plot generator.

Make compelling stories, engrossing scenes, and memorable characters by utilizing AI's in-depth knowledge of narrative structures. Simplify the writing process and use AI to realize your creative vision.

2. **Copy AI** (https://www.copy.ai/)

AI content tools allow librarians to spend less time writing from scratch and more time curetting and customizing generated text. This means we can create more marketing materials, instruction guides, and handouts - all of which help patrons make the most of our resources and services.

3. **Canva AI** (https://www.canva.com/ai-art-generator/)

Librarians can use Canva's AI features to quickly design eye-catching visuals for marketing library events, programs, and services. Beautiful graphics and images help attract patrons and increase engagement.

Canva Pro Features

1. Background Remover. Ideal for transparent PNGs, headshots, and product photographs, click to eliminate image backgrounds.
2. High-end media. Get free access to whole image, element, video, and audio library.
3. Instantaneous animation;
4. Social media scheduling;
5. Templates.
6. Images those are transparent.
7. Adjust design sizing.
8. Adhere to your brand.

4. Craiyon (https://www.craiyon.com/)

Craiyon allows librarians to transform abstract concepts into vivid illustrations that bring library collections, stories, and themes to life. AI-generated images can enhance newsletters, handouts, and signage.

Key Features:

1. No sign-up needed; this web app is free to use.
2. An intuitive interface for text prompts.
3. Produce imaginative, superior AI artwork.
4. Paintings, drawings, digital art, and photorealistic pictures.
5. Manage the composition, styles, and features of the image.
6. Get watermark-free versions of the created photographs.

5. AnyWord (https://anyword.com/)

AnyWord can help librarians write catchy headlines, compelling social media posts, and engaging descriptions that attract more patrons. AI-assisted copywriting ensures library communications stand out and motivate action.

6. Midjourney (https://www.midjourney.com/)

Librarians can use Midjourney to create interactive experiences that immerse patrons in the world of library collections. AI-generated art and visuals can enhance story times, book discussions, and exhibits - sparking imagination and learning. The generative artificial intelligence application and service, developed and hosted by the San Francisco-based independent research lab Midjourney, Inc. Similar to OpenAI's DALL-E and Stability AI's Stable Diffusion, it's uses natural language prompts to produce images.

7. Lexica - AI (https://lexica.art/)

AI art tools allow librarians to explore new ways of visualizing and representing library collections. AI-generated images inspired by library materials can add aesthetic appeal to communications and spark creative thinking. Lexical AI can distinguish between and within data sets of people, locations, and objects (drugs, illnesses, gadgets, therapies, and organizations). Using cutting edge machine learning and computational semantic models, messy data is automatically cleaned and linked.

8. Chatsonic - AI (https://writesonic.com/chat)

An AI tool like Chat GPT but enhanced to stay on top of current and recent events. Aids in easy access of information and inspiration for librarians aiming on incorporating creative strategies in promoting their library services.

Key Features:

1. Provides a selection of templates for speedy content creation
2. Has an integrated plagiarism detector to guarantee that the information is original.

3. Offers recommendations on word choice, tone, and sentence structure
4. Features an intuitive UI for entering ideas allows for real-time content language switching using "language switching."
5. Connects to other programs, such Word Press and Google Docs

9. Tableau (https://www.tableau.com/products/tableau-ai)

Data visualization tools help librarians transform complex statistics into easy-to-understand graphics and dashboards. This allows library stakeholders to make more informed decisions based on data, leading to improved services, operations, and outcomes.

Potentiality and Limitations of AI Application in Library

Enhanced Access: Making massive knowledge repositories easier to access by utilizing AI-powered search and recommendation systems. Giving users access to individualized material. The revolution in collaboration that will turn traditional library spaces into hotspots for AI-enabled collaboration, promoting information sharing and teamwork virtually.

Data management: AI-driven metadata tagging and classification that optimizes data organization and preservation, ensuring effective information retrieval.

User Experience: Improving user experience with interactive interfaces and virtual assistants powered by AI, supplying assistance and simple navigation.

Among Librarians, Scholars, and Technologists, there has been a lot of interest in and discussion about the future of libraries in the age of AI. There is rising fear that the traditional function of libraries as stores of knowledge and information may become obsolete given the rapid breakthroughs in artificial intelligence (AI) and machine learning. AI gives a chance for libraries to evolve and adapt to the changing demands of their customers and the larger society, rather than predicting the demise of libraries.

Automation of various procedures and processes is one of the most important ways AI is anticipated to affect libraries. For instance, using AI-powered systems to sort and categorize massive amounts of data would make it simpler for librarians to manage and preserve their collections. By focusing on more strategic and user-centric tasks like creating new services and programs to fulfil their clients' needs, this can free up significant time and resources for librarians to devote to other tasks.

It is more crucial than ever to take into account the user's interaction with AI because libraries and users are closely intertwined. Libraries are struggling to remain relevant in a digital world that has long sought to demonstrate the field's obsolescence. Librarians who work hard to enhance their users' experiences have demonstrated the resilience of libraries. Academic libraries must strive to integrate AI awareness and applications into their spaces, just as they did with maker spaces.

AI can help libraries in the delivery of individualized services, which is another area where it can be useful. AI algorithms can assist libraries in delivering individualized information and recommendations to their users by assessing user data and preferences. Increasing user involvement and happiness through this can assist. Additionally, AI can significantly improve the accessibility of library resources, especially for users with disabilities. To make audio and video content more accessible to people who are hard of hearing or deaf, for instance, AI-powered solutions can be used to automatically generate captions and transcripts for audio and video content. AI may also be used to create text-to-speech systems that make it easier for people with visual impairments to access textual content.

In the age of AI, libraries can also serve as hubs for the creation and transfer of AI knowledge. Libraries may assist in supplying its users with the information and abilities they need to survive and thrive in a society that is becoming more and more AI-driven by providing seminars, courses, and other learning opportunities. This may aid in positioning. This can help position libraries as vital hubs for lifelong learning and innovation, and strengthen their role as community anchors.

Overcoming Challenges: Integrating Artificial Intelligence in Libraries

Before implementing artificial intelligence (AI) in libraries, there are a number of problems that need to be carefully considered. Financial limitations are a notable obstacle because implementing AI calls for a strong infrastructure and state-of-the-art technological resources. Libraries might find it difficult to successfully assist AI without sufficient resources **(Ajani, 2022)**.

Another major challenge is resistance to change. It is possible that certain librarians would not readily embrace new technology, which will hinder the smooth incorporation of AI into library services. This problem is made worse by unfavorable opinions about librarians' IT competence, since a lack of knowledge can prevent AI from being used successfully **(Vijayakumar and Sheshadri, 2019)**.

Additionally, challenges such as poor networking, unreliable power supply, insufficiently trained personnel, and reliance on outdated technologies compound the difficulties associated with AI implementation **(Echedom and Okuonghae, 2022)**. Moreover, the high costs associated with acquiring and maintaining technological tools present further economic barriers.

Accepting AI, though, has the potential to revolutionize library operations despite these obstacles. AI has the capacity to provide quick and effective services to both current and past customers, from improving information delivery services to saving time and money.

In conclusion, even if there are a lot of obstacles in the way of integrating AI in libraries, these issues may be resolved with careful planning and financial support, opening the door to a day when these technologies will be used by libraries to improve services and connect with their local communities.

But there are also certain ethical and privacy issues with the incorporation of AI into libraries. For instance, concerns over user privacy and data security may arise when AI algorithms are used to evaluate user data and offer customised services. Libraries will need to strike a careful balance between using AI to enhance their services and upholding the faith of their patrons. Furthermore, if AI systems proliferate in libraries, there is a chance that they could unintentionally reinforce current prejudices and inequality. The reinforcement of prejudices and discriminatory behaviours, for instance, may result from AI systems that were trained on biased data. Libraries will need to be watchful in making sure that their AI systems are created and implemented in a way that supports fairness, inclusivity, and diversity.

CONCLUSION

To sum up, the incorporation of artificial intelligence (AI) into library operations is a critical step towards enhancing the caliber and reach of library services in the digital era. The dynamic future of librarianship is being shaped by the collaborative relationship between human competency and AI capabilities, which streamlines operations and frees up librarians to work on more difficult jobs. In conclusion, the integration of AI into library operations represents a pivotal step in improving the quality and accessibility of library services in the digital age. By streamlining processes and freeing up librarians to focus on more challenging assignments, the collaborative link between human competence and AI capabilities is shaping a dynamic future for the field of librarianship.

AI tools for librarians have a lot of potential, but if they are not created in an inclusive and ethical manner, there may be problems. We must support AI that empowers all users and leaves no one behind as information professionals. It is imperative that we make sure the human element, which is fundamental to any library, is enhanced rather than replaced by this new technology. It might be prudent to place more emphasis on the potential advantages of AI for academic libraries, highlighting chances to streamline labor-intensive processes and reallocate funds to initiatives that help advance libraries up the institutional value chain. Giving AI prominence in academic library planning seems like a smart way to embrace AI, while also allowing time for experimentation and indicating an understanding of the potential for significant change **(Huang et al., 2023)**.

The future of libraries ultimately lies not in the power of machine learning, but rather in our common humanity and the relationships we build with one another through the exchange of knowledge. The functions that librarians play should be enhanced by these technologies, not replaced, so that we can continue to serve our communities for many years to come.

Active exploration is unquestionably justified if new technologies can speed up goal-achieving or increase the effectiveness of professional processes. However, concrete application needs to take into account other factors, like financial availability, value generated, institutional support, and librarians' technical expertise. Technology may not be embraced if there are significant obstacles or if conventional approaches still function well. The inclusion of AI in HE agendas these days, however, should encourage a certain amount of active participation with an emphasis on practical and moral applications.

In conclusion, the future of libraries in the AI era is both promising and difficult. While AI has the potential to improve libraries in a variety of ways, it also raises a number of ethical and practical issues that should be properly studied and resolved. Libraries can develop and continue to be relevant in a world that is changing quickly by embracing AI and its potential. However, they must also uphold their fundamental principles of stimulating learning, facilitating access to information, and acting as welcoming spaces for all people of their communities.

REFERENCES

Ajani, Y. A., Tella, A., Salawu, K. Y., & Abdullahi, F. (2022). Perspectives of librarians on awareness and readiness of academic libraries to integrate artificial intelligence for library operations and services in Nigeria. *Internet Reference Services Quarterly*, *26*(4), 1–18. doi:10.1080/10875301.2022.2086196

Altmami, N. I., & Menai, M. E. B. (2020). Automatic summarization of scientific articles: A survey. *Journal of King Saud University. Computer and Information Sciences*, *34*(4), 1011–1028. https://creativecommons.org/licenses/by-nc-nd/4.0/. doi:10.1016/j.jksuci.2020.04.020

Angela, O. N., Adekoya, O. M., & Zajime, B. N. (2021). Integration of artificial intelligence into library and information workflow for enhanced services in developing economies. *Ahmadu Bello University Library Complex International Conference Book of Proceedings*, 663–671.

Asemi, A., & Asemi, A. (2018). Artificial Intelligence (AI) application in Library Systems in Iran: A taxonomy study. Library Philosophy and Practice (e-journal). https://digitalcommons.unl.edu/libphilprac/1840

Bairagi, M., & Lihitkar, S. Empowering Libraries: AI-Driven Tools and Techniques for Digital Transformation and Sustainable Innovation. UPA. *National Journal*, *10*(1), 388–396.

Banerjee, M. S. (2022). Advantage and disadvantage of artificial intelligence in library services. *International Journal of Creative Research Thought*, *10*(11).

Bhatia, S., & Mitra, P. (2012). Summarizing figures, tables and algorithms in scientific publications to augment search results. *ACM Transactions on Information Systems*, *30*(1), 1–24. doi:10.1145/2094072.2094075

Chen, X., Xie, H., & Hwang, G. (2020). A multi-perspective study on Artificial Intelligence in Education: Grants, conferences, journals, software tools, institutions, and researchers. *Computers & Education*, *1*, 1–11. doi:10.1016/j.caeai.2020.100005

De Silva, S. M. (1997). A review of expert systems in library and information science. *Malaysian Journal of Library and Information Science*, *2*(2), 57–92.

Dheshan, M., & Teja, D. S. (2022). Application of artificial intelligence in content management systems. *International Journal of Recent Advances in Science & Engineering*, *1*(1). https://www.ijrase.com

Divayana, D., Gede, H., Ariawan, P. W., Sugiarta, M., & Wayan, A. I. (2015). Digital library of expert system based at Indonesia technology university. *International Journal of Advanced Research in Artificial Intelligence*, *4*(3). https://www.ijarai.thesai.org

Echedom, A. U., & Okuonghae, O. (2021). Transforming academic library operations in Africa with artificial intelligence: opportunities and challenges: a review paper. *New Review of Academic Librarianship*, *27*(2), 243–255. doi:10.1080/13614533.2021.1906715

Frackiewicz, M. (2023). The Future libraries in the age of AI. Retrieved September 25, 2023. https://ts2.space/en/the-future-of-libraries-in-the-age-of-ai/

Goksel, N., & Bozkurt, A. (2019). Artificial intelligence in education: Current insights and future perspectives. In S. Sisman-Ugur & G. Kurubacak (Eds.), *Handbook of research on learning in the age of transhumanism* (pp. 224–236). IGI Global., doi:10.4018/978-1-5225-8431-5.ch014

Hervieux, S., & Wheatley, A. (2021). Perceptions of artificial intelligence: A survey of academic librarians in Canada and the United States. *Journal of Academic Librarianship*, *47*(1), 102270. doi:10.1016/j.acalib.2020.102270

Hewitt, J. A. (1991). Intelligent library systems: Artificial intelligence technology and library automation systems. Advances in Library Automation and Networking. http://www.elsevier.com. In JAI Press, 4 (pp. 1–23).

Hongwei, M. (2018). Thinking on the Ethical Problems of Strong Artificial Intelligence and Weak Artificial Intelligence. *Science and Society*, *8*(1).

Huang, Y. C. A. M., Cox, J., & Cox, J. (2023). Artificial Intelligence in academic library strategy in the United Kingdom and the Mainland of China. *Journal of Academic Librarianship*, *49*(6), 102772. doi:10.1016/j.acalib.2023.102772

Jaillant, L., & Rees, A. (2023). Applying AI to digital archives: Trust, collaboration and shared professional ethics. *Digital Scholarship in the Humanities*, *38*(2), 571–585. doi:10.1093/llc/fqac073

Kaijun, Y., Gong, R., Sun, L. & Chunguo, J. The application of artificial intelligence in smart library. Advances in Economics, Business and Management Research, 100, 708–713. doi:10.2991/icoi-19.2019.124

Lee, S. (2023). 7 Ways Librarians Can Prepare for the Future and Start Using AI at Work. Retrieved September 25, 2023. https://grtech.com/blog/ways-librarians-can-use-ai-for-future

Li, R., Huang, Z., Kurniawan, E., & Ho, C. K. (2015). AuRoSS: An autonomous robotic shelf scanning system. *IEEE/RSJ International Conference on Intelligent Robots and Systems (IROS)*, 6100–6105. DOI: 10.1109/IROS.2015.7354246

Liu, H. (2016). *Artificial Intelligence and Its Evolution*. Science Press.

Llanasas, R. (2020). "How AI and Machine Learning are Transforming Mobile Technology." Retrieved December 26, 2023 Greenbook Blog: https://www.greenbook.org/mr/market-research-technology/how-ai-is-transforming-mobile-technology/

J. McCarthy, M. Minsky & N. Rochester(2019). A Proposal for the Dartmouth Summer Research Project on Artificial Intelligence, 1(12).

Michos, S., Stamatatos, E., & Fakotakis, N. (1999). Supporting multilinguality in library automation systems using ai tools. *Applied Artificial Intelligence*, *13*(7), 679–703. doi:10.1080/088395199117243

Mogali, S. S. (2014). Artificial Intelligence and its applications in Libraries. Retrieved January2nd, 2024 https://www.researchgate.net/publication/287878456

Omame, I. M, and Alex-Nmecha (2020). Artificial intelligence in libraries (pp. 120–144). Jackson College. doi:10.4018/978-1-7998-1116-9.ch008

Park, S. (2017). The Fourth Industrial Revolution and Implications for Innovative Cluster Policies. *AI & Society*, *2017*, 1–13.

Pence, H. E. (2014). What is Big Data and Why is it Important? *Journal of Educational Technology Systems*, *43*(2), 159–171. doi:10.2190/ET.43.2.d

Rhanoui, M., Mikram, M., Yousfi, S., Kasmi, A., & Zoubeidi, N. (2022). A Hybrid recommender system for patron driven library acquisition and weeding. *Journal of King Saud University. Computer and Information Sciences*, *34*(6), 2809–2819. doi:10.1016/j.jksuci.2020.10.017

Rubin, V. L., Chen, Y., & Thorimbert, L. M. (2010). Artificially intelligent conversational agents in libraries. *Library Hi Tech*, *28*(4), 496–522. doi:10.1108/07378831011096196

Tiwari, A. (2018). Data analytics in Library and Information Centers. Retrieved January 4th, 2024. https://www.researchgate.net/publication/327389981

Vijaykumar, S., & Sheshadri, K. N. (2019). Applications of artificial intelligence in academic libraries. *International Journal on Computer Science and Engineering*, *7*(16), 136–140. doi:10.26438/ijcse/v7si16.136140

Vysakh, C., & Babu, R. H. (2019). Application of Artificially Intelligent Robot in Libraries. E-Proceedings. Reshaping of librarianship, innovations and transformation. ICRLIT.60-63. https://www.researchgate.net/publication/338712408

Warwick K (2011). Artificial Intelligence. Hoboken:Taylor& amp;Francis. 13-59.

Yasar, K., & Botelho, B. (2023). Retrieved January 3rd, 2024. https://www.techtarget.com/searchcustomerexperience/definition/virtual-assistant-AI-assistant

Yi, Z. (2021). Research on intelligent service mode of digital library based on data intelligence 4th International Conference on Advanced Electronic Materials, Computers and Software Engineering (AEMCSE). 10.1109/AEMCSE51986.2021.00192

Zhang, K., & Zhang, J. (2017). New District, Misunderstanding, Blind Zone and Forbidden Zone in the Application and Research of Artificial Intelligence Education. *Journal of Distance Education*, *5*, 54–63.

Zhang, Q., Lu, J., & Jin, Y. (2021). Artificial intelligence in recommender systems. *Complex & Intelligent Systems*, *7*(1), 439–457. doi:10.1007/s40747-020-00212-w

KEY TERMS AND DEFINITIONS

Artificial Intelligence Tools: A software program that employs artificial intelligence algorithms to carry out particular duties and resolve issues is known as an AI tool.AI solutions can be used to automate processes, analyze data, and enhance decision-making across a range of industries, including marketing, finance, healthcare, and education.

Big Data: Big data refers to vast and varied databases that have enormous volumes and expand quickly over time. In order to address business issues and make wise judgments, big data is utilized in predictive modeling, machine learning, and other advanced analytics.

Data Analytics: Analyzing unprocessed data to identify patterns and provide answers is known as data analytics. It covers a wide range of fields. This process involves a wide range of methods and objectives that vary depending on the industry.

Expert System: An expert system is a computer program that mimics the decision-making and actions of a person or a group of people with knowledge and experience in a certain area by utilizing artificial intelligence (AI) technologies. Typically, the goal of expert systems is to support human experts rather than to replace them.

Natural Language Processing: The goal of natural language processing (NLP), a subfield of computer science, linguistics, and artificial intelligence, is to enable computers to understand human language—including speech and text. Numerous commonplace goods and services employ natural language processing. Voice-activated digital assistants on smart phones, email scanning apps that detect spam, and translation apps that interpret foreign languages are a few of the most popular applications of natural language processing (NLP).

Chapter 9
AI-Powered Recommendation Systems and Resource Discovery for Library Management

R. Sivasankari
https://orcid.org/0000-0002-4862-3077
SRM Institute of Science and Technology, India

J. Shyamala Devi
https://orcid.org/0000-0002-6265-8380
SRM Institute of Science and Technology, India

S. Suriya
https://orcid.org/0000-0002-2297-4426
SRM Institute of Science and Technology, India

J. Dhilipan
SRM Institute of Science and Technology, India

S. Sindhu
https://orcid.org/0000-0002-2133-6377
SRM Institute of Science and Technology, India

ABSTRACT

Libraries face the difficulty of maintaining huge volumes of information while offering users effective resource discovery in the fast-expanding digital world. The incorporation of artificial intelligence (AI) has emerged as a significant change in library administration. This chapter explores the use of AI, with an emphasis on recommendation systems and knowledge discovery. AI-powered recommendation systems provide personalized ideas, increasing user engagement and making content

DOI: 10.4018/979-8-3693-1573-6.ch009

research easier. AI-powered resource discovery technologies extract important insights from enormous collections, assisting in trend analysis and resource summaries. The collaboration of these AI-powered technologies transforms the library experience, making it more user-centric, efficient, and enriching. This chapter demonstrates how AI-powered recommendation systems and resource discovery may convert libraries into dynamic, responsive organizations at the forefront of information distribution.

INTRODUCTION

This twenty-first century is an era for technologization and digitalization; there is a technological change in every field, and this also includes the library. Traditional libraries with shelves full of books with tightly packed silent readers and limited numbers of books to lend and borrow, with time limits and fines, have also changed. This change is happening because of the exponential growth in digital information, where books, magazines, journals, research articles, and even text books have evolved from traditional books to digital books. This evolution is also positive, as it provides readers with an abundance of knowledge compared to traditional methods. With this abundance of information from a variety of domains, it is easy for the readers to stay updated and knowledgeable in a variety of domains that are of interest to them.

In traditional methods of library management, there are several standard ways of organizing, cataloguing, indexing, and maintaining the library's resources of library. Due to digitalization, digital contents and information now contribute to the major resources in libraries. Now there is a problem with the methods for maintaining, organizing, cataloguing, and indexing digital resources. The library is loaded with an abundance of knowledge, and this puts readers in a difficult situation about choosing the correct and relevant resource required and the questions such as how and where to find such relevant resources. This difficulty in traditional library management is considerably low because every reader can easily access the physical resources available with proper indexing and cataloguing by the librarian. To face such difficulties in digital resources, Artificial Intelligence (AI) is being used in various services of libraries, which include cataloguing, assisting, resource recommendation, text summarization, knowledge discovery, etc., for the administration of libraries. The most common problems with the digitalization of libraries for users are: technical issues, platform independence, search and discovery of resources, lack of standardization etc., that can be addressed with the employment of AI in libraries. To summarize, modern libraries should employ more AI technologies to achieve efficiency in searching and utilizing the resource and to attract the users to engage in library to acquiring new knowledge.

AI Technologies for Library Administration

AI technology may be used to improve a number of common library services. Here are some examples (Halburagi and Mukarambi, 2023).

1. ***Chatbots***: Chatbots can be used in libraries to reduce the workload of librarians on primary tasks like finding a book, answering frequently asked queries, and suggesting free schedules for users. Also, these chatbots assist the users in recommending the latest resources.
2. ***Recommender systems***: With the help of the recommender system, it is easy for users to find new resources that may be useful to them. These recommendations are personalized based on the habits and patterns of the user. Resources that are computed to be interesting to users are generated as recommendations. These systems basically analyse the past reading histories of the user to generate new recommendations that could be interesting to them.
3. ***Natural Language Processing (NLP)***: There are situations where users cannot find quality time to skim through bulk digital data for the desired content. Using NLP, it is possible to do tasks such as classification, summarization, and key concept identification automatically with less effort from the user. It helps users to quickly locate the needed resource by searching the bulk content.
4. ***Image recognition:*** With the help of image recognition technologies, users can save time searching for books by providing the cover page of the books to the image recognition system. These systems can also be capable of identifying the book category using the cover page and recommending books in similar categories.
5. ***Digital assistants:*** The library automation of basic tasks such as users, inquiries, reminders, language, and accessibility can be done using digital assistants. They are capable of answering basic and frequently asked queries for users. They can alert and notify users about due dates and fine details. By using language translators, it can easily interact with users in multiple languages. Using text-to-voice tools is a better interaction tool for visually challenged people.
6. ***Sentiment analysis:*** Sentiment analysis can be used by librarians to collect feedback and reviews from library users for analysis. In libraries, sentiment analysis can be useful for librarians to understand the thoughts of users, and based on the analysis, it is easy to identify the areas in which library development should be strengthened. Sentimental analysis acts as a primary component to identify the weak structures in the library that require development.

This chapter primarily discusses the role of two powerful tools, recommendation systems and knowledge discovery, in effective library management. This chapter focuses on types of recommendation systems and how these systems play an important role in recommending books and resources of interest for users based on their habits and patterns. Similarly, knowledge discovery is another powerful tool used for gathering specific, content-based, in-depth searches based on keywords and textual contents. Using recommendation systems and knowledge discovery makes libraries more fun and efficient for users, assists libraries in making smart choices about their resources, and keeps them updated with the digital world. Although both concepts seem similar, they have different functionalities in the library management system.

LITERATURE REVIEW

Huang, Chung, Ong, and Chen (2002) presented a novel recommender system that combines content-based and collaborative filtering, two well-known recommendation techniques. To efficiently accomplish this integration, they employ the Hopfield network method. The recommender system functions by taking into account the connections between books and users. It considers both the interactions between books and users (book-user connections) as well as high-degree linkages between users and books (user-user relationships). This strategy is put into practice using a two-layer network. In the first layer, capturing connections and relationships between books is the main goal. Understanding user or customer connections is emphasized in the second layer. By doing this, the recommender system may provide recommendations that are more accurate and pertinent based on both the content of the items (books) and the user's behavior and preferences. By taking into account a wider range of linkages and associations, this novel technique seeks to increase suggestion accuracy while also improving the user experience and satisfaction with the offered recommendations.

A fuzzy linguistic recommender system was proposed by Porcel, Moreno, and Herrera-Viedma (2009) as a hybrid system that combines a recommender system with multi-granular fuzzy linguistic modeling to handle flexible information using linguistic labels. Fuzzy linguistics is used to enhance the University Digital Library's performance for researchers. It recommends specialized resources in the user's research area and complementary resources from related fields, fostering collaboration. It filters information and provides it to the right users, benefiting new users. Additionally, it suggests resources for collaboration, improving the user-system interaction and interpretability of system activities in the University Digital Library.

Jia and Shi (2013) presented a collaborative filtering algorithm to recommend books in libraries. The authors used The Chinese Library Classification System uses secondary categories to classify books into specific areas. For interdisciplinary subjects, books are grouped together. Readers are also categorized based on their ratings. Also, readers are classified based on the reader score generated. If a reader is classified into 2–3 categories, then the algorithm aims to find one target for generating an accurate result. Then, based on the similarity score and impact factors computed, books are recommended to the readers.

Tejeda-Lorente et al. (2014) proposed a hybrid fuzzy linguistic recommender system based on quality of the items that helps users access relevant research resources. A hybrid fuzzy linguistic recommender system based on item quality was proposed by Tejeda-Lorente et al. (2014) to assist users in finding pertinent research materials. In order to take user experiences and social knowledge into account, it employs a hybrid technique that alternates between content-based and collaborative suggestions. Users can add or remove subjects from their profiles as part of the feedback process, and researchers rate how satisfied they are with the resources they propose. This two-step procedure guarantees suggestions for high-quality and pertinent research resources. A re-ranking module that takes item quality and relevance into account is part of the system. Overall, the addition of satisfaction ratings enhances the feedback process.

Zhang (2016) introduced a personalized book recommendation algorithm that uses time-sequenced collaborative filtering along with students' learning trajectories. Unlike traditional recommendation methods that rely on user ratings, this algorithm considers the time sequence of borrowed books and how often books are checked out. This approach eliminates the need for users to rate books, making it more effective with a sparse rating matrix. The algorithm can be applied to library management systems, providing recommendations without user input. Its key benefit is that it combines the knowledge-learning systems of college students from various majors, offering a novel approach for university book recommendation systems. The authors Gao et al. (2016) introduced an improved collaborative filtering algorithm that combines the Top-N algorithm to enhance recommendation accuracy. It calculates similarity, obtains a nearest neighbour set, and then combines it with the similarity of the knowledge scenario, resulting in a refined similarity value for target users or items. This approach reduces recommendation errors and enhances accuracy. The framework for a personalized learning recommendation system based on knowledge situation selection is also presented. The choice of representative hidden situational characteristics plays a crucial role in recommendation performance.

The authors Tian et al. (2019) proposed an intelligent book recommendation system for university libraries based on big data analytics. As user and book volumes increase, traditional systems face challenges, such as slow performance and computational burdens during simultaneous recommendations for multiple users. To address these issues, the paper introduces the Spark big data platform, leveraging memory-based computing and parallelization algorithms for faster execution. The system utilizes Spark Core for algorithm parallelization, Hadoop Yarn for cluster management, and HDFS for distributed book data storage. Recommendations are personalized by analysing user borrowing history and book content data, enhancing library services for new and returning users.

Ghafarian et al. (2020) proposed research that focuses on designing a personalized recommendation system for the Digital Library of Astan-e Quds-e Razavi using the Basket Analysis pattern and the FP-Growth algorithm in data mining. By extracting frequent user item sets and employing RapidMiner software, this study aims to enhance information resource retrieval, provide valuable services to users, and increase their engagement with the website. Almaghrabi and Chetty (2020) presented a method for building a digital library recommendation system using deep machine learning for Arabic and English. It involves classifying metadata using support vector machines, convolutional neural networks, recurrent neural networks, and long short-term memory networks, followed by text pre-processing and semantic similarity methods. The system can handle various inputs and generate subjects from titles and abstracts. The authors Nugraha, Ardiansyah, Junaeti, and Riza (2020) created a digital library system with a recommendation feature to help users find interesting books. It employs machine learning and user-based collaborative filtering to provide book recommendations based on book value, user behavior, and borrowing data.

In this study by Zhao (2021), a digital library recommendation system including user preferences is introduced. It estimates user-interested topics using a Latent Dirichlet Allocation (LDA) model and suggests subjects with high preference ratings. Users may now obtain item listings based on their interests. The study applies a content filter to user-generated material, uses LDA to represent user preferences in social networks, and optimizes by taking user impact on conversation themes into account. Digital libraries use user choices to suggest appropriate books, periodicals, and magazines. The research by Wang, Wang, Guo, Xu, Gao, Liu, and Li (2021) introduced hierarchical reinforcement learning into the digital library's book recommendation. The primary aim of this work is to tackle data sparsity and noise issues in book recommendations within school digital libraries. It accomplishes this by utilizing hierarchical reinforcement learning and clustering to address sparse data challenges effectively.

A deep belief network model was proposed by Liu (2022) to aid in multimodal feature learning and produce a customized system for recommending library resources. To precisely represent user interests and provide semantic tailored suggestions, it integrates the creation of a semantic user interest model with a personalized recommendation algorithm. This study improves library services by using the deep belief network-based recommendation service, which shifts the focus from passive to scenario-based service delivery. This strategy emphasizes the individualized elements of digital library services while meeting the various information demands of users via smart mobile devices. It essentially creates a deep belief network-based customized library resource recommendation system, advancing the theoretical foundation of knowledge services.

A hybrid recommender system for digital libraries was created by Jomsri, Prangchumpol, Poonsilp, and Panityakul (2023) to recommend e-books by connecting knowledge sources from various digital libraries and online publishers. It uses a combination of collaborative filtering and content-based filtering and considers factors like book category and user reading habits. The system was evaluated by gathering user feedback and comparing it to traditional methods. The hybrid model, consisting of 80 percent collaborative filtering and 20 percent content-based filtering, proved more efficient and effective than conventional approaches, improving the recommendation process.

The scenario that is used throughout this chapter for understanding the concepts is illustrated in Scenario 1.

Figure 1.

Scenario 1: Consider a library named "Wisdom" which is one of the biggest libraries near the residence of a girl named "Lilly" doing her masters in the subject "Computer Science". The Wisdom Library boasts an extensive and diverse collection of books, periodicals, and other publications, covering a wide range of subjects including literature, history, science, and more. It has adapted to the digital age, offering access to e-books, e-journals, and other online resources for the past five years. It also provides membership cards and login credentials for every individual member of this library. so that every member of the library can access the book from the library or access e-resources and e-books provided by the library through

the internet. Lilly has been a member of Wisdom Library for the past seven years, and she visits the library often. The area of specialization of Lilly includes data mining and image processing; also, one of her hobbies is reading. She loves to read contemporary literature from this library.

Figure 2.

Table 1 presents the list of books read by Lilly from Wisdom for the past four months through books and e-books. Table 1 uses the title of the book mentioned only to understand the workings of the recommendation system and knowledge discovery in the upcoming sections of this chapter.

Table 1. Borrowed history of Lilly for past four months

Computer Science	Contemporary literature
"Artificial Intelligence and Machine Learning" by John Smith "Data Structures and Algorithms in C++" by Lisa Brown "Python Programming for Beginners" by Sarah Davis "Web Development with HTML and CSS" by David Wilson "Java: The Complete Reference" by Emily Turner "Machine Learning and Pattern Recognition" by Robert Moore "Big Data Analytics: Methods and Applications" by Laura Lee Data Mining for Business Intelligence" by James Williams "Image Processing and Analysis" by Sarah Adams "Practical Data Mining Techniques" by David Clarke "Fundamentals of Image Processing" by Emily Turner "Data Mining with Python" by Michael Davis "Digital Image Processing Essentials" by Laura Wilson "Pattern Recognition and Machine Learning" by Robert Moore "Image Compression and Analysis" by Karen White "Data Mining for Healthcare" by Daniel Johnson	The Unseen Stars" by Emma Miller "Voices in the Night" by Liam Johnson "Shadows of Tomorrow" by Ava Davis "Whispers of the Heart" by Olivia Wright "Fragments of Eternity" by Ethan Taylor "The Art of Letting Go" by Lucas Turner "In Search of Serendipity" by Noah Adams "Echoes of Yesterday" by Lily Foster "The Songbird's Melody" by Sophia Clark "Brushstrokes of Life" by Lucas Turner "The Lost Hours" by Mia Harris "Midnight Conversations" by Aiden Brown "Under the Crescent Moon" by Harper Mitchell "The Secrets We Keep" by Nora Anderson

[**NOTE**: The title of the book and name of the authors presented in Table 1 are synthetic data and do not represent any real-world books or authors.]

AI-POWERED RECOMMENDATION SYSTEMS FOR PERSONALIZING THE SEARCH EXPERIENCE

A recommendation is a AI tool that is used in a variety of applications to analyse the behaviour of the user, and based on the discovered pattern, it recommends personalized list of items that users could find useful and interesting to them. These personalized recommendations are based on patterns such as users' behaviour, preferences, and other metadata of the user. The purpose of these Recommendation Systems (RS) is to help users find useful products, contents, services, and items that are hard to acknowledge from bulk data. These RS are most commonly used in recommending similar products in e-commerce; music and movies in entertainment; books, courses, and materials in education; and so on. In the context of the Library Management System (LMS), it is used for the purpose of recommending books and e-contents for the user based on individual interests. Basically, recommendation systems can be classified into collaborative filtering, content – based filtering and hybrid recommendation systems.

Content based (CB) recommendation systems: Content-based recommendation systems are used to recommend relevant items to users based on the user profile and item properties. In LMS, content-based recommendations are employed to recommend books and e-resources that are similar to the books previously read by the user. Here, the properties that are used for the purpose of recommendations are the user's borrowed history and the properties of the books. Book properties include the title of the book, the description of the book, the theme of the book, the author's profile, and the publisher's profile. To make recommendations, the system compares the user's borrowing history with the properties of the books. It looks for similarities between the books the user has borrowed and the properties of other books in the library. Based on this analysis, the system recommends books or e-resources that are similar in content or theme to the ones the user has previously borrowed.

Based on Scenario 1, let us consider that the Wisdom Library has employed Content-Based Recommendation System (CBRS) to recommend new relevant books to Lilly to enhance Lilly's library experience by suggesting relevant books based on her borrowing history. This system analyzes her past preferences, focusing on her primary reading themes, which include computer science and contemporary literature. The process involves comparing the properties of the books she has borrowed, such as titles, authors, and book descriptions, with the attributes of unread books and e-resources in the library's extensive database. By assessing the similarity between these attributes, the CBRS generates personalized recommendations tailored to Lilly's interests. For example, the CBRS identifies that Lilly has a keen interest in data mining and image processing, likely inferred from her past borrowing history. With this insight, the system scours the library database for books and resources with themes akin to these topics. Furthermore, the CBRS goes beyond thematic recommendations. It takes into account Lilly's specific reading behavior. In this case, it recognizes her affinity for the contemporary literature collection of the author Lucas Turner. If a new book by Lucas Turner becomes available in the library's collection, the system promptly brings it to Lilly's attention.

CBRS is good at making recommendations by analyzing patterns in user behaviour, but with this RS, it is hard to address problems like lack of serendipity, cold start, high-profile maintenance, and lack of trend analysis.

- **Lack of Serendipity**: Serendipity is one of the greatest advantages of the digitalization era. Digitalization provides great opportunities to explore various interests with less effort. But in the case of CBRS, it is not possible because the search is limited to the previous interests of the user, so there is no chance for them to explore new items that can be of interest to the user.

Even if the user has a desire to learn new themes and genres, it is not possible with CBRS.

- **Cold-Start**: When a new user joins the recommendation system, the cold start problem occurs. This creates a hurdle for Content-Based Recommendation Systems (CBRS), which rely on a user's borrowing history to produce book recommendations. When a user is new and hasn't borrowed any books yet, the system lacks the historical data needed to provide appropriate recommendations. As a result, CBRS finds it challenging to provide relevant recommendations to new users. To deal with this issue, the algorithm must first learn about the user's behavior and interests, as high-quality book recommendations require data and patterns.
- **Higi-Profile Maintenance**: Content-Based Recommendation Systems (CBRS) use information about what users like and details about library books to suggest the right ones. When a new book is added, its information must be kept up to date, along with the data about users. As the data gets bigger, we need more space to store it properly because libraries collect many books, so keeping good records for each one can be a lot of work. We must have enough space to handle all this information as it keeps growing. Adequate storage capacity must be available to manage this ever-expanding data.
- **Lack of Trend Analysis**: CBRS is not recommended in environments that are time-sensitive because it will not recommend topics of current trend. Instead, it only focuses on recommending items based on past history. For example, if the analysis finds a user interested in C programming, it will only recommend books related to the C programming language, where the current world has moved to other advanced languages like Java, GO, and Python. This change in trend cannot be analyzed using CBRS, so it is hard for users to stay updated and connected with current trends.

Collaborative filtering (CF) -based recommendation systems: Collaborative filtering-based recommendation systems (CFRS) recommends relevant items to users based on the similarity between two users or items. CFRS can be either item-based or user-based. In user-based CFRS, it recommends an item to users based on the similarity between the items consumed by users. An example of user-based CFRS is recommending items to users based on similarities between their rating patterns. Similarly, in item-based CFRS, it recommends items based on the similarity between different items to recommend an item to users. An example of item-based CFRS is recommending items to users based on the similarity between the items they consume.

Figure 1 illustrates the workings of CFRS for LMS. Lilly and Akash are users of the same library. Book 1, Book 2, Book 3, Book 4, and Book 5 are books read by

Lilly, and Book 1, Book 2, Book 4, Book 6, and Book 7 are books read by Akash. If we employ CFRS to recommend books to read for Lilly and Akash, it will check for similarity in users reading patterns. CFRS then detects that Book 1, Book 2, and Book 4 are read by both users; based on this, it will recommend Book 6 and Book 7 to Lilly and Book 3 and Book 5 to Akash.

Figure 3. An example of CFRS to recommend book for users in LMS

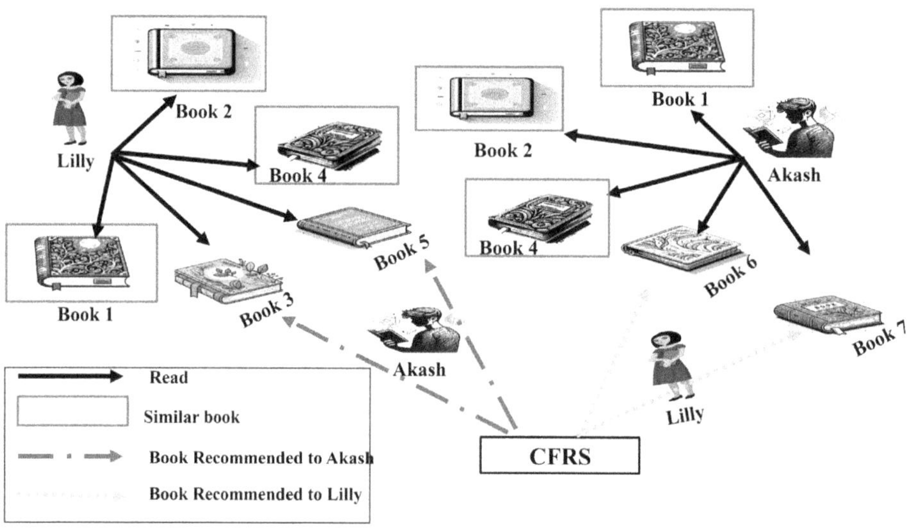

By using the similarity between different users or products, it is possible to explore different items that could be of interest to the users, and it has a high chance of serendipity and helps users stay in trend compared with CBRS. Although it has the ability to overcome a lack of serendipity and a lack of trend analysis, it also suffers from cold start problems similar to CBRS. Apart from the cold start problem, it faces other challenges like data sparsity, popularity bias and scalability

- **Cold-start problem**: CFRS also suffers from a cold-start problem similar to CBRS whenever a new user logs in to the system. For new users, there was no borrowed book history, which makes it challenging to find similar users.
- **Data sparsity:** Data sparsity is a problem that occurs when the data is too sparse to handle. That is, there are numerous numbers of books and users, but only a few books are read by a few authors, and a few books are not all read by any authors. Thus, these books cannot be used by recommendation systems. As an example, Lilly is the only one to read around 20 contemporary literature books with 200 books in the library, and no other users from the total

of 3000 members of this library have read any book from this genre. In this case, the system suffers from data sparsity because there are a large number of users and books, but only 20 books were used by a single user among 200 books. So, the remaining number of books will not even be considered for recommendation because they are not at all borrowed.

- **Scalability**: CFRS requires significant computational resources to handle numerous amounts of data from both users and books. The increase in computational time may decrease the performance and effectiveness of the system.
- **Popularity bias:** Popular items are more likely to be recommended to everyone, regardless of whether they truly match a user's likes. This bias develops because content filtering systems frequently rely on item popularity across the total user population. As a result, goods that are already popular likely to gain even more attention, but specialized or lesser-known items may not get the attention they deserve.

Hybrid recommendation systems: To overcome the disadvantages of both collaborative filtering and content-based filtering methods, hybrid recommendation systems have been developed. It combines the workings of both CB and CF methods to produce accurate and effective recommendations.

From Scenario 1, assume that Wisdom Library decides to update the LMS with a hybrid recommendation system. Now Lilly RS can use the borrowed book history to generate a content-based recommendation system. Every time users return a book, this LMS system gets feedback and ratings for the book. Based on user feedback and ratings, user-based CFRS can be employed to produce recommendations based on similarity between Lilly and other users. This helps Lilly find books that are more engaging and interesting, and she has a chance to explore diversified books from different fields to gain more knowledge.

Advantages of using Hybrid recommendation systems compared to pure collaborative filtering (CF) or content-based (CB) systems are:

- **Improved Recommendation Accuracy:** One of the primary advantages of hybrid systems is their ability to provide more accurate recommendations. By combining CF and CB methods, they can leverage the strengths of both approaches and mitigate the weaknesses, resulting in more precise and relevant recommendations.
- **Enhanced Diversity**: Hybrid systems can provide a broader range of recommendations. They can balance user-based collaborative filtering, which prefers popular items, with content-based filtering, which prefers items

based on their features. As a result, the suggestions become more diversified, presenting users to new and possibly interesting items.

- **Mitigation of Cold Start Problem**: Cold start issues are effectively addressed by hybrid systems. When dealing with new users who do not have enough interaction data, the content-based component can give suggestions based on the item's features and attributes.
- **Personalization**: Hybrid systems are capable of providing highly tailored recommendations. They may adjust suggestions to particular user preferences by taking into account both user behavior (CF) and item characteristics (CB).
- **Reduced Popularity Bias**: Traditional CF techniques have a tendency to recommend items that appeal to a large number of users, resulting in popularity bias. This bias can be reduced in hybrid systems by taking item characteristics into account in addition to user-item interactions.
- **Effective for Both New and Active Users**: Hybrid systems are equally useful for new users with little interaction history as they are for experienced users with substantial histories. The content-based component benefits new users, while active users receive specific recommendations based on previous interactions.

With this AI-powered recommendation system, a library management system can be enhanced to provide personalized recommendations with a better understanding of each individual. Also, LMS can be further enhanced with virtual librarians for engaging library experiences that allow every user to stay connected with the current trend, gain knowledge in a desired field, and experience interesting discoveries. This RS can be implemented in libraries to provide personalized recommendations, aid recommendation engines in retrieving relevant research content, and make real-time updates regarding the field of interest.

AI POWERED RESOURCE DISCOVERY FOR INTELLIGENT SEARCH

A digital library with various resources such as books, articles, journals, documents, multimedia content, and other forms of digital contents makes it hard to access specific resources from electronic sources, databases, websites, and repositories. The most common types of digital content accessed through a library are subscriptions, local databases, and open access. To make the search and retrieval process easy, resource discovery services are utilized in libraries. Resource discovery is the process of finding, accessing, and retrieving information from electronic sources. To retrieve information, it uses AI tools such as search engines, e-catalogs, and databases.

Why Do We Need Resource Discovery in Library?

A vast amount of digital data is spread across different electronic information sources, such as databases, websites, and repositories, which makes it hard to access the required information. The problem with accessing different electronic resources is that it requires users to search each individual resource separately. So, to make this process easier, a single resource discovery tool is used. It is capable of searching the user query across different electronic sources with a single click using tools like search engines and interfaces. To put it simply, it allows us to access vast amounts of information from different types of material stored across the internet or locally.

For example, if Lilly is searching for a research article titled "Enhanced big data mining techniques," a simple search technique searches for this topic in the major database of the library. But when AI-enhanced resource discovery is employed in Wisdom Library from Scenario 1, the system can search for this topic using a search engine provided by the library across different databases like IEEE, Research Scholar, Semantic Scholar, Scopus, and PubMed with a single click. This system then searches and lists all the articles that match Lilly's query with less effort and time.

Through resource discovery, it is possible for users to access the entire text of the available electronic content quickly using local and centralized indexing mechanisms. The data collected through resource discovery tools is always accurate because these systems are implemented using AI techniques for performing autocomplete suggestions, correcting spelling errors, and offering results that are contextually relevant even when the user's query is imprecise. They can translate the content of the source into the desired language. Natural language processing (NLP) and Machine Learning (ML) are the primary AI tools to support these language supporting services in resource discovery.

Using these resource discovery tools offers several advantages over the traditional online public access catalog (OPAC) system. While using traditional OPAC, users can only obtain information about locally available books, articles, and journals in the library, and it cannot be used for searching electronic sources. For this reason, OPAC today has been replaced with resource discovery interfaces. The catalog service provided by OPAC is also available in the resource discovery service. Apart from this, it provides a faceted search for smart search filtering, which allows users to perform a more specific search.

For resource discovery many different types of interfaces are developed, that can be classified as either commercial or open source. Commercial interfaces are typically developed and sold by private companies, while open-source interfaces are created collaboratively and are freely available for use and modification by the public.

Commercial Interfaces

EBSCO Discovery Service (EDS): Many libraries utilize EBSCO's commercial resource discovering service. It offers a single search interface for a wide variety of library materials, such as books, journals, and more.

ProQuest OneSearch: Another commercial discovery tool is ProQuest's OneSearch, which allows users to explore and access a variety of academic resources such as dissertations, journals, and newspapers.

Ex Libris Primo: Ex Libris, a ProQuest business, produces Primo. It is a commercial discovery and distribution tool that libraries employ in order to connect people to their resources.

Open-Source Interfaces

VuFind: VuFind is an open-source library resource discovery system. It provides a user-friendly and customizable interface for finding and accessing library content.

Koha: Koha is best known as an open-source integrated library system (ILS). It also features a discovery module that allows users to search for and locate library items.

Blacklight: Blacklight is an open-source discovery interface built using the Apache Solr search platform. It provides a highly customizable search experience for libraries.

INTEGRATING RESOURCE DISCOVERY IN RECOMMENDATION SYSTEM

Although Recommendation systems and resource discovery seems to be similar, they both perform different tasks in library management system. The primary goal of the resource discovery is to locate the content among different available resources either local or global, while that of the recommendation system is to pick the top number of matches from the retrieved content and recommend them to user. Both of them have significant contribution to the enhancement of the user experience in the library. If both integrated together can further improve the automation process done for enriching the metadata, content tagging and resources classification. The advances of integrating the Recommendation system and resource discoveries are as follows.

Enhanced User Experience: By integrating content discovery, users can not only search for specific items in the library but also receive personalized recommendations. This creates a seamless experience, where users can discover new documents while searching for specific resources. Also, to further ease the work of user's notifications and alerts can be sent to users.

Personalization: Based on the reading habits, interactions, and feedback received from users, this system can generate personalized recommendations. This helps users stay focused and updated in their area of interest. New resources that are found to be matched with the interests of users can be recommended to them. This process can increase the involvement of users in the library, and it helps users explore uncovered library resources.

Open Access Integration: Using Resource discovery services integrates the resources from subscription-based resources with open access resources. This helps users to easy access all available resources using one interface.

User Analytics: To understand the needs of users, libraries can collect and analyze the data gathered from individual users. This collected data can be used for further development of the library.

Accessibility: Compared to the traditional OPAC system, resource discovery interfaces have been enhanced with language skills. These skills are mostly used by people with disabilities to aid them in the library without any special requirements.

Adaptive Recommendations: The system continuously adapts and refines recommendations as users interact with the library. It learns from user behavior and evolves its suggestions over time.

By integrating resource discovery with the recommendation system, users' engagement in the library can be improved. From Scenario 1, if Wisdom Library uses this system, Lilly can have the possibility of reading all the relevant useful resources to write her assignment for her college project. This system can recommend articles and journals relevant to Lilly based on her recent actions, where resource discovery can locate items that match Lilly's interests, and the recommendation system presents recommendations of top matches. After a period of time, if Lilly changes her area of interest from contemporary literature to modern literature, this system can adopt the change in pattern to generate new list resource recommendations.

CONCLUSION

This chapter presents the major roles of two important AI components of LMS: the recommendation system and resource discovery. It explains different types of recommendation systems and lists the advantages and challenges involved in them. It also summarizes the need for and types of resource discovery tools in libraries. Additionally, it explores the advantages of integrating these systems to improve the efficiency and performance of the LMS. Traditional library systems have evolved into digital library systems with an increased volume of digital resources, which provides better convenience to library users. There is a unique challenge that is addressed by the AI-powered recommendation and resource discovery system, that is the finding required and relevant content. In a traditional library management system, we can easily access resources using indexing and cataloging methods by visiting the library physically, but only limited resources available in the library can be accessed. To address this challenge, libraries are integrated with various available databases and repositories through the internet on the basis of subscriptions or open access. This makes more content available, but again, there is a problem finding the required information from the vast collection. To retrieve relevant content, the recommendation system and resource discovery system are utilized. This enhances the search and optimizes the result with user queries using different AI tools and techniques.

REFERENCES

Ali, M. Y., Naeem, S. B., & Bhatti, R. (2020). Artificial intelligence tools and perspectives of university librarians: An overview. *Business Information Review*, *37*(3), 116–124. doi:10.1177/0266382120952016

Almaghrabi, M., & Chetty, G. (2020, December). Deep Machine Learning Digital library recommendation system based on Metadata for Arabic and English Languages. In *2020 IEEE Asia-Pacific Conference on Computer Science and Data Engineering (CSDE)* (pp. 1-6). IEEE. 10.1109/CSDE50874.2020.9411525

Asemi, A., Ko, A., & Nowkarizi, M. (2020). Intelligent libraries: A review on expert systems, artificial intelligence, and robot. *Library Hi Tech*, *39*(2), 412–434. doi:10.1108/LHT-02-2020-0038

Bisht, S., Nautiyal, A. P., Sharma, S., Sati, M., Bathla, N., & Singh, P. (2023, May). The role of Artificial Intelligence in shaping Library Management and its Utilization. In *2023 International Conference on Disruptive Technologies (ICDT)* (pp. 467-472). IEEE. 10.1109/ICDT57929.2023.10150520

Chen, L. C., Kuo, P. J., & Liao, I. E. (2015). Ontology-based library recommender system using MapReduce. *Cluster Computing*, *18*(1), 113–121. doi:10.1007/s10586-013-0342-z

Collins, A., Tkaczyk, D., Aizawa, A., & Beel, J. (2018). A study of position bias in digital library recommender systems. arXiv preprint arXiv:1802.06565.

Das, R. K., & Islam, M. S. U. (2021). Application of artificial intelligence and machine learning in libraries: a systematic review. arXiv preprint arXiv:2112.04573.

Dhiman, A. K. (2011). Knowledge discovery in databases and libraries. *DESIDOC Journal of Library and Information Technology*, *31*(6), 446–451. doi:10.14429/djlit.31.6.1319

Dumouchel, B., & Demaine, J. (2006). Knowledge Discovery in the Digital Library: Access tools for mining science. *Information Services & Use*, *26*(1), 39–44. doi:10.3233/ISU-2006-26105

Folorunso, A. L., & Momoh, E. O. (2020). Application of artificial intelligence and robotics in libraries: A review of literature. *ILIS Journal of Librarianship and Informatics*, *3*(2), 93–98.

Gao, X., Huang, W. X., Wang, N., Yang, Y. C., & Yan, Y. (2016). A top-N algorithm-based personalized learning recommendation system for digital library. [iJET]. *International Journal of Emerging Technologies in Learning*, *11*(11), 55–59. doi:10.3991/ijet.v11i11.6256

Gasparini, A. A., & Kautonen, H. (2022). Understanding Artificial Intelligence in Research Libraries: An Extensive Literature Review. LIBER Quarterly. *Te Journal of European Research Libraries*, *32*(1), 1–36.

Genovesi, S., Kaesling, K., & Robbins, S. (2023). Introduction: Understanding and Regulating AI-Powered Recommender Systems. In *Recommender Systems: Legal and Ethical Issues* (pp. 1–9). Springer International Publishing. doi:10.1007/978-3-031-34804-4_1

Geyer-Schulz, A., Neumann, A., & Thede, A. (2003). An architecture for behavior-based library recommender systems. *Information Technology and Libraries*, *22*(4), 165.

Ghafarian, S., Jalali, M., Babolhavaeji, F., Hariri, N., & Khademi, M. (2020). Designing a Personalized Service Model with an Approach to Recommender System in Astan-e Quds-e Razavi Digital Library Software. *Library and Information Sciences*, *23*(2), 5–24.

Guo, G., Zhang, J., Sun, Z., & Yorke-Smith, N. (2015, June). Librec: A java library for recommender systems. In UMAP workshops (Vol. 4, pp. 38-45).

Halburagi, S., & Mukarambi, P. (2023). *Use of Artificial Intelligence (AI).* Technology Futures in Library.

Huang, Y. H. (2022). Exploring the implementation of artificial intelligence applications among academic libraries in Taiwan. *Library Hi Tech*. doi:10.1108/LHT-03-2022-0159

Huang, Z., Chung, W., Ong, T. H., & Chen, H. (2002, July). A graph-based recommender system for digital library. In *Proceedings of the 2nd ACM/IEEE-CS joint conference on Digital libraries* (pp. 65-73). 10.1145/544220.544231

Huanyu, Z., & Xin, L. (2017, July). Research on the Application of Knowledge Discovery in Digital Library Service. In *2017 7th International Conference on Social Network, Communication and Education (SNCE 2017)* (pp. 817-820). Atlantis Press. 10.2991/snce-17.2017.166

Jia, F., & Shi, Y. (2013). Library management system based on recommendation system. In *Information Computing and Applications: 4th International Conference, ICICA 2013*, (vol 392 pp. 488-497). Springer Berlin Heidelberg. 10.1007/978-3-642-53703-5_50

Jomsri, P., Prangchumpol, D., Poonsilp, K., & Panityakul, T. (2023). Hybrid recommender system model for digital library from multiple online publishers. *F1000 Research*, *12*, 1140. doi:10.12688/f1000research.133013.1

Kronenfeld, M. R., & Bright, H. S. IV. (2015). Library resource discovery. *Journal of the Medical Library Association: JMLA*, *103*(4), 210–213. doi:10.3163/1536-5050.103.4.011 PMID:26512224

Liu, M. (2022). Personalized Recommendation System Design for Library Resources through Deep Belief Networks. *Mobile Information Systems*, *2022*, 2022. doi:10.1155/2022/7870724

Massis, B. (2018). Artificial intelligence arrives in the library. *Information and Learning Science*, *119*(7/8), 456–459. doi:10.1108/ILS-02-2018-0011

Nugraha, E., Ardiansyah, T., Junaeti, E., & Riza, L. S. (2020). Enhanced Digital Library with Book Recommendations Based on Collaborative Filtering. *Journal of Engineering Education Transformations, 34*(Special Issue).

Okunlaya, R. O., Syed Abdullah, N., & Alias, R. A. (2022). Artificial intelligence (AI) library services innovative conceptual framework for the digital transformation of university education. *Library Hi Tech*, *40*(6), 1869–1892. doi:10.1108/LHT-07-2021-0242

Panyadee, P., & Wita, R. (2021, May). Integrating Graph-Based Document Recommendation in Digital Libraries of Theses Collection. In *International Conference on Computing and Information Technology* (pp. 223-232). Cham: Springer International Publishing. 10.1007/978-3-030-79757-7_22

Porcel, C., Moreno, J. M., & Herrera-Viedma, E. (2009). A multi-disciplinar recommender system to advice research resources in university digital libraries. *Expert Systems with Applications*, *36*(10), 12520–12528. doi:10.1016/j.eswa.2009.04.038

Richardson, W. R., Srinivasan, V., & Fox, E. A. (2008). Knowledge discovery in digital libraries of electronic theses and dissertations: An NDLTD case study. *International Journal on Digital Libraries*, *9*(2), 163–171. doi:10.1007/s00799-008-0046-9

Rubin, V. L., Chen, Y., & Thorimbert, L. M. (2010). Artificially intelligent conversational agents in libraries. *Library Hi Tech*, *28*(4), 496–522. doi:10.1108/07378831011096196

Simović, A. (2018). A Big Data smart library recommender system for an educational institution. *Library Hi Tech*, *36*(3), 498–523. doi:10.1108/LHT-06-2017-0131

Sun, Z., & Stranieri, A. (2020). A knowledge discovery in the digital age. *PNG UoT BAIS*, *5*(1), 1–11.

Tejeda-Lorente, Á., Porcel, C., Peis, E., Sanz, R., & Herrera-Viedma, E. (2014). A quality based recommender system to disseminate information in a university digital library. *Information Sciences*, *261*, 52–69. doi:10.1016/j.ins.2013.10.036

Tian, Y., Zheng, B., Wang, Y., Zhang, Y., & Wu, Q. (2019). College library personalized recommendation system based on hybrid recommendation algorithm. *Procedia CIRP*, *83*, 490–494. doi:10.1016/j.procir.2019.04.126

Vijayakumar, S., & Sheshadri, K. N. (2019). Applications of artificial intelligence in academic libraries. *International Journal on Computer Science and Engineering*, *7*(16), 136–140.

Wang, X., Wang, Y., Guo, L., Xu, L., Gao, B., Liu, F., & Li, W. (2021). Exploring clustering-based reinforcement learning for personalized book recommendation in digital library. *Information (Basel)*, *12*(5), 198. doi:10.3390/info12050198

Weng, C. H. (2016). Knowledge discovery of digital library subscription by RFC itemsets. *The Electronic Library*, *34*(5), 772–788. doi:10.1108/EL-06-2015-0086

Wiil, U. K., & Hicks, D. L. (2001, July). Tools and services for knowledge discovery, management and structuring in digital libraries. In *Proceedings of the Eighth ISPE International Conference on Concurrent Engineering: Research and Applications* (pp. 580-589). IEEE.

Wu, C. H., Lee, T. Z., & Kao, S. C. (2004). Knowledge discovery applied to material acquisitions for libraries. *Information Processing & Management*, *40*(4), 709–725. doi:10.1016/j.ipm.2003.08.010

Yu, J. (2021, December). Construction of Smart Library Based on the Big Data Mining and Knowledge Discovery. In *2021 Smart City Challenges & Outcomes for Urban Transformation (SCOUT)* (pp. 57-61). IEEE.

Zhang, F. (2016). A personalized time-sequence-based book recommendation algorithm for digital libraries. *IEEE Access : Practical Innovations, Open Solutions*, *4*, 2714–2720. doi:10.1109/ACCESS.2016.2564997

Zhao, L. (2021). Personalized recommendation by using fused user preference to construct smart library. *Internet Technology Letters*, *4*(3), e273. doi:10.1002/itl2.273

KEY TERMS AND DEFINITIONS

Cataloguing: Cataloguing is the process of creating and maintaining bibliographic and authority records in the library catalog, the database of books, serials, sound recordings, moving images, cartographic materials, computer files, e-resources etc. that are owned by a library.

Chatbots: A computer program designed for performing a humanlike interactive conversation, providing information, and responding to the queries of the users.

Natural Language Processing: It is an AI programed to understand, interpret, and generate human language in an efficient way.

Serendipity: Serendipity can be defined as the act of finding unplanned discoveries that are useful and interesting.

Synthetic Data: Synthetic data refers to artificially generated data that mimics real-world data but is not obtained from actual observations or measurements.

Chapter 10
Future Trends and Emerging Technologies in AI and Libraries

S. Priya
SRM Institute of Science and Technology, India

R. Ramya
https://orcid.org/0000-0002-8071-9343
SRM Institute of Science and technology, India

ABSTRACT

This abstract investigates how libraries are changing in the age of artificial intelligence (AI). It explores how new technologies are changing how libraries operate and provide services. Recommendation systems driven by artificial intelligence (AI), natural language processing (NLP) for improved user engagement, text analysis and data mining for knowledge discovery, AI-driven metadata management, and AI-driven preservation initiatives are some of the major themes in this field. Furthermore, RPA, or robotic process automation, simplifies library operations. The chapter focuses on how these technologies are transforming user experience, library administration procedures, and information access, so influencing how libraries will function in the digital era.

DOI: 10.4018/979-8-3693-1573-6.ch010

INTRODUCTION

Libraries have traditionally functioned as knowledge and information archives, developing in tandem with technological breakthroughs. Libraries have long been used as information and knowledge archives, developing in tandem with technological breakthroughs. The use of Artificial Intelligence (AI) has resulted in notable changes to library services and operations in recent times. The future trends and cutting-edge technology influencing the nexus between AI and libraries are examined in this introduction.

Artificial intelligence (AI)-powered recommendation systems are becoming indispensable resources for libraries due to the growth of digital material and the increasing need for personalised experiences. By analysing user preferences and behaviour, these systems provide customised recommendations that increase user pleasure and engagement.

Moreover, Natural Language Processing (NLP) makes it possible for libraries to create intelligent interfaces that can comprehend and reply to user questions in natural language, such chatbots and virtual assistants.

Artificial intelligence (AI)-powered text analysis and data mining technologies are essential for extracting insights and accelerating knowledge discovery as libraries continue to gather enormous volumes of digital data.

Artificial intelligence (AI) technology also support preservation efforts, efficient operations, and information management in libraries. By automating monotonous work, robotic process automation, or RPA, frees up resources for more strategic endeavours.

Recent developments in artificial intelligence (AI) point to a dramatic change in the direction of increasingly complex and specialized uses across a range of industries. The field of natural language processing (NLP) and understanding is advancing at a rapid pace. Furthermore, AI-driven automation is becoming more and more common, especially in sectors like manufacturing, healthcare, and finance where autonomous systems and robotic process automation (RPA) are improving efficiency and streamlining operations. In order to address concerns about bias, privacy, and fairness, another developing field is responsible AI, which focuses on ethics, transparency, and responsibility in AI development and deployment.

Artificial intelligence (AI) is becoming more and more ingrained in daily life and has a significant impact on a wide range of businesses. Furthermore, the emergence of edge AI—made possible by edge computing and IoT devices—is boosting productivity and enabling real-time decision-making through local data processing. Initiatives for responsible AI research and deployment are being prompted by the growing importance of ethical AI considerations, which aim to reduce hazards like prejudice and privacy infringement. Anticipating the future, cutting-edge technologies such as neuromorphic computing, federated learning, and AI-driven drug discovery hold the potential to significantly influence AI's trajectory and bring about a period of unparalleled innovation and social change.

How AI Is Used in Libraries

Improved Search and Recommendation Systems: AI algorithms are used to enhance the search capabilities of library catalogues, providing more relevant results based on user preferences and behaviour.

AI aids in the effective organisation and labelling of digital resources, improving content discoverability and accessibility. This is known as content curation and metadata management.

Virtual Assistants and Chatbots: Libraries utilise chatbots or virtual assistants driven by artificial intelligence to help patrons instantly by responding to their questions and directing them to the resources and services offered by the library.

Automated Cataloguing: AI reduces manual labour and increases catalogue accuracy by automatically adding descriptive metadata to recently acquired objects, streamlining the cataloguing process.

Libraries are using artificial intelligence (AI) more and more to improve user experiences, operations, and services in a number of areas. Information retrieval and search engine optimization are two main areas where AI is used in libraries. In order to provide individualized recommendations and search results, AI-powered search engines and recommendation systems analyze user queries, preferences, and browsing activity. This makes it easier for users to access relevant information.

Chatbots and virtual assistants can now offer instantaneous, interactive assistance to library customers by using natural language processing (NLP) techniques to answer questions, help with research inquiries, and direct users through the library's resources and services. Additionally, artificial intelligence (AI) is used to automate metadata management and classification chores, such as labeling, categorizing, and organizing library resources to increase accessibility and discoverability.

AI-powered analytics technologies also make libraries possible to conduct demographic, usage, and trend analyses in order to support data-driven decision-making for resource allocation, collection development, and service planning. All things considered, AI gives libraries the ability to provide their patrons with more effective, customized, and responsive services, strengthening their position in the digital era.

Components of Artificial Intelligence

Natural Language Processing (NLP): NLP makes it possible for computers to comprehend and produce human language, which makes activities like chatbots, sentiment analysis, and language translation easier.

Expert systems are rule-based programmes designed to mimic human experts' decision-making processes in particular fields. They address issues by applying logic and rules.

Robotics: Artificial intelligence (AI)-driven robotics entails incorporating AI methods into robots to allow them to sense their surroundings, make choices, and carry out activities on their own .

Knowledge Representation and Reasoning: The emphasis of this component is on the representation of knowledge by AI systems and its application to problem-solving and decision-making. Semantic networks and ontologies are two methods used in knowledge representation .

AI systems employ planning and optimisation methodologies to ascertain the optimal approach for accomplishing particular objectives. This entails creating algorithms that can effectively look for potential answers.

Deep Learning: Deep learning is a branch of machine learning that makes use of multi-layered neural networks. It has shown impressive performance in a variety of AI applications, and it is especially useful for tasks like speech and picture recognition.

Training AI agents to interact with their surroundings and learn from feedback in the form of rewards or penalties is known as reinforcement learning. It is utilised in applications including autonomous vehicles, robots, and gaming.

Computer Vision: By using deep learning models like convolutional neural networks (CNNs), computer vision libraries provide functionality for applications like image categorization, object identification, picture segmentation, and facial recognition.

Techniques for Search and Optimisation: Artificial intelligence libraries provide search and optimisation techniques like breadth-first search and A*, which help with problem-solving and decision-making. Examples of these algorithms are gradient descent, simulated annealing, and genetic algorithms.

Reinforcement Learning: Certain libraries include capabilities for reinforcement learning, which let agents discover the best behaviours in dynamic situations by making mistakes. This is helpful for activities like controlling robots and playing games.

Data Pre-processing and Feature Engineering: Artificial intelligence libraries include tools for normalisation, dimensionality reduction, and missing value imputation, among other methods, to prepare datasets for model training.

Artificial Intelligence and Ranganathan Principles of Librarianship

Information Organisation: Ranganathan's categorization methods are applied by AI algorithms to help library materials be arranged systematically and make retrieval simple.

User-Centric Services: Ranganathan's notion of service to users is aligned with AI-driven personalisation, which offers personalised suggestions and help based on individual requirements.

Automation of Routine jobs: In keeping with Ranganathan's principle of economy in library operations, AI automates repetitive jobs like cataloguing and indexing, enabling librarians to concentrate on higher-level activities.

User Education and Engagement: Ranganathan's idea of encouraging the use of library resources is supported by AI-driven chatbots and virtual assistants.

LITERATURE SURVEY

Thayyib et al. (2023) analyzed 711 bibliometric articles from various fields to provide an overview of reviews on AI and Big Data Analytics in five domains. The study found that the USA had the most influence with 101 documents and 5405 citations, while China was the most productive with 204 documents and 2371 citations. Symbiosis International University in India was the most productive institution, with 32 documents .

Das and Islam (2021) conducted a systematic literature review to summarize empirical studies on using AI and machine learning in libraries. The study analyzed 32 papers from various databases and found that logistic regression, KNN, and AdaBoost are commonly used for metadata generation, resource discovery, and book acquisition. SVM and association rule techniques are applied for circulation recommender systems. AI and ML technologies also support various activities such as cataloging, classification, indexing, document analysis, and text recognition. Additionally, advanced techniques like pattern recognition and MAS are utilized for library security, user identification,

Yusuf et al. (2022) explore the implementation of AI in Nigerian academic libraries; the study accomplishes that AI can enhance library services, but its adoption in developing countries like

Nigeria needs to be higher. The authors recommend collaboration between the government and library management to develop AI adoption strategies and training programs for library staff to improve their AI proficiency for delivering library services.

AI FOR CATALOGUING

Because descriptive cataloguing is thought to be rule-based, its use in AI has focused on it (AACR2). There are two ways to use artificial intelligence algorithms to information material cataloguing. First, a human-computer interface where the intermediary (a human) and the support system (an AI) split the cataloguing effort; and second, a fully cataloguing system integrated with an electronic publishing system where text is generated digitally, passed through knowledge-based systems, and catalogued with minimal or no human intervention. Every attempt by researchers to convert AACR2 into the highly structured standards needed for system coding has been met with fierce resistance (Afolayan, et al., 2020). Expert systems can be employed by digital libraries to facilitate the process of classifying and examining digital resources.Through the online system, users will be able to browse the collection, peruse the available resources, and obtain the information of their choice by utilising this expert system based on a digital library. The utilisation of intelligent library retrieval in cataloguing procedures is facilitated by the application of data mining. Additionally, data mining may be utilised in online library systems to determine the information demands of customers. They help library patrons in selecting the right term or phrase for information retrieval They help library patrons in selecting the right term or phrase for information retrieval. Numerous research concentrate on the user-centered design of recommender systems for different library divisions as well as for library catalogues (Mogali, 2014).

Additionally, categorization is a crucial step in the knowledge organisation process. The use of AI technologies for categorization in the library include the following: BIOSIS is a knowledge-base-based indexing tool that was created. In order to automatically assign information items to topic classes, it also requires a significant amount of procedural expertise. In order to assign as many classifications as possible to biological materials, BIOSIS uses the information in their titles, much like a human indexer would. The structured indexing languages and practical information representation that are available are well-utilized by AI applications. Coal SORT is a conceptual browser intended for searching or indexing purposes; it lacks procedural expertise. The majority of coal SORT is made up of the software that users need to show certain aspects of it, as well as a framework-based semantical network and the conceptual structure. The EP-X, or Environmental Pollution Expert, resembles a coal SORT. Each system uses a Knowledge-Based methodology to focus on interface improvement.

Semantic analysis of texts and multimedia objects has been accomplished using a variety of approach types. Among the often employed methods are artificial neural networks, symbolic machine learning, multivariate analysis based on statistics, graph-based grouping and classification, and evolution-based programming. According to scholars, these methods will serve as effective replacements for conventional methods of processing, analysing, and summarising vast volumes of dynamic, varied multimedia data in the information era. A semantic analysis procedure's output might be expressed as rules, predicate logic, semantic networks, or judgements. Distribution of activation-based inferencing techniques is frequently employed to traverse different large-scale knowledge systems, which can aid in the classification and cataloguing of information resources found in libraries (Afolayan, et al, 2020).

The OPAC's circulation area can make it easier to retrieve library resources with the use of artificial intelligence. NLP may help break down linguistic barriers and aid retrieve pertinent information from databases, indexes, and catalogues. When requesting information, users may express their needs in their native tongue, which facilitates and improves the effectiveness of the search and retrieval process. Users may now specify intricate retrieval languages thanks to this. Users of libraries might not realise how unclear their search and retrieval strategy/method is; this can be fixed by incorporating artificial intelligence (AI) assistive technology into search tools. Library patrons would be able to search Dialogue databases directly with little to no help from information specialists if natural language processing (NLP) was used for these searches. A customer use an online catalogue in a library would want the catalogue to comprehend a specific term or a whole phrase. Because they are proficient in both natural language and search and inquiry, human librarians have an edge over machines and may serve as a liaison between the latter and the library's patrons. In order to properly get the required information resources, certain URLs or site addresses additionally include special instructions that must be followed or are case-sensitive. To utilise these new resources in the library, patrons must become computer literate (Afolayan, et al, 2020).

Even though libraries still purchase a significant amount of printed information items, they are now offering a wider range of digital resources and services. A lot of libraries, especially university or research libraries, are facing significant space and skill restrictions as a result of the combined need to provide both print and electronic information resources and services.

These issues can be resolved with the use of AI technologies. The Johns Hopkins University Library in the United States has an on-demand and batch scanning technology called Comprehensive Access to Printed Material (CAPM), which allows users to browse printed materials in real time via an online interface

e. The user activates the CAPM system, which sends a robot to get the specified item. The information material will be transferred by the robot to another robotic device, which will automatically open the material and flip the pages. Through the use of current scanners, indexing software created by the Digital Knowledge Base, and optical character recognition (OCR) software, the CAPM system will enable both text image scanning and the full-text analysis and searching that results from the pictures. (2019; Yu, Gong, Sun, and Jiang)

AI for Reference Services

Intelligent systems are designed to direct users of the library to internal information sources that are most likely to have the answers to their reference questions. To enable users to obtain information resources and have their reference queries answered in real-time through developed digital reference resources and services in libraries, more work has been done on systems for reference services than on any other service or section in the library (Chemulwo and Sirorei, 2020). These systems are designed to direct library users towards an appropriate reference source, particularly in situations where a librarian is not on hand to assist them. While some reference referral systems encompass knowledge as a whole (wide reference in its scope), others cover a specific or limited topic area (highly specialised domain or subject area). Any library must provide a reference service, and artificial intelligence technologies will work in tandem with the reference librarian to enhance their services. Here are a few instances of how artificial intelligence techniques are being used for reference services: AMSWERMAN is a knowledge-based system for agriculture that responds to inquiries concerning agricultural subjects or references. Through a succession of options, it refines the query's topic and the kind of instrument required. It can serve as a consultation system with CD-ROM reference resources or as a front end to external databases (Mogali, 2014).

A recommendation tool designed for public libraries is called PLEXUS. It is informed about certain topic areas, the library's patrons, information retrieval, reference sources, and the reference procedure. A recommender system called REFSEARCH gives users suggestions for information sources to check out in response to specific queries. The system may be used to instruct users in reference skills. Additionally, practicing reference librarians and other information experts can utilise it as a computerised tool. One of the earliest successful practical uses of artificial intelligence for reference services was POINTER. This computer-assisted reference tool directs library patrons to the precise reference materials they require. Online Reference Assistance (ORA) simulates the services of an academic reference librarian for low- and medium-level queries using a variety of technologies, including video-text, computer-assisted teaching modules, and knowledge-based systems. Directional transactions, such as library locations, services, and policies, make up ORA. According to Mogali (2014), the aforementioned systems are all advisory systems for accessing reference information resources.

AI for Indexing

AI technologies are also being developed for the indexing of library resources, particularly periodicals. Indexing is the foundation for document retrieval. Enhancing recall (the proportion of relevant content retrieved) and accuracy (ensuring that the fraction of recovered material is acceptable) are the goals of indexing. When a searcher enters these keywords into the electronic database in the correct order, the system will produce the citation for an article or other material. These keywords have been determined by an expert (indexer) or a body to be fundamental to human thought on a particular topic. The process of indexing a monthly article involves determining its essential elements, converting them into spoken descriptions, and selecting and assigning controlled vocabulary terms that are conceptually equivalent to the spoken descriptions. Improving index quality and consistency is the goal of automating the cognitive aspects of indexing. Based on the information supplied, the indexing systems may automatically choose the suitable preferred words to assign the necessary subdivisions.

In this network-centric information age, a number of well-known information retrieval difficulties have grown significantly more crucial as the applications get larger, more urgent, and more diverse. The most important IR approach is the identification of critical material properties. Texture, colour, or shape-based indexing and segmentation techniques are commonly used to identify photographs, while automatic indexing and natural language processing are widely used to extract important words or phrases on the fly from information sources. Important descriptions in audio and video streams can be found using speech recognition, voice recognition, and scene separation techniques in audio and video applications. The intelligent system is capable of interpretation and appropriate action depending on the conclusions drawn. One example of an AI indexing system in operation is the Med Index. for tasks related to indexing in the library. The range of ways a subject can be expressed is the indexing system's primary limitation (Afolayan et al., 2020)

AI FOR COLLECTION DEVELOPMENT

AI technologies can be used to choose book dealers or suppliers for library supplies. Based on prior successful transactions in supplying publications of a certain sort, an intelligent system to identify a vendor or book seller may be built. These kinds of technologies would be especially useful for acquiring information items that are not as common, including conference proceedings, publications in other languages or other nations, and specific technical reports, to name a few. Furthermore, research has shown that artificial intelligence (AI) technologies have been created specifically for the librarianship field to help with the selecting process. Among these systems are: One creative attempt to use this emerging technology to create library information resources is the Monograph Selection Advisor. The technology specifically replicated the item-by-item decision-making process that a topic bibliographer uses to choose monographic materials. In order to guarantee that the library can get the intended outcomes from the AI system, the system's knowledge base must be large enough and its interface features must be sufficiently straightforward.

Artificial intelligence is a vast and all-encompassing subject of research that can be challenging for non-specialists to understand without some foundational understanding. AI has created new opportunities for advancing research across the board. Researchers are already creating new technologies that can imitate the mental processes of librarians and display hitherto unattainable human characteristics. ICT gadgets, computer systems, and other devices are evolving technologically to the point where they are designed to think and act like people. At the same time, the concept of human intelligence (HI) is evolving into artificial intelligence (AI). To create an intelligent system, implicit human knowledge must be retrieved. This means that before creating an AI device, pertinent traits and information must be taken from human specialists; these traits and knowledge are frequently heuristic in nature. Applications and uses for computer-based goods and services include a range of library operations procedures, the provision of diverse library services, and the creation of output products. Artificial intelligence applications will aid in simulating human decision-making. AI technologies are used by library intelligent systems to deliver knowledge-based services to users (Asemi and Asemi, 2018).

Given its widespread use, artificial intelligence ought to be embraced and used in libraries. Its adoption in libraries is sluggish, particularly in Africa. The majority of the time, academic libraries employ these intelligent systems by utilising a variety of library procedures. The actual relevance of artificial intelligence (AI) on our civilization is demonstrated by its main applications, not by its technological triumphs. Automating human labour is what artificial intelligence applications aim to do. Up until recently, a number of people have started to recognise that robots are capable of doing tasks that are as challenging as self-driving vehicles or interpretation (ALA, 2019).

FUTURES OF AI IN LIBRARIES

Enhancement of Metadata: Artificial Intelligence (AI) technologies enable the automated tagging, classification, and enrichment of metadata for library materials, leading to increased search precision and retrieval effectiveness

Virtual Assistants: AI-powered virtual assistants may be used by libraries to improve accessibility and user happiness by answering questions from users, assisting with navigation.

Predictive analytics: By using AI models to forecast user demands, resource consumption trends, and library usage patterns, proactive resource allocation and collection development are made possible.

Automation of Routine Tasks: By streamlining repetitive library operations like inventory control, circulation management, and cataloguing, AI automation frees up staff time for additional high-value services.

Enhanced Accessibility: By offering text-to-speech capabilities, audio explanations, and alternate formats, AI technology may be used to make websites more accessible to people with impairments .

AI in libraries has the potential to completely transform the way that information is stored, accessed, and used in the future. With the use of conversational interfaces, tailored recommendations, and sophisticated search algorithms, AI-driven solutions have the potential to significantly improve user experiences and enable smooth interaction between library users and resources. Furthermore, libraries will be able to gain greater insights into user behavior and preferences thanks to AI-powered analytics, which will help them with collection development strategies and resource allocation decisions.

Advent of AI in Libraries

An important trend that is changing how libraries function and the services they provide is the introduction of artificial intelligence (AI) into libraries. The following are some significant ways that AI is affecting libraries:

Better Information Retrieval: Algorithms driven by AI improve the precision and effectiveness of information retrieval. Artificial intelligence (AI) systems have the capability to provide more pertinent search results by examining large volumes of data and user behaviour.

Intelligent Resource Management: Libraries can digitise resources, automate cataloguing procedures, and efficiently arrange information thanks to AI technologies like machine learning and natural language processing. This facilitates administrative work and increases resource accessibility, opening them out to a larger audience. By examining consumption trends and forecasting future demand for certain resources, AI may also aid in the optimisation of collection development.

Chatbots and Virtual Assistants: AI-driven chatbots and virtual assistants give library patrons immediate assistance. They can help with research inquiries, provide answers to often asked questions, and direct users to the resources and services offered by the library. These virtual assistants provide round-the-clock assistance, enhancing user experience overall and guaranteeing that researchers and students get help quickly.

Data Analytics for Better Decision-Making: AI helps libraries to take use of data analytics' potential. AI algorithms may offer insights into resource utilisation by examining consumption trends. This allows libraries to better manage their budgets, optimise their resources, and customise their services to their patrons' demands.

Content Classification and Tagging: AI systems categorise and tag library materials according to their content, genre, subject, or format by using machine learning algorithms. This improves discoverability by facilitating effective resource organisation and retrieval.

Duplicate Detection and Removal: By examining metadata and content similarities, AI systems are able to locate duplicate items in library catalogues. This facilitates the preservation of data integrity and expedites the cataloguing procedure.

Improved Search and Suggestion: Artificial intelligence (AI)-enabled search engines employ natural language processing (NLP) to comprehend user queries and deliver more precise and pertinent search results. Furthermore, AI recommendation systems enhance user experience by making similar item suggestions based on browsing history and user preferences.

Preservation and Restoration: By scanning, evaluating, and improving degraded documents, photos, and audio-visuals recordings, artificial intelligence (AI) systems help preserve and restore archive assets.

Library Operations

Throughout the lengthy and intricate history of the institution, library management systems have developed in tandem with associated technological advancements. Initially, the focus was on integrating routine processes such as allocating late fines and monitoring book loans.

Automation of libraries began with the potential to transform these manual methods into computerised ones with the development of computer technology. Again, rule-based software and artificial intelligence developments are propelling library management systems forward.

Automation of Robotic Processes

Robotic process automation (RPA) is already being used, for instance, by certain libraries to handle standard administrative duties including data transfer, shelf management, form processing, and email marketing. While some others are testing out automated storage and retrieval,

Clever Libraries

A "Smart Library," which is open to users without a physical staff, is the vision of artificial intelligence in library operations in the future. Remote controls will be used to operate self-service kiosks, doors, lights, and desktop PCs. Personal digital assistants (PDAs) will be used by patrons to look up and retrieve items.

Services for Users

One of the main goals of libraries and library professionals has always been to offer dependable and beneficial services that are customised for certain user groups. These services may appear static since they involve essential elements of every library, such as Collection Development, Circulation, Reference, Interlibrary Loans, and Programming. However, in practice, they are incredibly flexible, always adjusting to dynamic pressures such as user needs and emerging technology.

Artificial intelligence is being used in libraries worldwide to address these two issues. AI-powered chatbots are showing promise in facilitating quick and highly-personalized information requests for users who may be used to text messaging and round-the-clock support. Additionally, they are developing programming that educates users how to use AI tools securely and appropriately, as well as introducing them to new tools.

Plans are being made by libraries to accommodate the demands of user groups as artificial intelligence is sure to grow and influence them in the future. More individualised and user-friendly services will be provided by integrating AI technologies into its circulation services, such as recommendation systems that provide suggestions based on customers' past searches and borrowing habits. By detecting sensitive information, it may also provide more accessibility to born-digital resources, enabling libraries to democratise the non-sensitive portions.

KNOWLEDGE OF DATA AND AI

Libraries and academic institutions have emphasised the value of information literacy since the 1970s. Information literacy is usually understood to be a set of abilities required to find and utilise information for problem solving and decision making. The American Library Association formally proposed in 1989 to guarantee the inclusion of information literacy in national research, curricula, and policy.

The basic idea of information literacy has gained additional dimensions as information has changed in terms of format and distribution methods. Among the additions are:

Literacy with resources
Research Proficiency
proficiency with computers and more.

Library Statistics

In libraries, data analysis often uses static data that is obtained from circulation and usage statistics, saved for further examination, and then altered to address certain queries such as:

Which book is absent from this assortment?

"When is the average library visitation period?"

This strategy is not only labor-intensive and ineffectual, but it also ensures that the data that is provided is irrelevant and out-of-date.

It makes sense to include artificial intelligence into library analytics. Its objective is to use data to find patterns in situations that are almost real-time. Professionals at libraries may use this data to create planning and management plans that will improve the services they offer.

The AI Revolution in Public Library Systems

Libraries Using AI Applications

The use of AI in public libraries is undergoing a fascinating revolution that is changing how these establishments run and interact with their users. An extensive examination of the several AI in libraries can be found here:

AI for Classification and Cataloguing

Artificial Intelligence has the ability to completely transform library cataloguing and categorization procedures. Conventional cataloguing is a labor-intensive procedure that necessitates a thorough comprehension of intricate standards and regulations. This procedure can be automated by AI, which will speed up and improve accuracy. Books, journals, and multimedia resources are just a few examples of the various items that AI may be trained to identify and classify.

AI can also improve library patrons' search and discovery experiences. Artificial Intelligence (AI) can enhance the relevancy of search results and offer tailored suggestions by examining user behaviour and preferences. This can improve patrons' entire library experience by making it simpler for them to locate the materials they require.

Artificial Intelligence for User Services

AI has the potential to greatly improve library user services. Using chatbots for customer support is one of the most popular uses of AI in this field. These AI-powered chatbots can answer a variety of questions, from straightforward ones about library hours to trickier ones about resources that are accessible. They can react quickly, enhancing customer service effectiveness and freeing up library employees to work on more difficult assignments.

AI is also capable of giving people customised recommendations. Artificial intelligence (AI) may recommend materials that users may find interesting or helpful by examining user behaviour and preferences. Users may find new resources through this that they would not have located on their own.

AI may also be applied to improve accessibility in libraries. AI may be used, for example, to transcribe audio materials so that those with hearing problems can access them. In order to make materials available to a larger audience, it may also be used to translate them into other languages.

Using AI in Predictive Analysis

Through predictive analysis, AI may offer insightful information. AI is able to forecast future demands and preferences by examining user behaviour and patterns. This can aid libraries in more efficiently allocating their resources and services.

AI, for example, can forecast which resources will be in high demand in the future by analysing borrowing trends. By doing this, libraries may better manage their holdings and make sure the appropriate resources are available when they're needed.

AI's Potential Advantages for Libraries

Artificial intelligence has a plethora of revolutionary potential advantages for libraries. By offering individualised services based on user behaviour and interests, such customised book suggestions, AI may greatly improve the user experience. With technologies that can transform visual resources into formats that are readable by those with visual impairments, it can help increase accessibility. Another major advantage of AI is efficiency, since it can automate repetitive processes like loan administration and cataloguing, freeing up employees to work on more difficult jobs. AI may also help with data-driven decision making by evaluating vast amounts of data to offer insightful information about resource popularity and consumption patterns. Libraries may use this to help them make well-informed operational choices. Let's examine a few of the advantages in greater detail:

Improved User Experience

The application of artificial intelligence (AI) in libraries has the potential to completely change patron experience. AI systems are capable of providing individualised suggestions and services by learning from user behaviour and preferences. AI can, for example, examine a user's reading preferences and recommend materials or books that fit their interests. Users may find the library experience more enjoyable and engaging with this degree of personalisation.

AI can also increase library accessibility. For people with limited vision, Facebook's Automatic Alternative Text service, for instance, utilises AI to recognise items in a photo and generate a description that can be read out by a text-to-speech engine. Libraries might employ similar technologies to improve visually impaired patrons' access to visual resources.

Data-Informed Decision Making

AI is capable of analysing vast volumes of data to produce insights that help libraries make decisions. AI, for instance, may examine use statistics to spot trends and patterns, such the most popular resources or the busiest times of day. These observations can assist libraries in making better-informed choices about the distribution of resources, hours of operation, and other related issues.

AI can also assist libraries in navigating and comprehending the expanding corpus of public research. For example, the Semantic Scholar search engine from the Allen Institute for Artificial Intelligence leverages AI to enhance the way researchers find publications online. This might be utilised in libraries to assist patrons in more quickly locating pertinent research.

The Difficulties of Using AI in Libraries

Libraries are not left behind in the need to change and adapt as we move farther into the digital era. A breakthrough that has the potential to completely transform library operations is the incorporation of Artificial Intelligence (AI) into systems. This will enable data-driven decision-making, enhanced efficiency, and personalised user experiences. But there are obstacles in the way of this digital transformation path. Libraries confront several obstacles in their efforts to integrate and utilise artificial intelligence, ranging from technology limitations to privacy and ethical considerations. In order to highlight the difficulties in integrating AI into the library industry, this section explores a number of these issues.

Strong data and artificial intelligence (AI) knowledge is becoming more and more important in a variety of fields as businesses use these tools to spur innovation, obtain new insights, and make decisions. AI systems are constructed using data, which is composed of both organized and unstructured information that is gathered, processed, and analyzed to find relevant patterns and connections. Artificial intelligence (AI) methods like computer vision, machine learning, and natural language processing allow enterprises to obtain actionable intelligence and improve operational efficiency by automatically extracting insights from large datasets. To ensure the responsible and fair use of data-driven technologies, however, a comprehensive understanding of data governance, ethics, and bias is necessary to negotiate the ethical and regulatory challenges surrounding AI adoption. Consequently, a thorough understanding of data AI promotes ethical stewardship and societal benefit in a society that is becoming more and more data-driven, in addition to helping with strategic decision-making and competitive advantage.

LIMITATIONS OF TECHNOLOGY

The limitations of technology provide libraries with their biggest obstacle when incorporating AI. Many libraries lack the resources needed to install and operate AI systems, especially smaller ones or those located in underdeveloped areas. This is a worldwide problem, not one that is exclusive to libraries. For example, a recent Indian news article described how rural schools are finding it difficult to implement digital learning because of a lack of infrastructure and resources. This is a reflection of the inadequate or nonexistent financing for cutting-edge technology like artificial intelligence in many libraries throughout the globe.

Despite continuous progress, technology has limitations in many areas. Emerging technologies and future trends in artificial intelligence (AI) and libraries present both obstacles and promising answers. AI-driven automation, such as chatbots for user help and personalized recommendations, is becoming increasingly important in streamlining library operations and improving user experiences. However, there might be restrictions on the moral use of AI, such as worries about algorithmic bias and data privacy. Additionally, due to resource limitations and the requirement for specialized expertise, libraries may encounter difficulties adopting and integrating these technologies as AI continues to progress. However, continuous advances in AI, such as those in machine learning and natural language processing, have the potential to completely change how libraries organize and make knowledge available, opening up new possibilities for creativity and better services in the digital era. But there are still issues with guaranteeing the moral application of AI and reducing possible biases in algorithmic decision-making in library settings. To properly traverse these intricacies, further research, cooperation, and community involvement are required.

The potential for technology to exacerbate preexisting biases and inequality is another important drawback. Digital technologies can unintentionally reinforce or magnify social biases despite efforts to promote inclusivity. This is especially true for AI systems that were created without diverse representation or that were trained on biased datasets. This restriction highlights the necessity of continuing efforts to provide equitable access to technology and digital literacy abilities, as well as the significance of addressing problems of justice, transparency, and accountability in AI development and deployment. In addition, new trends in AI and libraries point to the need to keep utilizing AI for predictive analytics and data-driven decision-making in order to maximize resource allocation and library services. AI integration into metadata management and library cataloging procedures is another recent development that improves the effectiveness and precision of information organizing and retrieval. But there are still issues with guaranteeing the moral application of AI and reducing possible biases in algorithmic decision-making in library settings. To properly traverse these intricacies, further research, cooperation, and community involvement are required.

Concerns About Ethics and Privacy

There are serious ethical and privacy issues with the introduction of artificial intelligence (AI) technology into several industries, including libraries. These issues are not exclusive to libraries; they are a worldwide problem that has an impact on a number of industries, including social media, healthcare, and banking.

For AI systems to work well, massive volumes of data are frequently required. There may be sensitive user information in this data, which raises concerns regarding data security and user privacy. AI is utilised, for example, in the healthcare industry to forecast illness and suggest therapies. However, the need for these technologies to access private patient information raises questions about data security and privacy. Similar to this, AI is utilised in the financial industry for fraud detection and credit rating, which also entails

Concerns About Ethics and Privacy

Artificial intelligence (AI) technology integration has prompted serious ethical and privacy concerns in a number of industries, including libraries.

Examples of AI Use Cases in Libraries

All throughout the world, libraries are looking for new and creative methods to improve their operations and services. An increasingly popular innovation in library systems is the incorporation of Artificial Intelligence (AI). AI has the potential to completely transform library services because of its capacity for learning, reasoning, and self-correction. AI is poised to completely transform the way libraries operate, from automating repetitive operations to delivering individualised user experiences. This post will examine some actual instances of AI being used in libraries to show how this technology has the ability to completely change the library environment.

Applications:

Improved User Experience: By offering individualised suggestions and help with research, AI-powered virtual assistants can enhance patron experiences in libraries.

Data Management and Analysis: Artificial Intelligence can help libraries manage and analyse massive volumes of data by organising, cataloguing, and extracting insights from digital collections.

information Curation and Recommendation: AI systems have the capacity to choose and suggest pertinent information to consumers based on their browsing history and preferences, which improves discoverability.

Predictive analytics: AI can identify patterns in library usage, which helps libraries better manage resources and anticipate patron requirements.

BENEFITS OF ARTIFICIAL INTELLIGENCE IN LIBRARIES

AI Boosts Efficiency and Effectiveness in Operations

By improving information resource provision and service efficacy and lowering operational costs through automation, digital asset management, and improved research data governance, libraries may assess and improve the organisational effectiveness and efficiency of library services. The integration of artificial intelligence technologies into library procedures and services can lead to many benefits such as collection analysis, visualisation, conservation and preservation, and cost reduction. Putting intelligent technologies into place to provide library services and resources may foster creativity and innovation, which will increase operational effectiveness and efficiency.

Assists Librarians in Reaching Their New Objectives

When AI approaches are applied, human errors and inefficiencies are reduced. Examples of these routines include daily searches and reference operations. These intelligent systems can free up library staff members to work on other worthwhile projects, such as helping patrons create reading lists, teaching patrons how to do better scientific research, developing library information resources, and so on.

Chatbots and Virtual Agents Powered by AI: Combining RPA with AI chatbots improves customer service by automating answers to commonly asked inquiries and carrying out duties like making appointments.

Intelligent Document Processing (IDP): IDP automates document-centric tasks like contract management and invoice processing by using AI algorithms for data extraction, categorization, and validation Process

Mining and Discovery: To find automation possibilities and streamline workflows, AI-driven process discovery technologies examine user interactions and data logs

Self-Learning Bots: RPA bots with artificial intelligence (AI) capabilities are able to learn from user interactions and data trends in order to gradually increase the accuracy and flexibility of their automation

Improved Information Retrieval and Search

By using algorithms that examine user queries, preferences, and browsing habits to provide more precise and pertinent search results, artificial intelligence enhances library search capabilities. With the use of natural language processing (NLP) techniques, search engines powered by artificial intelligence (AI) may better comprehend user intent and give customized answers to complicated searches. Furthermore, AI-powered recommendation systems make relevant resource recommendations based on user behavior and interests, which promotes accidental discovery and improves the user experience in general.

Automating Typical Tasks

By automating repetitive processes like cataloging, indexing, and metadata management, AI automation simplifies library operations. With the use of machine learning algorithms, library resources can be analyzed and categorized more quickly, saving manual work and enhancing the consistency and accuracy of metadata tagging. Additionally, administrative duties like issuing past-due reminders and updating patron information can be automated by robotic process automation (RPA), freeing up library staff members to concentrate on higher-value activities like user engagement and community outreach.

Customized User Interfaces

By evaluating user data and preferences, AI helps libraries to provide individualized user experiences by customizing messaging, services, and suggestions. Artificial intelligence (AI)-powered chatbots and virtual assistants offer consumers individualized support by responding to questions, suggesting resources, and assisting them in navigating the library's resources in a conversational style. Additionally, AI-powered content curation increases user happiness and engagement by providing personalized content recommendations based on browsing history, feedback, and preferences.

Customized User Interfaces

By evaluating user data and preferences, AI helps libraries to provide individualized user experiences by customizing messaging, services, and suggestions. Artificial intelligence (AI)-powered chatbots and virtual assistants offer consumers individualized support by responding to questions, suggesting resources, and assisting them in navigating the library's resources in a conversational style. Additionally, AI-powered content curation increases user happiness and engagement by providing personalized content recommendations based on browsing history, feedback, and preferences.

CHALLENGES OF ARTIFICIAL INTELLIGENCE IN LIBRARIES

Uncertainty in Finances

Libraries and other cultural organisations typically see cuts to their funding anytime public revenue and budgets decline and socioeconomic or political developments take place on a global scale. Libraries are unable to justify funding or exhibit cost-effective procedures, particularly if they do not leverage technology innovations to upgrade their physical spaces, launch novel services, and improve the overall experience of library patrons. All of these demand more financial resources. Libraries and library staff find it difficult to justify the integration of these new technologies into their systems due to a lack of proper information and understanding about the operational advantages and significant cost savings that the application of artificial intelligence techniques can provide to libraries. As a result, modern libraries frequently face budgetary constraints and are unable to demonstrate value without a significant financial outlay. Moreover, proprietary software powers the vast majority of AI systems. Libraries are not currently seeing a lot of interest in researching AI-based breakthroughs; further discussion and clarity among specialists are still needed.

Openness to Change

Throughout the world, most librarians are scared that AI will take over the work environment and render them jobless. Humans are notoriously resistant to change in operational processes and the introduction of advanced technologies. Staff in libraries frequently exhibit obstinance, even defensiveness, when it comes to technological transition. This might be due to a variety of beliefs, technophobia, or even fear of losing their jobs.

Technical expertise and gradual learning curves among library employees An increasing number of libraries are indicating a desire to use extremely creative procedures and technological applications. The majority of libraries, however, are unaware of how to use the tools, and staff acceptance rates are still rather low. Skill gaps in digital literacy are impeding the usage of AI tools and technology.

Privacy of Users

Artificial intelligence ultimately learns to detect particular data sets through machine learning when it is fed enormous volumes of data. Nowadays, personal data is a commodity that may be utilised for evil purposes. AI has the potential to compromise data privacy, which has always been a vital asset to libraries and is much more so in the current technological world. Librarians must safeguard users' privacy by enabling anonymous communication between users and AI systems. Furthermore, since searches and inquiries are logged, this data might be used against specific people. There is a risk while requesting and receiving communications from artificial intelligence systems since machine learning might collect private information.

Language Proficiencies

The limited memory and processing power of chatbots make it impossible for them to grasp a wide vocabulary or range of conversational styles. Developers face a difficult task in any multilingual country since dialects differ by location and preprogrammed interactional styles might not be suitable for every kind of communication. They must anticipate the forms of interaction and create acceptable responses to them.

Recognising Users' Feelings

Because AI is so efficient, human creativity and empathy would be diminished. This would lead to a future in which the library's community ties and other important human qualities would be valued and in short supply. Because they have feelings and are able to sense each other's emotions, humans are superior to robots. A crucial quality for any library employee is empathy, which improves the delivery of information resources and services and helps users' information requirements be met. Artificial intelligence should be used to help and do tasks in a new way rather than being permitted to diminish values based on the interchange and availability of information.

Integration Complexity: It might be difficult and complex to integrate AI technology into library systems in a seamless manner with the current infrastructure.

Data Security and Privacy: Libraries manage sensitive user data, which presents security and privacy issues when using AI-driven solutions. Ensuring adherence to data protection rules while utilising artificial intelligence presents notable obstacles.

Digital Divide: The use of AI may make the divide worse since some library patrons would not have access to cutting-edge technology or the necessary digital literacy abilities to take advantage of services

Ethical Concerns: AI systems have the potential to reinforce biases seen in training data, which might result in unjust outcomes or discriminatory actions. It is imperative to address prejudice and guarantee algorithmic fairness in AI applications used in libraries.

Resource Constraints: It might be difficult to invest in and maintain AI projects at libraries since they frequently have limited funds and resources. One major challenge is overcoming resource limitations while preserving AI infrastructure and knowledge.

User Acceptance and Trust: It's critical to increase user acceptance and trust of AI technology in library services. Building trust and promoting use of AI requires educating library employees and users about its potential, constraints, and ethical ramifications.

Other difficulties include commercial organisations, which may result in discrepancies in librarianship, and prejudice, which arises when algorithms are created to operate based on developer bias. As a result, concerns are raised about the accountability and transparency of artificial intelligence systems. Furthermore, two primary factors that determine an artificial intelligence system's quality level or intelligence are its corpus capacity, which is data-related, and its logical algorithms, which are technical in nature. Because technology is advancing so quickly, an increasing number of sophisticated algorithms are being created and improved upon. More crawlers would be required to capture the internet and increase its intelligence in order to stay up.

AI Algorithm Bias and Ethical Issues

By enacting transparency policies and embracing inclusive practices, libraries can address moral questions and lessen bias in AI systems. This entails giving consumers a clear understanding of how artificial intelligence (AI) systems operate and the data they rely on, empowering them to accept and comprehend the suggestions and judgments made by AI. Libraries may guarantee that AI systems take into account the requirements and viewpoints of a variety of user groups by emphasizing inclusion and diversity in algorithm design and data collection. Furthermore, continuous assessment and monitoring of AI algorithms can support the accountability and fairness of AI-powered library services by assisting in the identification and correction of biases or unexpected outcomes.

Digital Gap and AI-Powered Service Access

Libraries can conduct outreach initiatives and give resources to marginalized areas in order to close the digital gap and guarantee fair access to AI-driven library services. Offering digital literacy training courses could be one way to enable customers to efficiently use AI-powered technology. Libraries can also work with educational institutions and community organizations to give underprivileged communities access to computer networks and other technology infrastructure. Additionally, libraries can promote digital inclusion as a vital aspect of library services by lobbying for laws and financing programs that enable equitable access to technology and digital resources.

Risks to Data Security and Privacy

By placing a high priority on user privacy and putting strong data protection measures in place, libraries can manage the privacy and data security threats connected with AI. This involves minimizing the amount of sensitive user data that AI algorithms are exposed to by implementing privacy-preserving AI approaches including federated learning, differential privacy, and encryption. Additionally, libraries can set up explicit data governance policies and processes for managing and safeguarding user data, guaranteeing adherence to pertinent privacy laws like the CCPA and GDPR. Furthermore, libraries have the ability to teach patrons about their rights and choices regarding the management of their personal data, enabling them to make knowledgeable choices regarding the sharing of their data with AI-powered library services.

CONCLUSION

AI's Role in Public Libraries

Public libraries might undergo a dramatic change as a result of artificial intelligence (AI), becoming more effective, user-friendly, and data-driven. It's obvious that artificial intelligence (AI) will become more and more integral to how libraries function and serve their communities in the future.

Enhancing information retrieval is one of the main areas where artificial intelligence may have an impact. AI-powered algorithms can analyse enormous volumes of data and user behaviour to improve the efficiency and accuracy of information retrieval. This can produce more pertinent search results, assisting library patrons in swiftly and effectively locating the information they want. This enhances the user experience overall and saves important time.

Within the subject of librarianship, artificial intelligence applications are a growing technology. Artificial Intelligence has great promise for simplifying and enhancing the availability, handling, utilisation, and safety of library resources. To address issues with teaching and research pertaining to the use of AI in libraries, LIS researchers should work with AI specialists. Opportunities in librarianship will arise from this, and library patrons will receive effective and efficient information resources and services. Although artificial intelligence is being used in the library in many different contexts, the majority of these applications are still in the theoretical stage, which means they are more or less restricted and cannot be put into practice. This is because there is a lack of investment in artificial intelligence hardware and research for libraries, challenges with big data collection and mining, a shortage of talent for library AI, and a lack of artificial intelligence thinking in the library industry, particularly in the Global South nations like Nigeria. Instead than being afraid that these sophisticated technologies would replace them, librarians should be prepared to increase their level of expertise so they can interact with these systems and work more productively.

REFERENCES

Afolayan, J. O., Ogundokun, R. O., Afolabi, A. G., & Adegun, A. A. (2020). Artificial intelligence,cloud librarianship, and infopreneurship initiatives for Inclusiveness. In Managing and Adapting Library Information Services for Future Users. IGI Global. doi:10.4018/978-1-5225-9034-7.ch003

Ali, M. Y., Naeem, S. B., & Bhatti, R. (2020). Artificial intelligence tools and perspectives of university librarians: An overview. *Business Information Review*, *37*(3), 1–9. doi:10.1177/0266382120952016

Asemi, A., & Asemi, A. (2018). Artificial Intelligence (AI) application in Library Systems in Iran: A taxonomy study. *Library Philosophy and Practice (e-journal)*. https://digitalcommons.unl.edu/libphilprac/1840

Chemulwo, M. J., & Sirorei, E. C. (2020). Managing and adapting library information services for future users: Applying AI in libraries. In Managing and Adapting Library Information Services for Future Users. IGI Global

Cox, A. M., Pinfield, S., & Rutter, S. (2019). The intelligent library: Thought leaders' views on the likely impact of artificial intelligence on academic libraries. *Library Hi Tech*, *37*(3), 418–435. doi:10.1108/LHT-08-2018-0105

Gujral, G., Shivarama, J. & Choukimath, P. A. (2019) Perceptions and Prospects of Artificial Intelligence Technologies for Academic Libraries: An Overview of Global Trends. *12th International CALIBER-2019*. Research Gate.

IFLA. (2016). *IFLA Trend Report 2016*. IFLA.

Kim, B. (2019). AI and Creating the First Multidisciplinary AI Lab. In J. Griffey (Ed.), *Artificial Intelligence and Machine Learning in Libraries. American Library Association*. ALA.

Kumar, S. V., & Sheshadri, K. N. (2019). Applications of artificial intelligence in academic libraries. *International Journal on Computer Science and Engineering*, *7*(16), 136–140. doi:10.26438/ijcse/v7si16.136140

Mogali, S. S. (2014). *Artificial Intelligence and its applications in Libraries*. Academic Press.

Omame, I. M., & Alex-Nmecha, J. C. (2020). Artificial intelligence in libraries. In Managing and Adapting Library Information Services for Future Users. IGI Global. doi:10.4018/978-1-7998-1116-9.ch008

Otterlo, M. (2016). Project BLIIPS: Making the Physical Public Library more Intelligent through Artificial Intelligence. *Qualitative and Quantitative Methods in Libraries*, *5*, 287–300.

Thayyib, P. V., Mamilla, R., Khan, M., Fatima, H., Asim, M., Anwar, I., Shamsudheen, M. K., & Asif Khan, M. (2023). State-of-the-art of artificial intelligence and big data analytics reviews in five different domains: A bibliometric summary. *Sustainability (Basel)*, *15*(5), 42. doi:10.3390/su15054026

Vysakh, C. & Rajendra Babu, H. (2019). Application of Artificially Intelligent Robot in Libraries. *ICRLIT – 2019: e-Proceedings*, (pp. 59-63). ICRLIT.

Whitehair, K. (2016). *Libraries in an Artificially Intelligent World*. Public Libraries. http://publiclibrar-iesonline.org/2016/02/libraries-in-an-artificially-intelligent-world/

Yu, K., Gong, R., Sun, L., & Jiang, C. (2019). *The application of artificial intelligence in smart library*.

Yusuf, T. I., Adebayo, O. A., Bello, L. A., & Kayode, J. O. (2022). Adoption of artificial intelligence for effective library service delivery in academic libraries in Nigeria. *Library Philosophy & Practice* 6804:1–13. https://digitalcommons.unl.edu/libphilprac/6804

Compilation of References

Abdulwahid, A. H., Pattnaik, M., Palav, M. R., Tilak Babu, S. B. G., Manoharan, G., & Pandi Selvi, G. (2023). Library Management System Using Artificial Intelligence. *2023 Eighth International Conference on Science Technology Engineering and Mathematics (ICONSTEM)*, Chennai, India. 10.1109/ICONSTEM56934.2023.10142904

Adakawa, M. I., Al-hassan, Z. M., & Auyo, M. A. (2020). Now and Future of Libraries: the Necessity to Equip Librarians with Cybersecurity Skills. In *Management of Library and Information Centers in the Era of Global Insecurity*. https://www.researchgate.net/publication/346967054

Adejo, A. A & Misau, A.Y.(2021), Application of artificial intelligence in academic libraries in Nigeria. *Library philosophy and practice(e-journal), 6639.*

Adetayo, A. J. (2023). Artificial intelligence chatbots in academic libraries: The rise of ChatGPT. *Library Hi Tech News*, *3*(3), 18–21. doi:10.1108/LHTN-01-2023-0007

Afolayan, J. O., Ogundokun, R. O., Afolabi, A. G., & Adegun, A. A. (2020). Artificial intelligence,cloud librarianship, and infopreneurship initiatives for Inclusiveness. In Managing and Adapting Library Information Services for Future Users. IGI Global. doi:10.4018/978-1-5225-9034-7.ch003

Aguilar, I., Valdivizo-Diaz, P., & Riofrio, G. (2017). (2017). A general framework for intelligent recommender systems. *Applied Computing and Informatics*, *13*(2), 147–160. doi:10.1016/j.aci.2016.08.002

Ahmed, M., Mukhopadhyay, M., & Mukhopadhyay, P. (2023). Automated Knowledge Organisation: AI/ML-based Subject Indexing System for Libraries. *DESIDOC Journal of Library and Information Technology*, *43*(1), 45–54. doi:10.14429/djlit.43.01.18619

Aithal, S & Aithal, P.S (2023). *Effects of AI-based ChatGPT on Higher Education libraries.*

Ajani, Y. A., Tella, A., Salawu, K. Y., & Abdullahi, F. (2022). Perspectives of librarians on awareness and readiness of academic libraries to integrate artificial intelligence for library operations and services in Nigeria. *Internet Reference Services Quarterly*, *26*(4), 1–18. doi:10.1080/10875301.2022.2086196

Ajie, I. (2019). A Review of Trends and Issues of Cybersecurity in Academic Libraries. *Library Philosophy and Practice (E-Journal)*, 1–20. https://digitalcommons.unl.edu/libphilprac/2523

Akakpo, M. G. (2023, November 09). Skilled for the Future: Information Literacy for AI Use by University Students in Africa and the Role of Librarians. *Internet Reference Services Quarterly*. doi:10.1080/10875301.2023.2280566

Alberico, R. (2011). The future of expert systems and artificial intelligence technologies in. *The Application of Expert Systems in Libraries and Information Centres*, 194.

Al-Daihani, S. M & Abrahams, A. (2015). A text mining analysis of academic libraries tweets. *The Journal of Academic Librarianship, 42(2016), 135-143.*

Alhaif, A. M. (2023). Training Needs of Information Specialists at Saudi Universities Libraries to Achieve Cybersecurity Requirements. *International Journal of Education and Information Technologies*, *17*, 38–50. doi:10.46300/9109.2023.17.5

Ali, M. Y., Naeem, S. B., & Bhatti, R. (2020). Artificial intelligence tools and perspectives of university librarians: An overview. *Business Information Review*, *37*(3), 116–124. doi:10.1177/0266382120952016

Allison, D. (2012). Chatbots in the library: Is it time? *Library Hi Tech*, *30*(1), 95–107. doi:10.1108/07378831211213238

Almaghrabi, M., & Chetty, G. (2020, December). Deep Machine Learning Digital library recommendation system based on Metadata for Arabic and English Languages. In *2020 IEEE Asia-Pacific Conference on Computer Science and Data Engineering (CSDE)* (pp. 1-6). IEEE. 10.1109/CSDE50874.2020.9411525

Altmami, N. I., & Menai, M. E. B. (2020). Automatic summarization of scientific articles: A survey. *Journal of King Saud University. Computer and Information Sciences*, *34*(4), 1011–1028. https://creativecommons.org/licenses/by-nc-nd/4.0/. doi:10.1016/j.jksuci.2020.04.020

Alzubaidi, A. (2021). Measuring the level of cyber-security awareness for cybercrime in Saudi Arabia. *Heliyon*, *7*(1), e06016. doi:10.1016/j.heliyon.2021.e06016 PMID:33537477

American Library Association [ALA]. (2023). *AI Empowerment for Library Staff: Ethical, Equitable, and Engaging Solutions*. ALA. https://elearning.ala.org/local/catalog/view/product.php?productid=940

Amini, M., & Jahanbakhsh Javid, N. (2023). A Multi-Perspective Framework Established on Diffusion of Innovation (DOI) Theory and Technology, Organization and Environment (TOE) Framework Toward Supply Chain Management System Based on Cloud Computing Technology for Small and Medium Enterprises. *International Journal of Information Technology and Innovation Adoption*, *11*, 1217–1234.

Amram, T., Malamud, R. G., & Hollingsworth, C. (2023). Response to" From ChatGPT to CatGPT. *Information Technology and Libraries*, *42*(4). doi:10.5860/ital.v42i4.16983

Anday, A., Francese, E., Huurdeman, H. C., Yılmaz, M., & Zengenene, D. (2012). Information Security Issues in a Digital Library Environment: A Literature Review. *Bilgi Dünyası, 13*(1), 117–137. doi:10.15612/BD.2012.171

Angela, O. N., Adekoya, O. M., & Zajime, B. N. (2021). Integration of artificial intelligence into library and information workflow for enhanced services in developing economies. *Ahmadu Bello University Library Complex International Conference Book of Proceedings*, 663–671.

Archer, L., Godec, S., Calabrese Barton, A., Dawson, E., Mau, A., & Patel, U. (2021). Changing the field: A Bourdieusian analysis of educational practices that support equitable outcomes among minoritized youth on two informal science learning programs. *Science Education*, *105*(1), 166–203. doi:10.1002/sce.21602 PMID:34588711

Ardagna, C. A., De Capitani di Vimercati, S., & Samarati, P. (2006). Enhancing user privacy through data handling policies. In *Data and Applications Security XX: 20th Annual IFIP WG 11.3 Working Conference on Data and Applications Security, Sophia Antipolis, France, July 31-August 2, 2006. Proceedings 20* (pp. 224-236). Springer Berlin Heidelberg. https://link.springer.com/chapter/10.1007/11805588_16

Aregbesola, A., & Nwaolise, E. (2023). Securing Digital Collections: Cyber Security Best Practices for Academic Libraries in Developing Countries. *Library Philosophy and Practice (E-Journal)*, 1–13. https://digitalcommons.unl.edu/libphilprac/7822

Aronson, A. R., Mork, J. G., Gay, C. W., Humphrey, S. M., & Rogers, W. J. (2004). The NLM indexing initiative's medical text indexer. In *MEDINFO 2004* (pp. 268–272). IOS Press.

Arshad, M., Khan, A., Ahmed, P. & Shah, N.A(2020). *Next-Generation Data.*

Asemi, A., & Asemi, A. (2018). Artificial Intelligence (AI) application in Library Systems in Iran: A taxonomy study. Library Philosophy and Practice (e-journal). https://digitalcommons.unl.edu/libphilprac/1840

Asemi, A., & Asemi, A. (2018). Artificial Intelligence (AI) application in Library Systems in Iran: A taxonomy study. *Library Philosophy and Practice, 2.*

Asemi, A., Ko, A., & Nowkarizi, M. (2020). Intelligent libraries: A review on expert systems, artificial intelligence, and robot. *Library Hi Tech*, *39*(2), 412–434. doi:10.1108/LHT-02-2020-0038

Ashikuzzaman, M. D (2022). *Reference services of the library and its types.*

Aslam, F. (2023). The impact of artificial intelligence on chatbot technology: a study of the current advancements and leading innovations. *European Journal of Technology.*

Bairagi, M., & Lihitkar, S. (•••). Empowering Libraries: AI-Driven Tools and Techniques for Digital Transformation and Sustainable Innovation. UPA. *National Journal*, *10*(1), 388–396.

Balleste, R. (2002). The future of Artificial Intelligence in your virtual libraries. *Computers in Libraries*, *22*(9), 10–15.

Balleste, R. (2006). *Technology Trends in Law Libraries*. Law Librarianship for the Twenty-First Century.

Banerjee, M. S. (2022). Advantage and disadvantage of artificial intelligence in library services. *International Journal of Creative Research Thought*, *10*(11).

Bartolomé, J., & Garaizar, P. (2022). Design and Validation of a Novel Tool to Assess Citizens' Netiquette and Information and Data Literacy Using Interactive Simulations. *Sustainability (Basel)*, *14*(6), 3392. doi:10.3390/su14063392

Bawden, D., & Robinson, L. (2018). The dark side of information: Overload, anxiety and other paradoxes and pathologies. *Journal of Information Science*, *44*(6), 745–747.

Beaman, C., Barkworth, A., Akande, T. D., Hakak, S., & Khan, M. K. (2021). Ransomware: Recent advances, analysis, challenges and future research directions. *Computers & Security*, *111*(1), 102490. doi:10.1016/j.cose.2021.102490 PMID:34602684

Bender, E. M., Gebru, T., McMillan-Major, A., & Shmitchell, S. (2021, March). On the Dangers of Stochastic Parrots: Can Language Models Be Too Big? In *FAccT '21: Proceedings of the 2021 ACM Conference on Fairness, Accountability, and Transparency* (pp. 610–623). ACM. https://dl.acm.org/doi/abs/10.1145/3442188.3445922

Benslimane, Y., & Yang, Z. (2008, December). Project management trends in IS development: A study of the IT sector in China. In *2008 IEEE International Conference on Industrial Engineering and Engineering Management* (pp. 1759-1763). IEEE. 10.1109/IEEM.2008.4738174

Bhatia, S., & Mitra, P. (2012). Summarizing figures, tables and algorithms in scientific publications to augment search results. *ACM Transactions on Information Systems*, *30*(1), 1–24. doi:10.1145/2094072.2094075

Bisht, S. R., Nautiyal, A. P., Sharma, S., Sati, M. D., Bathla, N., & Singh, P. (2023). The role of Artificial Intelligence in shaping Library Management and its Utilization. *2023 International Conference on Disruptive Technologies (ICDT),* (pp. 467-472). IEEE. 10.1109/ICDT57929.2023.10150520

Blackman, R. (2020). A practical guide to building ethical AI. *Harvard Business Review*, 15.

Boden, M. (1987). Artificial intelligence: Cannibal or missionary? *AI & Society*, *1*(1), 17–23. doi:10.1007/BF01905886

Bogosavljević, M (2019). Protection of personal data in documents: Application of the law on personal data protection in serbia and abroad. *Moderna arhivistika* *2*(1), 106–15. http://dx.doi.org/. doi:10.54356/MA/2019/GHKV7413

Bradley, F. (2022). Representation of libraries in artificial intelligence regulations and implications for ethics and practice. *Journal of the Australian Library and Information Association*, *71*(3), 189–200. doi:10.1080/24750158.2022.2101911

Breeding, M. (2015). Smarter Libraries through Technology: Protecting the Privacy of Library Patrons. *Smart Libraries Newsletter, 35*. https://journals.ala.org/index.php/sln/issue/download/261/19

Breeding, M. (2016). *Privacy and security for library systems*. ALA TechSource. https://journals.ala.org/index.php/ltr/issue/viewFile/549/303

Brown, C. (2020, October 27). *How can library and information services protect people against cyber attacks?* https://www.vable.com/blog/cyber-security-what-your-library-needs-to-know

Brzustowicz, R. (2023). From ChatGPT to CatGPT: The implications of artificial intelligence on library cataloging. *Information Technology and Libraries*, *42*(3). doi:10.5860/ital.v42i3.16295

Bubinger, H., & Dinneen, J. D. (2021). Actionable approaches to promote ethical AI in libraries. *Proceedings of the Association for Information Science and Technology*, *58*(1), 682–684. doi:10.1002/pra2.528

Bui, M., & Noble, S. U. (2020). We're missing a moral framework of justice in artificial intelligence. *The Oxford handbook of ethics of AI*, 163-179. https://books.google.com/books

Butkovich, N. J., Taylor, K. L., Dent, S. H., & Moore, A. S. (2019). An expert system at the reference desk: Impressions from users. In *Expert Systems in Reference Services* (pp. 61–70). Routledge. doi:10.4324/9780429352539-5

Butters, A. (2007). RFID systems, standards and privacy within libraries. *The Electronic Library*, *25*(4), 430–439. doi:10.1108/02640470710779844

Chatila, R., Firth-Butterfield, K., & Havens, J. C. (2018). Ethically aligned design: A vision for prioritizing human well-being with autonomous and intelligent systems (version 2). *University of southern California Los Angeles*. https://apps.dtic.mil/sti/citations/AD1170922

Chemulwo, M. J., & Sirorei, E. C. (2020). Managing and adapting library information services for future users: Applying AI in libraries. In Managing and Adapting Library Information Services for Future Users. IGI Global

Chen, H., Hussain, S. U., Boemer, F., Stapf, E., Sadeghi, A. R., Koushanfar, F., & Cammarota, R. (2020, July). Developing privacy-preserving AI systems: The lessons learned. In *2020 57th ACM/IEEE Design Automation Conference (DAC)* (pp. 1-4). IEEE. 10.1109/DAC18072.2020.9218662

Chen, E., Bullard, J., & Giustini, D. (2023). Automated indexing using NLM's Medical Text Indexer (MTI) compared to human indexing in Medline: A pilot study. *Journal of the Medical Library Association: JMLA*, *111*(3), 684–695. doi:10.5195/jmla.2023.1588 PMID:37483360

Chen, L. C., Kuo, P. J., & Liao, I. E. (2015). Ontology-based library recommender system using MapReduce. *Cluster Computing*, *18*(1), 113–121. doi:10.1007/s10586-013-0342-z

Chen, X., Xie, H., & Hwang, G. (2020). A multi-perspective study on Artificial Intelligence in Education: Grants, conferences, journals, software tools, institutions, and researchers. *Computers & Education*, *1*, 1–11. doi:10.1016/j.caeai.2020.100005

Chen, Y., & Yan, F. (2016). Centuries of sociology in millions of books. *The Sociological Review*, *64*(4), 872–893. doi:10.1111/1467-954X.12399

Cihon, P., Kleinaltenkamp, M. J., Schuett, J., & Baum, S. D. (2021). AI Certification: Advancing Ethical Practice by Reducing Information Asymmetries. *IEEE Transactions on Technology and Society*, *2*(4), 200–209. doi:10.1109/TTS.2021.3077595

Coleman, C. N. (2020). Managing bias when library collections become data. *International Journal of Librarianship*, *5*(1), 8–19. doi:10.23974/ijol.2020.vol5.1.162

Collins, A., Tkaczyk, D., Aizawa, A., & Beel, J. (2018). A study of position bias in digital library recommender systems. arXiv preprint arXiv:1802.06565.

Committee on National Security Systems (CNSS). (2010). *National Information Assurance Glossary. CNSS Instruction No. 4009.* CNSS. http://www.ncix.gov/publications/policy/docs/CNSSI_4009.pdf

Conroy, G. (2023). How generative AI could disrupt scientific publishing. *Nature*, *622*(7982), 235. doi:10.1038/d41586-023-03144-w

Cordell, R. (2022). *Machine learning + libraries. A report on the state of the field.* Library of Congress.

Corredera, A., Romero, M., & Moya, J. M. (2017). Affective computing for smart operations: A survey and comparative analysis of the available tools, libraries and web services. *International Journal of Innovative and Applied Research*, *5*(9).

Cox, A. (2022). *The rise of AI: implications and applications of artificial intelligence in academic libraries (ACRL publications in librarianship, no. 78)* (S. Hervieux & A. Wheatley, Eds.). Association of College and Research Libraries. doi:10.1080/24750158.2022.2103917

Cox, A. M., Kennan, M. A., Lyon, L., Pinfield, S., & Sbaffi, L. (2019). Maturing research data services and the transformation of academic libraries. *The Journal of Documentation*, *75*(6), 1432–1462. doi:10.1108/JD-12-2018-0211

Cox, A. M., & Mazumdar, S. (2022). Defining artificial intelligence for librarians. *Journal of Librarianship and Information Science*, •••, 09610006221142029.

Cox, A. M., Pinfield, S., & Rutter, S. (2019). The intelligent library: Thought leaders' views on the likely impact of artificial intelligence on academic libraries. *Library Hi Tech*, *37*(3), 418–435. doi:10.1108/LHT-08-2018-0105

Craigen, D., Thibault, N. D., & Purse, R. (2014). Defining Cybersecurity [Review of *Defining Cybersecurity*]. *Technology Innovation Management Review*, 13–21. https://www.researchgate.net/publication/267631801

Curtis, N. (2023). To ChatGPT or not to ChatGPT? The impact of artificial intelligence on academic publishing. *The Pediatric Infectious Disease Journal*, *42*(4), 275. doi:10.1097/INF.0000000000003852 PMID:36757192

CybSafe. (2019, April 23). *7 reasons why security awareness training is important.* CybSafe. https://www.cybsafe.com/blog/7-reasons-why-security-awareness-training-is-important/

Dark, M., Kaza, S., & Taylor, B. (2018). CLARK – The Cybersecurity Labs and Resource Knowledge-base – A Living Digital Library. *2018 USENIX Workshop on Advances in Security Education, ASE 2018, Co-Located with USENIX Security 2018.* Unsenix. https://www.usenix.org/conference/ase18/presentation/dark

Das, R. K., & Islam, M. S. U. (2021). Application of artificial intelligence and machine learning in libraries: a systematic review. *arXiv preprint arXiv:2112.04573.*

Das , R. K., & Islam, M. S. U. (2021). Application of artificial intelligence and machine learning in libraries: a systematic review. *arXiv preprint arXiv:2112.04573.* https://doi.org/ doi:10.48550/arXiv.2112.04573

Davies, R., & James, B. (1984). Towards an expert system for cataloguing: Some experiments based on AACR2. *Program, 18*(4), 283–297. doi:10.1108/eb046882

De Cremer, D., & Kasparov, G. (2021). AI should augment human intelligence, not replace it. *Harvard Business Review, 18*, 1.

de Leon, L. C. R., Flores, L. V., & Alomo, A. R. L. (2024). Artificial Intelligence and Filipino Academic Librarians: Perceptions, Challenges and Opportunities. *Journal of the Australian Library and Information Association*, 1-18.

De Silva, S. M. (1997). A review of expert systems in library and information science. *Malaysian Journal of Library and Information Science, 2*(2), 57–92.

Dempsey, M. (2011). Blending the trends: A holistic approach to reference services. *Public Services Quarterly, 7*(1/2), 3–17. doi:10.1080/15228959.2011.572769

Deshmukh, A., Hegde, G., Lathi, R., & Govikarn, S. (2012, June). A literature survey on latent semantic indexing. In *International Conference on Computing* (p. 100). IEEE.

Dhelim, S., Aung, N., & Ning, H. (2020). Mining user interest based on personality-aware hybrid filtering in social networks. *Knowledge-Based Systems, 206*, 106227. doi:10.1016/j.knosys.2020.106227

Dheshan, M., & Teja, D. S. (2022). Application of artificial intelligence in content management systems. *International Journal of Recent Advances in Science & Engineering, 1*(1). https://www.ijrase.com

Dhiman, A. K. (2011). Knowledge discovery in databases and libraries. *DESIDOC Journal of Library and Information Technology, 31*(6), 446–451. doi:10.14429/djlit.31.6.1319

Dilmaghani, S., Brust, M. R., Danoy, G., Cassagnes, N., Pecero, J., & Bouvry, P. (2019, December). Privacy and security of big data in AI systems: A research and standards perspective. In *2019 IEEE International Conference on Big Data (Big Data)* (pp. 5737-5743). IEEE. 10.1109/BigData47090.2019.9006283

Divayana, D., Gede, H., Ariawan, P. W., Sugiarta, M., & Wayan, A. I. (2015). Digital library of expert system based at Indonesia technology university. *International Journal of Advanced Research in Artificial Intelligence*, *4*(3). https://www.ijarai.thesai.org

Dixon, L., Duncan, C., Fegan, J. C., Mandernach, M., & Warlick, S. E. (2010, Winter). Finding articles and journals via Google Scholar, journal portals and link resolvers: Usability study results. *Reference and User Services Quarterly*, *50*(2), 170–181. doi:10.5860/rusq.50n2.170

Dixon, P. (2008). Ethical issues implicit in library authentication and access management: Risks and best practices. *Journal of Library Administration*, *47*(3-4), 141–162. doi:10.1080/01930820802186480

Dohrmann, E., Hügi, J., Scheurer, N., Trummer, A., Schneider, R., & Eggenberg, C. (2010). *Bridging the virtual and the physical space: Kornelia–a chatbot for public libraries.*

Dumouchel, B., & Demaine, J. (2006). Knowledge Discovery in the Digital Library: Access tools for mining science. *Information Services & Use*, *26*(1), 39–44. doi:10.3233/ISU-2006-26105

Echedom, A. U., & Okuonghae, O. (2021). Transforming academic library operations in Africa with artificial intelligence: opportunities and challenges: a review paper. *New Review of Academic Librarianship*, *27*(2), 243–255. doi:10.1080/13614533.2021.1906715

Ehrenpreis, M., & DeLooper, J. (2022). Implementing a chatbot on a library website. *Journal of Web Librarianship*, *16*(2), 120–142. doi:10.1080/19322909.2022.2060893

Emiri, O. T. (2023). *Adoption and utilisation of artificial intelligence by librarians in university libraries in Southern Nigeria. Library Philosophy and Practice (e-journal).* Libraries at the University of Nebraska.

Epstein, M. (2018). That thing is so annoying: How proactive chat helps us reach more users. *College & Research Libraries News*, *79*(8), 436. doi:10.5860/crln.79.8.436

Ercegovac, Z., & Borko, H. (1992). Design and implementation of an experimental cataloging advisor-Mapper. *Information Processing & Management*, *28*(2), 241–257. doi:10.1016/0306-4573(92)90048-5

Eroğlu, Ş., & Çakmak, T. (2020). Personal data perceptions and privacy in Turkish academic libraries: An evaluation for administrations. *Journal of Academic Librarianship*, *46*(6), 102251. doi:10.1016/j.acalib.2020.102251

European Parliamentary Research Service [EPRS]. (2020). The ethics of artificial intelligence: Issues and initiatives. *Panel for the Future of Science and Technology*. EPRS. https://www.europarl.europa.eu/stoa

Fan, S. C., Fought, R. L., & Gahn, P. C. (2017). Adding a feature: Can a pop-up chat Does the box enhance virtual reference services? *Medical Reference Services Quarterly*, *36*(3), 220–228. doi:10.1080/02763869.2017.1332143 PMID:28714818

Farid, G., Warraich, N. F., & Iftikhar, S. (2023). Digital information security management policy in academic libraries: A systematic review (2010–2022). *Journal of Information Science*. doi:10.1177/01655515231160026

Feldman, J. D., Lopez, E., Gaspard, C. S., Barton, K. D., & Barcenes, L. F. III. (2018). Making it work for everyone: An evolving reference service. *Medical Reference Services Quarterly*, *37*(1), 10–18. doi:10.1080/02763869.2018.1404381 PMID:29327989

Feng, W. (2021). The Applications of Artificial Intelligence in Reading Promotion in Chinese University Libraries. *Diversity, Divergence, Dialogue - iConference 2021, 16th International Conference on Information,* Beijing, China. https://www.ideals.illinois.edu/handle/2142/109662

Filion, P., Moos, M., & Sands, G. (2023). Urban neoliberalism, smart city, and big tech: The aborted sidewalk labs Toronto experiment. *Journal of Urban Affairs*, *45*(9), 1625–1643. doi:10.1080/07352166.2022.2081171

Folorunso, A. L., & Momoh, E. O. (2020). Application of artificial intelligence and robotics in libraries: A review of literature. *ILIS Journal of Librarianship and Informatics*, *3*(2), 93–98.

Fortier, A., & Burkell, J. (2015). Hidden online surveillance: What librarians should know to protect their own privacy and that of their patrons. *Information Technology and Libraries*, *34*(3), 59–72. doi:10.6017/ital.v34i3.5495

Frackiewicz, M. (2023). The Future libraries in the age of AI. Retrieved September 25, 2023. https://ts2.space/en/the-future-of-libraries-in-the-age-of-ai/

Froehlich, A. (2022, July). *What is a data breach?* SearchSecurity. https://www.techtarget.com/searchsecurity/definition/data-breach

Gabriel, A. (2019). Artificial intelligence in scholarly communications: An Elsevier case study. *Information Services & Use*, *39*(4), 319–333. doi:10.3233/ISU-190063

Gao, X., Huang, W. X., Wang, N., Yang, Y. C., & Yan, Y. (2016). A top-N algorithm-based personalized learning recommendation system for digital library. [iJET]. *International Journal of Emerging Technologies in Learning*, *11*(11), 55–59. doi:10.3991/ijet.v11i11.6256

Gasparini, A. A., & Kautonen, H. (2022). Understanding Artificial Intelligence in Research Libraries: An Extensive Literature Review. LIBER Quarterly. *Te Journal of European Research Libraries*, *32*(1), 1–36.

Generative AI in Scholarly Communications: Ethical and practical guidelines for the use of generative AI in the publication process. (2023, December 5). STM. https://www.stm-assoc.org/new-white-paper-launch-generative-ai-in-scholarly-communications/

Genovesi, S., Kaesling, K., & Robbins, S. (2023). Introduction: Understanding and Regulating AI-Powered Recommender Systems. In *Recommender Systems: Legal and Ethical Issues* (pp. 1–9). Springer International Publishing. doi:10.1007/978-3-031-34804-4_1

Geyer-Schulz, A., Neumann, A., & Thede, A. (2003). An architecture for behavior-based library recommender systems. *Information Technology and Libraries*, *22*(4), 165.

Ghafarian, S., Jalali, M., Babolhavaeji, F., Hariri, N., & Khademi, M. (2020). Designing a Personalized Service Model with an Approach to Recommender System in Astan-e Quds-e Razavi Digital Library Software. *Library and Information Sciences*, *23*(2), 5–24.

Gillis, A. (2020, May). *What is Phishing? How it Works and How to Prevent it*. SearchSecurity. https://www.techtarget.com/searchsecurity/definition/phishing

Goh, E., & Sigala, M. (2020). Integrating Information & Communication Technologies (ICT) into classroom instruction: Teaching tips for hospitality educators from a diffusion of innovation approach. *Journal of Teaching in Travel & Tourism*, *20*(2), 156–165. doi:10.1080/15313220.2020.1740636

Goksel, N., & Bozkurt, A. (2019). Artificial intelligence in education: Current insights and future perspectives. In S. Sisman-Ugur & G. Kurubacak (Eds.), *Handbook of research on learning in the age of transhumanism* (pp. 224–236). IGI Global., doi:10.4018/978-1-5225-8431-5.ch014

Gondek, C. (n.d.). *The Cybersecurity Risks of Using Outdated Software*. https://originstamp.com/blog/the-cybersecurity-risks-of-using-outdated-software/

Gu, Q., & Liu, P. (2012). Denial of Service Attacks. In Handbook of Computer Networks (pp. 454–468). Springer. doi:10.1002/9781118256107.ch29

Gujral, G., Shivarama, J. & Choukimath, P. A. (2019) Perceptions and Prospects of Artificial Intelligence Technologies for Academic Libraries: An Overview of Global Trends. *12th International CALIBER-2019*. Research Gate.

Gundakanakanal, S. S., & Kaddipujar, M. (2019). Intelligent libraries: New horizons with artificial intelligence. *Journal of Information Management and Educational Technology*, *3*(2&3).

Guo, G., Zhang, J., Sun, Z., & Yorke-Smith, N. (2015, June). Librec: A java library for recommender systems. In UMAP workshops (Vol. 4, pp. 38-45).

Guy, J., Pival, P. R., Lewis, C. J., & Groome, K. (2023). *Reference chatbots in Canadian academic libraries*. Information Technology and Librarians. doi:10.5860/ital.v42i4.16511

Halburagi, S., & Mukarambi, P. (2023). *Use of Artificial Intelligence (AI)*. Technology Futures in Library.

Hanna, K. T. (2021, September). *What is a brute-force attack? - Definition from TechTarget*. SearchSecurity. https://www.techtarget.com/searchsecurity/definition/brute-force-cracking

Harisanty, D., Anna, N. E. V., Putri, T. E., Firdaus, A. A., & Noor Azizi, N. A. (2023). Is adopting artificial intelligence in libraries urgency or a buzzword? A systematic literature review. *Journal of Information Science*. doi:10.1177/01655515221141034

Harisanty, D., Anna, N. E., Putri, T. E., & Firdaus, A. A. (2023). Leaders, practitioners and scientists awareness of artificial intelligence in libraries: A pilot study. *Library Hi Tech.*

Head, A. J., Fister, B., & MacMillan, M. (2020). *Information Literacy in the Age of Algorithms: Student Experiences with News and Information, and the Need for Change*. Project Information Literacy.

Hervieux, S., & Wheatley, A. (2021). Perceptions of Artificial Intelligence: A Survey of Academic Librarians in Canada and the United States. *Journal of Academic Librarianship*, *47*(1), 102270. doi:10.1016/j.acalib.2020.102270

Hewitt, J. A. (1991). Intelligent library systems: Artificial intelligence technology and library automation systems. Advances in Library Automation and Networking. http://www.elsevier.com. In JAI Press, 4 (pp. 1–23).

Hjerppe, R., & Olander, B. (1989). Cataloging and expert systems: AACR2 as a knowledge base. *Journal of the American Society for Information Science*, *40*(1), 27–44. doi:10.1002/(SICI)1097-4571(198901)40:1<27::AID-ASI4>3.0.CO;2-R

Hodonu-Wusu, J. O. (2024). The rise of artificial intelligence in libraries: The ethical and equitable methodologies, and prospects for empowering library users. *AI and Ethics*, 1–11. doi:10.1007/s43681-024-00432-7

Hoffmann, A. L., Roberts, S. T., Wolf, C. T., & Wood, S. (2018). Beyond fairness, accountability, and transparency in the ethics of algorithms: Contributions and perspectives from LIS. *Proceedings of the Association for Information Science and Technology*, *55*(1), 694–696. doi:10.1002/pra2.2018.14505501084

Hongwei, M. (2018). Thinking on the Ethical Problems of Strong Artificial Intelligence and Weak Artificial Intelligence. *Science and Society*, *8*(1).

Houston, A. B., & Corrado, E. M. (2023). Embracing ChatGPT: Implications of Emergent Language Models for Academia and Libraries. *Technical Services Quarterly*, *40*(2), 76–91. doi:10.1080/07317131.2023.2187110

Huang, L. (2023). Ethics of artificial intelligence in education: Student privacy and data protection. *Science Insights Education Frontiers*, *16*(2), 2577–2587. doi:10.15354/sief.23.re202

Huang, Y. C. A. M., Cox, J., & Cox, J. (2023). Artificial Intelligence in academic library strategy in the United Kingdom and the Mainland of China. *Journal of Academic Librarianship*, *49*(6), 102772. doi:10.1016/j.acalib.2023.102772

Huang, Y.-H. (2022, July). Exploring the Implementation of Artificial Intelligence Applications among Academic Libraries in Taiwan. *Library Hi Tech.*. doi:10.1108/LHT-03-2022-0159

Huang, Z., Chung, W., Ong, T. H., & Chen, H. (2002, July). A graph-based recommender system for digital library. In *Proceedings of the 2nd ACM/IEEE-CS joint conference on Digital libraries* (pp. 65-73). 10.1145/544220.544231

Huanyu, Z., & Xin, L. (2017, July). Research on the Application of Knowledge Discovery in Digital Library Service. In *2017 7th International Conference on Social Network, Communication and Education (SNCE 2017)* (pp. 817-820). Atlantis Press. 10.2991/snce-17.2017.166

Hussain, A. (2023). Use of artificial intelligence in the library services: Prospects and challenges. *Library Hi Tech News*, *40*(2), 15–17. doi:10.1108/LHTN-11-2022-0125

Hwang, S. Y., & Hanson, M. (2021). Learning analytics and privacy: A library perspective. *Internet Reference Services Quarterly*, *25*(3), 69–72. doi:10.1080/10875301.2021.1946456

IFLA. (2016). *IFLA Trend Report 2016*. IFLA.

IFLA. (2022). *IFLA Statement on Cybersecurity* (pp. 1–5). IFLA. https://repository.ifla.org/bitstream/123456789/1912/1/IFLA%20Statement%20on%20Cybersecurity.pdf

Igbinovia, M. O., & Ishola, B. C. (2023). Cyber security in university libraries and implication for library and information science education in Nigeria. *Digital Library Perspectives*, *39*(3), 248–266. doi:10.1108/DLP-11-2022-0089

IMF-International Monetary Fund. (2024). *Gen-AI: Artificial Intelligence and the Future of Work. IMF Staff Discussion Notes*. IMF. https://www.imf.org/en/Publications/Staff-Discussion-Notes/Issues/2024/01/14/Gen-AI-Artificial-Intelligence-and-the-Future-of-Work-542379?cid=bl-com-SDNEA2024001

Imperva. (2019). *What is Social Engineering | Attack Techniques & Prevention Methods*. Learning Center. https://www.imperva.com/learn/application-security/social-engineering-attack/

International Federation of Library Associations and Institutions [IFLA]. (2020). *IFLA statement on libraries and artificial intelligence*. IFLA Publications. https://repository.ifla.org/handle/123456789/1646

International Telecommunication Union (ITU). (2009). *X.1205: Overview of cybersecurity*. ITU. https://www.itu.int/rec/T-REC-X.1205-200804-I/en

Iqbal, N., Jamil, F., Ahmad, S., & Kim, D. (2020). Toward effective planning and management using predictive analytics based on rental book data of academic libraries. *IEEE Access : Practical Innovations, Open Solutions*, *8*, 81978–81996. doi:10.1109/ACCESS.2020.2990765

Ivashkevych, O. (2023). *Artificial Intelligence in Acoustics of Library Functioning in Ukraine. Scientific journal "Library Science*. Record Studies. Informology.

J. McCarthy, M. Minsky & N. Rochester(2019). A Proposal for the Dartmouth Summer Research Project on Artificial Intelligence, 1(12).

J., & Kim, Y. (2019). Automated metadata extraction and enrichment for digital libraries: A survey. Journal of Information Science, 45(6), 715–734.

Jaillant, L., & Rees, A. (2023). Applying AI to digital archives: Trust, collaboration and shared professional ethics. *Digital Scholarship in the Humanities*, *38*(2), 571–585. doi:10.1093/llc/fqac073

Jamieson, T., & Salinas, G. (2018). Protecting human subjects in the digital age: Issues and best practices of data protection. *Survey Practice*, *11*(2), 1–10. https://digitalcommons.unomaha.edu/emergencyservicespublications/1/. doi:10.29115/SP-2018-0028 PMID:37201036

Jarrahi, M. H., Askay, D., Eshraghi, A., & Smith, P. (2023). Artificial intelligence and knowledge management: A partnership between human and AI. *Business Horizons*, *66*(1), 87–99. doi:10.1016/j.bushor.2022.03.002

Jeske, M., Intahchomphoo, C., Landriault, E., & Bioni, B. R. (2016). The intersection of freedom of information, privacy legislation and library services in Canadian jurisdictions. *Legal Information Management*, *16*(1), 14–21. doi:10.1017/S1472669616000050

Jha, S. K. (2023). Application of artificial intelligence in libraries and information centers services: Prospects and challenges. *Library Hi Tech News*, *40*(7), 1–5. doi:10.1108/LHTN-06-2023-0102

Jia, F., & Shi, Y. (2013). Library management system based on recommendation system. In *Information Computing and Applications: 4th International Conference, ICICA 2013*, (vol 392 pp. 488-497). Springer Berlin Heidelberg. 10.1007/978-3-642-53703-5_50

Johnson, B. (2018). Libraries in the age of artificial intelligence. *Computers in Libraries*, *38*(1), 14–16.

Johnston, M., & Weckert, J. (1990). Selection advisor: An expert system for collection development. *Information Technology and Libraries*, *9*(3), 219.

Jomsri, P., Prangchumpol, D., Poonsilp, K., & Panityakul, T. (2023). Hybrid recommender system model for digital library from multiple online publishers. *F1000 Research*, *12*, 1140. doi:10.12688/f1000research.133013.1

Jones, K. M. L., Briney, K. A., Goben, A., Salo, D., Asher, A., & Perry, M. R. (2020). A Comprehensive Primer to Library Learning Analytics Practices, Initiatives, and Privacy Issues. *College & Research Libraries*, *81*(3), 570–591. https://ssrn.com/abstract=3567955. doi:10.5860/crl.81.3.570

Joo., Y. J., Lim, K. Y., ve Lim, E. (2014). Investigating the structural relationship among perceived innovation attributes, intention to use and actual use of mobile learning in an online university in South Korea. *Australasian Journal of Educational Technology*, *30*(4), 427–439.

Kaijun, Y., Gong, R., Sun, L. & Chunguo, J. The application of artificial intelligence in smart library. Advances in Economics, Business and Management Research, 100, 708–713. doi:10.2991/icoi-19.2019.124

Kastrin, A., & Hristovski, D. (2021). Scientometric analysis and knowledge mapping of literature-based discovery (1986–2020). *Scientometrics*, *126*(2), 1415–1451. doi:10.1007/s11192-020-03811-z

Katz, W. A. (2001). *Introduction to Reference Works. 2vols*. McGraw-Hill.

Kaushal, V., & Yadav, R. (2022). The role of chatbots in academic libraries: An experience-based perspective. *Journal of the Australian Library and Information Association*, *71*(3), 215–232. do i:10.1080/24750158.2022.2106403

Kelly, S., Kaye, S.-A., & Oviedo-Trespalacios, O. (2023). What Factors Contribute to the Acceptance of Artificial Intelligence? A Systemic Review. *Telematics and Informatics*, *77*, 101925. doi:10.1016/j.tele.2022.101925

Kennedy, M. L. (2019). What do artificial intelligence (AI) and ethics of AI mean in the context of research libraries. *Research Library Issues, 299*, 3-13. https://publications.arl.org/18nm1db/

Khaiser, F. K., Saad, A., & Mason, C. (2023). Sentiment analysis of students' feedback on institutional facilities using text-based classification and natural language processing (NLP). *Journal of Language and Communication*, *10*(1), 101–111. doi:10.47836/jlc.10.01.06

Khan, A., Ibrahim, M., & Hussain, A. (2021). An exploratory prioritization of factors affecting current state of information security in Pakistani university libraries. *International Journal of Information Management Data Insights*, *1*(2), 100015. doi:10.1016/j.jjimei.2021.100015

Khurana, S. (2017). A Review Paper on Cyber Security. [IJERT]. *International Journal of Engineering Research & Technology (Ahmedabad)*, *5*(23). doi:10.17577/IJERTCONV5IS23011

Kim, B. (2016b, August 24). *Keeping Up With... Cybersecurity, Usability, and Privacy*. Association of College & Research Libraries (ACRL). https://www.ala.org/acrl/publications/keeping_up_with/cybersecurity

Kim, B. (2016a). Cybersecurity and digital surveillance versus usability and privacy1: Why libraries need to advocate for online privacy. *College & Research Libraries News*, *77*(9), 442–451. doi:10.5860/crln.77.9.9553

Kim, B. (2019). AI and Creating the First Multidisciplinary AI Lab. In J. Griffey (Ed.), *Artificial Intelligence and Machine Learning in Libraries. American Library Association*. ALA.

Kont, K.-R. (2023). Libraries and cyber security: the importance of the human factor in preventing cyber attacks. *Library Hi Tech News*. doi:10.1108/LHTN-03-2023-0036

Kronenfeld, M. R., & Bright, H. S. IV. (2015). Library resource discovery. *Journal of the Medical Library Association: JMLA*, *103*(4), 210–213. doi:10.3163/1536-5050.103.4.011 PMID:26512224

Kumar, V. & Sheshandri, K. (2019). Application of artificial intelligence in academic libraries.

LaBrie, R. C., & Steinke, G. (2019). Towards a framework for ethical audits of AI algorithms. In *Ethical Audits of AI Algorithms*. https://scholar.archive.org/work/wv7pfbs3uve5xegh336ffeeuta/access/wayback/https://aisel.aisnet.org/cgi/viewcontent.cgi?article=1398&context=amcis2019

Lancaster, F. W., & Smith, L. C. (1990). *Artificial Intelligence and Expert Systems: Will They Change the Library?* Papers Presented at the Annual Clinic on Library Applications of Data Processing, Urbana, Illinois.

Lapidusa, M., Bond, I., Wentza, E., King, S. B., & Mahnken, S. S. (2020). Measuring the quality of reference services provided by paraprofessionals at an academic library. *Journal of Academic Librarianship*, *46*(5), 102198. doi:10.1016/j.acalib.2020.102198

Lee, S. (2023). 7 Ways Librarians Can Prepare for the Future and Start Using AI at Work. Retrieved September 25, 2023. https://grtech.com/blog/ways-librarians-can-use-ai-for-future

Lee, T.-T. (2004). Nurses' adoption of technology: Application of Rogers' innovation-diffusion model. *Applied Nursing Research, 17*(4), 231-238. doi:10.1016/j.apnr.2004.09.001

Leikas, J., Koivisto, R., & Gotcheva, N. (2019). Ethical framework for designing autonomous intelligent systems. *Journal of Open Innovation*, *5*(1), 18. doi:10.3390/joitmc5010018

Lemos, A. N. L. E., & Passos, E. (2020). A adequação das bibliotecas à Lei Geral de Proteção de Dados. *Cadernos de Informação Jurídica (Cajur), 7*(1), 85-103. http://cajur.com.br/index.php/cajur/article/view/265

Lin, X., Sun, Y., & Zhang, Y., & R, K.M. (2023). Application of AI in Library Digital Reading Promotion Service. *2023 IEEE International Conference on Integrated Circuits and Communication Systems (ICICACS),* (pp. 1-6). IEEE.

Li, R., Huang, Z., Kurniawan, E., & Ho, C. K. (2015). AuRoSS: An autonomous robotic shelf scanning system. *IEEE/RSJ International Conference on Intelligent Robots and Systems (IROS)*, 6100–6105. DOI: 10.1109/IROS.2015.7354246

Lisedunetwork. (2019, September 26). *Library and Information Services*. Library & Information Science Network. https://www.lisedunetwork.com/library-and-information-services/

Litsey, Y., & Mauldin, W. (2018). Knowing What the Patron Wants: Using Predictive Analytics to Transform Library Decision Making. *Journal of Academic Librarianship*, *44*(1), 140–144. doi:10.1016/j.acalib.2017.09.004

Liu, H. (2016). *Artificial Intelligence and Its Evolution*. Science Press.

Liu, M. (2022). Personalized Recommendation System Design for Library Resources through Deep Belief Networks. *Mobile Information Systems*, *2022*, 2022. doi:10.1155/2022/7870724

Liu, M., Zhao, C., Peng, X., Yu, S., Wang, H., & Sha, C. (2023). Task-Oriented ML/DL Library Recommendation Based on a Knowledge Graph. *IEEE Transactions on Software Engineering*, *49*, 4081–4096. doi:10.1109/TSE.2023.3285280

Liu, P., Xu, Z., & Zhao, X. (2019). Road tests of self-driving vehicles: Affective and cognitive pathways in acceptance formation. *Transportation Research Part A, Policy and Practice*, *124*, 354–369. doi:10.1016/j.tra.2019.04.004

Llanasas, R. (2020). "How AI and Machine Learning are Transforming Mobile Technology." Retrieved December 26, 2023 Greenbook Blog: https://www.greenbook.org/mr/market-research-technology/how-ai-is-transforming-mobile-technology/

Lund, B. (2023). The prompt engineering librarian. *Library Hi Tech News*, *40*(8), 6–8. doi:10.1108/LHTN-10-2023-0189

Lund, B. D., Omame, I., Tijani, S., & Agbaji, D. (2020). Perceptions toward artificial intelligence among academic library employees and alignment with the diffusion of innovations' adopter categories. *College & Research Libraries*, *81*(5), 865. doi:10.5860/crl.81.5.865

Lund, B. D., & Wang, T. (2023). Chatting about ChatGTPT: How may artificial intelligence impact on academia and libraries. *Library Hi Tech News*. doi:10.1108/LHTN-01-2023-0009

Luo, L., & Buer, V. B. (2015). Reference service evaluation at an African academic library: The user perspective. *Library Review*, *64*(8/9), 552–566. doi:10.1108/LR-04-2015-0046

Mamun, A. A., Ibrahim, J. B., & Mostofa, S. M. (2021). Cyber Security Awareness in Bangladesh: An Overview of Challenges and Strategies. *International Journal of Computer Science and Information Technology Research*, *9*(1), 88–94. https://www.researchpublish.com/upload/book/paperpdf-1611555745.pdf

Manuel, K. (2002). Teaching Information Literacy to Generation. *Journal of Library Administration*, *36*(1-2), 1–2, 195–217. doi:10.1300/J111v36n01_12

Maranchak, N. (2023). The Use of Artificial Intelligence in Digital Marketing of the Library Industry in Ukraine: Foreign Experience and Prospects. *Digital Platform: Information Technologies in Sociocultural Sphere*. IEEE.

Margetis, G., Ntoa, S., Antona, M., & Stephanidis, C. (2021). Human-centered design of artificial intelligence. Handbook of Human Factors and Ergonomics, 1085-1106.

Massis, B. (2018). Artificial intelligence arrives in the library. *Information and Learning Science*, *119*(7/8), 456–459. doi:10.1108/ILS-02-2018-0011

McCulloch, W. S., & Pitts, W. (1943). A logical calculus of the ideas immanent in nervous activity. *The Bulletin of Mathematical Biophysics*, *5*(4), 115–133. doi:10.1007/BF02478259

McDonald, J. D., & Levine-Clark, M. (Eds.). (2017). *Encyclopedia of Library and Information Sciences*. CRC Press. doi:10.1081/E-ELIS4

McNeal, M., & Newyear, D. (2013). Introducing chatbots in libraries, Streamlining Information Services Using Chatbots (Library TechnologyReports). ALATechSource, Chicago, IL.

Meador, J. M., & Cline, L. S. (1991). *Collection Development in an Era of Networking: The Bibliographer's Workstation*.

Meng, C., Rombach, R., Gao, R., Kingma, D., Ermon, S., Ho, J., & Salimans, T. (2023). On distillation of guided diffusion models. In *Proceedings of the IEEE/CVF Conference on Computer Vision and Pattern Recognition* (pp. 14297-14306). IEEE.

Meurisch, C., & Mühlhäuser, M. (2021). Data protection in AI services: A survey. *ACM Computing Surveys*, *54*(2), 1–38. doi:10.1145/3440754

Miao, Z. (2019). Investigation on human rights ethics in artificial intelligence researches with library literature analysis method. *The Electronic Library*, *37*(5), 914–926. doi:10.1108/EL-04-2019-0089

Michos, S., Stamatatos, E., & Fakotakis, N. (1999). Supporting multilinguality in library automation systems using ai tools. *Applied Artificial Intelligence*, *13*(7), 679–703. doi:10.1080/088395199117243

Mimecast. (n.d.). *What is Cyber Awareness Training?* Mimecast. https://www.mimecast.com/content/cyber-security-awareness-training/#:~:text=Cyber%20awareness%20refers%20to%20the

Min, S., So, K. K. F., & Jeong, M. (2021). Consumer adoption of the Uber mobile application: Insights from diffusion of innovation theory and technology acceptance model. In *Future of tourism marketing* (pp. 2–15). Routledge. doi:10.4324/9781003176039-2

Miranda, M. Q., & Farias, J. S. (2016). Technology Adoption in Diffusion of Innovations Perspective: Introduction of an ERP System in a Non-Profit Organization. *RAI Revista de Administração e Inovação, 13*, 48-57.

Mishra, S. (2023). Ethical ımplications of artificial ıntelligence and machine learning in libraries and ınformation centers: a frameworks, challenges, and best practices. *Library Philosophy and Practice (e-journal)*. https://digitalcommons.unl.edu/libphilprac/7753

Mogali, S. S. (2014). Artificial Intelligence and its applications in Libraries. Retrieved January2nd, 2024 https://www.researchgate.net/publication/287878456

Mogali, S. S. (2014). *Artificial Intelligence and its applications in Libraries*. Academic Press.

Moore, G. C., & Benbasat, I. (1991). Development of an instrument to measure the perceptions of adopting an information technology innovation. *Information Systems Research*, *2*(3), 192–222. doi:10.1287/isre.2.3.192

Mo, P. K. H., Luo, S., Wang, S., Zhao, J., Zhang, G., Li, L., Li, L., Xie, L., & Lau, J. T. (2021). Intention to receive the COVID-19 vaccination in China: Application of the diffusion of innovations theory and the moderating role of openness to experience. *Vaccines*, *9*(2), 129. doi:10.3390/vaccines9020129 PMID:33562894

Mork, J. G., Jimeno-Yepes, A., & Aronson, A. R. (2013). The NLM Medical Text Indexer System for Indexing Biomedical Literature. *BioASQ@ CLEF, 1*.

Muraszkiewcz, M. (2019). The synergetic impact of artificial intelligence, the Internet of Things and 5G on information literacy and education. *ZIN*, *57*(2), 7–22.

Musangi, P, S. (2015). Redefining reference services in academic libraries: A critical review. *An International Peer Reviewed Bilingual E-Journal of Library And Information Science, 2*(04).

Nardi, B. A., & O'Day, V. (1996). Intelligent agents: what we learned at the library.

NaudéW.DimitriN. (2021). Public procurement and ınnovation for human-centered artificial ıntelligence. IZA Discussion (Paper No. 14021), https://ssrn.com/abstract=3762891

Nayyer, K., & Rodriguez, M. (2022). Ethical implications of implicit bias in AI: Impact for academic libraries. Chicago: ACRL. In S.Hervieux & A.Wheatley (Eds.), The Rise of AI: Implications and applications of Artificial Intelligence in academic libraries (165-174). ACRL.

Ng, D. T. K., Leung, J. K. L., Chu, S. K. W., & Qiao, M. S. (2021). Conceptualizing AI literacy: An exploratory review. *Computers and Education: Artificial Intelligence*, *2*, 100041.

Ngwum, N. I., Raina, S., Aguon, S., Taylor, B., & Kaza, S. (2020). A Model for Security Evaluation of Digital Libraries: A Case Study on a Cybersecurity Curriculum Library. *Journal of the Colloquium for Information Systems Security Education*, *7*(1), 1–12. https://www.researchgate.net/publication/344357576

Nikolinakos, N. T. (2023). Ethical Principles for Trustworthy AI. In: EU Policy and Legal Framework for Artificial Intelligence, Robotics and Related Technologies - The AI Act. Springer. doi:10.1007/978-3-031-27953-9_3

Nißen, M., Selimi, D., Janssen, A., Cardona, D. R., Breitner, M. H., Kowatsch, T., & von Wangenheim, F. (2022). See you soon again, chatbot. A design taxonomy to characterise user-chatbot relationships with different time horizons. *Computers in Human Behavior*, *107043*(127), 107043. doi:10.1016/j.chb.2021.107043

Noh, Y. (2013). A study on the next-generation digital library using context awareness technology. *Library High Tech.31*(2).

Noh, Y. (2014). Digital library user privacy: Changing librarian viewpoints through education. *Library Hi Tech*, *32*(2), 300–317. doi:10.1108/LHT-08-2013-0103

Nordhoff, S., Malmsten, V., van Arem, B., Liu, P., & Happee, R. (2021). A structural equation modeling approach for the acceptance of driverless automated shuttles based on constructs from the Unified Theory of Acceptance and Use of Technology and the Diffusion of Innovation Theory. *Transportation Research Part F: Traffic Psychology and Behaviour*, *78*, 58–73. doi:10.1016/j.trf.2021.01.001

Nugraha, E., Ardiansyah, T., Junaeti, E., & Riza, L. S. (2020). Enhanced Digital Library with Book Recommendations Based on Collaborative Filtering. *Journal of Engineering Education Transformations, 34*(Special Issue).

Numarasi, K. (2016). The Law on Protection of Personal Data. *T.C. Resmi Gazete (Official Gazette of the Republic of Turkey)* (number: 29677) https://www.mevzuat.gov.tr/MevzuatMetin/1.5.6698.pdf

Okpokwasili, N. (2019). *Artificial Intelligence in Libraries and Users Satisfaction in Higher Institutions in Nigeria. International Journal of Research in Informative Science Application & Techniques*. IJRISAT.

Okunlaya, R. O., Syed Abdullah, N., & Alias, R. A. (2022). Artificial intelligence (AI) library services innovative conceptual framework for the digital transformation of university education. *Library Hi Tech*, *40*(6), 1869–1892. doi:10.1108/LHT-07-2021-0242

Olmstadt, W. (2000). *Cataloging expert systems: Optimism and frustrated reality.*

Olusegun Oyetola, S., Oladokun, B. D., Ezinne Maxwell, C., & Obotu Akor, S. (2023). *Artificial intelligence in the library: Gauging the potential application and implications for contemporary library services in Nigeria*. Data & Metadata.

Omame, I. M, and Alex-Nmecha (2020). Artificial intelligence in libraries (pp. 120–144). Jackson College. doi:10.4018/978-1-7998-1116-9.ch008

Ong, D. C. (2021, September). An ethical framework for guiding the development of affectively-aware artificial intelligence. In *2021 9th International Conference on Affective Computing and Intelligent Interaction (ACII)* (pp. 1-8). IEEE. 10.1109/ACII52823.2021.9597441

Ormeño, P., Mendoza, M., & Valle, C. (2021). Topic models ensembles for ad-hoc information retrieval. *Information (Basel)*, *12*(9), 360. doi:10.3390/info12090360

Otterlo, M. (2016). Project BLIIPS: Making the Physical Public Library more Intelligent through Artificial Intelligence. *Qualitative and Quantitative Methods in Libraries*, *5*, 287–300.

Oxford University Press. (2014). Cybersecurity | Meaning of Cybersecurity by Lexico. In *Oxford Online Dictionary*. Oxford Press. http://www.oxforddictionaries.com/definition/english/Cybersecurity

Oyelana, O., Kamanzi, J., & Richter, S. (2021). A critical look at exclusive breastfeeding in Africa: Through the lens of diffusion of innovation theory. *International Journal of Africa Nursing Sciences*, *14*, 100267. doi:10.1016/j.ijans.2020.100267

Oyelude, A. A. (2017). What's trending in the library cybersphere–Recent conferences and posts focus on data and information literacy. *Library Hi Tech News*, *34*(6), 21–22. doi:10.1108/LHTN-06-2017-0040

Oyelude, A. A. (2021). AI and libraries: Trends and projections. *Library Hi Tech News*, *38*(10), 1–4. doi:10.1108/LHTN-10-2021-0079

Oyetoloa, S.O., Oladokun, D.D., Maxwell, C. E., & Akor, S.O. (2023). *Artificial intelligence in the library: gauging the potential application and implications for contemporary library services in Nigeria.*

Panda, S & Chakravarty. (2021). Implementing conversational AI in libraries: A practical approach. In *Impact of COVID-19 in academic institutions,* 124-145. Springer.

Panda, S., & Chakravarty, R. (2022). Adapting intelligent information services in libraries: A case of smart AI chatbots. *Library Hi Tech News*, *39*(1), 12–15. doi:10.1108/LHTN-11-2021-0081

Panyadee, P., & Wita, R. (2021, May). Integrating Graph-Based Document Recommendation in Digital Libraries of Theses Collection. In *International Conference on Computing and Information Technology* (pp. 223-232). Cham: Springer International Publishing. 10.1007/978-3-030-79757-7_22

Park, D. H., Kim, H. K., Choi, I. Y., & Kim, J. K. (2012). A literature review and classification of recommender systems research. *Expert Systems with Applications*, *39*(11), 10059–10072. doi:10.1016/j.eswa.2012.02.038

Park, S. (2017). The Fourth Industrial Revolution and Implications for Innovative Cluster Policies. *AI & Society*, *2017*, 1–13.

Pauletto, C. (2021). Options towards a global standard for the protection of individuals with regard to the processing of personal data. *Computer Law & Security Report*, *40*, 105433. doi:10.1016/j.clsr.2020.105433

Pence, H. E. (2014). What is Big Data and Why is it Important? *Journal of Educational Technology Systems*, *43*(2), 159–171. doi:10.2190/ET.43.2.d

Peterson, T. (2020). *Improve online learning and more with artificial intelligence.*

Piano, S. (2020). Ethical principles in machine learning and artificial intelligence: Cases from the field and possible ways forward. *Humanities & Social Sciences Communications*, *7*(1), 1–7. https://www.nature.com/articles/s41599-020-0501-9. doi:10.1057/s41599-020-0501-9

Pinho, C., Franco, M., & Mendes, L. (2021). Application of innovation diffusion theory to the E-learning process: Higher education context. *Education and Information Technologies*, *26*(1), 421–440. doi:10.1007/s10639-020-10269-2

Porcel, C., López-Herrera, A. G., & Herrera-Viedma, E. (2009). A recommender system for research resources based on fuzzy linguistic modeling. *Expert Systems with Applications*, *36*(3), 5173–5183. doi:10.1016/j.eswa.2008.06.038

Porcel, C., Moreno, J. M., & Herrera-Viedma, E. (2009). A multi-disciplinar recommender system to advice research resources in university digital libraries. *Expert Systems with Applications*, *36*(10), 12520–12528. doi:10.1016/j.eswa.2009.04.038

Rashid, M. H. A. (2023, September 10). *Role of Libraries in Promoting Information Literacy and Critical Thinking Skills in the Digital Age*. Library & Information Management. https://limbd.org/role-of-libraries-in-promoting-information-literacy-and-critical-thinking-skills-in-the-digital-age/

Rhanoui, M., Mikram, M., Yousfi, S., Kasmi, A., & Zoubeidi, N. (2022). A Hybrid recommender system for patron driven library acquisition and weeding. *Journal of King Saud University. Computer and Information Sciences*, *34*(6), 2809–2819. doi:10.1016/j.jksuci.2020.10.017

Richardson, W. R., Srinivasan, V., & Fox, E. A. (2008). Knowledge discovery in digital libraries of electronic theses and dissertations: An NDLTD case study. *International Journal on Digital Libraries*, *9*(2), 163–171. doi:10.1007/s00799-008-0046-9

Ridley, M., & Pawlick-Potts, D. (2021). Algorithmic literacy and the role for libraries. *Information Technology and Libraries*, *40*(2). doi:10.6017/ital.v40i2.12963

Rieh, S. Y. (1999). Changing reference service environment: A review of perspective from managers, librarians and users. *Journal of Academic Librarianship*, *25*(3), 178–186. doi:10.1016/S0099-1333(99)80197-9

Rodríguez-García, M. Á., García-Sánchez, F., & Valencia-García, R. (2021). Knowledge-based system for crop pests and diseases recognition. *Electronics (Basel)*, *10*(8), 905. doi:10.3390/electronics10080905

Rodriguez, S., & Mune, C. (2022). Uncoding library chatbots: Deploying a new virtual reference tool at the San Jose State University library. *RSR. Reference Services Review*, *50*(3/4), 392–405. doi:10.1108/RSR-05-2022-0020

Rogers, E. M. (1983). *Diffusion of innovations* (3rd ed.). Free Press of Glencoe.

Rubin, V. L., Chen, Y., & Thorimbert, L. M. (2010). Artificially intelligent conversational agents in libraries. *Library Hi Tech*, *28*(4), 496–522. doi:10.1108/07378831011096196

Saeidnia, H. R. (2023). Ethical artificial intelligence (AI): Confronting bias and discrimination in the library and information industry. *Library Hi Tech News*. Advance online publication. doi:10.1108/LHTN-10-2023-0182

Safder, I., Hassan, S. U., Visvizi, A., Noraset, T., Nawaz, R., & Tuarob, S. (2020). Deep learning-based extraction of algorithmic metadata in full-text scholarly documents. *Information Processing & Management*, *57*(6), 102269. doi:10.1016/j.ipm.2020.102269

Sakala, L. C., & Chigona, W. (2020). How lecturers neutralize resistance to the implementation of learning management systems in higher education. [Springer US.]. *Journal of Computing in Higher Education*, *32*(2), 365–388. doi:10.1007/s12528-019-09238-7

Šauperl, A., & Saye, J. D. (2011). Pebbles for the mosaic of cataloging expertise: What do problems in expert systems for cataloging reveal about cataloging expertise? *Library Resources & Technical Services*, *43*(2), 78–94. doi:10.5860/lrts.43n2.78

Schmager, S., Pappas, I., & Vassilakopoulou, P. (2023, September). Defining Human-centered AI: a comprehensive review of HCAI literature. In *Proceedings of the Mediterranean Conference on Information Systems*. IEEE.

Scott, S. D., Plotnikoff, R. C., Karunamuni, N., Bize, R., & Rodgers, W. (2008). Factors influencing the adoption of an innovation: An examination of the uptake of the Canadian Heart Health Kit (HHK). *Implementation Science : IS*, *3*(1), 41. doi:10.1186/1748-5908-3-41 PMID:18831766

Shazly, H., Ferraro, A., & Bennet, K. (2020, November). Ethical Concerns: An overview of Artificial Intelligence System Development and Life Cycle. In *2020 IEEE International Symposium on Technology and Society (ISTAS)* (pp. 33-42). IEEE. 10.1109/ISTAS50296.2020.9462201

Shi, Y., Sun, F., Zuo, H. & Peng, F. (2023). Analysis of Learning Behavior Characteristics and Prediction of Learning Effect for Improving College Students' Information Literacy Based on Machine Learning. *IEEE Education Society section*. IEEE.

Shreiner, T. L., & Dykes, B. M. (2021). Visualizing the teaching of data visualizations in social studies: A study of teachers' data literacy practices, beliefs, and knowledge. *Theory and Research in Social Education*, *49*(2), 262–306. doi:10.1080/00933104.2020.1850382

SifatI. (2023). Artificial Intelligence as an Institution: Impacts, Integration Strategies, and Policy Directions (August 18, 2023). Available at SSRN: https://ssrn.com/abstract=4545403 doi:10.2139/ssrn.4545403

Siguenza-Guzman, L., Saquicela, V., Avila-Ordóñez, E., Vandewalle, J., & Cattrysse, D. (2015). Literature Review of Data Mining Applications in Academic Libraries. *Journal of Academic Librarianship*, *41*(4), 499–510. doi:10.1016/j.acalib.2015.06.007

Silverstein, C., & Shieber, S. M. (1996). Predicting individual book use for off-site storage using decision trees. *The Library Quarterly*, *66*(3), 266–293. doi:10.1086/602885

Simović, A. (2018). A Big Data smart library recommender system for an educational institution. *Library Hi Tech*, *36*(3), 498–523. doi:10.1108/LHT-06-2017-0131

Singh, B. (2019). SIS: Smart identify systems for library books. *International Journal for Modern Trends in Science and Technology*, *5*(11).

Singh, D. K., Singh, B. K., & Dube, Y. P. (1996). Expert Systems and their Application in Library and Information Systems. *DESIDOC Bulletin of Information Technology*, *16*(4), 9–12. doi:10.14429/dbit.16.4.3272

Singley, E. (2020). A holistic approach to user privacy in academic libraries. *Journal of Academic Librarianship*, *46*(3), 102151. doi:10.1016/j.acalib.2020.102151

Sinha, K. (2023). The Metaverse and Digital Libraries. In B. Holland (Ed.), Handbook of Research on Advancements of Contactless Technology and Service Innovation in Library and Information Science (pp. 1–22). IGI Global. doi:10.4018/978-1-6684-7693-2.ch001

Slatter, D., & Howard, Z. (2013). A place to make, hack, and learn: Makerspaces in Australian public libraries. *The Australian Library Journal*, *62*(4), 272–284. doi:10.1080/00049670.2013.853335

Slavkovik, M. (2020, November). Teaching AI Ethics: Observations and Challenges. In *Norsk IKT-konferanse for forskning og utdanning,* (4). https://hdl.handle.net/11250/2764233

Souchet, A. D., Lourdeaux, D., Burkhardt, J. M., & Hancock, P. A. (2023). Design guidelines for limiting and eliminating virtual reality-induced symptoms and effects at work: A comprehensive, factor-oriented review. [Lee]. *Frontiers in Psychology*, *14*, 1161932. doi:10.3389/fpsyg.2023.1161932 PMID:37359863

Spanning Cloud Apps. (2022, June 30). *Cybersecurity Awareness: Definition, Importance & More*. Spanning. https://spanning.com/blog/cybersecurity-awareness/

Stahl, B., Mohnke, J., & Seeliger, F. (2018). Roboter ante portas? About the deployment of a humanoid robot into a library. *Proceedings of the IATUL, Conference Paper 6*. Research Gate.

Strzalkowski, T., Perez-Carballo, J., & Marinescu, M. (1996, April). Natural language information retrieval in digital libraries. In *Proceedings of the First ACM International Conference on Digital libraries* (pp. 117-125). ACM. 10.1145/226931.226954

Sturges, P., Davies, E., Dearnley, J., Iliffe, U., Iliffe, U., Oppenheim, C., & Hardy, R. (2003). User privacy in the digital library environment: An investigation of policies and preparedness. *Library Management*, *24*(1/2), 44–50. doi:10.1108/01435120310454502

Sturges, P., Teng, V., & Iliffe, U. (2001). User privacy in the digital library environment: A matter of concern for information professionals. *Library Management*, *22*(8/9), 364–370. doi:10.1108/01435120110406309

Subaveerapandiyan, A. (2023). Application of Artificial Intelligence (AI) In Libraries and Its Impact on Library Operations Review. *Library Philosophy and Practice (e-journal), 7828*. https://digitalcommons.unl.edu/libphilprac/7828

Sun, Z., & Stranieri, A. (2020). A knowledge discovery in the digital age. *PNG UoT BAIS*, *5*(1), 1–11.

Suqri, M. N. A., & Fatuyi, E. A. (2012). Information Security and Privacy in Digital Libraries: Challenges, Opportunities and Prospects. *International Journal of Digital Library Systems, 3*(4), 54–61. https://www.researchgate.net/publication/260174707

Tait, E., & Pierson, C. M. (2022). Artificial intelligence and robots in libraries: Opportunities in LIS curriculum for preparing the librarians of tomorrow. *Journal of the Australian Library and Information Association*, *71*(3), 256–274. doi:10.1080/24750158.2022.2081111

Tang, J., Zhang, J., Yao, L., Li, J., Zhang, L., & Su, Z. (2008). *ArnetMiner: Extraction and Mining of Academic Social Networks*. KDD'08, Las Vegas, Nevada, USA.

Taylor, B., Kaza, S., & Dark, M. (2022). Designing a Cybersecurity Curriculum Library: Best Practices from Digital Library Research. In K.-K. R. Choo, T. Morris, G. Peterson, & E. Imsand (Eds.), *National Cyber Summit (NCS) Research Track 2021. NCS 2021. Lecture Notes in Networks and Systems* (pp. 47–59). Springer. doi:10.1007/978-3-030-84614-5_5

Tejeda-Lorente, Á., Porcel, C., Peis, E., Sanz, R., & Herrera-Viedma, E. (2014). A quality based recommender system to disseminate information in a university digital library. *Information Sciences*, *261*, 52–69. doi:10.1016/j.ins.2013.10.036

Tella, A. (2020). Robots are coming to libraries: Are libraries ready to accommodate them? *Library Hi Tech News*, *2*(8), 13–17. doi:10.1108/LHTN-05-2020-0047

Tella, A. (2022). Teaching information literacy in Nigerian universities using advanced technologies. *Regional Journal of Information and Knowledge Management*, *7*(2), 38–53.

Tella, A. (2023). Application of Artificial Intelligence for Reference Services in Academic Libraries: A Global Overview through a Systematic Review of Literature. *Journal of Library Resource Sharing*, *32*(1-5), 11–26. doi:10.1080/26915979.2023.2281668

Teredesai, A., Ahmad, M. A., & Eckert, C. (2020). *Fairness, Accountability, Transparency in AI at Scale: Lessons from National Programs, School of Engineering and Technology Publications*. Digital Commons. https://digitalcommons.tacoma.uw.edu/tech_pub/394/

Thayyib, P. V., Mamilla, R., Khan, M., Fatima, H., Asim, M., Anwar, I., Shamsudheen, M. K., & Asif Khan, M. (2023). State-of-the-art of artificial intelligence and big data analytics reviews in five different domains: A bibliometric summary. *Sustainability (Basel)*, *15*(5), 12. doi:10.3390/su15054026

Tian, Y., Zheng, B., Wang, Y., Zhang, Y., & Wu, Q. (2019). College library personalized recommendation system based on hybrid recommendation algorithm. *Procedia CIRP*, *83*, 490–494. doi:10.1016/j.procir.2019.04.126

Tikkinen-Piri, C., Rohunen, A., & Markkula, J. (2018). EU General Data Protection Regulation: Changes and implications for personal data collecting companies. *Computer Law & Security Report*, *34*(1), 134–153. doi:10.1016/j.clsr.2017.05.015

Tiwari, A. (2018). Data analytics in Library and Information Centers. Retrieved January 4th, 2024. https://www.researchgate.net/publication/327389981

Tornatzky, L. G., & Fleischer, M. (1990). *The Processes of Technological Innovation*. Lexington Books.

Tyckoson, D. A. (2011). Issues and trends in the management of reference services: A historical perspective. *Journal of Library Administration*, *51*(3), 259–278. doi:10.1080/01930826.2011.556936

Tzanou, M. (Ed.). (2020). *Personal data protection and legal developments in the European Union*. IGI Global. https://www.igi-global.com/publish/ doi:10.4018/978-1-5225-9489-5

Vickery, A., Brooks, H., Robinson, B., & Vickery, B. (1987). A reference and referral system using expert system techniques. *The Journal of Documentation*, *43*(1), 1–23. doi:10.1108/eb026798

Vincze, J. (2017). Virtual reference librarians (chatbots). *Library Hi Tech News*, *34*(4), 5–8. doi:10.1108/LHTN-03-2017-0016

Viyakuma, S., & Sheshadri, K. N. (2019). Applications of artificial intelligence in academic libraries. *International Journal on Computer Science and Engineering*, *7*(16).

Vysakh, C. & Rajendra Babu, H. (2019). Application of Artificially Intelligent Robot in Libraries. *ICRLIT – 2019: e-Proceedings*, (pp. 59-63). ICRLIT.

Vysakh, C., & Babu, R. H. (2019). Application of Artificially Intelligent Robot in Libraries. E-Proceedings. Reshaping of librarianship, innovations and transformation.ICRLIT.60-63. https://www.researchgate.net/publication/338712408

Wagstaff, K. L., & Liu, G. Z. (2018). Automated classification to improve the efficiency of weeding library collections. *Journal of Academic Librarianship*, *44*(2), 238–247. doi:10.1016/j.acalib.2018.02.001

Wallace, N., & Feeney, M. (2018). An Introduction to Text Mining: How Libraries Can Support Digital Scholars. [QQML]. *Qualitative and Quantitative Methods in Libraries*, *7*, 23–30.

Wang, X., Wang, Y., Guo, L., Xu, L., Gao, B., Liu, F., & Li, W. (2021). Exploring clustering-based reinforcement learning for personalized book recommendation in digital library. *Information (Basel)*, *12*(5), 198. doi:10.3390/info12050198

Wang, Y., Gu, J., Wang, S., & Wang, J. (2019). Understanding consumers' willingness to use ridesharing services: The roles of perceived value and perceived risk. *Transportation Research Part C, Emerging Technologies*, *105*, 504–519. doi:10.1016/j.trc.2019.05.044

Warwick K (2011). Artificial Intelligence. Hoboken:Taylor& amp;Francis. 13-59.

Web Master. (2022, June 9). *What Is an Insider Threat? Malicious vs. Negligent Threats*. Vera. https://www.vera.com/intellectual-property-protection/insider-threat/

Weigert, V. (2020). *Chatbots in libraries*. Library Services. https://libraryservices.jiscinvolve.org/wp/2020/09/chatbots-in-libraries/

Wei, X., & Croft, W. B. (2006, August). LDA-based document models for ad-hoc retrieval. In *Proceedings of the 29th Annual International ACM SIGIR Conference on Research and Development in Information Retrieval* (pp. 178-185). ACM.

Weng, C. H. (2016). Knowledge discovery of digital library subscription by RFC itemsets. *The Electronic Library*, *34*(5), 772–788. doi:10.1108/EL-06-2015-0086

Whitehair, K. (2016). *Libraries in an Artificially Intelligent World.* Public Libraries. http://publiclibrar-iesonline.org/2016/02/libraries-in-an-artificially-intelligent-world/

Wiil, U. K., & Hicks, D. L. (2001, July). Tools and services for knowledge discovery, management and structuring in digital libraries. In *Proceedings of the Eighth ISPE International Conference on Concurrent Engineering: Research and Applications* (pp. 580-589). IEEE.

Winkler, B., & Kiszla, P. (2022). Views of Academic Library Directors on Artificial Intelligence: A Representative Survey in Hungary. *New Review of Academic Librarianship*, *28*(3), 256–278. doi:10.1080/13614533.2021.1930076

Wojcik, M. (2021). Augmented intelligence technology. The ethical and practical problems of its implementation in libraries. *Library Hi Tech*, *39*(2), 435–447. doi:10.1108/LHT-02-2020-0043

Wolfram, D. (2016, June). Bibliometrics, information retrieval and natural language processing: natural synergies to support digital library research. In *Proceedings of the Joint Workshop on Bibliometric-Enhanced Information Retrieval and Natural Language Processing for Digital Libraries (BIRNDL)* (pp. 6-13). ACM.

Wolfram, S. (2023). *What Is ChatGPT Doing... and Why Does It Work?* Stephen Wolfram Media.

Wu, X., Duan, R., & Ni, J. (2023). Unveiling security, privacy, and ethical concerns of chatgpt. *Journal of Information and Intelligence.*

Wu, C. H., Lee, T. Z., & Kao, S. C. (2004). Knowledge discovery applied to material acquisitions for libraries. *Information Processing & Management*, *40*(4), 709–725. doi:10.1016/j.ipm.2003.08.010

Wu, J., Liang, C., Yang, H., & Giles, C. L. (2016, June). Citeseerx data: Semanticizing scholarly papers. In *Proceedings of the International Workshop on Semantic Big Data* (pp. 1-6). ACM.

Wu, J., Williams, K. M., Chen, H. H., Khabsa, M., Caragea, C., Tuarob, S., & Giles, C. L. (2015). Citeseerx: AI in a digital library search engine. *AI Magazine*, *36*(3), 35–48. doi:10.1609/aimag.v36i3.2601

Xiao, J., & Gao, W. (2020). Connecting the Dots: Reader Ratings, Bibliographic Data, and Machine-Learning Algorithms for Monograph Selection. *The Serials Librarian*, *78*(1-4), 1–4, 117–122. doi:10.1080/0361526X.2020.1707599

Xie, I., & Matusiak, K. (2016). *Discover digital libraries: Theory and practice*. Elsevier.

Xing, Y., He, W., Zhang, J., & Cao, G. (2022). AI Privacy Opinions between US and Chinese People. *Journal of Computer Information Systems*, *63*(3), 492–506. doi:10.1080/08874417.2022.2079107

Xu, Z. (2023). *Research on the application of artificial intelligence in the library sector. International Conference on Artificial Intelligence and Computer Engineering (ICAICE 2022)*, Wuhan, China. 10.1117/12.2671477

Yan, R., & Zhao, X. (2023). Chatbots in libraries. A systematic literature review. *Education for information,* Research Gate.

Yasar, K., & Botelho, B. (2023). Retrieved January 3rd, 2024. https://www.techtarget.com/searchcustomerexperience/definition/virtual-assistant-AI-assistant

Yi, Z. (2021). Research on intelligent service mode of digital library based on data intelligence 4th International Conference on Advanced Electronic Materials, Computers and Software Engineering (AEMCSE). 10.1109/AEMCSE51986.2021.00192

Yoon, J. W., Andrews, J. E., & Ward, H. L. (2022). Perceptions on Adopting Artificial Intelligence and Related Technologies in Libraries: Public and Academic Librarians in North America. *Library Hi Tech*, *40*(6), 1893–1915. doi:10.1108/LHT-07-2021-0229

Yu, J. (2021, December). Construction of Smart Library Based on the Big Data Mining and Knowledge Discovery. In *2021 Smart City Challenges & Outcomes for Urban Transformation (SCOUT)* (pp. 57-61). IEEE.

Yu, K., Gong, R., Sun, L., & Jiang, C. (2019). *The application of artificial intelligence in smart library.*

Yusuf, T. I., Adebayo, O. A., Bello, L. A., & Kayode, J. O. (2022). Adoption of artificial intelligence for effective library service delivery in academic libraries in Nigeria. *Library Philosophy & Practice* 6804:1–13. https://digitalcommons. unl.edu/libphilprac/6804

Yusuf, R. A., & Awoyemi, O. O. (2022). Cyber Security and Its Implication on Library Users' Privacy. *Owena Journal of Library and Information Science*, *9*(1), 1–13.

Zanin-Yost, A. (2004). Digital reference: What the past has taught us and what the future will hold. *Library Philosophy & Practice*, *7*(1), 1–16.

Zeng, J., Cao, S., Chen, Y., Pan, P., & Cai, Y. (2023). Measuring the interdisciplinary characteristics of Chinese research in library and information science based on knowledge elements. *Aslib Journal of Information Management*, *75*(3), 589–617. doi:10.1108/AJIM-03-2022-0130

Zhang, C., & Lu, Y. (2021). Study on artificial intelligence: The state of the art and future prospects. *Journal of Industrial Information Integration*, *23*, 100224. doi:10.1016/j.jii.2021.100224

Zhang, F. (2016). A personalized time-sequence-based book recommendation algorithm for digital libraries. *IEEE Access : Practical Innovations, Open Solutions*, *4*, 2714–2720. doi:10.1109/ACCESS.2016.2564997

Zhang, K., & Zhang, J. (2017). New District, Misunderstanding, Blind Zone and Forbidden Zone in the Application and Research of Artificial Intelligence Education. *Journal of Distance Education*, *5*, 54–63.

Zhang, Q., Lu, J., & Jin, Y. (2021). Artificial intelligence in recommender systems. *Complex & Intelligent Systems*, *7*(1), 439–457. doi:10.1007/s40747-020-00212-w

Zhang, Y., Wu, M., Tian, G. Y., Zhang, G., & Lu, J. (2021). Ethics and privacy of artificial intelligence: Understandings from bibliometrics. *Knowledge-Based Systems*, *222*, 106994. doi:10.1016/j.knosys.2021.106994

Zhao, L. (2021). Personalized recommendation by using fused user preference to construct smart library. *Internet Technology Letters*, *4*(3), e273. doi:10.1002/itl2.273

Zielinski, C., Winker, M. A., Aggarwal, R., Ferris, L., Heinemann, M., Florencio, J., & Habibzadeh, F. (2023). WAME recommendations on chatbots and generative artificial intelligence in relation to scholarly publications. *Global Journal of Medicine & Public Health*, *12*(2). PMID:38089825

Ziyue, X., & Ya, C. (2020, August). The Research on User Privacy Protection of library Intelligent Service. In *2020 International Symposium on Computer Engineering and Intelligent Communications (ISCEIC)* (pp. 200-205). IEEE. 10.1109/ISCEIC51027.2020.00050

About the Contributors

Iman Magdy Khamis is a data scientist and director of the library at Northwestern Qatar. Prior to joining Northwestern Qatar, she worked at Bibliotheca Alexandrina. Iman's research interests include machine learning and artificial intelligence in libraries. She is the author of two chapters on the concepts used by data scientists to build chatbots and book recommender systems in the Handbook of Research on Advancements of Contactless Technology and Service Innovation in Library and Information Science. She is currently enrolled in EdD at Johns Hopkins University.

***

Mandira Bairagi, a Ph.D. research scholar in the Department of Library and Information Science at Rashtrasant Tukadoji Maharaj Nagpur University, holds degrees in MLISc and MPhil in the same field. With a solid 17 years of experience in practical library work, she currently serves as a Librarian at DVR & Dr HS MIC College of Technology in Andhra Pradesh. Mandira has contributed to scholarly discourse by publishing several seminar and conference papers and is a Life member of both the Indian Library Association and the LIS Academy.

Younes Benslimane is an Associate Professor at the School of Information Technology, York University in Toronto, Canada. He received his PhD in Information Systems (IS) from University of Quebec in Montreal, Canada. His research interests include IS analysis and design, business process management, methodologies and best practices for IS development and management, and skills requirements for IT professionals. His work has been published in refereed journals and conference

Prosper Bernard is a professor of management at the University of Quebec in Montréal where he was previously vice-rector and member of the BOARD of TRUSTEES of the university. He is also Chairman of the Board of the University Consortium of the Americas in Florida. He holds several degrees including a PhD from City University of New York. He has served successively as Director of the

PHD program in management, and managed a PHD consortium including McGill university,Director of the department of management and technology, Director of the MBA program locally and abroad, namely in China, the only one Executive MBA officially recognized by the Chinese government. Lately, China's Jiangsu Province presented him with the prestigious Friendship Medal and the Labor Prize for his contribution to university education. He has published numerous books and articles in academic conferences and scopus, IEEE and other prestigious journals

Dhilipan J has completed M.Sc, MBA, and MPhil and completed his Doctorate in 2014. He has 23 years of Teaching Experience and 9 years of Research Experience. His area of interest is Cloud Computing, Machine Learning, E Commerce & Data Analysis. He has published 57 research articles in reputed journals and Conferences.He is currently guiding 8 research scholars in the areas of Machine learning, Deep Learning and Cloud Computing. He has attended many conferences conducted in India and around the globe. He has organized International Conference in association with Foreign Universities, International FDP/Workshop/STTP every year and collaborating with many industries for providing Internship & Placement offers for the Students. He received various awards from recognized organizations. Apart from these, he has completed several consultancy projects with the leading IT industries as a contribution to society. He is an active participant who is very keen on rendering his helping hands through various outreach programs.

Shyamala Devi J, Assistant Professor at SRM IST, Ramapuram campus, Department of Computer Applications having 25 years of Experience. Working on domains like Information Extraction and Machine Learning and presented paper at Internal conference and published paper at more than ten journals.

Navkiran Kaur is currently serving as Assistant Professor in the Department of Library and Information Science, Punjabi University, Patiala (Punjab, India). She was awarded Ph.D. in 2014 on the topic "Role of Medical College Libraries in Health Information Literacy in Punjab and Chandigarh: An Analytical Study". She has contributed more than 30 research papers in journals, conference proceedings, and edited books. She has jointly edited two books. Dr. Kaur has traveled to different parts of the country for academic and professional assignments. She has been actively participating in national and international conferences, seminars, workshops, webinars, and training programmes. She is a life member of the Indian Library Association (ILA), Indian Association of Teachers of Library and Information Science (IATLIS) and Punjab Library Association (PLA). Her areas of interest are Health Information Literacy, Information Literacy, Information Sources and

Services, Knowledge Organization and Information Processing, Information Storage and Retrieval, and Information Analysis, Consolidation and Repackaging.

Ali Kavak completed his doctoral education in Information and Document Management; his master's degrees in Information and Document Management and Turkish Education. His undergraduate studies took place in Aviation Management, Public Relations and Advertising, Information and Document Management Department, and Turkish Language and Literature branches. He has master's theses on the information literacy skills of teacher candidates and the effects of library services on users. His doctoral thesis is on information security management in university libraries and a guide proposal. His academic research areas include library and information science, librarianship, information systems, documentation, information security, information literacy, and artificial intelligence. Additionally, he has articles published in journals indexed in SSCI.

Shalini Lihitkar is a distinguished LIS professional with an illustrious 21-year career, presently serving as a Professor at RTM Nagpur University. Holds a Gold Medal from Nagpur University, having demonstrated exceptional leadership as Head of the LISc Department at both Rashtrasant Tukadoji Maharaj Nagpur University and Shivaji University, Kolhapur. Academic Achievements: An accomplished educator with expertise in competitive examinations, guiding 15 scholars to Ph.D., and currently mentoring 7 Ph.D. researchers. Proven commitment to academic excellence and professional growth. Research and Publications: Prolific researcher with over 230 publications in journals and conferences, including 10 authored books. Successfully completed projects with UNESCO and SALIS, and a UGC-Minor Research Project, ICSSR and ICMR extramural research project. Organised and edited 18 conferences and workshops, contributing significantly to the academic discourse. Administrative Leadership: Demonstrated administrative prowess as the Head of LISc, leading the department at both Nagpur and Kolhapur universities. Organized workshops and coordinated UGC-Refresher Courses, showcasing effective management skills. International Recognition: An international presence through paper presentations at global conferences. Holds editorial roles in various journals, further establishing a reputation as a thought leader in the field. Awards and Recognitions: Recipient of prestigious awards, including the "Young LIS Professional" award from the Karnataka State Library Professionals Association, the Best Paper Award from KISTI, and the Professional Excellence Award from SRFLIS. Acknowledged for outstanding contributions to the LIS community. A dynamic professional with a comprehensive skill set encompassing research, teaching, administration, and mentoring. Strives for excellence, leaving an indelible mark on the academic and professional landscape of Library and Information Science.

Geetha Manoharan is currently working in Telangana as an assistant professor at SR University. She is the university-level PhD programme coordinator and has also been given the additional responsibility of In Charge Director of Publications and Patents under the Research Division at SR University. Under her tutelage, students are inspired to reach their full potential in all areas of their education and beyond through experiential learning. It creates an atmosphere conducive to the growth of pupils into independent thinkers and avid readers. She has more than ten years of experience across the board in the business world, academia, and the academy. She has a keen interest in the study of organisational behaviour and management. More than forty articles and books have been published in scholarly venues such as UGC-refereed, SCOPUS, Web of Science, and Springer. Over the past six-plus years, she has participated in varied research and student exchange programmes at both the national and international levels. A total of five of her collaborative innovations in this area have already been published and patented. Emotional intelligence, self-efficacy, and work-life balance are among her specialties. She organises programmes for academic organizations. She belongs to several professional organizations, including the CMA and the CPC. The TIPSGLOBAL Institute of Coimbatore has recognised her twice (in 2017 and 2018) for her outstanding academic performance.

Aslı Gül Öncel is a faculty member of the Department of Management and the Director of the Business Research Center at Galatasaray University in İstanbul, Turkey. She is also a member of the academic council of ATINER institute in Athens, Greece. She earned her bachelor's degree in Electrical Engineering from Yıldız Technical University and master's degree in Industrial Engineering from Galatasaray University. She received her Ph.D. in Information and Communication Sciences from Picardie Jules Verne University in Amiens, France and completed a one-year of post-doctorate at University of Québec at Trois Rivières (UQTR) in Canada. Dr. Aslı Gül Öncel served as the organizing committee member of the 2013 European Academy of Management (EURAM) conference in İstanbul. Since 2009, she has been teaching statistics, mathematics, and courses on energy and environment politics at Galatasaray University. Her primary research interests are focused on climate change, the environment, and quantitative techniques.

Subhajit Panda is currently pursuing his Ph.D. at Punjabi University, Patiala, and concurrently holds the position of Assistant Librarian at the Central Library, Chandigarh University. He earned his B.Sc. (Non-Med.) in 2017 and was honored with the University Gold Medal for his BLIS & MLIS Degrees from Panjab University, Chandigarh, in 2018 and 2019, respectively. Mr. Panda boasts an impressive publication record, including 37 National & International Journal Articles (6 Scopus Indexed), 20 Book Chapters (5 Scopus Indexed), 1 Book, and 8 Conference

Proceedings (1 International). He is a life member of esteemed organizations such as the Indian Library Association (ILA), Madras Library Association (MALA), and Bengal Library Association (BLA). Mr. Panda has also served as an associate editor for The International Journal of Information Studies & Libraries (IJISL). His expertise lies in Digital Literacy, Information Retrieval, Library Management, and Subject Analysis. His research interests encompass e-Learning, Change Management, Cloud Computing, Open Access, Web Accessibility, Virtual & Augmented Reality, and Metrics Studies.

Michel Plaisent is a full professor in the University of Québec at Montréal (Canada). After a bachelor in Information technology, a M.Sc. in project management and a Ph.D. in Information Technology Management, he joined the Business school in 1980 where he held different position while developing his research career, namely IT program director for 6 years. His doctoral research was pioneer as he studied the use of computer mediated communication systems by CEO. Since then, Dr. Plaisent's researches continue to focus human factors of IT, namely cognitive ergonomics, learning problems and personal productivity tools for managers. Among his new researches namely: Education 4.0 concepts and tools, and more broadly the impact of internet on life and society. He has published more than 25 books and more than one hundred of articles in international conferences and academic indexed journals. He is engaged in China EMBA program and he manages for UQAM research collaboration protocols with three South-Asia universities.

Ramya R. completed her B.E and M.E degree in Computer science and engineering. She had 14 years of teaching experience in various Engineering colleges. She pursuing PhD in computer science and engineering and published many articles and book chapters in her domain. She specialises in edge computing, cloud computing, Machine learning, artificial intelligence, Quality of services and resource management.

Sivasankari.R. received her bachelor's degree in B.Sc. computer science at Fatima College, Madurai, in 2011, and completed her master's in MCA at Velammal College of Engineering and Technology, Madurai, in 2014. She has more than five years of experience as an assistant professor. She is currently pursuing a Ph.D. in computer science at SRM Institute of Science and Technology. Her specialization includes recommendation systems, semantic technologies, ontologies, citation networks, and IoT

Sindhu S is an assistant professor, Department of BCA, SRM IST, Ramapuram. She received her bachelor's degree in BCA Computer Application at Bharathi

Women's Arts and Science College, Kallakurichi, 2009. And completed a Master's in Computer Applications at Dhanalakshmi Srinivasan College of Arts and Science, Perambalur, 2011. She is currently doing a Ph.D. in Computer Science at SRM IST. She has more than six years of teaching experience in computer science. Her specializations include the Internet of Things, Image processing and segmentation, and machine learning

S. Suriya is an assistant professor, Department of Computer Applications (BCA), SRM IST, Ramapuram. She completed her master's degree in 2014. Her areas of interest are network security and WSN.

Daniel Tomiuk is a tenured professor at the University of Quebec in Montreal (UQAM), Canada, specializing in e-commerce, e-learning, online sales strategies, serious games and user behaviour, social media in collaborative work, and online service recovery. He obtained his PhD from McGill University (Montreal, Quebec, Canada) in 2005. He worked in the A&M university system (Texas) as an assistant professor and has taught at Zhejiang University (Hangzhou, China) as a visiting professor. He has received multiple best paper awards and has been published in renowned journals such as Information & Management. He was recently involved in an SSHRC-funded project focused on building an online community of practice to foster improved networking and knowledge exchange for women in STEM.

Stefka Tzanova is the Science Librarian at York College Library, CUNY. Her research interests include academic librarianship, scientific literacy, science education, history of science and technology, STEM, open educational resources, scholarly communications, and patents. Professor Tzanova has a strong background in the hard sciences and holds Master's degrees in engineering and in library science.

Cataldo Zuccaro obtained a Ph.D. in marketing at the University of Quebec in Montreal in 1999. He is a professor of marketing at the University of Quebec in Montreal. He had been a director of the MBA Research and the chair of the department of business strategies. Dr. Cataldo Zuccaro is a specialist in Data Analysis, Business Analytics and Marketing. His areas of research are marketing research methods, business modeling, customer scoring and segmentation, business analytics and research methods. He has taught and continues to teach in the university's Executive MBA program in such countries as Romania, Poland, France, Morocco, Algeria, Tunisia, Lebanon, Mexico and Peru. He has also consulted for large multinational corporations and government agencies. Dr. Zuccaro has published his research in such journals as Recherches sociologiques Revue des sciences administratives du Canada, Journal of the market research society Journal of social psychology, International journal of market research, Journal of modelling management, International journal of bank marketing, Social research indicators and the Journal of Economics and Economic Education Research. He is the winner, in 2010, of the silver medal for the best paper in the International Journal of Market Research.

Index

O

P

R

S

T

U

www.ingramcontent.com/pod-product-compliance
Lightning Source LLC
LaVergne TN
LVHW081335300926
849161LV00008B/1976